PSYCHOLOGY OF DECISION MAKING

PSYCHOLOGY OF DECISION MAKING

PAUL M. GARRISON
EDITOR

Nova Science Publishers, Inc.
New York

Copyright © 2008 by Nova Science Publishers, Inc.

All rights reserved. No part of this book may be reproduced, stored in a retrieval system or transmitted in any form or by any means: electronic, electrostatic, magnetic, tape, mechanical photocopying, recording or otherwise without the written permission of the Publisher.

For permission to use material from this book please contact us:
Telephone 631-231-7269; Fax 631-231-8175
Web Site: http://www.novapublishers.com

NOTICE TO THE READER

The Publisher has taken reasonable care in the preparation of this book, but makes no expressed or implied warranty of any kind and assumes no responsibility for any errors or omissions. No liability is assumed for incidental or consequential damages in connection with or arising out of information contained in this book. The Publisher shall not be liable for any special, consequential, or exemplary damages resulting, in whole or in part, from the readers' use of, or reliance upon, this material. Any parts of this book based on government reports are so indicated and copyright is claimed for those parts to the extent applicable to compilations of such works.

Independent verification should be sought for any data, advice or recommendations contained in this book. In addition, no responsibility is assumed by the publisher for any injury and/or damage to persons or property arising from any methods, products, instructions, ideas or otherwise contained in this publication.

This publication is designed to provide accurate and authoritative information with regard to the subject matter covered herein. It is sold with the clear understanding that the Publisher is not engaged in rendering legal or any other professional services. If legal or any other expert assistance is required, the services of a competent person should be sought. FROM A DECLARATION OF PARTICIPANTS JOINTLY ADOPTED BY A COMMITTEE OF THE AMERICAN BAR ASSOCIATION AND A COMMITTEE OF PUBLISHERS.

LIBRARY OF CONGRESS CATALOGING-IN-PUBLICATION DATA
Available upon request

ISBN 978-1-60021-869-9

Published by Nova Science Publishers, Inc. ✣ New York

CONTENTS

Preface vii

Short Communication

    Coronary Pressure Measurement in Decision Making for
Equivocal Left Main Coronary Artery Disease   1
Kohichiro Iwasaki

Research and Review Chapters

Chapter 1   Antiterrorist Emergency Ventilation: System,
Strategy and Decision-Making   9
Xianting Li, Hao Cai and Lina Zhao

Chapter 2   Decision-Making in a Structured Connectionist
Agent Architecture   81
Carter Wendelken and Lokendra Shastri

Chapter 3   Cognitive Dysfunction in Cocaine Abuse: Evidence for
Impairments in Impulse Control and Decision-Making   107
Laurie M. Rilling and Bryon Adinoff

Chapter 4   Expert Systems, GIS, and Spatial Decision Making:
Current Practices and New Trends   123
Khalid Eldrandaly

Chapter 5   Development of Response Inhibition and Decision-Making
Across Childhood: A Cognitive Neuroscience Perspective   145
Wery P. M. van den Wildenberg and Eveline A. Crone

Chapter 6   Enabling Pregnant Women to Participate in Informed
Decision-Making Regarding their Labour Analgesia   165
Camille Raynes-Greenow, Christine Roberts and Natasha Nassar

Chapter 7   Adolescent Decision-Making about Substance Use:
A Video-Based Assessment   177
Kristen G. Anderson and Sara J. Parent

Chapter 8	Interprofessional Decision Making in Elderly Care: Morality, Criteria and Help Allocation *Pirjo Nikander*	**197**
Chapter 9	Analysing the Effects of Mortality Salience on Prejudice and Decision-Taking *Agustin Echebarria-Echabe and Francisco J. Valencia Gárate*	**211**
Index		**225**

PREFACE

In a fast-moving world, the necessity of making decisions, and preferably good ones, has become even more difficult. One reason is the variety and number of choices perhaps available which often arenot presented or understood. Alternatives are often unclear and complex paths to them confusing and misleading. Thus the process of decision making itself requires analysis on an ongoing basis. Decision making is often made based on cultural factors whereas the best alternative might be quite different. The subject touches ethics aspects as well as psychological considerations. This new book presents important research on the psychology of decision making.

Short Communication - It is often difficult for equivocal left main coronary artery (LMCA) disease to make decision about coronary artery bypass surgery (CABG). The authors investigated the usefulness of coronary pressure measurement for decision making for CABG to equivocal LMCA disease. They measured coronary pressure in 16 patients with equivocal LMCA disease. Fractional flow reserve (FFR) was calculated at the maximal hyperemia from the simultaneously recorded aortic (Pa) and distal coronary pressure (Pd) by the ratio of Pd/Pa. If FFR of LMCA was <0.75 the authors selected CABG and if it was ≥0.75 they selected medical therapy. The authors followed these patients for 26.5±10.8 (13-39) months. Eight patients underwent medical therapy (medical group) and eight patients underwent CABG (surgical group). The FFR of LMCA was 0.91±0.01 in medical group and 0.61±0.03 in surgical group (p<0.0001). There were no significant differences in reference vessel diameter (3.63±0.71 vs 3.31±0.86mm), minimal lumen diameter (1.84±0.26 vs 1.69±0.45mm), percent diameter stenosis (48.4±7.8 vs 48.9±9.0%) between the medical and surgical groups. During follow up no patient in medical group had cardiac event and two patients in surgical group hospitalized for congestive heart failure. In conclusion coronary pressure measurement for equivocal left main coronary artery disease is clinically useful to make decision about CABG.

Chapter 1 - There are two kinds of antiterrorist emergency ventilation system. One is to defend indoor environment against chemical and biological agent (CBA) attacks. The other is to supply calmative gas to incapacitate terrorists when they hold hostages in public buildings. What kind of system and ventilation strategy can be used for antiterrorism, and how to make decision are introduced in the chapter. There are six sections in the chapter. How the emergency ventilation systems work is introduced in the first section. The second section is on the theory of contaminant dispersion and identification of contaminant source. For the theory of contaminant dispersion, both computational fluid dynamics (CFD) method and analytical formula of contaminant distribution are introduced. For the theory of contaminant source identification, an algorithm to identify the position and intensity of contaminant source with limited number of sensors is proposed and demonstrated for its effectiveness. The third section is on the evacuation model and evaluation of exposure risk. Both cellular automata (CA) model and spatial-grid evacuation model (SGEM) are introduced for modeling evacuation process. The relative exposure risk index, EFCS, and absolute exposure risk index, PIR, are introduced to evaluate the exposure risk of contaminant. Both the second section and third section are the fundamental of emergency ventilation. Based on section 2 and 3, the ventilation strategy and decision-making are introduced for emergency ventilation against contaminant suddenly released in public building in section 4 and for emergency ventilation to rescue hostages held by terrorists in section 5, respectively. Section 6 is the summary of the whole chapter.

Chapter 2 - To understand the mapping between networks of neurons and the mental constructs that underlie complex cognition and behavior is a central problem for the field of neurocomputing. The structured connectionist approach tackles this problem directly by investigating the relation between connectionist circuits and cognitive operations. One structured connectionist model, SHRUTI, has demonstrated how a system of simple, neuron-like elements can encode a large body of relational causal knowledge and provide a basis for rapid inference. The SHRUTI model explored the use of spreading activation across structured representations and temporal synchrony variable binding within a connectionist network. This article will describe the transformation of the SHRUTI model into a decision-making agent architecture. Key contributions of this effort include the development of a connectionist encoding of goals and utility and of connectionist mechanisms for cognitive control that support goal-oriented behavior. Specific connectionist circuits encode long-term goals or drives, associate value with possible events, and propagate utility from effects to possible causes. Together, these mechanisms support reactive planning and simple goal-driven decision-making. However, successful operation in more complex decision scenarios, such as those involving conflicting subgoals, requires top-down control mechanisms. Several such control mechanisms are described; it is then shown that each can be implemented via some combination of a small set of control primitives. Each of these control primitives -- including monitoring, filtering, selection, maintenance, organization, and manipulation – is implemented as a simple connectionist circuit.

Chapter 3 - Cocaine is one of the most widely abused psychoactive substances in the United States, with an estimated 1.3 million Americans using the drug on a regular (at least monthly) basis. Even occasional cocaine use can result in serious medical complications, such as cardiac damage, vascular ischemia, respiratory failure, and persistent alterations in neural function. In this chapter, the authors examine the most recent research on impulsivity and decision-making in cocaine use. First, the authors will present a brief overview of the cognitive processes affected by cocaine use. Next, they review the relevant literature detailing the status of inhibitory control and decision-making in cocaine users, as well as their proposed neuroanatomical correlates. Finally, they integrate these findings with the current view of cocaine addiction and relapse, with an emphasis on the role of impulsivity and decision-making in continued cocaine use despite the elevated risk of negative consequences.

Chapter 4 - Spatial decision making is a routine activity that is common to individuals and to organizations. Spatial decision making problems are multi-facetted challenges. Not only do they often involve numerous technical requirements, but they may also contain economical, social, environmental and political dimensions that could have conflicting objectives. Solving these complex problems requires an integrative use of information, domain specific knowledge and effective means of communication. Although geographic information systems (GIS) and expert systems (ES) have played important roles in solving spatial decision problems, each of these tools has its own limitations in dealing with such problems. For instance, GIS is a great tool for handling physical suitability analysis. However, it has limited capabilities of incorporating the decision maker's preferences, experiences, intuitions, and judgments into the problem-solving process. Expert Systems, which is capable of addressing heuristic analysis, lacks the capabilities of handling spatial data/knowledge that are crucial to spatial analysis. The need for improvement of the performance of these tools in solving highly complex spatial decision-making problems has promoted the integration of GIS and ES. Numerous mechanisms enabling interoperability between GIS and ES have appeared over the years. Examples range from primitive solutions such as simple, loose coupling to much more sophisticated approaches, such as COM technology and Ontology. In this study, both primitive and advanced techniques for integrating GIS and ES are discussed.

Chapter 5 - Recent advances within the field of neuroimaging and psychophysiological recording techniques have enabled the identification of key brain regions that contribute to developmental changes in cognitive control and decision-making. This chapter will focus on two influential paradigms in the field of experimental cognitive neuroscience that have contributed to our understanding of the nature of the increasing ability in children to control their own thoughts and actions as they grow older. The first section reviews the current cognitive developmental theories of behavioral inhibition. Response inhibition comes into play when prepotent, overlearned, or ongoing responses have to be suppressed in favor of executing an alternative response and is generally considered an important element of cognitive control and flexibility. These theories are supported by neuroimaging studies that identify the lateral prefrontal cortex as being relevant in tasks that require the on-line manipulation of information and the suppression of responses. The second part of this chapter provides an account of the development of cognitive processes involved in decision-making. Decision-making is required for a variety of behavior and often involves the consideration of multiple alternatives and reasoning about distant future consequences. According to the somatic-marker theory, the possible outcomes of a choice are mediated by emotions that are accompanied by anticipatory somatic activity. The theory underlying emotional self-regulation assigns an important role to the ventromedial prefrontal cortex. Finally, the examination of developmental changes in cognitive control functions from the perspective of cognitive neuroscience has also led to better characterizations of behavioral deficits found in disordered child populations.

Chapter 6 – The pain of labour is a central part of women's experience of childbirth. Many factors are considered influential in determining women's experience of and her satisfaction with childbirth. Women's expectations of the duration and level of pain suffered, quality of her care-giver support, and involvement in labour decision making are the most commonly reported factors.[1]

Significantly, there have been more clinical trials of pharmacological pain relief during labour and childbirth than of any other intervention in the perinatal field[2] however to what degree this evidence is available or discussed with pregnant women before labour is unclear.

Chapter 7 - Adolescence is a period characterized by rapid cognitive and social change. As youth move through adolescence, they are faced with a myriad of decisions regarding risky behavior, including substance involvement. Given the importance of the social sphere for teens, these decisions are often influenced by peers. There is a growing body of research into the processes underlying adolescent decision-making regarding alcohol and drug use. However, few process-oriented assessment approaches have been developed to understand how youth make these decisions in the moment. This chapter briefly reviews the literature on adolescent decision-making regarding alcohol and drugs, presents a social-information processing model for adolescent substance use, and describes the development of a novel video-based approach to assessing adolescent decision-making. This assessment integrates methods traditionally used in the educational setting as well as those developed for clinical populations of youth. Preliminary data from the development phase of the assessment will be presented. The implications for adolescent research in risk taking, substance involvement and intervention with youth will be discussed.

Chapter 8 - In terms of its methodological stance, the current chapter draws on prior work on discourse analysis, categorization in institutional settings as well as work that analyses categorization in talk more broadly. It provides numerous illustrations and detailed analyses of professional care allocation. Doing this, the chapter hopefully shows how the criteria and morality of decision making are jointly constructed in interaction, and how the responsibilities of professionals as well as the rights and responsibilities of elderly clients and of their carers are discursively carved and talked into being in institutional meeting talk. Special focus in the chapter will be given to the ways in which professionals use *imageries and ideals concerning the caring relationship and the life course* as part of their descriptive work.

In the remaining sections of this chapter I will first introduce the data and the institutional setting in which they were collected. Following this, I will then move to the analysis of two elderly client cases and provide several data excerpts on both. To conclude, I will briefly discuss possible benefits and practical implications of discursive analyses of professional argumentation.

Chapter 9 - Recently (Echebarria & Fernandez, 2006) the authors carried out a quasi-experimental study on the effects of the terrorist attacks against the railways in Madrid and found that these attacks provoked a generalized prejudice directed not only against groups regarded as the responsible of the attacks but also against other non-related group (Jews). A generalized displacement toward more conservative values and political options was also found. Here they present two follow-up experimental studies designed to analyse the socio-psychological processes that might underlie these changes. The first study manipulated, through pictures, the salience of death- related thoughts without involving any personal or group based threat. The generalized increment of prejudices and group bias are reproduced but only at an implicit level. The second study proved that mortality salience affects how social dilemmas are approached. Participants assigned to the mortality salient condition approached a health related dilemma in terms of losses, independently of how it was experimentally framed. In contrast, control participants shifted their choices in function of the experimental manipulation. The authors discuss the implications of these results in terms of understanding the effects of terrorism from the Terror Management Theory.

In: Psychology of Decision Making
Editor: Paul M. Garrison

ISBN 978-1-60021-869-9
© Nova Science Publishers, Inc.

Short Communication

CORONARY PRESSURE MEASUREMENT IN DECISION MAKING FOR EQUIVOCAL LEFT MAIN CORONARY ARTERY DISEASE

Kohichiro Iwasaki

Department of Cardiology, Okayama Central Hospital, Okayama, Japan

ABSTRACT

It is often difficult for equivocal left main coronary artery (LMCA) disease to make decision about coronary artery bypass surgery (CABG). We investigated the usefulness of coronary pressure measurement for decision making for CABG to equivocal LMCA disease. We measured coronary pressure in 16 patients with equivocal LMCA disease. Fractional flow reserve (FFR) was calculated at the maximal hyperemia from the simultaneously recorded aortic (Pa) and distal coronary pressure (Pd) by the ratio of Pd/Pa. If FFR of LMCA was <0.75 we selected CABG and if it was ≥0.75 we selected medical therapy. We followed these patients for 26.5±10.8 (13-39) months. Eight patients underwent medical therapy (medical group) and eight patients underwent CABG (surgical group). The FFR of LMCA was 0.91±0.01 in medical group and 0.61±0.03 in surgical group (p<0.0001). There were no significant differences in reference vessel diameter (3.63±0.71 vs 3.31±0.86mm), minimal lumen diameter (1.84±0.26 vs 1.69±0.45mm), percent diameter stenosis (48.4±7.8 vs 48.9±9.0%) between the medical and surgical groups. During follow up no patient in medical group had cardiac event and two patients in surgical group hospitalized for congestive heart failure. In conclusion coronary pressure measurement for equivocal left main coronary artery disease is clinically useful to make decision about CABG.

INTRODUCTION

A large part of myocardium of the left ventricle is perfused by the left main coronary artery (LMCA). Although acute obstruction of the LMCA is not frequently observed [1], acute LMCA obstruction causes severe hemodynamic deterioration, frequently results in catastrophic event [2-4]. Thus evaluation of LMCA stenosis is important with respect to avoid severe ischemia and prevent acute LMCA obstruction.

Assessment of LMCA disease by coronary angiography is often suboptimal [5-6]. It is often difficult for equivocal LMCA disease to make decision whether coronary revascularization is required or not.

Fractional flow reserve (FFR), calculated from coronary pressure measurement, represents physiological coronary reserve and has been reported to be a useful index to determine the functional severity of coronary artery disease [7-8].

Thus we investigated the usefulness of coronary pressure measurement for decision making for CABG to equivocal LMCA disease.

METHODS

We measured coronary pressure in 16 patients with equivocal LMCA stenosis, defined as LMCA stenosis of more than 25% but less than 75% by visual assessment. They consisted of 14 men and two women aged 37 to 78 (mean 67.6 ± 7.5) years old.

The patients' medication was continued until cardiac catheterization. At the beginning of cardiac catheterization all patients were given 100 IU/kg of heparin intravenously and additional heparin was administered if the procedure lasted more than 90 minutes.

Coronary angiography was performed using multiple views by the standard percutaneous transluminal method using a femoral approach.

The angiographic severity of the LMCA was measured by quantitative coronary angiography with an automated edge detection algorithm (Super DF Series, Digital Fluoroscopy System, Toshiba, Tokyo, Japan). The reference vessel diameter was obtained from the diameter of the guiding catheter. Two orthogonal projections of the coronary arterial lesion during the end-diastolic phase were used to perform biplane analysis of the minimal lumen diameter and the percent stenosis of the coronary artery diameter.

Isosorbide dinitrate (2.5mg) was administered into the coronary artery every 30 minutes throughout the procedure. A pressure guide wire (Wave Wire, Volcano Therapeutics Inc., Rancho Cordova, CA, USA) was zeroed, calibrated and advanced through the catheter into the coronary artery and positioned as distally as possible. Maximal hyperemia was then induced by intravenous continuous infusion of adenosine triphosphate (150 µg/kg/min).

Fractional flow reserve (FFR) was then calculated at the maximal hyperemia from the simultaneously recorded aortic (P_a) and distal coronary pressure (P_d) by the ratio of P_d/P_a. Thereafter the pullback pressure tracing from a point as distal as possible to the proximal part of the left anterior descending coronary artery (LAD) or left circumflex coronary artery (LCX) under steady-state maximal hyperemia was obtained and recorded at paper speed of 5mm/sec. We calculated the FFR of LMCA by correcting the pressure gradient across the other part of the coronary artery.

A value of the FFR <0.75 was considered significant with respect to physiological criteria, based on previously reported studies [7,8].

Patients with FFR <0.75 across the LMCA lesion were assigned for CABG and those with FFR ≥0.75 across the LMCA lesion were assigned for medical therapy, including statin, angiotensin converting enzyme inhibitor, and life style modification. We followed these patients for 26.5±10.8 (13-39) months.

STATISTICAL ANALYSIS

To study the differences in angiographic and pressure measurements between the two groups, we used Student's unpaired t-test. The chi-square test or Fisher's exact probability test was used to compare proportional data between the two groups. All values are expressed as means±SD, and p values less than 0.05 were considered significant.

RESULTS

Among 16 patients, eight patients underwent medical therapy (medical group) and eight patients underwent CABG (surgical group).

The FFR of LMCA was 0.91±0.01 in medical group and 0.61±0.03 in surgical group (p<0.0001). There were no significant differences in reference vessel diameter, minimal lumen diameter, and percent diameter stenosis between the medical and surgical groups (Table 1).

Table 1. Clinical, angiographic, and pressure measurement characteristics of patients in medical and surgical groups

	medical group	surgical group	p
n	8	8	
age(years old)	65.5±8.1	70.0±6.4	NS
male	7	7	NS
coronary risk factors			
hypertension	4	4	NS
diabetes	4	5	NS
hyperlipidemia	7	5	NS
smoking	2	3	NS
obesity	1	1	NS
angiographic findings			
RVD(mm)	3.63±0.71	3.31±0.87	NS
MLD(mm)	1.84±0.26	1.69±0.45	NS
%DS(%)	48.4±7.8	48.9±9.0	NS
coronary pressure			
for LMCA	0.91±0.01	0.61±0.03	<0.0001

Table 1. (Continued)

	medical group	surgical group	p
n	8	8	
for LAD-LMCA	0.86±0.10	0.61±0.03	<0.0001
for LCX-LMCA	0.92±0.07	0.82±0.03	<0.05
follow-up period (months)	18.1±9.8	14.7±10.0	NS

Abbreviations: LAD: left anterior descending coronary artery, LCX: left circumflex coronary artery, LMCA: left main coronary artery, MLD: minimal lumen diameter, RVD: reference vessel diameter, %DS: percent diameter stenosis

Table 2. Clinical, angiographic, and pressure measurement characteristics and follow-up clinical events of patients in medical group

No	age	sex	diagnosis	RVD	MLD	%DS	location	LMCA-FFR	F/U	event
1	70	M	MI	4.4	1.8	59	orifice	0.82	4	none
2	73	M	MI	2.9	1.5	48	distal	0.85	22	none
3	58	M	AP	2.8	1.8	36	orifice	0.85	29	none
4	66	M	MI	2.8	1.6	43	distal	0.90	21	none
5	52	M	MI	4.5	2.0	56	distal	0.90	25	none
6	60	M	AP	3.8	1.7	55	orifice	0.93	27	none
7	75	M	AP	3.7	2.0	46	distal	0.99	12	none
8	70	F	AP	4.1	2.3	44	orifice	1.00	5	none

Abbreviations: AP: angina pectoris, F/U: follow-up (months), LMCA: left main coronary artery, MI: myocardial infarction, MLD: minimal lumen diameter, RVD: reference vessel diameter, %DS: percent diameter stenosis

Table 3. Clinical, angiographic, and pressure measurement characteristics and follow-up clinical events of patients in surgical group

No	age	sex	diagnosis	RVD	MLD	%DS	location	LMCA-FFR	F/U	event
1	66	M	MI	2.1	1.3	38	body	0.56	31	CHF
2	66	M	AP	4.0	1.8	55	distal	0.58	7	none
3	73	M	MI	2.9	1.4	52	distal	0.59	9	none
4	75	M	MI	2.5	1.5	40	body	0.62	27	none
5	64	M	AP	3.5	1.7	51	distal	0.61	10	none
6	75	M	AP	3.6	1.9	47	body	0.62	8	none
7	76	M	AP	4.6	2.5	46	distal	0.64	13	CHF
8	59	M	AP	3.3	1.2	64	orifice	0.65	8	none

Abbreviations: AP: angina pectoris, CHF; chronic heart failure, F/U: follow-up (months), LMCA: left main coronary artery, MI: myocardial infarction, MLD: minimal lumen diameter, RVD: reference vessel diameter, %DS: percent diameter stenosis

One patient in medical group underwent coronary angioplasty in the proximal lesion of LAD. The FFR of LMCA of that patient was 0.90 (Figure 5). In medical group no cardiac event was observed during follow-up (Table 2). In surgical group two patients hospitalized for congestive heart failure because of depressed left ventricular function (Table 3).

DISCUSSION

Our results clearly showed that coronary pressure measurement for equivocal LMCA disease was clinically useful for decision making of optimal treatment strategy.

There are some problems dealing with LMCA stenosis. First, our result showed that coronary angiography could not distinguish patients with normal FFR from those with abnormal FFR. Actually accurate assessment of the stenosis severity is often difficult for LMCA stenosis. Coronary angiography has some limitations for assessment of coronary artery stenosis. Pathological studies demonstrated that atherosclerosis involves coronary artery diffusely and recent intravascular ultrasound (IVUS) studies confirmed this finding in vivo [9-10]. And intravascular ultrasound studies found that coronary remodeling frequently occurs, which prevent narrowing of coronary arterial lumen by compensatory enlargement of the coronary artery [11]. These findings suggest that true reference segment cannot be identified by coronary angiography. Cameron et al studied the reliability of angiographic assessment of the LMCA stenosis [6]. They reviewed 106 coronary angiograms and found that there was only 41% to 59% agreement on the severity of the lesion among three groups of angiographers. Garber et al performed intravascular ultrasound study in 60 patients [12]. While significant LMCA stenosis was present in 2 patients IVUS demonstrated plaques in 27 of 60 LMCAs, six of them in patients with normal angiograms. When the LMCA lesion was immeasurably short, diffusely diseased, or obscured by overlapping vessels, determination of severity of the LMAC by angiography was especially difficult. Therefore angiographic assessment is not enough for the accurate evaluation of LMCA stenosis.

Second, if LMCA stenosis is not functionally significant bypass graft will be occluded and unnecessary bypass surgery will be performed. Abizaid et al followed 122 patients with moderate ($\geq$50% diameter stenosis) LMCA stenosis for one year [13]. The lesion site minimum lumen diameter by quantitative coronary angiography correlated moderately with IVIS (r=0.364) and they found that one-year event rate was only 14%, only four patients died. This study suggests that most patients with moderate LMCA stenosis do not benefit from CABG and these patients may not have functionally significant LMCA stenosis. Our results demonstrated that coronary pressure measurement could identify patients who benefit from CABG. We found that any patients with medication showed no symptoms due to LMCA lesion.

Third, if LMCA stenosis is not functionally significant and functionally significant coronary stenosis exists in the other part of coronary artery percutaneous coronary intervention for this lesion should be the appropriate treatment. LMCA stenosis has been known to be frequently associated with coronary stenosis in the other part of coronary artery [14]. This situation actually happened in one of our patients in medical group.

Fourth, non-invasive tests, such as myocardial perfusion imaging, often fail to differentiate between ischemia caused by LMCA stenosis and that caused by coronary stenosis located in the other part of the coronary artery.

By coronary pressure measurement most of these problems can be solved.

There are one report which selected treatment strategy by FFR results in patients with equivocal LMCA disease [15]. Bech et al measured FFR in 54 patients with equivocal LMCA stenosis and assigned 24 patients with FFR$\geq$0.75 to medical treatment and 30 patients with FFR <0.75 to CABG. Event-free survival at three years was not significantly different between the medical group and surgical group (76% vs 83%, respectively). In medical group two patients underwent coronary angioplasty and three patients underwent CABG. In contrast we found no cardiac event in our medically treated patients. The discrepancy of their and our findings was obscure.

It is mandatory to emphasize the importance of careful follow-up of patients with medical therapy. Rupture of coronary plaque in the LMCA followed by thrombus formation will likely to result in catastrophic event [2-4]. Therefore we observed patients in medical group carefully with intensive medical therapy, including statin and ACE inhibitors.

As for coronary pressure measurement of LMCA stenosis, the position of the catheter is critical for the accurate assessment. The tip of the catheter should not be engaged in LMCA and rather should be slightly removed from the ostium of LMCA, which enabled us to measure precisely the proximal coronary pressure of the LMCA stenosis. Then pressure wire is gradually pulled back under fluoroscopy. Caution should be made not to allow deep engagement of the tip of the catheter into the LMCA during gradual pull-back of pressure wire. These careful coronary pressure measurements provided precise FFR measurement across the LMCA lesion

There are several limitations in the present study. One of them is that the present study included relatively small number of patients because the LMCA stenosis is not frequently encountered. Careful follow-up, including coronary angiography, may partially compensate for this limitation.

CONCLUSION

Coronary pressure measurement for equivocal left main coronary artery disease was clinically useful to make decision for CABG.

REFERENCES

[1] de Feyter PJ, Serruys PW. Thrombolysis of acute total occlusion of the left maincoronary artery in evolving myocardial infarction. *Am J Cardiol* 1984;53:1727-1728.

[2] Goldberg S, Grossman W, Markis JE, Cohen MV, Baltave HA, Levin DC. Total occlusion of the left main coronary artery. A clinical, hemodynamic and angiographic profile. *Am J Med* 1978;64:3-8.

[3] Ward DE, Valantine H, Hui W. Occluded left main stem coronary artery. Report of five patients and review of published reports. *Br Heart J* 1983;49:276-279.

[4] Iwasaki K, Kusachi S, Hina K, Nishiyama O, Kondo J, Kita T, Hata T, Taniguchi G, Tsuji T. Acute left main coronary artery obstruction with myocardial infarction--reperfusion strategies, and the clinical and angiographic outcome. *Jpn Circ J* 1993;57:891-897.

[5] Johnston PW, Fort S, Cohen EA. Noncritical disease of the left main coronary artery: limitations of angiography and the role of intravascular ultrasound. *Can J Cardiol* 1999;15:297-302.

[6] Cameron A, Kemp HG, Jr., Fisher LD, Gosselin A, Judkins MP, Kennedy JW, Lesperance J, Mudd JG, Ryan TJ, Silverman JF, Tristani F, Vlietstra RE, Wexler LF. Left main coronary artery stenosis: angiographic determination. *Circulation* 1983;68:484-489.

[7] Pijls NH, Van Gelder B, Van der Voort P. Fractional flow reserve. A useful index to evaluate the influence of an epicardial coronary stenosis on myocardial blood flow. *Circulation* 1995;92:3183-3193.

[8] Pijls NH, De Bruyne B, Peels K, van der Voort PH, Bonnier HJR, Bartunek J, Koolen JJ. Measurement of fractional flow reserve to assess the functional severity of coronary-artery stenoses. *N Engl J Med* 1996;334:1703-1708.

[9] Grodin CM, Dydra I, Pasternac L, Bourassa MG. Discrepancies between cineangiographic and post-mortem findings in patients with coronary artery disease and recent myocardial revascularization. *Circulation* 1974;49:703-709.

[10] Blankenhorn DH, Curry PJ. The accuracy of arteriography and ultrasound imaging for atherosclerosis measurement: a review. *Arch Pathol Lab Med* 1982;106:483-490.

[11] Glagov S, Weisenberg E, Zarins CK, Stankunavicius R, Kolettis GJ. Compensatory enlargement of human atherosclerotic coronary arteries. *N Engl J Med* 1987;316:1371-1375.

[12] Gerber TC, Erbel R, Gorge G, Ge J, Ruprecht HJ, Meyer J. Extent of atherosclerosis and remodeling of the left main coronary artery determined by intravascular ultrasound. *Am J Cardiol* 1994;73:666-671.

[13] Abizaid AS, Mintz GS, Abizaid A, Mehran R, Lansky AJ, Pichard AD, Satler LF, Wu H, Kent KM, Leon MB. One-year follow-up after intravascular ultrasound assessment of moderate left main coronary artery disease in patients with ambiguous angiograms. *J Am Coll Cardiol* 1999;34:707-715.

[14] Sukhija R, Yalamanchili K, Aronow WS. Prevalence of left main coronary artery disease, of three- or four-vessel coronary artery disease, and of obstructive coronary artery disease in patients with and without peripheral arterial disease undergoing coronary angiography for suspected coronary artery disease. *Am J Cardiol* 2003;92:304-305.

[15] Bech GJ, Droste H, Pijls NH, De Bruyne B, Bonnier JJ, Michels HR, Peels KH, Koolen JJ. Value of fractional flow reserve in making decisions about bypass surgery for equivocal left main coronary artery disease. *Heart* 2001;86:547-552.

In: Psychology of Decision Making
Editor: Paul M. Garrison

ISBN 978-1-60021-869-9
© Nova Science Publishers, Inc.

Chapter 1

ANTITERRORIST EMERGENCY VENTILATION: SYSTEM, STRATEGY AND DECISION-MAKING

Xianting Li[1*], Hao Cai[1,2] and Lina Zhao[1]

[1]Department of Building Science, School of Architecture, Tsinghua University, Beijing, 100084, China

[2]Engineering Institution of Engineering Corps, PLA University of Science and Technology, Nanjing, 210007, China

ABSTRACT

There are two kinds of antiterrorist emergency ventilation system. One is to defend indoor environment against chemical and biological agent (CBA) attacks. The other is to supply calmative gas to incapacitate terrorists when they hold hostages in public buildings. What kind of system and ventilation strategy can be used for antiterrorism, and how to make decision are introduced in the chapter. There are six sections in the chapter.

How the emergency ventilation systems work is introduced in the first section.

The second section is on the theory of contaminant dispersion and identification of contaminant source. For the theory of contaminant dispersion, both computational fluid dynamics (CFD) method and analytical formula of contaminant distribution are introduced. For the theory of contaminant source identification, an algorithm to identify the position and intensity of contaminant source with limited number of sensors is proposed and demonstrated for its effectiveness.

The third section is on the evacuation model and evaluation of exposure risk. Both cellular automata (CA) model and spatial-grid evacuation model (SGEM) are introduced for modeling evacuation process. The relative exposure risk index, EFCS, and absolute exposure risk index, PIR, are introduced to evaluate the exposure risk of contaminant.

Both the second section and third section are the fundamental of emergency ventilation. Based on section 2 and 3, the ventilation strategy and decision-making are introduced for emergency ventilation against contaminant suddenly released in public

---

[*] Corresponding author: Xianting Li, Department of Building Science, School of Architecture, Tsinghua University, Beijing, 100084, P.R. China. Tel: +86-10-62785860; Fax: +86-10-62773461; E-mail: xtingli@tsinghua.edu.cn

building in section 4 and for emergency ventilation to rescue hostages held by terrorists in section 5, respectively.

Section 6 is the summary of the whole chapter.

Keywords: Emergency ventilation, Contaminant dispersion, Source identification, Evacuation model, Exposure risk, Decision-making, Antiterrorism

NOMENCLATURE

$A_{ci,p}$	accessibility of contaminant source to an arbitrary point p from the ith source
$A_{ci}(\beta_j,\tau)$	accessibility of contaminant source at position α_i to sensor β_j in any time period τ
$A_{c*}(\beta_j,\tau)$	accessibility of contaminant source at position α^* to sensor β_j in any time period τ
$A_{si,p}$	accessibility of supply air to an arbitrary point p from the ith inlet
a	constant
BEC_i	basic exposure cell
b	constant
C	mass concentration of contaminant
$C_{e,i}$	average exhausted concentration of tracer gas under steady-state conditions only when the i-th source exists
$C_i(\beta_j,t)$	concentration of contaminant at sensor β_j at moment t
$C^*(\beta_j,t)$	concentration of contaminant at sensor β_j when there is a contaminant source at position α^* with intensity S^*
$\overline{C}_{1,i}(t)$	volume-averaged concentration for one-layer model
$\overline{C}_{3,i}(t)$	volume-averaged concentration of all layers for three-layers model
$\overline{C}_i(t)$	contaminant concentration in the exposure cell EC_i at time t
$C_{in,i}$	concentration of tracer gas at the ith supply inlet
$C_p(t)$	concentration of tracer gas at an arbitrary point p at moment t
C_0	initial conconcentration
$\overline{C}_R$	average exhausted concentration of contaminant under steady-state conditions
$C_{s,i}$	contaminant concentration of supply air at the i-th inlet
$C_{s,max}$	maximum contaminant concentration of supply air at all inlets
$CN_j(t)$	serial number of exposure cell in which the j-th person stays at time t
D	crowded density (number of persons/m^2) of the calculated grid☐decision space
$D(x,y,z)$	occupied density
$D_h(x,y,z)$	occupied density of hostages

$D_t(x,y,z)$	occupied density of terrorists
d^*	optimal decision alternative under the state of nature S_j
d_i	decision alternative
E	toxic exposure
$E(d_i)$	expected payoff
$E(d^*)$	maximum expected payoff
EC_i	exposure cell
$EFCS1_i(\tau)$	influence of contaminant source on the occupants who once stayed in EC_i in the period τ
$EFCS2_i(\tau)$	influence of contaminant source on the j-th occupant in the period τ
$EFCS3_i(\tau)$	influence of contaminant source on the whole population ever indoors in the period τ
$EFCS3(\tau,d_i,S_j)$	value of EFCS3 for the combination of the decision alternative d_i and the state of nature S_j in the period τ
ER_j	injured degree of the j-th occupant in the period τ
f	friction probability
f_1	friction probability when 2-4 pedestrians move vis-à-vis
f_2	friction probability for the conflict between a moving pedestrian and a standstill one
f_w	friction probability for the conflict between a moving pedestrian and a wall
g_x	acceleration of gravity in the x-axis
g_y	acceleration of gravity in the y-axis
g_z	acceleration of gravity in the z-axis
$H(d_i)$	Hurwicz criterion
$H(d^*)$	the maximum of Hurwicz criterion
h	air enthalpy
$ID^i(x,y,z)$	individual occupied density of the i-th occupant at each point in the room
$IR(x,y,z,\tau)$	injury risk of the vulnerable people
k	turbulent kinetic energy
$L2$	injury proportion for people suffering from exposed concentrations as high as AEGL2
$L3$	injury proportion for people suffering from exposed concentrations as high as AEGL3
M	number of control volumes
m	number of the individuals, $m=1,2,\cdots,N$; number of pedestrians involved in the conflict
$mark_i$	mark for the identification system to identify the ith source
N	number of occupants indoors; number of sensors
n	aggregating number of people in a certain domain at the individual's location
OD^i_j	individual occupied density of the i-th occupant for j-th region indoors
P	exposure risk probit

$P(d_i, S_j)$	payoff of the decision alternative d_i under the state of nature S_j
$P(d^*, S_j)$	maximum (or minimum) value of the payoffs
PIR	population injury rate
$PIR(\tau)$	average injured degree of the whole occupants in the period τ
$PIR(\tau, d_i, S_j)$	value of PIR for the combination of the decision alternative d_i and the state of nature S_j in the period τ
$PIR_h(\tau)$	population injury rate of hostages
$PIR_t(\tau)$	population injury rate of terrorists
$PNC_i(t)$	number of indoor occupants in the exposure cell EC_i at time t
ΔPIR	injury difference between hostages and terrorists
p	air pressure
p_i	moving probability of each pedestrian
p_j	probability of state S_j
p_{stay}	stay probability
Q	total airflow rate for the ventilated space
RES	average of the absolute values of the relative errors
RES_i	relative error of the identification system for the i-th source intensity
r	repulsion probability
r_1	repulsion probability when 2-4 pedestrians move together
r_2	repulsion probability for the conflict between a moving pedestrian and a standstill one
r_w	repulsion probability for the conflict between a moving pedestrian and a wall
S_0	known source of contaminant
S_c	contaminant source
$S_{C,k}$	the kth source of tracer gas
S_h	heat source
S_i	intensity of each contaminant source
S_j	state of nature
T	air temperature
TAC_j	average exposure concentration of the j-th occupant in the period τ
T_{ref}	reference temperature
Δt	time step
U	speed of an individual
U_j	three velocity components, i.e., u, v, w, when j=1, 2, 3 respectively
U_m	velocity component of the person at time step t in the x direction
U_0	speed of an individual when he/she does not encounter any crowd obstruction
u	velocity component in the x direction
$\vec{u}$	velocity vector
V	vulnerability intensity; relative speed
V_m	velocity component of the person at time step t in the y direction
V_j	volume of the j-th region of the room

v	velocity component in y-axis; absolute speed
w	velocity component in z-axis
x_j	three directions of axis, i.e., x, y, z, when $j=1, 2, 3$ respectively
$x(m,t)$	geometrical coordinates of the person whose number is m at time step t in the x direction
Y	probit variable
$y(m,t)$	geometrical coordinates of the person whose number is m at time step t in the y direction
Z	total score of the judgements from the identification system
Z_i	score of the identifion system for the i-th source
Z_k	mark of the identificaton system for the k-th source location

Greek Letters

α	hardness degree; coefficient of optimism
α_i	center position of the i-th control volume
β	volumetric coefficient of expansion
β_j	position of the j-th sensor
θ	friction coefficient reflecting the roughness of pedestrian and wall; angle between the direction and x-axis
ε	dissipation rate of turbulent kinetic
ϕ	dependent variable
$\phi_i^T(\tau)$	probability that the source is located at the i-th control volume
φ	relative error
$\varphi_i(\beta_j,\tau)$	relative error for all the relative distances from sensor β_j
ρ	density
γ	time-averaged ratio
$\gamma_i(\beta_j,\tau)$	time-averaged ratio between $A_{ci}(\beta_j,\tau)$ and $A_{c*}^0(\beta_j,\tau)$
$\bar{\gamma}_i(\tau)$	averaged ratio
δ	relative distance
$\delta_i(\beta_j,\tau)$	relative distance from the ratio between $A_{ci}(\beta_j,\tau)$ and $A_{c*}^0(\beta_j,\tau)$ to $\gamma_i(\beta_j,\tau)$
τ	time period; elapsed time
τ_j	occupied time of the j-th occupant in the room
μ_{eff}	effective viscosity
μ_l	laminar viscosity
μ_t	turbulence viscosity

ABBREVIATIONS

ACS	Accessibility of Contaminant Source
AEE	Air Exchange Efficiency
AEGL	Acute Exposure Guideline Level
ASA	Accessibility of Supply Air
CA	Cellular Automata
CAD	Computer Aided Design
CBA	Chemical and Biological Agent
CBWA	Chemical and Biological Warfare Agent
CFD	Computational Fluid Dynamics
EC	Exposure Cell
EFCS	Efficiency Factor of Contaminant Source
EFSA	Efficiency Factor of Supply Air
EPA	Environmental Protection Agency
FEMA	Federal Emergency Management Agency
FVM	Finite Volume Method
IACS	Integrated Accessibility of Contaminant Source
IR	Injury Risk
LEV	Local Exhaust Ventilation
MMRS	Metropolitan Medical Response Systems
NIOSH	National Institute for Occupational Safety and Health
OD	Occupied Density
PD	Position Danger Grade
PIR	Population Injury Rate
RANS	Reynolds Average Navier-Stokes
SGEM	Spatial-Grid Evacuation Model
SQP	Sequential Quadratic Programming
SVE	Scale for Ventilation Effectiveness
USPS	United States Postal Service

1. WHY IS ANTITERRORIST EMERGENCY VENTILATION NEEDED?

1.1. Background

Following the events of September 11, 2001 in New York, deadly bombings killed 190 and wounded 1200 people in Madrid on March 11, 2004 and killed dozens and injured hundreds seriously in London on July 7, 2005. All these events demonstrate that terrorist attacks are becoming more frequent and deadlier. Never, not even in the Cold War era, was there a threat of deliberate release of chemical and biological agent (CBA), comparable to the one that exists today.

In order to know whether people are prepared for a deliberate release of CBA, Rivera and Char (2004) made a survey in St Louis, Missouri to see whether emergency department providers are familiar with the Metropolitan Medical Response Systems (MMRS) which are one form of targeted funding aimed at improving regional preparedness and response. The conclusions show that many emergency department providers are aware of the heightened concern about disaster preparedness. However, our ability to respond effectively remains limited. Pooransingh and Hawkera (2006) made a similar survey in West Midlands, UK. Findings revealed that plans delineating action to take during an incident do exist. However, staff training (40%) in acute trusts and testing of plans in primary care trusts (45%) could be improved. The scenarios may be much worse in other countries all over the world.

Are our buildings prepared for such kind of deliberate release of CBA? Researchers from the National Institute for Occupational Safety and Health (NIOSH) have conducted several evaluations of local exhaust ventilation (LEV) systems for the United States Postal Service (USPS) since autumn 2001 when (a) terrorist(s) employed the mail system for acts of bioterrorism. The conclusion is the development and installation of LEV onto USPS mail-processing equipment can reduce future exposures to operators from potentially hazardous contaminants, such as anthrax, which might be emitted during the processing of mail (Bryan R. Beamer, 2004). Although NIOSH released guidelines for protecting ventilation systems in commercial and government buildings from chemical, biological and radiological attack (NIOSH, 2002), Chen (2004) believes there is a long way to go to protect our buildings from CBA attacks.

On the other hand, in October 26, 2002, the Russian military used an anesthetic "gas" to incapacitate Chechen rebels in rescuing hostages at Moscow Dubrovka Theater Center (Wax et al., 2003). Although there are debates on whether such kind of calmative "gas" should be used, more and more attentions are paid on what kind of incapacitating gas we should use and how to use the gas to incapacitate terrorists when they hold hostages. Obviously, such kind of technology should be closely combined with ventilation systems in buildings.

Therefore, ventilation systems in buildings should not only act as the provider for healthy, comfortable indoor environment, but also take important role against CBA attacks or in supplying calmative gas to incapacitate terrorists.

For the former purpose, many kinds of indices have been proposed to evaluate the ventilation effectiveness, such as air age (Sandberg and Sjoberg, 1983), air exchange efficiency (AEE) (Sandberg and Sjoberg, 1983; Sandberg 1983), contamination removal efficiency (Sandberg, 1981), scale for measuring ventilation effectiveness in a room (SVE) (Murakami, 1992; Kato et al., 1994), etc., which can be a guide for ventilation system designing or ventilation strategy decision-making. However, all these indices are appropriate for evaluating the ventilation performance in steady conditions and cannot be applied for contaminant dispersion in a short period.

Since ventilation for the latter purpose will not be used frequently, it belongs to range of emergency ventilation. Although we have emergency ventilation system for fire safety in buildings, the purpose of aforementioned emergency ventilation is different from fire safety and therefore it should be different from the traditional emergency ventilation. Here we call it antiterrorist emergency ventilation system.

1.2. Antiterrorist Emergency Ventilation System

The antiterrorist emergency ventilation systems can be divided into two categories.

One is immediate, portable emergency ventilation system which can be used for on-scene medical response. Unfortunately, current capabilities for providing simple respiratory assistance for hundreds or even thousands of victims of CBA attacks do not exist. However, lightweight, portable ventilator and medical diagnostic systems for the treatment of far-forward battlefield and mass civilian casualties can be available. (Kerechanin II et al., 2004)

The other is the emergency ventilation system in existing buildings. As NIOSH (2002) emphasized, industrial facilities, military facilities, subway systems, and law enforcement facilities are higher risk facilities to be attacked by terrorists. Governmental buildings, including offices, laboratories, hospitals, retail facilities, schools, transportation terminals, and public venues (for example, sports arenas, malls) are more possibly attacked by terrorists. Therefore, emergency ventilation systems are very important to these buildings.

Since the attacks to important buildings will have both wide and deep influence, we focus on the emergency ventilation systems in existing public buildings in this chapter.

1.2.1. Previous Studies

The previous work related to antiterrorist emergency ventilation systems will be introduced briefly here.

Bailey et al. (2004) suggested that existing technologies must be identified and validated before their implementation against CBA attacks. They believe the following sub-areas are very important to emergency ventilation: (1) modeling and simulation of airborne chemical/biological contaminant dispersion in a building, (2) intelligent building control, and (3) CBA-related whole building diagnostics.

Chen (2004) discussed the important issues related to emergency ventilation to protect buildings from CBWA (chemical and biological warfare agent) attacks. One is sensors and sensor systems, which are crucial for obtaining the necessary information. Since both biological and chemical sensors are expensive, one could not afford to place such sensors or sensor systems everywhere in most buildings. It is important to install limited number sensors to get the necessary information. The other is how to predict the transportation and distribution of CBA in buildings. Computational fluid dynamics (CFD), multi-zone models, and zonal models are available methods. However, accurate methods need too much computing time, and fast ones are not accurate. A reliable and fast method has yet to be developed for the prediction of CBA dispersion in and around buildings.

In order to know how flow pattern influence the dispersion of contaminant in limited time period, Li and Zhao (2004) proposed the concept of accessibility. Two indices, accessibility of supply air (ASA) and accessibility of contaminant source (ACS) were proposed to describe the distributed contribution of supply air and contaminant source to the dispersion of contaminant quantitatively.

Based on the index of ACS, Zhao et al. (2004a) integrated the concept of Occupied Density (OD) (Zhao et al. 2003c) with ACS and took the integrated accessibility of contaminant source (IACS) as an index to evaluate what kind of ventilation strategy will be better to defend indoor environment against contamination. Chen et al (2005) further analyzed the influence of contaminant source location, occupant distribution and air distribution on emergency ventilation strategy numerically.

In order to calculate the dispersion of contaminant distribution quickly, Yang et al (2004) proposed an analytical formula to predict the transient dispersion of contaminant. The essence of the formula is to replace the time-consuming CFD simulation with indices of ASA and ACS. Therefore, the formula is with almost the same accuracy as CFD simulation, but much less computing time, provided the flow field is steady.

Based on the analytical formula, Li et al (2005) proposed a strategy to optimize the building ventilation system to aid rescue of hostages held by terrorists.

In order to consider the influence of evacuation process on the exposure of occupants, Cai (2006) proposed two set of indices, efficiency factor of contaminant source (EFCS) and efficiency factor of supply air (EFSA). Two algorithms to identify contaminant source were also proposed based on one sensor and two sensors respectively.

Based on these previous studies, the antiterrorist emergency ventilation systems are proposed in following sections.

1.2.2. Emergency Ventilation System against Contaminant Suddenly Released in Public Building

Since biological agent attack is much complicated, we will show the emergency ventilation system based on chemical agent in the chapter. In order to protect people in public buildings, the emergency ventilation system must have the following functions:

(1) Detect contaminant release online;
(2) Guide people to shelter in place or evacuate;
(3) Switch to emergency ventilation mode.

For contaminant detection, we need not only if there is contaminant release, but also the position and intensity, so that optimal ventilation strategy can be implemented. In order to guide people's evacuation, we need to know how people will evacuate and start the best ventilation strategy to protect people from contaminant exposure. All these work will be finished in seconds rather than minutes by the emergency ventilation system. Therefore, only work with less computing time can be done on-site. There are three stages in such kind of emergency ventilation system:

(1) Stage 1: Pretreatment
   In this stage, all scenarios (for example, different ventilation mode, occupant distribution, typical contaminant sources) necessary and time-consuming will be simulated with accurate toolkits and the results will be stored in emergency ventilation system.
(2) Stage 2: Identification of contaminant online
   In this stage, readings of sensors will be transferred to emergency ventilation system. Software on contaminant identification will decide whether there is contaminant release and tell the position and intensity of contaminant source if there is.
(3) Stage 3: Execution of emergency ventilation
   In this stage, emergency ventilation system will decide whether to shelter in place or evacuate based on the contaminant detected, and the corresponding

emergency ventilation mode will be started to protect occupants from contaminant exposure until the emergency is over.

All the stages will be related to the dispersion of contaminant, evacuation of occupants, optimal ventilation strategy and decision-making, which will be introduced in the following sections.

1.2.3. Emergency Ventilation System for Rescuing Hostages Held by Terrorists

When anesthetic gas is supplied to rescue hostages held by terrorists, the most important concerns are: (1) whether the dose is enough to incapacitate terrorists, (2) whether there is lethal influence on hostages. Therefore, the concentration of anesthetic gas in supply air, in which mode to supply air, and the time period for injection should be analyzed, and injury to both terrorists and hostages should be evaluated before decision-making.

In this case, it seems that we will have more time for computation than what we have in emergency ventilation system against contaminant suddenly released in public building. However, since we will compare a lot of different scenarios to get an optimal result, the possible computing time is still limited. Therefore, there are three stages in such kind of emergency ventilation system:

Stage 1: Pretreatment
In this stage, the flow fields of all possible ventilation modes will be simulated and stored in computer so that such kind of time-consuming work will not be done when emergency occurs.

Stage 2: Determine optimal strategy
In this stage, different anesthetic gas, ventilation modes, concentration of supply air and injection period will be simulated and the injury to terrorists and hostages will be evaluated. The optimal strategy will be made based on the comparisons of different scenarios.

Stage 3: Execution of emergency ventilation
In this stage, the optimal strategy will be executed and other information, such as on-scene medical response, will be provided by emergency ventilation system.

The simulation of flow fields and method to determine optimal strategy will be introduced in detail in the following sections.

2. MODELING OF CONTAMINANT DISPERSION AND SOURCE IDENTIFICATION

The method to predict contaminant dispersion and to identify contaminant source is of importance to antiterrorist emergency ventilation.

Traditionally, there are three methods to predict contaminant dispersion in buildings, i.e., CFD, multi-zone models, and zonal models. Since the distribution of contaminant rather than the average concentration is important to the ventilation strategy, CFD method is the best one for predicting the contaminant distribution in buildings and will be introduced here. The main problem for CFD method is that it needs too much computing time. Therefore, new method with same accuracy but much less computing time as CFD method will be introduced then.

For identification of contaminant source, a method with limited number of sensors is introduced, which can identify the position and intensity of contaminant source online.

2.1. CFD Method

Generally speaking, CFD is a method to predict what will happen, quantitatively, when fluids flow. For contaminant dispersion in buildings, CFD method will show us the movement of air and the distribution of temperature, humidity and contaminant at any time.

There are two radically different states of air flows: laminar flow and turbulent flow. The air flow in buildings is seldom laminar flow. Therefore, only CFD method for turbulent flow is introduced here.

2.1.1. Physical and Mathematical Modeling

The air flow in buildings can usually be taken as incompressible turbulent fluid. The three-dimensional time-averaged equations of conservation of mass, momentum, thermal energy and chemical species can be written in the following general form:

$$\frac{\partial}{\partial t}(\rho\phi) + div(\rho \vec{u} \phi - \Gamma_\varphi grad\phi) = S_\phi \qquad (2.1.1-1)$$

where ϕ is a dependent variable, ρ is the density, $\vec{u}$ is the velocity vector. The details of ϕ, Γ_φ and S_ϕ are given in Table 2.1.1-1, where u, v, w are the three velocity components in x, y, z directions respectively. μ_l, μ_t, μ_{eff} are laminar, turbulence and effective viscosity respectively; p is air pressure, h is air enthalpy and C is the mass concentration of contaminant; k, ε are the turbulent kinetic energy and its dissipation rate respectively; g_x, g_y, g_z are acceleration of gravity in x, y, z directions respectively; β is volumetric coefficient of expansion, T is air temperature, T_{ref} is the reference temperature; S_h and S_C are the heat source and contaminant source respectively.

The above equations can be solved numerically after initial and boundary conditions are given.

2.1.2. Numerical Method

These governing equations are highly non-linear and self-coupled, and analytical solutions for engineering problems are seldom available. Therefore, to obtain the solution of the conservative governing equations it is necessary to use numerical technique. The main process to solve these equations is as follows:

(1) Generation of grid(s)
(2) Discretization of governing partial differential equations
(3) Solutions of algebraic equations
(4) Iteration for convergence.

**Table 2.1.1-1. The governing equations for air flow
and contaminant dispersion in buildings**

ϕ	Γ_φ	S_ϕ
1	0	0
u	μ_{eff}	$-\dfrac{\partial p}{\partial x}+\dfrac{\partial}{\partial x}(\mu_{eff}\dfrac{\partial u}{\partial x})+\dfrac{\partial}{\partial y}(\mu_{eff}\dfrac{\partial v}{\partial x})+\dfrac{\partial}{\partial z}(\mu_{eff}\dfrac{\partial w}{\partial x})+\rho\beta g_x(T_{ref}-T)$
v	μ_{eff}	$-\dfrac{\partial p}{\partial y}+\dfrac{\partial}{\partial x}(\mu_{eff}\dfrac{\partial u}{\partial y})+\dfrac{\partial}{\partial y}(\mu_{eff}\dfrac{\partial v}{\partial y})+\dfrac{\partial}{\partial z}(\mu_{eff}\dfrac{\partial w}{\partial y})+\rho\beta g_y(T_{ref}-T)$
w	μ_{eff}	$-\dfrac{\partial p}{\partial z}+\dfrac{\partial}{\partial x}(\mu_{eff}\dfrac{\partial u}{\partial z})+\dfrac{\partial}{\partial y}(\mu_{eff}\dfrac{\partial v}{\partial z})+\dfrac{\partial}{\partial z}(\mu_{eff}\dfrac{\partial w}{\partial z})+\rho\beta g_z(T_{ref}-T)$
k	$\dfrac{\mu_{eff}}{\sigma_k}$	$G_k-\rho\varepsilon$
ε	$\dfrac{\mu_{eff}}{\sigma_\varepsilon}$	$\dfrac{\varepsilon}{k}[G_k C_1 - C_2\rho\varepsilon]$
h	$\dfrac{\mu_{eff}}{\sigma_h}$	S_h
C	$\dfrac{\mu_{eff}}{\sigma_c}$	S_C

$\mu_{eff}=\mu_l+\mu_t$, $\mu_t=C_D\rho\, k^2/\varepsilon$ for standard k-ε model

$\mu_t=0.03874\rho vl$ for zero-equation model (Chen and Xu, 1998)

$G_k=\mu_t\{2[(\dfrac{\partial u}{\partial x})^2+(\dfrac{\partial v}{\partial y})^2+(\dfrac{\partial w}{\partial z})^2]+(\dfrac{\partial u}{\partial z}+\dfrac{\partial w}{\partial x})^2+(\dfrac{\partial w}{\partial y}+\dfrac{\partial v}{\partial z})^2+(\dfrac{\partial u}{\partial y}+\dfrac{\partial v}{\partial x})^2\}$

$C_1=1.44, C_2=1.92, C_D=0.09, \sigma_k=1.0, \sigma_\varepsilon=1.3, \sigma_h=1.0, \sigma_c=1.0$

The details of the solving process has been completely described by Patankar (1980). Now a lot of commercial CFD tools are available to solve air flow and contaminant dispersion in buildings. The main process to use these tools is as follows:

(1) Generate grids
(2) Prescribe boundary conditions
(3) Prescribe initial conditions (for unsteady problem)
(4) Select turbulence model
(5) Select numerical parameters and post-processing variables
(6) Execute CFD code
(7) Post-process

In this chapter, two CFD tools will be used for simulation.
One is STACH-3, developed by Tsinghua University (Li and Yan, 1995; Zhao *et al.* 2003b). There are two turbulence models: $k-\varepsilon$ turbulence model and a zero-equation

turbulence model (Chen and Xu, 1988) available in STACH-3. The Reynolds Average Navier-Stokes (RANS) equations are discretized by finite volume method (FVM). The difference scheme is power law scheme. Semi-Implicit Method for Pressure-Linked Equations (SIMPLE) algorithm is adopted while momentum equations are solved on non-uniform staggered grids (Patankar, 1980). For $k-\varepsilon$ turbulence model, wall functions are employed; for the zero-equation turbulence model, the algebraic equation of eddy viscosity is adopted directly in the near wall region. The reliability of STACH-3 to predict air flow and contaminant dispersion has been validated by Zhao et al. (2000, 2001, 2002, 2003a, 2003b, 2004b).

The other is a commercial CFD program AIRPAK (http://airpak.fluent.com/), which is a customized version of the general-purpose program FLUENT (http://www.fluent.com/) tailored for accurately modeling airflow, heat transfer, contaminant transport, and thermal comfort in ventilation systems as well as external building flows. AIRPAK uses the FLUENT solver engine for thermal and fluid-flow calculations. The solver engine provides complete mesh flexibility, and allows users to solve complex geometries using unstructured meshes. The multigrid and segregated solver algorithms provide robust and quick calculations (Fluent Inc., 2002). The reliability of AIRPAK has been validated on numerous occasions for indoor air flow and contaminant dispersion studies, such as that reported by Architectural Energy Corporation and Halton Company (2004).

2.2. Modeling of Contaminant Dispersion

Usually it takes only seconds to build the air flow pattern indoors, but hours for the contaminant dispersion. For emergency ventilation, the heat sources indoors can be taken as unchangeable during the period of emergency ventilation. Therefore, the air flow field can be treated as steady.

For chemical contaminant, the dispersion has little influence on the air flow. Since it is usually turbulent flow indoors, and the turbulence diffusion will be much greater than the molecular diffusion, most of the chemical gas can be treated as passive contaminant in ventilation rooms. In this case, the dispersion of contaminant can be calculated without numerical iteration when the air flow field is given and kept steady.

2.2.1. Concept of Accessibility

(1) Accessibility of Supply Air (ASA)

When the flow field is steady, the accessibility of supply air to an arbitrary point p from the ith inlet is defined by tracer gas concentration in the case with the following initial and boundary conditions:

$$\begin{cases} C_{in,i} = C_{s,i} & \text{for the ith inlet} \\ C_{in,j} = 0 & \text{for all the other inlets} (j \neq i) \\ S_{C,k} = 0 & \text{for all the sources} \end{cases} \quad (2.2.1\text{-}1)$$

Initial condition:

$$C_p(t)\big|_{t=0} = 0 \qquad (2.2.1\text{-}2)$$

where $C_{in,i}$ is the concentration of tracer gas at the ith supply inlet, $S_{C,k}$ is the kth source of tracer gas, $C_p(t)$ is the concentration of tracer gas at an arbitrary point p at moment t.

The accessibility of supply air to an arbitrary point p from the ith inlet is then defined as (Yang et al, 2004):

$$A_{si,p}(\tau) = \frac{\int_0^{\tau} C_p(t)dt}{C_{s,i} \cdot \tau} \qquad (2.2.1\text{-}3)$$

where τ is the time period from moment $t=0$.

ASA quantifies how easily the air from a supply inlet is continuously delivered into an indoor location. It is a function of the flow characteristic and has nothing to do with contaminant type and source. ASA can be easily calculated by the definition with CFD tools when the flow field is available.

(2) Accessibility of Contaminant Source (ACS)

When the flow field is steady, the accessibility of contaminant source to an arbitrary point p from the ith source is defined by tracer gas concentration in the case with the following boundary conditions (the initial condition is same with Eq. (2.2.1-2)):

$$\begin{cases} C_{in,j} = 0 & \text{for all the inlets} \\ S_{C,i} = S_i & \text{for the ith inlet} \\ S_{C,k} = 0 & \text{for all the sources}(k \neq i) \end{cases} \qquad (2.2.1\text{-}4)$$

The accessibility of contaminant source to an arbitrary point p from the ith source is then defined as (Yang et al, 2004):

$$A_{ci,p}(\tau) = \frac{\int_0^{\tau} C_p(t)dt}{C_{e,i} \cdot \tau} \qquad (2.2.1\text{-}5)$$

$$C_{e,i} = \frac{S_i}{Q} \qquad (2.2.1\text{-}6)$$

where $C_{e,i}$ is the average exhausted concentration of tracer gas under steady-state conditions only when the ith source exists, Q is the total airflow rate for the ventilated space.

ACS quantifies how easily the contaminant is continuously diffused into an indoor location. It is a function of both the flow characteristic and the source location, and has nothing to do with the emission rate and contaminant type. ACS can be easily calculated by the definition with CFD tools when the flow field and source position are available.

2.2.2. Temporal and Spatial Distribution Formula of Contaminant

The contaminant dispersion can be described by the following species equation and boundary and initial conditions.

Species equation:

$$\frac{\partial C}{\partial t} + \frac{\partial (U_j C)}{\partial x_j} = \frac{\partial}{\partial x_j}(\Gamma_C \frac{\partial C}{\partial x_j}) + S_C \qquad (2.2.2\text{-}1)$$

where U_j and x_j are the three velocity components, i.e., u, v, w, and three directions of axis, i.e., x, y, z, when $j = 1, 2, 3$ respectively.

Boundary conditions:

$$\begin{cases} C_{in,i} = C_{s,i} & \text{for the ith inlet} \\ S_{C,i} = S_i & \text{for the ith source} \end{cases} \qquad (2.2.2\text{-}2)$$

Initial condition:

$$C_p(t)\big|_{t=0} = C_0 \qquad (2.2.2\text{-}3)$$

When the flow field is steady, Eq. (2.2.2-1) becomes a linear one and Superposition Theorem can be used. Usually the walls of ventilated space can be treated as adiabatic to contaminant and the outlets can be treated as unidirectional flow. So the contaminant concentration will be determined by the contaminant concentration of supply air at each inlet, position and intensity of each contaminant source, and the initial condition of contaminant.

When the contaminant is passive gas, the time-averaged concentration of contaminant at any point p can be calculated with following equation based on the definitions of ASA and ACS and Superposition Theorem (Yang et al, 2004):

$$\overline{C_p}(\tau) = C_0 + \sum_{i=1}^{M}\{(C_{s,i} - C_0)A_{si,p}(\tau)\} + \sum_{i=1}^{N}\left\{\frac{S_i}{Q}A_{ci,p}(\tau)\right\} \qquad (2.2.2\text{-}4)$$

The contaminant distribution at moment τ can be calculated as follows:

$$C_p(\tau) = \overline{C_p}(\tau) + \tau \frac{\partial \overline{C_p}(\tau)}{\partial \tau} \qquad (2.2.2\text{-}5)$$

The derivative of time-averaged concentration of contaminant can be calculated with the derivative of ASA and ACS:

$$\frac{\partial \overline{C_p}(\tau)}{\partial \tau} = \sum_{i=1}^{M}\left\{(C_{s,i} - C_0)\frac{\partial}{\partial \tau}A_{si,p}(\tau)\right\} + \sum_{j=1}^{N}\left\{\frac{S_j}{Q}\frac{\partial}{\partial \tau}A_{cj,p}(\tau)\right\} \qquad (2.2.2\text{-}6)$$

The derivative of ASA and ACS can be calculated by their definitions with CFD tools.

2.3. Identification of Contaminant Source

2.3.1. Introduction

Traditionally, we can predict the contaminant dispersion in buildings with many methods when the contaminant source is known. If the position and intensity of contaminant source are known, the solving of indoor contaminant concentration field is a typical direct problem. Sometimes, what we know is the contaminant dispersion in some points or the whole field; what we do not know is the position and intensity of contaminant source. Such kind of problem, i.e., solving the location and intensity of contaminant source based on the contaminant distribution, is an inverse problem. Although we can find publications on inverse problems in heat transfer, groundwater transport, and atmospheric constituent transport, only a little work has, to our knowledge, been published on the determination of indoor contaminant source.

The first kind of method to identify contaminant source is based on multi-zonal model. For example, Sohn et al. (2002) used Bayesian probability model to identify the contaminant source in a five-room building; Arvelo et al. (2002) employed genetic algorithm to interpret the computed data to locate the sources in a building with nine offices and a hallway. Since multi-zone model can only provide some macroscopic information about the contaminant transport, it cannot be used for accurate identification of location and intensity.

The second kind of method to identify contaminant source is based on CFD simulations. Zhang and Chen (2007) developed a model to solve the inverse problem directly. Their results show that the method could identify the contaminant source location but is not very accurate for intensity. This method is time-consuming and cannot be used for online and real-time identification.

A new method will be proposed for online identification of contaminant source based on the contaminant dispersion formula in section 2.2. Limited number of sensors will be used to limit the cost for identification. The main assumptions for the method are as follows:

(1) Air flow field is steady.
(2) Contaminant to be identified is passive.
(3) The release rate of contaminant source is steady.
(4) Only one contaminant source exists in the ventilated room.

The process of identification is:

(1) Divide the ventilated room into M control volumes and put N sensors in the room. The center position of the ith control volume is at point α_i. The position of the jth sensor is at point β_j.

(2) Put a known source S_0 at the center of ith control volume, we can get the concentration of contaminant versus time in each sensor, $C_i(\beta_j,t)$ by on-site experiment or with CFD simulation in advance.

(3) When there is a contaminant source, say at position α^* with intensity S^*, to be identified, the concentrations of sensors, $C^*(\beta_j,t)$, will be sent to identification system where the location and intensity of contaminant will be identified.

2.3.2. Method to Identify Source with Limited Number of Sensors

Firstly, the accessibility of contaminant source at α_i to any sensor in any time period τ can be calculated based on the definition equations (2.2.1-5) and (2.2.1-6) as follows:

$$A_{ci}(\beta_j,\tau) = \frac{\int_0^\tau C_i(\beta_j,t)dt}{S_0 \times \tau/Q} \tag{2.3.2-1}$$

The accessibility of contaminant source at α^* to any sensor in any time period τ can be expressed as:

$$A_{c*}(\beta_j,\tau) = \frac{\int_0^\tau C^*(\beta_j,t)dt}{S^* \times \tau/Q} = \frac{\int_0^\tau C^*(\beta_j,t)dt}{S_0 \times \tau/Q} \times \frac{S_0}{S^*} \tag{2.3.2-2}$$

Define $A_{c*}^0(\beta_j,\tau) = \dfrac{\int_0^\tau C^*(\beta_j,t)dt}{S_0 \times \tau/Q}$, which can be calculated with the readings from the sensors, then,

$$A_{c*}(\beta_j,\tau) = A_{c*}^0(\beta_j,\tau) \times \frac{S_0}{S^*} \tag{2.3.2-3}$$

Since the accessibility of contaminant source to one point has nothing to do with the intensity, the ratio between $A_{ci}(\beta_j,\tau)$ and $A_{c*}^0(\beta_j,\tau)$ will be always constant (equal to $\dfrac{S_0}{S^*}$) if the source to be identified is at α_i.

Calculate the ratio between $A_{ci}(\beta_j,\tau)$ and $A_{c*}^0(\beta_j,\tau)$ to find whether it is constant. The time-averaged ratio, $\gamma_i(\beta_j,\tau)$, between $A_{ci}(\beta_j,\tau)$ and $A_{c*}^0(\beta_j,\tau)$ is calculated by the following equation:

$$\gamma_i(\beta_j,\tau) = \frac{1}{\tau}\int_{t=0}^{\tau}\frac{A_{ci}(\beta_j,t)}{A_{c*}^0(\beta_j,t)}dt \tag{2.3.2-4}$$

The relative distance, $\delta_i(\beta_j,\tau)$, from the ratio between $A_{ci}(\beta_j,\tau)$ and $A_{c*}^0(\beta_j,\tau)$ to the time-averaged ratio, $\gamma_i(\beta_j,\tau)$, in the whole time period can be obtained by:

$$\delta_i(\beta_j,\tau) = \frac{1}{\gamma_i(\beta_j,\tau)\tau} \int_{t=0}^{\tau} \left| \frac{A_{ci}(\beta_j,t)}{A_{c*}^0(\beta_j,t)} - \gamma_i(\beta_j,\tau) \right| dt \qquad (2.3.2\text{-}5)$$

For all the relative distances from sensor β_j, we define the relative error, $\varphi_i(\beta_j,\tau)$, as follows:

$$\varphi_i(\beta_j,\tau) = \delta_i(\beta_j,\tau) \bigg/ \sum_{i=1}^{M} \delta_i(\beta_j,\tau) \qquad (2.3.2\text{-}6)$$

The less the relative error $\varphi_i(\beta_j,\tau)$ is, the more probability the source to be identified is located at α_i. The relative error $\varphi_i(\beta_j,\tau)$ satisfies:

$$0 \leq \varphi_i(\beta_j,\tau) \leq 1 \qquad (2.3.2\text{-}7)$$

$$\sum_{i=1}^{M} \varphi_i(\beta_j,\tau) = 1 \qquad (2.3.2\text{-}8)$$

Calculate all the relative errors for each volume from all sensors and define the non-dimensional score for each volume, $\phi_i^T(\tau)$, as follows:

$$\phi_i^T(\tau) = \frac{\sum_{j=1}^{N}(1 - \varphi_i(\beta_j,\tau))}{\sum_{i=1}^{M}\sum_{j=1}^{N}(1 - \varphi_i(\beta_j,\tau))} \qquad (2.3.2\text{-}9)$$

The higher the non-dimensional score, the more probability the source is located at the control volume. The non-dimensional score satisfies:

$$0 \leq \phi_i^T(\tau) \leq 1 \qquad (2.3.2\text{-}10)$$

$$\sum_{i=1}^{M} \phi_i^T(\tau) = 1 \qquad (2.3.2\text{-}11)$$

There are two ways to depict the position of source to be identified. One is deterministic way. The other is with probability.

In deterministic way, the control volume with the greatest non-dimensional score is the position of the source to be identified. In way with probability, the probability that the source is located at the ith control volume is $\phi_i^T(\tau)$. As there are M control volumes, we construct a vector as:

$$\vec{\phi}^T(\tau) = [\phi_1^T(\tau), \phi_2^T(\tau), \cdots, \phi_M^T(\tau)]^T \qquad (2.3.2\text{-}12)$$

Sort the elements in the set $A = \{\gamma_i(\beta_1,\tau), \gamma_i(\beta_2,\tau), \ldots, \gamma_i(\beta_N,\tau)\}$ in descending order to construct a new set $B = \{b_1, b_2, \ldots, b_N\}$.

The intensity of contaminant source can be calculated as follows:

$$\begin{cases} \overline{\gamma}_i(\tau) = \dfrac{1}{N}(\sum_{j=2}^{N-1} b_j + b_2 + b_{N-1}) & \text{if } N > 3 \\ \overline{\gamma}_i(\tau) = \dfrac{1}{N}\sum_{j=1}^{N} \gamma_i(\beta_j,\tau) & \text{if } N \leq 3 \end{cases} \qquad (2.3.2\text{-}13)$$

$$S^* = \frac{S_0}{\overline{\gamma}_i(\tau)} \qquad (2.3.2\text{-}14)$$

In equation (2.3.2-13), if N is greater than three, $\overline{\gamma}_i(\tau)$ is taken as the winsorized mean of the elements in the set A. In addition, if N is less than or equal to three, $\overline{\gamma}_i(\tau)$ is taken as the arithmetic mean of the elements in the set A. The winsorized mean is a robust estimate of the location of a sample, which eliminates the outliers at both ends of an ordered set of observations and replaces the outliers with observed values. If there are outliers in the data, the winsorized mean is a more representative estimate than the arithmetic mean.

In order to evaluate the accuracy of the identification method, we put contaminant source with different intensity in each control volume and present following indices for evaluation:

(1) Indices for Evaluating the Accuracy of the Identifications of Source Location

Sort the elements in $\vec{\phi}^T(\tau)$ in descending order for each given source location. Suppose that $\alpha_k \to \alpha^*$. The greater the value of $\phi_k^T(\tau)$ is, or the more forward $\phi_k^T(\tau)$ ranks, the more accurate the identification will be. To evaluate the accuracy of the identifications, we imitate the grading method of shooting competition as shown in Table 2.3.2-1.

Table 2.3.2-1. Standard of mark for evaluating the accuracy of identifications

RANKING	$\vec{\phi}^T(\tau)$	MARK
No.1	≥0.5	6
	<0.5	5
No.2	≥0.3	4
	<0.3	3
No.3	≥0.1	2
	<0.1	1
Others	--	0

When the ranking of $\phi_k^T(\tau)$ is No.1 in the sequence and $\phi_k^T(\tau) \geq 0.5$, we consider this judgement hits the bull's-eye and gets a mark of 6; the score of judgement declines with the decrease in the value or ranking of $\phi_k^T(\tau)$; when the ranking of $\phi_k^T(\tau)$ is No.4, or even behind, in the sequence, we consider this judgement is off target and gets a mark of 0. This is the mark, Z_k, of the identificaton system for the *k*th source location.

After we have identified all contaminant source locations given, the total score, Z, of the judgements from the identification system (one sensor or multiple sensors) can be obtianed as follows:

$$Z = \sum_{i=1}^{M} Z_i = \sum_{i=1}^{M} (mark_i + \phi_i^T(\tau)) \qquad (2.3.2\text{-}15)$$

where $mark_i$ is the mark for the identification system to identify the *i*th source according to Table 2.3.2-1; $\phi_i^T(\tau)$ is the non-dimensional score of the center α_i for the *i*th source; Z_i is the score of the identifion system for the i-th source, which equals the sum of $mark_i$ and $\phi_i^T(\tau)$.

The bigger value of the score Z_i indicates the higher accuracy of the identification system for the i-th source location while the bigger value of the total score Z indicates the higher accuracy of the overall identifications.

(2) Indices for Evaluating the Accuracy of the Identifications of Source Intensity

The relative error of the identification system for the i-th source intensity is defined as follows:

$$RES_i = \frac{(S_i^* - S^*)}{S^*} \qquad (2.3.2\text{-}16)$$

where S^* is the true value of the source intensity to be identified, S_i^* is the result of i-th identification.

For all the M given source in each control volume, the average of the absolute values of these relative errors is further defined as the following:

$$RES = \frac{1}{M} \sum_{i=1}^{M} |RES_i| \qquad (2.3.2\text{-}17)$$

The smaller value of RES_i indicates the higher accuracy of the identification system for the i-th source intensity while the smaller value of RES indicates the higher accuracy of the overall identifications.

With the help of indices Z_i, Z, RES_i, and RES, we may reasonably evaluate the accuracy of the idenfication method as well as optimize the layout of sensors.

2.3.3. Demonstration Cases of Source Identification

In the following paragraphs, we demonstrate how to use the method to identify contaminant source in a three-dimensional room.

(1) Cases Setup

The room is 5 m long(X), 3m high(Y) and 5m wide (Z) (see Fig. 2.3.3-1). Here, the walls, ceiling and floor are considered to be adiabatic for simplicity. In addition, there is no thermal source in the room, i.e., the room is under iothermal condition.

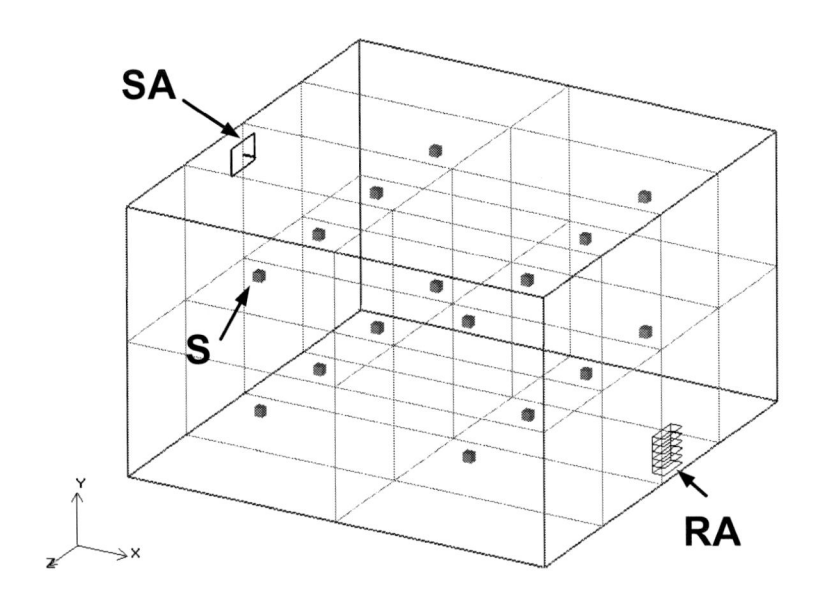

Figure 2.3.3-1. Schematic of the room (SA—supply air diffuser, RA—return air grill, S—Contaminant source locations to be identified.

Table 2.3.3-1. The positions of 16 volume centers

Center Symbol	Position X(m)	Y(m)	Z(m)	Volume Number	Center Symbol	Position X(m)	Y(m)	Z(m)	Volume Number
α_1	1.250	0.750	0.625	1	α_2	3.750	0.750	0.625	2
α_3	1.250	0.750	1.875	3	α_4	3.750	0.750	1.875	4
α_5	1.250	0.750	3.125	5	α_6	3.750	0.750	3.125	6
α_7	1.250	0.750	4.375	7	α_8	3.750	0.750	4.375	8
α_9	1.250	2.250	0.625	9	α_{10}	3.750	2.250	0.625	10
α_{11}	1.250	2.250	1.875	11	α_{12}	3.750	2.250	1.875	12
α_{13}	1.250	2.250	3.125	13	α_{14}	3.750	2.250	3.125	14
α_{15}	1.250	2.250	4.375	15	α_{16}	3.750	2.250	4.375	16

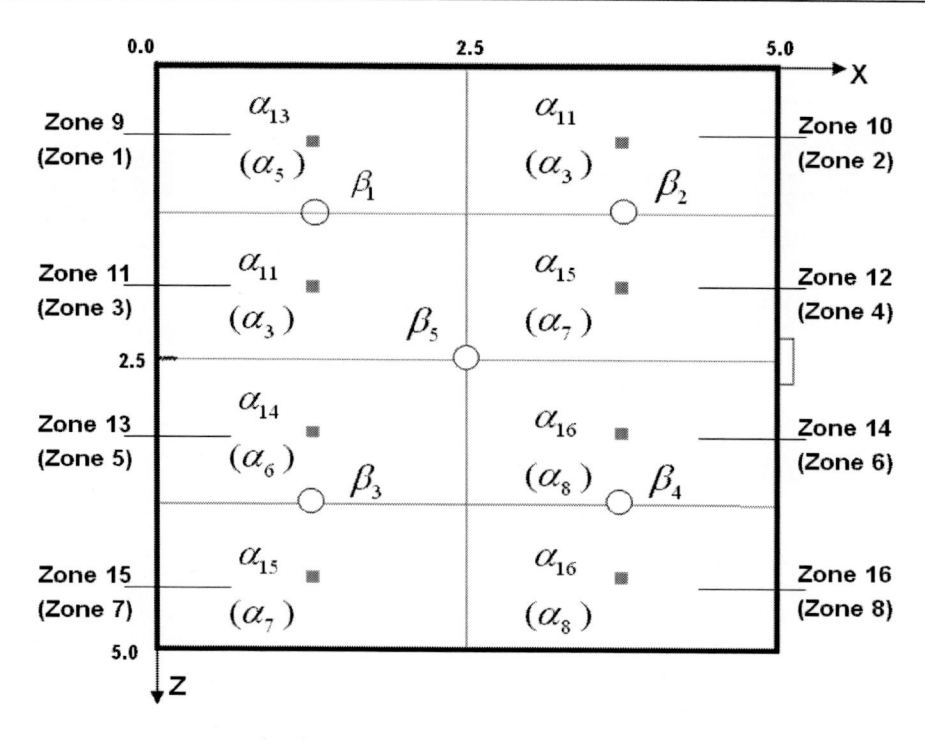

Figure 2.3.3-2. Layout of sources and sensors.

The room is divided into 16 volumes; X and Y directions are divided into two equal parts, while direction Z is divided into four equal parts. The centers of various volumes construct the set $A = \{\alpha_1, \alpha_2, \cdots, \alpha_{16}\}$. The specific positions of these centers are listed in Table 2.3.3-1.

The ventilation mode of the room under study is mixing type in which air change rate is 6 ACH. The size of inlet is 0.5 m (Z) × 0.3 m (Y), and the velocity of supply air is 0.83 m/s. The size of outlet is 0.4 m (Z) × 0.4 m (Y). Both the inlet and outlet are symmetrical about the centerline of the side wall. The inlet starts at 2.5 m (Y) and ends at 2.8 m (Y) while the outlet starts at 0.2 m (Y) and ends at 0.6 m (Y).

Table 2.3.3-2. The positions of five sensors

Sensor Number	Position		
	X(m)	Y(m)	Z(m)
1	1.25	2.25	1.25
2	3.75	0.75	1.25
3	1.25	0.75	3.75
4	3.75	2.25	3.75
5	2.50	1.50	2.50

Five sensors are placed in the room. Figure 2.3.3-2 depicts the layout of sources and sensors. The specific positions of these sensors are listed in Table 2.3.3-2. Note that the sensor numbered 5 is at the center of the room, sensors numbered 1 and 4 are located at higher level while that numbered 2 and 3 are located at lower level.

(2) Numerical Procedure

The CFD method was employed to simulate airflow and contaminant dispersion. An indoor zero-equation model (Chen and Xu, 1998) was used to account for the turbulent flow in the room. The commercial software AIRPAK 2.1 (Fluent Inc., 2002) was used as a simulation tool, which has been validated on numerous occasions for indoor air flow studies. The simulation of contaminant dispersion in each case is based on the unchanged flow field with the time step 0.5 s.

(3) Results and Discussion

According to the main assumptions for the identification method, all the cases under study share an identical airflow pattern which remain steady during the release event. The airflow pattern under steady state was simulated by AIRPAK, as shown in Figure 2.3.3-3.

With the steady-state airflow pattern, sixteen cases for contaminant release were simulated by the CFD method. For each case, the source with the intensity $S_0 = 100 \text{ mg/s}$ is located exactly at the center of each volume. That is, the center of each source is coincident with that of each volume. The size of these sources are 0.1 m (X) × 0.1 m (Y) × 0.1 m (Z). The positions of these source centers can be referred to Table 2.3.3.1. After the simulations, the concentration of contaminant at the positions of each sensor, $C_i(\beta_j, t)$, are sampled and stored with a constant time step 1 s. This is the data of pretreatment, which should be prepared before identification system starts to work.

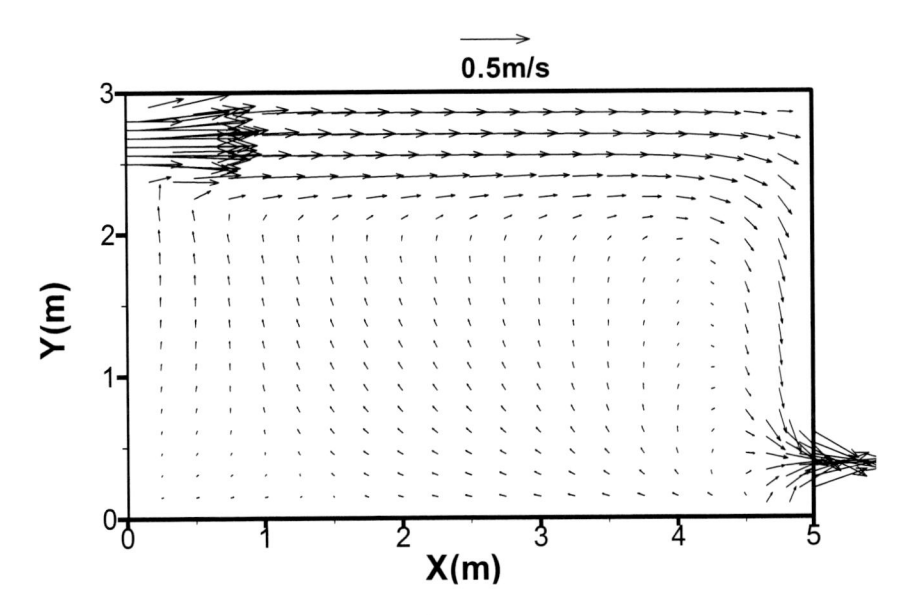

Figure 2.3.3-3. Flow pattern of the cases (Z=2.5 m).

First, let us examine the effect of identification method when the source to be identified is located exactly at the center of each volume. Sixteen cases standing for the actual release events were simulated. For each case, the source locations α_i^* to be determined is coincident with the volume center α_i, that is $\alpha_i^* = \alpha_i$, $(i=1,2,\cdots,16)$, and the intensity of the source to be determined is $S_i^* = 10 \text{ mg/s}$, $(i=1,2,\cdots,16)$. The sampling of sensors started at $t_1 = 0 \text{ s}$ when source was released and ended at $t_2 = 30 \text{ s}$. Then, the sampling duration of each sensor $\tau = t_2 - t_1 = 30 \text{ s}$. Although these data can only be obtained by sensors in practical project, it is appropriate to use CFD modeling here to generate them for demonstration purpose.

Table 2.3.3-3 summarizes the results of the non-dimensional score $\phi_i^T(\tau)$. The data in column j are the results of $\phi_i^T(\tau)$ for each volume center α_i, $(i=1,2,\cdots,16)$, when the source to be identified α_j^* is at α_j. In the deterministic view, we will obtain the correct output for source α_j^* provided the value in row j and column j is greater than all the others in the column. In the probabilistic view, the value in row i and column j represents the probability that the source α_j^* is located at the i-th volume center α_i.

Table 2.3.3-4 summarizes the results of source identifications by using the method with five sensors. All the 16 locations are identified correctly in the deterministic view with $Z = 81.064$ and $RES = 2.499\%$. It is shown that the method with five sensors could identify the source locations and intensities with quite high accuracy provided the sources to be identified are located exactly at the centers of the volumes.

Table 2.3.3-5 summarizes the results of source identifications by using the method with one sensor. A comparison between the results in the Table 2.3.3-4 and Table 2.3.3-5 shows that both the identification accuracy of source location and intensity are improved to a certain extent by increasing the number of sensors provided the sources to be identified are located exactly at the centers of the volumes.

Second, let us examine the effect of identification method when the source to be identified is located inside the volume but with an offset from its center. Sixteen cases standing for the actual release events were simulated. For each case, the source α_i^* to be determined is not coincident with the volume center α_i, that is $\alpha_i^* \neq \alpha_i$, $(i=1,2,\cdots,16)$, and the intensity of the source to be determined is $S_i^* = 10 \text{ mg/s}$, $(i=1,2,\cdots,16)$. The specific positions of each source α_i^* are listed in the Table 2.3.3-6. It is shown that source $\alpha_1^* - \alpha_8^*$ are offset from the corresponding volume centers by 20 cm in the positive direction of y-axis, while $\alpha_9^* - \alpha_9^*$ are offset by same distance in the negative direction of y-axis. The sampling of sensors started at $t_1 = 0 \text{ s}$ when source was released and ended at $t_2 = 30 \text{ s}$. The sampling duration is $\tau = t_2 - t_1 = 30 \text{ s}$ for each sensor.

Table 2.3.3-7 summarizes the results of source identifications by using the method with five sensors. Among the 16 locations to be identified, 15 are identified correctly in the deterministic view with $Z = 77.035$ and $RES = 84.363\%$. From the comparison between the results in the Table 2.3.3-4 and Table 2.3.3-7, it is shown that the degree of accuracy is declined slightly to identify the source location but decreased extraordinarily to determine the source intensity when the source to be identified is offset from the volume center.

Table 2.3.3-8 summarizes the results of source identifications by using the method with one sensor. A comparison between the results in the Table 2.3.3-7 and Table 2.3.3-8 shows that both the identification accuracy of source location and intensity are improved to a large extent by increasing the number of sensors provided the sources to be identified are offset from the centers of the volumes by a certain distance.

When the source to be identified is offset from the volume center, although the identification accuracy of source location is still high and acceptable, the identification of source intensity is very poor. Let us further examine the influence of the sampling duration τ, beginning time of the sampling t_1, and ending time of the sampling t_2 on the identification accuracy.

Table 2.3.3-9 summarizes the deterministic results of source location with five sensors. The first column lists the results when $t_1 = 0\,\text{s}$ and t_2 is changed from 30 to 180 s. The second column lists the results when $t_1 = t_2 - 30\,\text{s}$ and t_2 is changed from 30 to 180 s. In the probabilistic view, Figure 2.3.3-4 (a) depicts the variation of the total score Z with τ, t_1, and t_2. Two types of results indicate that: when $t_1 = 0\,\text{s}$, the increase of sampling time may have little influence on the identification accuracy of source location; however, when the sample duration $\tau = t_2 - t_1$ remains unchanged, the identification accuracy of source location may decrease greatly with increasing t_1 and t_2. Therefore, the data from the early period of sampling may be helpful for identifying source location.

Figure 2.3.3-4 (b) depicts the variation of RES with τ, t_1, and t_2. As previously defined in Eq. 2.3.2-17, the smaller value of RES indicates the higher accuracy of the overall identifications for source intensity. The results indicate that: A) The identification accuracy of source intensity may be improved with increasing t_2; B) The degree of improvement may be greater when the sample duration $\tau = t_2 - t_1$ remains unchanged than that when $t_1 = 0\,\text{s}$; C) Particularly, when $t_1 = 150\,\text{s}$ and $t_2 = 180\,\text{s}$, the identification accuracy of source intensity comes to be acceptable. Therefore, the data from the later period of sampling may be helpful for identifying source intensity, which is very different from the case for identifying source location.

Finally, this case study shows that all the computational tasks for identifying source during the event can be executed within a second by using an ordinary personal computer. Therefore, the presented method is characterized by quick response and can be used online since it completes the time-consuming CFD simulations before the release event.

Table 2.3.3-3. The non-dimensional score $\phi_i^T(\tau)$ for source identifications with five sensors ($\alpha_i = \alpha_i^*$, $\tau = 30s$)

Volume center number	\multicolumn{16}{c}{Actual position of source to be identified (Source number)}
	1	2	3	4	5	6	7	8	9	10	11	12	13	14	15	16
1	0.0665	0.0625	0.0629	0.0625	0.0619	0.0630	0.0625	0.0622	0.0621	0.0620	0.0616	0.0616	0.0618	0.0616	0.0627	0.0617
2	0.0631	0.0665	0.0619	0.0640	0.0616	0.0625	0.0629	0.0627	0.0628	0.0626	0.0614	0.0617	0.0613	0.0619	0.0633	0.0626
3	0.0625	0.0618	0.0663	0.0616	0.0633	0.0623	0.0618	0.0620	0.0615	0.0622	0.0625	0.0619	0.0634	0.0617	0.0619	0.0616
4	0.0628	0.0642	0.0627	0.0666	0.0625	0.0640	0.0627	0.0623	0.0626	0.0626	0.0618	0.0617	0.0619	0.0618	0.0633	0.0625
5	0.0616	0.0615	0.0632	0.0614	0.0667	0.0613	0.0635	0.0616	0.0617	0.0613	0.0628	0.0618	0.0632	0.0618	0.0617	0.0618
6	0.0630	0.0628	0.0630	0.0641	0.0628	0.0656	0.0630	0.0636	0.0625	0.0639	0.0619	0.0626	0.0626	0.0621	0.0628	0.0622
7	0.0614	0.0616	0.0621	0.0619	0.0634	0.0618	0.0667	0.0614	0.0614	0.0611	0.0614	0.0617	0.0618	0.0616	0.0618	0.0616
8	0.0633	0.0629	0.0624	0.0620	0.0621	0.0632	0.0629	0.0663	0.0618	0.0618	0.0620	0.0619	0.0627	0.0622	0.0625	0.0620
9	0.0624	0.0627	0.0622	0.0630	0.0622	0.0629	0.0621	0.0627	0.0666	0.0632	0.0634	0.0628	0.0622	0.0628	0.0630	0.0632
10	0.0623	0.0629	0.0616	0.0629	0.0618	0.0625	0.0620	0.0630	0.0628	0.0665	0.0613	0.0622	0.0612	0.0614	0.0630	0.0630
11	0.0616	0.0614	0.0627	0.0616	0.0627	0.0618	0.0615	0.0622	0.0625	0.0618	0.0667	0.0631	0.0642	0.0631	0.0616	0.0619
12	0.0613	0.0614	0.0610	0.0613	0.0610	0.0612	0.0609	0.0611	0.0616	0.0620	0.0621	0.0666	0.0613	0.0642	0.0610	0.0619
13	0.0617	0.0614	0.0629	0.0613	0.0629	0.0613	0.0618	0.0619	0.0621	0.0615	0.0646	0.0627	0.0666	0.0627	0.0612	0.0619
14	0.0611	0.0613	0.0611	0.0611	0.0612	0.0618	0.0612	0.0614	0.0621	0.0615	0.0624	0.0643	0.0614	0.0667	0.0609	0.0624
15	0.0631	0.0627	0.0623	0.0621	0.0624	0.0624	0.0628	0.0633	0.0630	0.0631	0.0622	0.0617	0.0623	0.0618	0.0665	0.0631
16	0.0623	0.0624	0.0615	0.0625	0.0615	0.0623	0.0619	0.0622	0.0629	0.0630	0.0619	0.0614	0.0619	0.0626	0.0629	0.0666
Results	1	2	3	4	5	6	7	8	9	10	11	12	13	14	15	16

Table 2.3.3-4. Summary of contaminant source identifications with five sensors
($\alpha_i = \alpha_i^*$, $\tau = 30s$)

Source number	$\phi_i^T(\tau)$ Value	Ranking	Determination of Location Right Y/N	Score (Z_i)	Determination of Intensity $\overline{\gamma}_i(\tau)$	S_i^*, mg/s	RES_i, %
1	0.066465	1	Y	5.066465	9.9886	10.011	0.11416
2	0.066523	1	Y	5.066523	9.9878	10.012	0.1218
3	0.066289	1	Y	5.066289	9.9849	10.015	0.1513
4	0.066627	1	Y	5.066627	9.9913	10.009	0.086676
5	0.066655	1	Y	5.066655	9.9999	10	0.000997
6	0.065599	1	Y	5.065599	10.16	9.8424	-1.5758
7	0.066655	1	Y	5.066655	9.9931	10.007	0.068637
8	0.066293	1	Y	5.066293	15.222	6.5694	-34.306
9	0.066613	1	Y	5.066613	9.9481	10.052	0.52192
10	0.066545	1	Y	5.066545	9.9762	10.024	0.23863
11	0.066655	1	Y	5.066655	10.001	9.9986	-0.01373
12	0.066639	1	Y	5.066639	10.016	9.9837	-0.16341
13	0.066579	1	Y	5.066579	10.066	9.934	-0.66013
14	0.066663	1	Y	5.066663	9.9965	10.003	0.034944
15	0.066541	1	Y	5.066541	9.8265	10.177	1.7659
16	0.066622	1	Y	5.066622	9.9833	10.017	0.16732

Total Score: $Z = 81.064$; Average of the absolute values of the relative errors (%) 2.499

Table 2.3.3-5. Summary of contaminant source identifications with one sensor
($\alpha_i = \alpha_i^*$, $\tau = 30s$)

Sensor symbol	The number of correct determinations	Total score (Z)	RES, %
β_1	16	81.0657	3.389881
β_2	14	74.05998	9.305037
β_3	15	79.0629	7.641423
β_4	16	81.066	3.510306
β_5	16	81.0672	2.496813

Table 2.3.3-6. The positions of 16 contaminant sources to be identified

Source Symbol	Positions of the Source Centers X(m)	Y(m)	Z(m)	Related Volume	Source Symbol	Positions of the Source Centers X(m)	Y(m)	Z(m)	Related Volume
α_1^*	1.250	0.950	0.625	1	α_2^*	3.750	0.950	0.625	2
α_3^*	1.250	0.950	1.875	3	α_4^*	3.750	0.950	1.875	4
α_5^*	1.250	0.950	3.125	5	α_6^*	3.750	0.950	3.125	6
α_7^*	1.250	0.950	4.375	7	α_8^*	3.750	0.950	4.375	8
α_9^*	1.250	2.050	0.625	9	α_{10}^*	3.750	2.050	0.625	10
α_{11}^*	1.250	2.050	1.875	11	α_{12}^*	3.750	2.050	1.875	12
α_{13}^*	1.250	2.050	3.125	13	α_{14}^*	3.750	2.050	3.125	14
α_{15}^*	1.250	2.050	4.375	15	α_{16}^*	3.750	2.050	4.375	16

Table 2.3.3-7. Summary of contaminant source identifications with five sensors ($a_i \neq a_i^*, \tau = 30s$)

Source Number	$\phi_i^T(\tau)$ Value	Ranking	Determination of Location Right Y/N	Score Z_i	Determination of Intensity $\bar{\gamma}_i(\tau)$	S_i^*, mg/s	RES_i, %
1	0.06447	1	Y	5.0645	45.457	2.1999	-78.001
2	0.065358	1	Y	5.0654	14.385	6.9515	-30.485
3	0.065149	1	Y	5.0651	4.3669	22.9	129
4	0.064774	1	Y	5.0648	143.5	0.69688	-93.031
5	0.064516	1	Y	5.0645	32.225	3.1032	-68.968
6	0.064341	1	Y	5.0643	253.17	0.39499	-96.05
7	0.064598	1	Y	5.0646	151.81	0.65871	-93.413
8	0.065201	1	Y	5.0652	22.532	4.4381	-55.619
9	0.064964	1	Y	5.065	24.799	4.0323	-59.677
10	0.064196	1	Y	5.0642	2.3207	43.09	330.9
11	0.064755	1	Y	5.0648	16.895	5.9188	-40.812
12	0.06473	1	Y	5.0647	37.748	2.6492	-73.508
13	0.064327	1	Y	5.0643	25.948	3.8538	-61.462

Table 2.3.3-7 (continued)

Source Number	$\phi_i^T(\tau)$ Value	Ranking	Determination of Location Right Y/N	Score Z_i	Determination of Intensity $\bar{\gamma}_i(\tau)$	S_i^*, mg/s	RES_i, %
14	0.063515	3	N	1.0635	97.083	1.03	-89.7
15	0.065411	1	Y	5.0654	15.03	6.6533	-33.467
16	0.064779	1	Y	5.0648	11.864	8.429	-15.71

Total Score: $Z = 77.035$; Average of the absolute values of the relative errors (%) 84.36

Table 2.3.3-8. Summary of contaminant source identifications with one sensor ($\alpha_i \neq \alpha_i^*$, $\tau = 30s$)

Sensor Symbol	Number of Correct Identifications	Total Score (Z)	RES, %
β_1	6	50.033	226.355
β_2	9	56.037	76.837
β_3	4	35.029	540.866
β_4	7	43.035	144.747
β_5	6	40.042	243.679

Table 2.3.3-9. Deterministic results of source location with five sensors ($\alpha_i \neq \alpha_i^*$, $\tau = t_2 - t_1$ s)

t_2, s	Number of Correct Identifications	
	$t_1 = 0$ s	$t_1 = t_2 - 30$ s
30	15	15
60	15	9
90	15	9
120	16	9
150	15	7
180	15	7

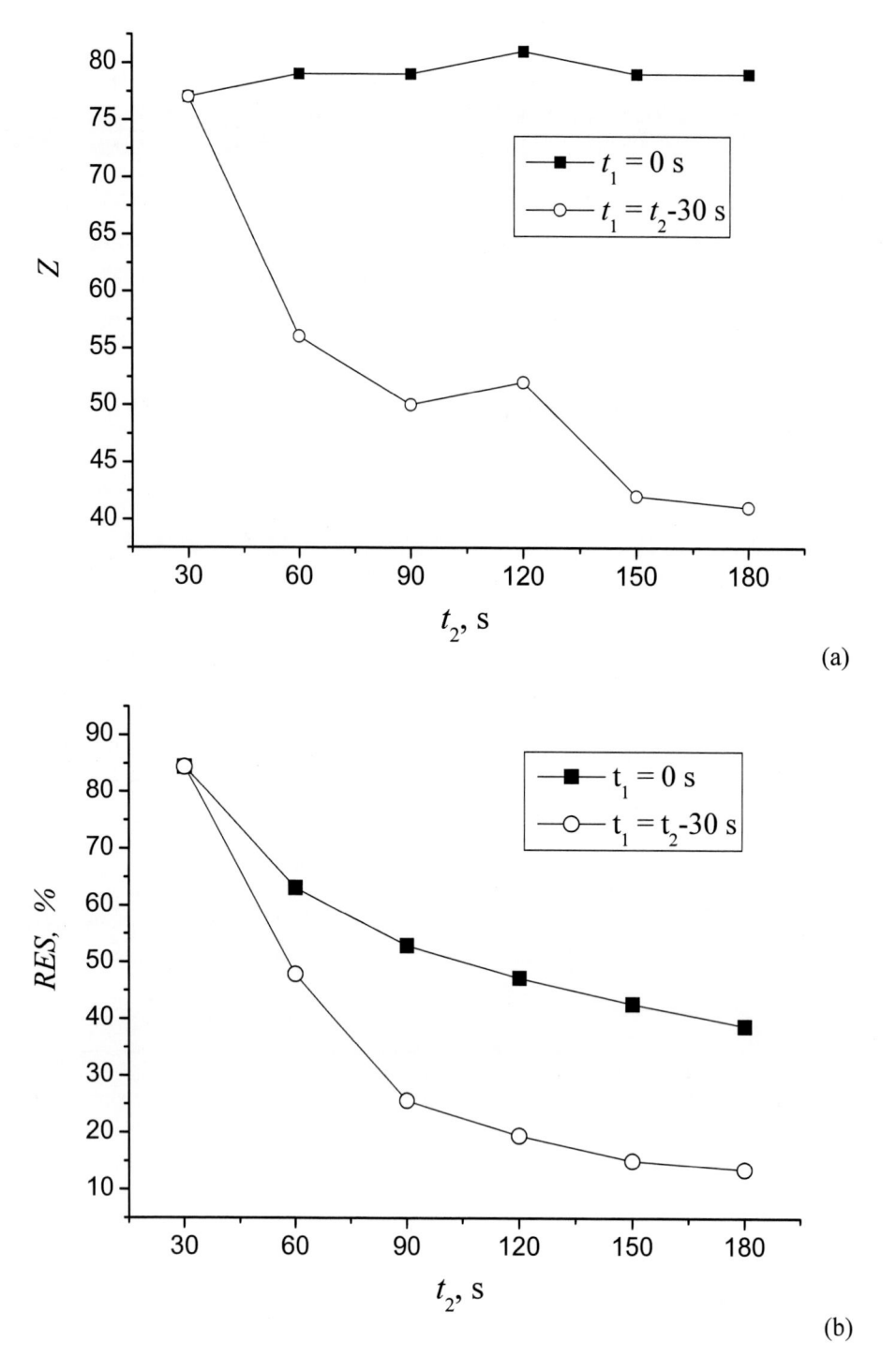

Figure 2.3.3-4. Variation of the identification accuracy with sampling time ($\tau = t_2 - t_1$), (a) Variation of total score Z; (b) Variation of RES.

3. EVACUATION MODEL AND EVALUATION OF EXPOSURE RISK

3.1. Modeling of Evacuation

3.1.1. Review of Existing Evacuation Models

Research on quantifying and modeling human movement and behavior in emergency event has been underway for many years. Since the first computer based evacuation model, which concerns the modeling of emergency egress during fires, appeared in 1982, great advances have been made both in the understanding of human response to emergency evacuation situations and in the attempts to model this response (Gwynne et al. 1999).

Sime (1994) identified two different ways to model people moving around buildings, in terms of movement of occupants or their behavior. The first way of modeling is called a 'physical science' or 'ball-bearing' model of human movement. The second way of modeling is called a 'social science' or psychological model of human reactions. People are assumed to be behaving irrationally in 'physical science' model whereas people in 'social science' model are thinking and acting accordingly.

Gwynne et al. (2002) investigated the behavioural aspects required for evacuation modeling. They have categorized four major factors that influenced evacuation performance and suggested those to be represented within an evacuation model. The four broad areas are: configuration of enclosure, environmental factors inside the structure, procedures implemented within the enclosure, and most important of all, behavior of the occupants. The influence of an occupant's personal attributes, such as physical, psychological and sociological, will be affected by the other three broad areas. It concludes that a model should consider the factors on which these decisions are based, rather than treating occupants as instinctive entities as would be the case in a 'ball-bearing' model. In terms of the methodologies of evacuation models, there are different approaches to the evacuation analysis. The approaches are based on nature of model application, population perspectives, behavioural perspective and enclosure representation respectively (Gwynne et al. 1999). In the lattermost approach, evacuation models could be identified as discretization models or continuity models.

For discretization models, there are two ways to represent a building space, using either a coarse network approach or a fine network approach. In each case, space is discretized into subregions, and each subregion is connected to its neighbors. The resolution of this subdivision distinguishes the two approaches. The former, which is similar with a 'physical science' or 'ball-bearing' model, represents a space as a node and an arc to connect to the next node. An arc represents the actual connection of the building space. Typically each node is used to represent a distinct space in the building such as a room. However, it is sometimes more appropriate to represent a space such as a long corridor with more than one node. There are several simulation-type evacuation models including CRISP (Ghosh and Fraser 1999), DONEGAN'S ENTROPY MODEL, EXIT89 (Fahy 1996), EXITT (Kostreva and Lancaster 1998), E-SCAPE (Reisser-Weston 1996), EVACSIM (Poon and Beck 1994, Poon 1995), EVACNET (Kisko and Francis, 1985), PAXPORT (Barton and Leather 1995, Buckmann and Leather 1994), TAKAHASHI'S MODEL (Takahashi et al. 1989) and WAYOUT (Shestopal and Grubits 1994). The second approach represents a space as an extensive network of nodes. Each node corresponds to a small area of the building space and allows a detailed description to be implemented in an evacuation model. This approach is usually an accurate representation of the building geometry and it often requires CAD drawings. There are several simulation-type evacuation models including Building EXODUS (Owen et al. 1997), BGRAF (Ozel 1992), EGRESS (Ketchell et al. 1993, Ketchell 1995), MAGNET MODEL (Okasaki and Matsushita 1993), SIMULEX (Thompson and Marchant 1994, Thompson and Marchant 1995, Thompson et al. 1996), VEGAS (Still 1993, Still 1994), SGEM (Lo and Fang 2000, Lo et al. 2004) and Cellular Automata (Yang et al. 2003, Yang et al. 2004).

For a continuity model, the social force model is based on the ecumenical dynamics model to simulate pedestrian's jam dynamics in nervous. It can describe the complex behaviors of emergent evacuation, for instance lances, jamming and faster-is-slower, but with low simulation speed (Song et al. 2005).

In this study, the purpose of evacuation model is to obtain the spatial and temporal distribution of indoor occupants. For this reason, the selected models must describe the evacuation process clearly and accurately. Comparing the above-mentioned models, fine networks are more able to accurately represent details during the occupant evacuation process than other models. Therefore, we choose SGEM and Cellular Automata model to simulate the occupant evacuation finally.

3.1.2. Spatial-grid Evacuation Model (SGEM)

In this section, the theoretical background of the SGEM (Lo and Fang, 2000; Wang, 2005) will be introduced. The model takes the spatial geometry of a building (or a room inside building) and divides it into planar grids. Each notional occupant in the building is represented by a relative co-ordinate and the individual's movement pattern in the setting is modeled by solving the representing differential equations. The inter-person influence and behavior can be taken into consideration.

(1) Computational Principles

The model treats the evacuation process with Lagrangian approach as follows:

$$x(m,t+1) = x(m,t) + U_m \Delta t \qquad (3.1.2\text{-}1)$$
$$y(m,t+1) = y(m,t) + V_m \Delta t \qquad (3.1.2\text{-}2)$$

where, m is the number of the individual, $m = 1, 2, \cdots, N$; $x(m,t)$ and $y(m,t)$ are the geometrical coordinates of the person whose number is m at time step t in x and y directions respectively; U_m and V_m are the velocity components of the person at time step t in x and y directions respectively; Δt represents the time step.

Accordingly, the trajectory of an individual can be determined by knowing the person's velocity vector at any time and his/her respective location. In order to simplify the computation, the model first assumes that the velocities of the people depend on their respective location and the crowd density in which the people move. Later, other adjustments in accordance with the individual's behavior can be added to the basic model. The speed of an individual can be expressed by a function of his/her location and the crowd density at this location.

$$U = f(x, y, n) \qquad (3.1.2\text{-}3)$$

where x and y are the coordinates of the individual, n is the aggregating number of people in a certain domain at the individual's location.

To find out the function of each individual, the model divides a room into a series of uniform grids as shown in Figure 3.1.2-1.

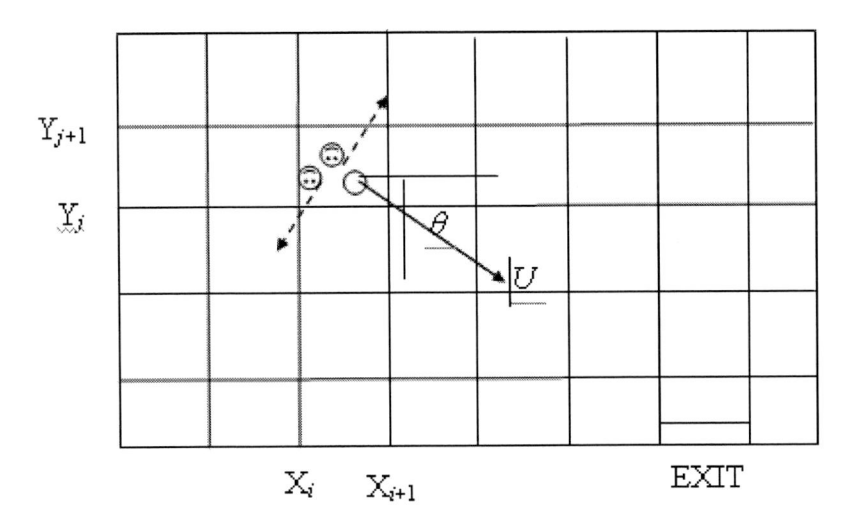

Figure 3.1.2-1. Analysis of an individual's movement in a grid (Lo and Fang, 2000).

When an individual, whose number is m, moves to a new place $x(m,t)$, $y(m,t)$, at the t time step, then he will move in the direction which can make him proceed to the exit at the next time step $t+1$ (Figure 3.1.2-1). The angle between the direction and x-axis is θ. The magnitude of the speed mainly depends on the individual's location and the number of people in the special domain around the respective grid. In general, an individual can move ahead at a speed U_0 when he/she does not encounter any crowd obstruction such as at bottleneck regions. When the time step is small enough and only one person in the grid, the person will proceed towards the exit at a speed U which is determined by the following empirical function (Thompson and Marchant, 1994; Ando et al. 1988):

$$U = U_0 \left(\sqrt{\frac{1}{D}} - 0.25 \right) \Big/ 0.87 \qquad (3.1.2\text{-}4)$$

where U_0 is the speed of an individual (m/s) when he/she does not encounter any crowd obstruction, D is crowded density (number of persons/m^2) of the calculated grid, which is based on the nine grids included around the calculated grid and itself.

If there is more than one person in the grid, a path-finding function is introduced in this model to adjust the movement of the person. The model assumes that only the person who is near to the exit can proceed at U. The others will either stay at the original grid or move to the side-grids. The path-finding function can be expressed as follows:

$$U_m = f_x(x,y,n) = \begin{cases} U\cos\theta & n=1 \\ \begin{cases} 0 \\ U\cos(\theta+\dfrac{\pi}{2}) \\ U\cos(\theta-\dfrac{\pi}{2}) \end{cases} & n \geq 2 \end{cases} \qquad (3.1.2\text{-}5a)$$

$$V_m = f_y(x,y,n) = \begin{cases} U\sin\theta & n=1 \\ \begin{cases} 0 \\ U\sin(\theta+\dfrac{\pi}{2}) \\ U\sin(\theta-\dfrac{\pi}{2}) \end{cases} & n \geq 2 \end{cases} \qquad (3.1.2\text{-}5b)$$

where θ is the angle between the direction of movement of an individual and the x-axis, m is the number of the individual.

Then, if the initial location of an individual is known, his/her trajectory of movement can be determined.

(2) Simulation Method

The algorithmic description of the simulation is as follows:

Step 1. Define the nodes of the building and the flow direction.
Step 2. In each node, divide grid x_i, y_j and calculate the direction of motion in each grid: angle (i,j).
Step 3. Set the original coordinate of each occupant $x(m,1), y(m,1)$ and the reaction time function of each person.
Step 4. Scan all the grids and determine the velocity vector of each individual according to the Eqs. 3.1.2-4 and 3.1.2-5.
Step 5. Calculate the new coordinate of each occupant at new time step by Eqs. 3.1.2-1 and 3.1.2-2.
Step 6. Determine whether the individual has left the respective zone. If not, increase one time step, and repeat Step 1–Step 5.
Step 7. Output the evacuation trajectory file and the results of evacuation time.

3.1.3. Cellular Automata Model

CA (Cellular Automata) is a discrete, decentralized and spatially extended system consisting of large numbers of simple identical components with local connectivity. CA is an alternative to differential equations to model the physical system. Because CA model can exhibit the artificial intelligence, they are usually called the artificial lift models (Yang et al. 2004).

In this study, we present CA models for simulating the four-directional occupant evacuation in emergency event, including a basic model and an extended model based on it.

(1) Basic Model

Basic model is developed to study the crowed, large, and open space. Considering a large room with one or two exits, the basic structure of the model is a two-dimensional (2D) grid. Each cell is either empty or occupied by one occupant. In basic 2D model, each cell has two states: 0 for no occupant, 1for occupant with the maximum velocity of 1. The size of a cell is 0.4m×0.4m (Burstedde et al. 2001), which is the typical space occupied by an occupant in a dense crowd. The synchronous update is performed for all occupants. Empirically the average velocity of an occupant in nervous can reach 1.50 m·s^{-1}, so the time step in this basic model is 0.4/1.5≈0.27s, which is in the order of the reaction time and consistent with microscopic rules.

In order to determine each occupant's moving direction, danger grade is introduced to describe the occupant's knowledge of danger in the emergence environment. The position danger grade (PD) is determined by the distance from the safety exit, i.e., the closer the position to the exit is, the less the PD of the cell is. An optional stage can be used to describe the more realistic evacuation, and we call it the familiar stage. During this stage, occupants are introduced into the room to get familiar with the structure and the PDs are determined. When one walks into a cell, he compares the cell's PD with those of the four adjacent cells. If the PD of the cell he occupied now is not the minimum, PD will be changed to the sum of 1 and the minimum value of the four adjacent PDs.

There are four parallel updating stages of the set for occupants in the basic model. Stage 1: For each cell occupied, check the neighboring cells according to the time steps he can premeditate, select a proper cell and assign the cell to be occupied. Stage 2: For each cell more than one occupant vying, it is randomly assigned to be occupied by one of the viers with each one having same chance and the other occupants stay where they were last time-step. Stage 3: Given each occupant, who has decided to move, the probability p_{stay} to stay. The introduction of p_{stay} is to simulate the occupant's unexpected behaviors, such as the suddenly stop for physical and other reasons. An experimental value, 0.05, is used, just to make the model more stochastic. It can be changed according to the real situations. Stage 4: Every occupant alters the dynamic danger grades of all the cells if necessary (Yang et al. 2003, Yang et al. 2004).

(2) Extended Model

Basic model have simple rules but low accuracy, thus are always focused on qualitative research.

In order to increase accuracy of the CA model, Song et al. (2005) build a new set of rules and a new model considering frictions and repulsions based on the predominance of social force model.

Usually pedestrians walk towards the exit in evacuation preferring the direction which bridges over the smallest distance without any obstacles. To represent the influence of movement destination, researchers have introduced a concept of "floor field". In extended model, we only considered the static floor field which can be calculated by the distance to exit. When pedestrians move from large value to small value of it, they can reach and pass the exit.

Repulsion occurs when a pedestrian is near other pedestrians or walls, as shown in Figure 3.1.3-1. There are three kinds of repulsion: that between moving pedestrians, that between a moving pedestrian and a standstill one, and that between a moving pedestrian and a wall. The result of repulsion is the action of slowdown and avoiding.

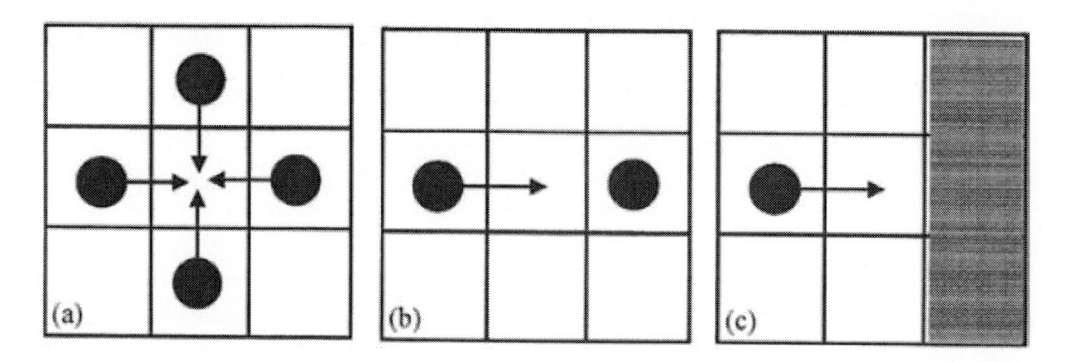

Figure 3.1.3-1. Occurrence of repulsion. (a) two-four pedestrians move together; (b) one moves and one stays; (c) interaction with wall (Song et al. 2005).

The repulsion probability r_1 is introduced to model the repulsion for Figure 3.1.3-1(a). The moving probability of each pedestrian is shown in formula (3.1.3-1).

$$p_i = (1-r_1)/m \quad (i=1,2\cdots m) \tag{3.1.3-1}$$

where m ($m \geq 2$) is the number of pedestrians involved in the conflict. All pedestrians involved in the conflict choose to stay with probability r_1, or move to the empty site with probability $1-r_1$, and each pedestrian's movement probability is the same.

Considering relative velocities between pedestrian-pedestrian and pedestrian-wall, as shown in Figure 3.1.3-1(b) and (c), the moving probabilities are determined with formulas (3.1.3-2) and (3.1.3-3).

$$p_i = (1-r_2) \tag{3.1.3-2}$$
$$p_i = (1-r_w) \tag{3.1.3-3}$$

where r_2 is repulsion probability for the conflict between a moving pedestrian and a standstill one, and r_w is repulsion probability for the conflict between a moving pedestrian and a wall. Once the value of r is obtained, the repulsion probability is calculated.

The value of repulsion is related to the relative speed. If the relative speed is greater than the threshold, the pedestrian always avoids it. The repulsion probability is determined with formula (3.1.3-4):

$$r = \frac{1-e^{-\alpha V}}{1+e^{-\alpha V}} \tag{3.1.3-4}$$

where V is relative speed, $\alpha \in [0, \infty]$ is the hardness degree. For the repulsion between two moving pedestrians, $V = 2 \cdot v$; for the repulsion between a moving pedestrian and a standstill pedestrian, $V = v$; and for that of between a moving pedestrian and wall, $V = v$. The hardness degree is corresponding to the pedestrian's endurance to physical collision, as well as the roughness of the pedestrian or wall.

In an emergent evacuation, friction is another key factor affecting evacuation behaviors. The result of friction is slowdown when two pedestrians, or a pedestrian and a wall, touch with each other. In CA model, the desired speeds of all pedestrians are the same, i.e., one grid in one time step, so that there are three types of friction, as shown in Figure 3.1.3-2.

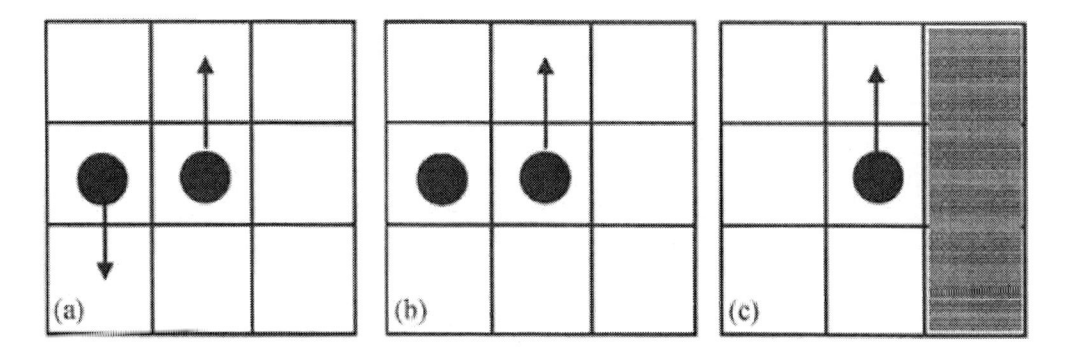

Figure 3.1.3-2. Occurrence of friction. (a) move vis-à-vis; (b) one moves and one stays; (c) interaction with wall (Song et al. 2005).

A concept "friction probability" is introduced to quantify the effects of friction. For the three conditions in Figure 3.1.3-2, the moving probabilities are calculated with formulas (3.1.3-5)-(3.1.3-7) respectively.

$$p_i = 1 - f_1 \tag{3.1.3-5}$$
$$p_i = 1 - f_2 \tag{3.1.3-6}$$
$$p_i = 1 - f_w \tag{3.1.3-7}$$

where f is the friction probability. The value of moving probability is calculated as soon as the friction probability is obtained.

The value of the friction probability is decided by relative distance, relative speed and friction coefficient. The friction probability is defined as formula (3.1.3-8).

$$f = \theta \cdot V \tag{3.1.3-8}$$

where V is relative speed and $\theta \in [0,1]$ is the friction coefficient reflecting the roughness of pedestrian and wall. For two moving pedestrians, $V = 2 \cdot v$; for a moving pedestrian and a standstill pedestrian, $V = v$; for a moving pedestrian and wall, $V = v$.

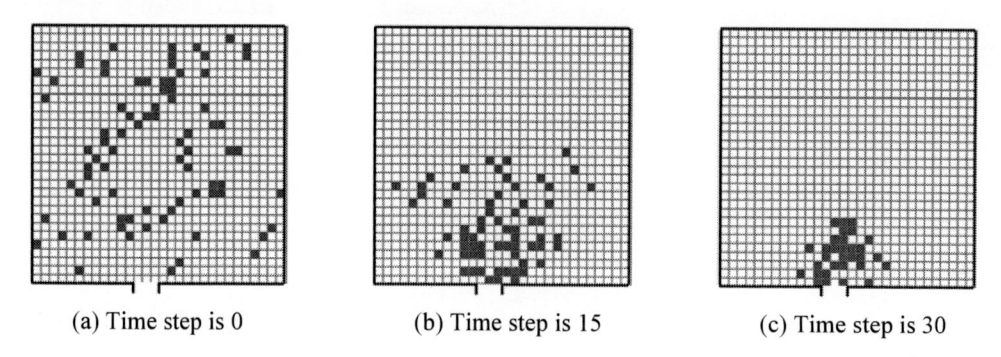

(a) Time step is 0   (b) Time step is 15   (c) Time step is 30

Figure 3.1.3-3. Simulation of occupants evacuating by extended CA model.

Figure 3.1.3-3 shows the application of extended CA model. In this case, the extended CA model is used in a one-exit, 12 m by 12 m room. The effective width of the exit is 1.2 m occupying 3cells. There are 80 pedestrians in the room. The desired velocity of pedestrians is 0.8 m/s. Other parameters used are as follows:

$$\alpha = \begin{cases} 1 & \text{(between 2 pedestrians)} \\ 2 & \text{(between pedestrian and wall)} \end{cases}$$

$$\theta = \begin{cases} 0.1 & \text{(between 2 pedestrians)} \\ 0.5 & \text{(between pedestrian and wall)} \end{cases}$$

The extended model can simulate the time of evacuation accurately, and describe the classical phenomena during the process of occupant evacuation perfectly, and therefore is used to calculate the distribution of occupants during the emergent evacuation.

3.2. Evaluation of Exposure Risk

3.2.1. Concept of Occupied Density, Exposure Cell and its Layered Model

(1) Occupied Density (OD)

To describe the occupant distribution in a room, OD is used to indicate the probability distribution of occupants in the room. The OD is defined as (Zhao et al. 2003c; Zhao et al. 2004a):

$$D(x,y,z) = \frac{\sum_{i=1}^{N} ID^i(x,y,z)}{N} \quad (3.2.1\text{-}1)$$

where N is the number of persons indoors, and $ID^i(x,y,z)$ is the individual occupied density of the i-th occupant at each point in the room. $ID^i(x,y,z)$ should satisfy the following equation for each region (V_j) indoors:

$$OD_j^i = \int_{V_j} ID^i(x,y,z) dxdydz \tag{3.2.1-2}$$

where OD_j^i is the individual occupied density of the i-th occupant for j-th region indoors, which is the ratio of occupied time of the person in the region to the whole time he/she spent in the room. If the occupied density is uniform for each point in the specified region, $ID^i(x,y,z)$ can be denoted as:

$$ID^i(x,y,z) = \frac{OD_j^i}{V_j} \tag{3.2.1-3}$$

where V_j is the volume of the j-th region of the room.

For example, if N persons are in an office and each has an 8 h stay, the i th occupant sits on the work region 6 h and walks in other regions of the room for 2 h, then the individual occupant density of this person in different regions are:

$$OD_j^i = \begin{cases} 6/8 = 0.75, & j \text{ stands for work region} \\ 2/8 = 0.25, & j \text{ stands for other region} \end{cases} \tag{3.2.1-4}$$

where x, y, z are Cartesian coordinates.

Since OD is independent of time for a specified period, it is reasonable to be used for steady case or for describing the occupant distribution when the numbers of occupants in different regions indoors have not greatly changed. If these numbers are changing with time remarkably, such as in the evacuation process of occupants indoors, the concept of exposure cell (EC) will be used for such purpose instead of OD.

(2) Exposure Cell and its Layered Model

Exposure cell (EC), which is an abstract spatial concept, represents the indoor spatial volume that caused occupant exposure, as shown in Figure 3.2.1-1 (Cai et al. 2007a). For different research aims, EC can be used to represent the volume occupied by single person, which is called Basic Exposure Cell and denoted by $BEC_i, (i = 1, 2...M)$, or a part of the room denoted by $EC_i, (i = 1, 2...M)$.

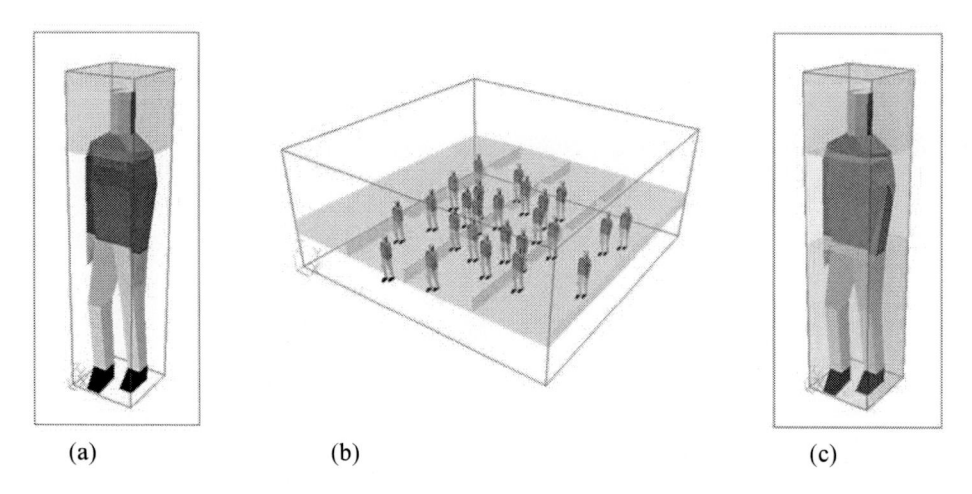

Figure 3.2.1-1. Exposure cell and its layered model. (a) Basic exposure cell (1-layer model) (b) The room is equally divided into 16 exposure cells in the range of $Z = 1.4m\sim1.8m$ (1-layer model) (c) Basic exposure cell (3-layers model).

EC can be further divided into several layers to distinguish different exposure route and effects of contaminants on indoor occupants at different heights. For the inhaled exposure, EC may only have one layer which represents the respiration region (Figs. 3.2.1-1a, b), and it is called one-layer model. For the contact exposure, EC can be divided into several layers in the height direction of human body. Figure 3.2.1-1c depicts an EC with three layers which is called three-layers model.

The contaminant concentration in the exposure cell EC_i at time t is represented by equivalent concentration $\overline{C}_i(t)$. The physical meaning of equivalent concentration is a completely uniform concentration in an imaginary exposure cell whose influence on the occupants within it is equal to that of the actual exposure cell in which the concentration is nonuniform. For one-layer model, the volume-averaged concentration $\overline{C}_{1,i}(t)$ is suggested as an approximation of $\overline{C}_i(t)$. For three-layers model, the volume-weighted-average concentration of all layers $\overline{C}_{3,i}(t)$ is proposed as an approximation of $\overline{C}_i(t)$. The number of indoor occupants in EC_i at time t is represented by $PNC_i(t)$ ($PNC_i(t) \geq 0$).

3.2.2. Relative Exposure Risk Index —Efficiency Factor of Contaminant Source

Efficiency factor of contaminant source (EFCS) is a set of indices, including EFCS1-EFCS3, which reflect the relative influence of indoor contaminant source on occupants in any period of time from three different angles. These indices are defined as (Cai et al. 2007b):

$$EFCS1_i(\tau) = \frac{\int_0^\tau \overline{C}_i(t)PNC_i(t)dt}{\overline{C}_R \int_0^\tau PNC_i(t)dt} \qquad (3.2.2-1)$$

$$EFCS2_j(\tau) = \frac{\int_0^\tau \overline{C}(CN_j(t),t)dt}{\overline{C}_R \tau} \qquad (3.2.2\text{-}2)$$

$$EFCS3(\tau) = \frac{\sum_{i=1}^{M} \int_0^\tau \overline{C}_i(t) PNC_i(t) dt}{\overline{C}_R \sum_{i=1}^{M} \int_0^\tau PNC_i(t) dt} \qquad (3.2.2\text{-}3)$$

where $EFCS1_i(\tau)$ indicates the influence of contaminant source on the occupants who once stayed in the exposure cell $EC_i, (i=1,2...M)$ in the period τ, $EFCS2_j(\tau)$ reflects the influence of contaminant source on the j-th occupant in the period τ, $EFCS3(\tau)$ reflects the influence of contaminant source on the whole population ever indoors in the period τ. $\overline{C}_R$ is the average exhausted concentration of contaminant under steady-state conditions, $PNC_i(t)$ is the number of occupants in EC_i at moment t. Set $ECS1_i(\tau) = 0$ when $PNC_i(t) \equiv 0$. $CN_j(t)$ is the serial number of exposure cell in which the j-th person stays at time t. For $CN_j(t) = i$, $\overline{C}(CN_j(t),t) = \overline{C}_i(t)$ holds. τ_j is the occupied time of the j-th occupant in the room. Set $\tau = \tau_j$ when $\tau \geq \tau_j$.

From the definition of EFCS, it is shown that these indices are non-dimensional parameters and can be used to quantify the relative exposure risk of occupants indoors. They are functions of the flow characteristic, the distribution of occupant, and the source location, while have nothing to do with the emission rate and contaminant type. The indices of EFCS can be easily calculated by combining the distribution of contaminant with that of occupants.

3.2.3. Absolute Exposure Risk Index —Population Injury Rate

The impact of contaminant agent on human body is dependent on both the inhaled concentration and exposure duration. The toxic exposure E can be calculated with Haber's Law (Haber, 1924):

$$E = C\tau \qquad (3.2.3\text{-}1)$$

where C is the contaminant concentration, τ is the exposure duration.

In emergency incidents, the contaminant concentration often varies with time, so the acute exposure is defined with the integration of whole time period, which was also adopted in fire protection engineering (Purser, 1996; Speitel, 1996):

$$E(x,y,z,\tau) = \int_0^\tau C(x,y,z,t)dt \qquad (3.2.3\text{-}2a)$$

$$E(x,y,z,\tau) = \overline{C}(x,y,z,\tau) \times \tau \qquad (3.2.3\text{-}2b)$$

In order to evaluate the exposure risk quantitatively, a well accepted probit model (Finney, 1971) is adopted:

$$P = \frac{1}{(2\pi)^{1/2}} \int_{-\infty}^{Y-5} \exp\left(-\frac{u^2}{2}\right) du \qquad (3.2.3\text{-}3)$$

where the probit variable Y, with an average value of 5 and a normal deviation of 1, is calculated by vulnerability intensity V together with constants a and b:

$$Y = a + b \ln V \qquad (3.2.3\text{-}4)$$

The probit model provides a measure of relating the received dose to the proportion of population with response. It has been widely used after the first Canvey report (HSE, 1978) and the Rijnmond report (Rijnmond Public Authority, 1982), both of which concerned person injury.

After replacing vulnerability intensity V with exposure E, we can get the probability of the vulnerable people, named as Injury Risk (IR) in this case, with the following equation:

$$IR(x, y, z, \tau) = \frac{1}{(2\pi)^{1/2}} \int_{-\infty}^{a+b\ln(E(x,y,z,\tau))-5} \exp\left(-\frac{u^2}{2}\right) du \qquad (3.2.3\text{-}5)$$

Constants a and b in the equation should be specified according to the nature of the chemical agent. Since the Acute Exposure Guideline Levels (AEGLs) (EPA, 1997) are well accepted to evaluate exposure risk, we take AEGL-1, -2, -3, the 3-level thresholds of one-time-only exposure values, to get the constants a and b. There are different kinds of exposure periods, such as 10 min, 30 min, 1 h, 4 h, to 8 hours, for different contaminant (EPA, 2001). For effect of anesthetic gas, as stated in AEGLs documents, the general population, including susceptible individuals, would not experience notable effects where the contaminant concentration is below AEGL1; the anesthetic effect will not probably occur until the concentration reaches AEGL2; it is the concentration threshold for life-threatening danger on most people when the contaminant concentration reaches AEGL-3 (EPA, 2000). In a given time period τ, after defining the injury proportion $L2$ and $L3$ as the expectation people suffering from exposed concentrations as high as AEGL2 and AEGL3, respectively, the constants a and b can be calculated as follows:

$$L2 = \frac{1}{(2\pi)^{1/2}} \int_{-\infty}^{Y_2-5} \exp\left(-\frac{u^2}{2}\right) du, \quad Y_2 = a + b\ln(\tau \times AEGL2) \qquad (3.2.3\text{-}6a)$$

$$L3 = \frac{1}{(2\pi)^{1/2}} \int_{-\infty}^{Y_3-5} \exp\left(-\frac{u^2}{2}\right) du, \quad Y_3 = a + b\ln(\tau \times AEGL3) \qquad (3.2.3\text{-}6b)$$

Then we can calculate the probability of injury for any exposure in the process. Since the exposure E is different for different position and the occupied density of occupant is also different, we integrate the $IR(x,y,z,\tau)$ in the whole space with occupied density $D(x,y,z)$ as the weight factors and get the population injury rate (PIR) as follows:

$$PIR(\tau) = \iiint_{V_{room}} IR(x,y,z,\tau)D(x,y,z)dxdydz \qquad (3.2.3\text{-}7)$$

When $PIR=0$, it means none of the occupants has significant clinical reactions; $PIR = L2$ indicates the occupants suffer a toxic injury rate corresponding to the adverse health effect due to exposure of AEGL2 level; and $PIR = 1$ indicates a lethal danger for all the people in concern.

During the evacuation process, the distribution of occupants will change time by time. The concept of EC rather than OD is preferred for quantitatively evaluating the absolute exposure risk. In this case, the PIR can be defined simply as:

$$TAC_j = \frac{\int_0^\tau \overline{C}(CN_j(t),t)dt}{\tau} \qquad (3.2.3\text{-}8)$$

$$ER_j = \begin{cases} 0 & \text{if } TAC_j \leq AEGL1 \\ \dfrac{TAC_j - AEGL1}{AEGL2 - AEGL1} \times L_2 & \text{if } AEGL1 < TAC_j < AEGL2 \\ L_2 & \text{if } TAC_j = AEGL2 \\ \dfrac{(TAC_j - AEGL2)\cdot(L_3 - L_2)}{AEGL3 - AEGL2} + L_2 & \text{if } AEGL2 < TAC_j < AEGL3 \\ L_3 & \text{if } AEGL3 \leq TAC_j \end{cases} \qquad (3.2.3\text{-}9)$$

$$PIR = \frac{\sum_{j=1}^{N} ER_j(\tau_j)}{N} \qquad (3.2.3\text{-}10)$$

where TAC_j indicates the average exposure concentration of the j-th occupant in the period τ; ER_j reflects the injured degree of the j-th occupant in the periods τ; PIR is the average injured degree of the whole occupants in the periods τ; N is the number of the whole occupants. Usually, the value of L_2 and L_3 is decided by toxicologists in practical application. Here we set L_3 as 0.99 and L_2 0.3~0.5 dependent on the type of contaminant.

4. EMERGENCY VENTILATION SYSTEM AGAINST CONTAMINANT SUDDENLY RELEASED IN PUBLIC BUILDING

4.1. Introduction

When chemical agent was suddenly released in a public building, it is of great significance to take proper response actions to mitigate damages and protect indoor occupants. In the reference manual released by Federal Emergency Management Agency

(FEMA), five possible protective actions are suggested after the presence of an airborne hazard is detected. In increasing order of complexity and cost, these actions are evacuation, sheltering in place, personal protective equipment, air filtration and pressurization, exhausting and purging (FEMA, 2003).

Among these actions, emergency ventilation plays an important role in protecting occupants indoors since it is a major measure to control the spatial and temporal distribution of air flow and contaminant indoors. For a specific chemical attack, the influence of contaminant on indoor occupants during the evacuation process depends heavily on both the distribution pattern of the contaminant and occupants indoors. In order to protect the occupants as much as possible, both the emergency ventilation and evacuation strategies should be comprehensively considered while the decision maker is determining the optimal response action.

If the contaminant source characteristics, such as the location, intensity, and type, are known with a reasonable degree of certainty, the effects of different combinations of emergency ventilation and evacuation mode can be predicted with certain outcomes. However, these characteristics may be identified with much more uncertainty in practical application due to various environmental disturbances. If the judgment of source is false, the corresponding strategy may produce reverse effects and cause even greater losses. Therefore, the response strategies usually accompany certain risks. In order to avoid the risks involved, the situations in which the certainty of contaminant source are incompletely certain and even completely uncertain should be carefully considered during the process of decision-making (Cai et al., 2007c).

Decision analysis provides a framework and methodology for rational response of the emergency ventilation system. In this section, the certainty of contaminant source is classified as completely certain, incompletely certain, and completely uncertain. According to such classification, three types of decision analysis models will be presented to guide the decision-making of emergency ventilation system. In addition, two examples are given to demonstrate the practical application of these models.

4.2. Decision Analysis Method for Emergency Ventilation System

4.2.1. Overview of Decision Analysis

Decision analysis refers to a broad quantitative field, overlapping operations research and statistics, which deals with modeling, optimizing and analyzing decisions made by individuals, groups and organizations (Clemen, 1996; Goodwin and Wright, 2004). The purpose of decision analysis is to assist decision makers in making better decisions in complex situations, usually under uncertainty. It is a rational approach to decision making that makes use of a formal model to represent alternative courses of action, potential states of nature relevant to the problem being analyzed, probability distributions of the states of nature, and expected payoffs to determine an optimal decision strategy.

In general, the decision problems include the following main elements:

(1) Decision maker: the person(s) responsible for making the decision.
(2) Decision alternative: a course of action that may be taken by a decision maker. Decision alternatives must be mutually exclusive (clearly distinct among themselves)

and, ideally, collectively exhaustive (cover all reasonable options). A set of all the available decision alternatives is called decision space. Determination of a realistic decision space demands creativity and experience on the nature of the problem under consideration. Decision alternatives are under the control of the decision maker.

(3) State of nature: an uncertain event which, if it occurs, partly determines the outcome of a decision. As with decision alternatives, states of nature must be mutually exclusive and, ideally, collectively exhaustive. A set of all the possible states of nature is called state space. Judgment and experience are indispensable in determining a realistic state space. States of nature are not controllable by the decision maker.

(4) Payoff: the net result (gain or loss) of taking a particular decision alternative combined with the occurrence of a particular state of nature; informally, the consequence of a decision.

(5) Decision criterion: a standard adopted by the decision maker to determine the optimal decision.

With above elements, a decision problem can be represented by a payoff matrix (a payoff table). A common format is the following:

Table 4.2.1-1. Payoff table for decision-making

Decision alternative	State of Nature			
	S_1	S_2	...	S_n
d_1	$P(d_1, S_1)$	$P(d_1, S_2)$	...	$P(d_1, S_n)$
d_2	$P(d_2, S_1)$	$P(d_2, S_2)$	...	$P(d_2, S_n)$
⋮	⋮	⋮	⋮	⋮
d_m	$P(d_m, S_1)$	$P(d_m, S_2)$	...	$P(d_m, S_n)$

where, d_i ($i = 1, 2, \cdots, m$) is the decision alternative; S_j ($j = 1, 2, \cdots, n$) is the state of nature; $P(d_i, S_j)$ is the payoff of the decision alternative d_i under the state of nature S_j.

The outcome of a decision problem depends on two things: the decision alternative chosen by the decision maker and the uncontrollable state of nature which happens to occur. The payoff table should be used for the decision maker to find an optimal alternative according to an appropriate decision criterion.

4.2.2. Modeling the Decision Problem of Emergency Ventilation System

In this section, we will formulate a model of emergency ventilation system with a decision matrix based on the theory of decision analysis.

(1) Decision Alternatives

As discussed in section 4.1, the effects of emergency ventilation depend largely on the distribution pattern of indoor occupants. Therefore, the decision alternatives are defined as all the available combinations of ventilation and evacuation modes. If there are m possible combinations, the decision space can be written as $D = \{d_1, d_2, \cdots, d_m\}$.

(2) States of Nature

Since the release of contaminant source is an uncertain event beyond the control of decision maker, the state of natures are defined as all the potential state of contaminant source. If there are n possible states, the state space can be written as $S = \{S_1, S_2, \cdots, S_n\}$. The state of contaminant source depends on three aspects of characteristics: location, intensity, and type.

If the intensity and type of the contaminant source are unknown to the decision maker, both of them must have no effect on the payoffs. Otherwise, they should be considered in the state space, which may result in that the size of the state space may be tremendously large, and furthermore, the decision problem can hardly be solved. From another point of view, if the intensity and type of the contaminant source have certain effect on the payoffs, they should be determined by the decision maker before the decision-making.

(3) Payoffs

Two kinds of indices, the relative index (Efficiency Factor of Contaminant Source, EFCS) and the absolute index PIR, are presented in section 3.2 to evaluate the exposure risk of occupants indoors. These indices will be employed here to quantitatively represent the payoff of a decision alternative under a certain state of nature.

A. Payoffs Based on the Relative Index

As presented in section 3.2.2, EFCS3 reflects the relative influence of contaminant source on the whole population ever indoors in a finite period of time. The greater the value of EFCS3, the greater the adverse influence of contaminant will be. Based on this index, the payoff which represents the gain of a decision is defined as follows:

$$P(d_i, S_j) = 1/EFCS3(\tau, d_i, S_j) \qquad (4.2.2\text{-}1)$$

where, $EFCS3(\tau, d_i, S_j)$ is the value of EFCS3 for the combination of the decision alternative d_i and the state of nature S_j in the period τ.

From the above definition, it is shown that the greater the value of a payoff, the smaller the resulting relative exposure risk, and then the greater the rewards of a decision alternative.

When the airflow pattern and evacuation mode is given, EFCS3 is only dependent on the location of the source, and has nothing to do with the intensity and type of the source. Therefore, the intensity and type of the source have no effect on the payoff defined by Eq. 4.2.2-1, and then only the location of source should be considered in the state space. As a result, the size of the state space is greatly reduced and the analysis process is remarkably simplified.

As already presented in Section 1.2.2, an integrated response process of emergency ventilation system can generally be divided into three stages. With the payoffs based on the relative index EFCS3, main tasks regarding decision-making in these stages are explained as follows:

Stage 1: Pretreatment

All scenarios, the combinations of decision alternatives and states of nature, will be simulated and the values of payoffs will be calculated. Here, the intensity of contaminants source is supposed to be S_0 for simulating contaminant dispersion. This time-consuming stage should be accomplished before the event and the payoff table will be stored in the emergency ventilation system.

Stage 2: Identification of contaminant source

Since the payoffs have nothing to do with the intensity and type of the source, only the location information of source is needed in this stage.

Stage 3: Execution of emergency ventilation

By using the payoff table constructed in stage 1, decision maker should find an optimal decision alternative according to an appropriate decision criterion. Following the optimal alternative, the emergency ventilation and evacuation modes will be started until the emergency is over.

B. Payoffs Based on the Absolute Index

As presented in section 3.2.3, PIR reflects the absolute influence of contaminant source on the indoor occupants in a finite period of time. The value of it directly reflects the average injured degree of the whole population. Based on this index, the payoff which represents the gain of a decision is defined as follows:

$$P(d_i, S_j) = 1 / PIR(\tau, d_i, S_j) \qquad (4.2.2\text{-}2)$$

where, $PIR(\tau, d_i, S_j)$ is the value of PIR for the combination of the decision alternative d_i and the state of nature S_j in the period τ.

The above definition shows that the greater the value of a payoff, the smaller the resulting average injured degree of the whole population (absolute exposure risk), and then the greater the rewards of a decision alternative. Since both the intensity and type of the source have effects on the payoff defined by Eq. 4.2.2-2, they should be identified before the calculation of payoffs in order to control the size of the state space.

With the payoffs based on the absolute index PIR, main tasks involved are explained as follows:

Stage 1: Pretreatment

All scenarios, the combinations of decision alternatives and states of nature, will be simulated. Here, the intensity of contaminants source is supposed to be S_0 for simulating contaminant dispersion. This time-consuming stage should be accomplished before the event and the data of contaminant and occupant distribution will be stored in the emergency ventilation system.

Stage 2: Identification of contaminant source

In order to calculate the payoffs based on the absolute index PIR, all the characteristics of the contaminant source including the location, intensity, and type must be identified. By using the analytical formula for fast calculation on the transient dispersion of contaminant presented in section 2.2, the data of contaminant distribution will be updated online with intensity S^* which is the intensity of the source identified by the method presented in section 2.3. Since all the computational tasks in this stage are mathematically simple, the payoff table can be established in real time.

Stage 3: Execution of emergency ventilation

With the payoff table constructed online in stage 2, decision maker should find an optimal decision alternative and start the corresponding emergency ventilation and evacuation modes until the emergency is over.

4.2.3. Decision under Certainty

When the location of the contaminant source is completely certain, the decision made by the decision maker is called decision under certainty. The procedure of it is to determine an optimal decision alternative d^* from the decision space which meets the following equation under the state of nature S_j:

$$\max_{d_i \in D} P(d_i, S_j) = P(d^*, S_j) \qquad (4.2.3\text{-}1)$$

where, d^* is the optimal decision alternative under the state of nature S_j, $P(d^*, S_j)$ is the maximum value of the payoffs, and D is the decision space.

4.2.4. Decision under Risk

When the location of contaminant source is incompletely certain, the corresponding decision-making is called decision under risk. For such kind of problems, decision-making can only be based on the experience or the probability results from source identification to set or presume the relative likelihood of the possible contaminant source locations. It is just an optimal decision with statistical meaning, and the decision maker therefore needs to take a risk for a specific decision-making. This section tackles this kind of decision analysis issues with the expected value criterion for the purpose of demonstration. Here the probability of state S_j is assumed to be p_j. When one of the strategies is adopted, the expected payoff can be calculated as follows:

$$E(d_i) = \sum_{S_j \in S} p_j \times P(d_i, S_j), \quad \forall d_i \in D \qquad (4.2.4\text{-}1)$$

where, $P(d_i, S_j)$ is the payoff for the decision alternative d_i under the state of nature S_j, and S is the state space.

The expected value criterion chooses the decision alternative with the maximum expected payoff. The first step is to calculate the expected value of the payoffs for each of the possible decision alternatives, and then to select the optimal decision alternative d^* from decision space which meets the following equation:

$$\max_{d_i \in D} E(d_i) = E(d^*) \tag{4.2.4-2}$$

where, $E(d^*)$ is the maximum expected payoff.

The advantage of the expected value criterion is that it incorporates all the available information, including all the payoffs and the best available estimates of the probabilities of the respective states of nature.

It is sometimes argued that these estimates of the probabilities necessary are largely subjective and so are too shaky to be trusted. This argument has some validity. The reasonableness of the estimates of the probabilities should be assessed in each individual situation.

Nevertheless, the method to identify source presented in section 2.3 could enable us to develop reasonable estimates of the probabilities. Using this information could provide better grounds for a sound decision than ignoring it.

4.2.5. Decision under Uncertainty

When the location of the contaminant source is completely uncertain, which represents the worst circumstance, and then the corresponding decision-making is called decision under uncertainty. For such kind of problems, the certainty of the information of the possible contaminant source is worst. In this case, the result of decision-making depends heavily on the subjective attitude or intuition of the decision maker. In the following, three decision criteria will be discussed to demonstrate the solution for this kind of issues.

(1) Maximax Criterion

The maximax criterion or optimistic criterion chooses the alternative with maximum of maximum payoff. This criterion assumes that the best possible outcome will occur for any choice. This criterion chooses the "best of the best." But it does not provide protection against the potentially worst outcomes. The decision maker who adopts this criterion is always full of optimism and the spirit of adventure, and will not give up any opportunity to get the best result. The procedure is to determine the optimal decision alternative d^* which meets the condition as:

$$\max_{d_i \in D} \max_{S_j \in S} P(d_i, S_j) = P(d^*, S^*) \tag{4.2.5-1}$$

(2) Maximin Criterion

The maximin criterion or pessimistic criterion maximizes the minimum payoff. This criterion assumes that the worst will happen no matter what alternative we select. From the conservative view, decision maker estimates the minimum returns for alternatives and pick up the maximum of them or the "best of the worst." Thus, it provides a way of avoiding the worst outcome. The procedure is to determine the optimal decision alternative which meets the following equation:

$$\max_{d_i \in D} \min_{S_j \in S} P(d_i, S_j) = P(d^*, S^*) \tag{4.2.5-2}$$

(3) Hurwicz Criterion

The Hurwicz criterion computes the weighted sum of the maximax and maximin evaluations by introducing a coefficient of optimism, $\alpha \in [0,1]$.

$$H(d_i) = \alpha \max_{S_j \in S} P(d_i, S_j) + (1-\alpha) \min_{S_j \in S} P(d_i, S_j), \quad \forall d_i \in D \qquad (4.2.5\text{-}3)$$

Then, choose the maximum of the weighted sum.

$$\max_{d_i \in D} H(d_i) = H(d^*) \qquad (4.2.5\text{-}4)$$

The Hurwicz criterion is a compromise between the maximax and maximin criteria. But it is difficult to determine the appropriate α for decision makers, since it varies from person to person. Therefore, it is a highly subjective criterion.

4.3. Demonstration Examples of Emergency Ventilation Decision-making

Two illustrative examples are given in this section to demonstrate the emergency ventilation decision-making process with two kinds of payoff functions, which are based on the relative exposure risk index, efficiency factor of contaminant source (EFCS), and the absolute exposure risk index, population injury rate (PIR), respectively.

4.3.1. Example 1: Decision Analysis Based on Relative Exposure Risk

(1) Case Setup

The room under study was 12 m long (X), 16 m wide (Y), and 12 m high (Z) (Figure 4.3.1-1 (a)). Three kinds of ventilation systems were equipped in the room that are normal system, emergency system for fire safety, and emergency system for antiterrorist. Here, the antiterrorist system is combined with normal one, which can switch the return air grills from normal mode to exhaust mode and employ them as exhaust grills when emergency occurs.

Assume there are five typical locations (S1-S5) of possible contaminant sources in the room as shown in Figure 4.3.1-1 (b), and the locations and intensity of them are listed in Table 4.3.1-1.

Table 4.3.1-1. Typical locations and intensity of possible contaminant sources

Contaminant Sources	Length Δx[m]	Width Δy[m]	High Δz[m]	Coordinate of Starting Point x[m]	y[m]	z[m]	Intensity
S1	0.1	0.1	0.1	8.8	14.4	0.1	3g/s
S2	0.1	0.1	0.1	8.8	1.5	0.1	3g/s
S3	0.1	0.1	0.1	3.1	14.4	0.1	3g/s
S4	0.1	0.1	0.1	3.1	1.5	0.1	3g/s
S5	0.1	0.1	0.1	5.6	8	0.1	3g/s

(a) Three-dimensional sketch map

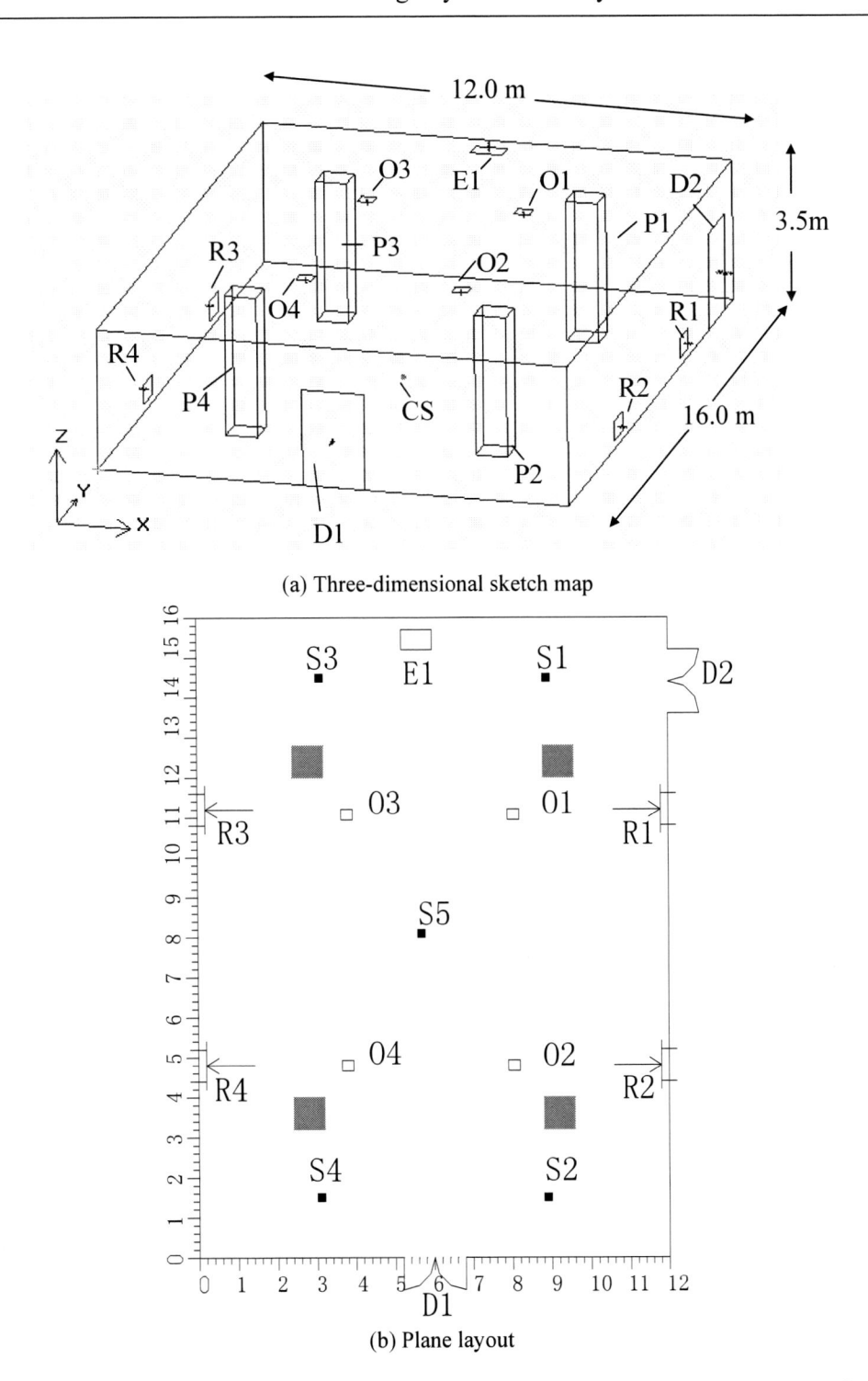

(b) Plane layout

Figure 4.3.1-1. Schematic of the ventilation room (O1~O4—supply air diffusers for normal ventilation, R1~R4—return air grills for normal ventilation, E1—exhaust for emergency ventilation, CS—contaminant source, P1~P4 — pillars, D1, D2 — exits for occupants).

Suppose there are generally 10 modes available for emergency ventilation during the incidents, as tabulated in Table 4.3.1-2. For the emergency ventilation modes V1 to V8, all the air openings are turned off except these in operation and supply air is supplied from exits D1 or D2. V8 represents smoke exhaust mode, V9 represents that the normal ventilation mode remains unchanged when emergency occurs, and V10 means that the ventilation is stopped and all the air openings are closed.

In addition, suppose that there are two evacuation modes available, mode A and mode B. For mode A, both the exits D1 and D2 are opened for evacuation; whereas, for mode B only the exit D1 is opened.

There are totally 100 scenarios which consist of ten emergency ventilation modes and two evacuation modes under five possible source locations. The nomenclature rules of these scenarios are described as follows. All the cases under source location S1 will be denoted by "Case-S1-*-*", in which two asterisks are wildcard characters for representing every ventilation and evacuation modes respectively. "Case-S*-V2-*" means all the cases with the ventilation mode V2 while "Case-S*-*-A" means that with the evacuation mode A. In addition, "Case-S*-V2-A" means all the cases with the combination of ventilation mode V2 and evacuation mode A under every possible source locations.

Table 4.3.1-2. Available emergency ventilation modes

Ventilation Modes	Openings In Operation	Vertical Air Inlets Velocity (m/s)	Air Flow Rate (m^3/h)
V1	R1	8.0	7200
V2	R2	8.0	7200
V3	R3	8.0	7200
V4	R4	8.0	7200
V5	R1,R2	4.0	7200
V6	R3,R4	4.0	7200
V7	R1,R2,R3,R4	2.0	7200
V8	E1	8.0	7200
V9	O1-O4, R1-R4	1.75	4032
V10	--	--	--

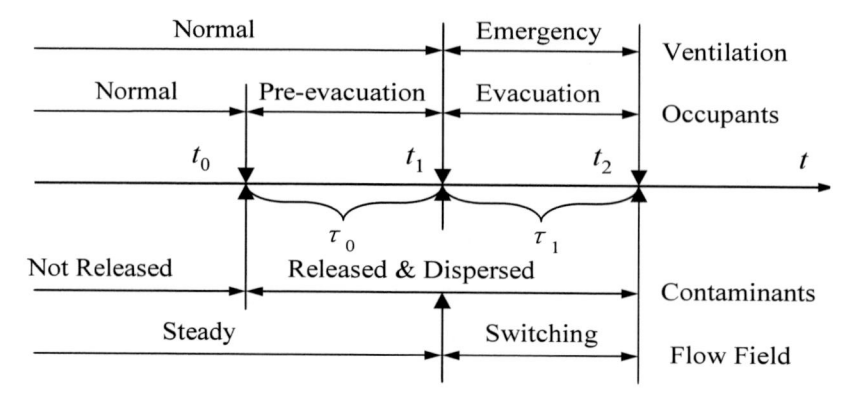

Figure 4.3.1-2. Developing process of emergency ventilation.

Figure 4.3.1-2 depicts the developing process of emergency ventilation. The contaminant source was released at time t_0, and occupants began to evacuate at time t_1 and the ventilation system switched to emergency mode at the same time. There were 120 persons indoors and stayed in random manner at initial moment.

(2) Numerical Procedure

The CFD method was employed to predict indoor contaminant dispersion. The commercial software Airpak2.1 (Fluent Inc., 2002) was used as a simulation tool, which has been validated on numerous occasions for indoor air flow studies.

The SGEM (Spatial-Grid Evacuation Model) was employed to simulate the evacuation process (Lo and Fang, 2000; Lo et al. 2004). SGEM has a full consideration of the characteristics of personal behavior during evacuation. This model has been well validated in practical projects.

The exposure cells were divided within the range of respiration region ($Z = 1.4\text{m}-1.8\text{m}$), and their size are $(\Delta X, \Delta Y, \Delta Z) = (0.8\text{m}, 0.8\text{m}, 0.4\text{m})$. The value of t_0 and t_1 in this solution are 300 s and 330 s, respectively. The CFD method was used to predict air flow and contaminant dispersion during $t_1 - t_2$, while SGEM was employed to simulate occupants evacuation during $t_1 - t_2$. The time step was 0.25s.

(3) Results and Discussion

The whole time were 126 time steps, that is $\tau_1 = 31.5\text{s}$, for evacuation mode A and 144 time steps ($\tau_1 = 36\text{s}$) for mode B by SGEM simulation.

According to the simulation results of contaminant dispersion and occupant's evacuation, we solved the payoffs ($1/EFCS3$) of 100 scenarios and then established the payoff table for decision analysis as shown in Table 4.3.1-3. The results in the table indicate that the evacuation modes have significant influence on the payoffs of indoor occupants. Therefore, the emergency response should combine the ventilation and evacuation strategy.

If the location of the contaminant source is completely certain, the decision-making model under certainty will be used to obtain the optimal decision alternative as shown in Table 4.3.1-4. The results in the table show that although evacuation mode B spends longer evacuation time than that of mode A, it is still a safer evacuation mode for most situations. It also indicates that the influence of the contaminant on occupants indoors may not always depend on the evacuation time. Decision maker should give careful consideration to the spatial and temporal distribution of contaminant, and organize occupants to steer clear of the region with higher concentration during the evacuation process.

If the location of contaminant source is incompletely certain, the model under risk should be employed. Assuming the probability distribution of different contaminant source locations is $p = (0.2, 0.1, 0.05, 0.2, 0.45)$. Table 4.3.1-5 summarizes the expected payoffs of each decision alternative by using the decision model with the expected value criterion. From the table, the decision maker can easily get that the optimal decision is D18 in this case. In other words, the best choice is the combination of ventilation mode V8 and evacuation mode B.

Table 4.3.1-3. Payoff table for the decision problem of emergency ventilation

Decision alternatives	States of Nature				
	S1	S2	S3	S4	S5
D1 (V1, A)	31.04	61.15	939.67	40.33	188.52
D2 (V2, A)	21.74	83.57	925.15	33.59	186.07
D3 (V3, A)	25.07	54.81	1598.26	41.70	193.69
D4 (V4, A)	22.39	47.15	932.14	52.04	191.32
D5 (V5, A)	20.86	71.29	931.19	38.22	186.64
D6 (V6, A)	23.69	51.08	1435.17	46.37	193.08
D7 (V7, A)	22.18	60.39	1274.03	41.12	189.79
D8 (V8, A)	35.17	65.80	691.75	38.29	170.33
D9 (V9, A)	18.89	50.04	946.79	36.02	184.70
D10 (V10, A)	21.71	50.54	948.23	35.24	183.36
D11 (V1, B)	2358.88	202.11	8884.94	91.23	26.28
D12 (V2, B)	2345.22	1100.86	9006.57	88.49	22.83
D13 (V3, B)	2452.72	178.79	10164.87	91.27	26.16
D14 (V4, B)	2394.92	143.07	8970.22	310.35	23.18
D15 (V5, B)	2368.21	663.66	8901.55	90.10	23.69
D16 (V6, B)	2427.30	160.23	9598.77	220.24	24.00
D17 (V7, B)	2403.21	357.94	9621.86	172.24	23.78
D18 (V8, B)	2299.43	202.71	11327.47	87.04	26.31
D19 (V9, B)	2368.21	124.79	8955.76	91.67	21.41
D20 (V10, B)	2361.11	114.42	9041.59	93.99	22.43

Table 4.3.1-4. Optimal decision alternative by decision analysis model under certainty

Source Locations	S1	S2	S3	S4	S5
Optimal Decision	D13	D12	D18	D14	D3
Ventilation Modes	V3	V2	V8	V4	V3
Evacuation Modes	B	B	B	B	A

Table 4.3.1-5. Expected payoffs of each decision alternative by decision analysis model with expected value criterion

Decision alternatives	Expected payoffs	Decision alternatives	Expected payoffs	Decision alternatives	Expected payoffs
D1	152.21	D8	132.51	D15	1013.77
D2	149.41	D9	146.44	D16	1036.27
D3	185.91	D10	146.37	D17	1042.68
D4	152.30	D11	966.31	D18	1075.78
D5	149.49	D12	1057.43	D19	961.88
D6	177.76	D13	1046.69	D20	964.64
D7	167.81	D14	1014.30	--	--

If the location of the contaminant source is completely uncertain, the model under uncertain should be adopted. With the maximax, maximin, and Hurwicz criteria, we obtained the optimal strategies as summarized in Table 4.3.1-6. In this specific example, the optimal decision alternative does not change with the coefficient of optimism. Nevertheless, this phenomenon should not be taken as a general conclusion. In general, the subjective attitude of decision maker has remarkable influence on the results of the decision problems under uncertain. To ensure the decision to be more objective, we should employ proper identification method to improve the certainty of contamination source and convert a completely uncertain problem into incompletely uncertain or certain one as much as possible.

Table 4.3.1-6. Optimal decisions by decision analysis models under uncertainty

Decision Criteria	Maximax	Maximin	Hurwicz (coefficient of optimism)			
			$\alpha = 0.2$	$\alpha = 0.4$	$\alpha = 0.6$	$\alpha = 0.8$
Optimal Decision	D18	D8	D18	D18	D18	D18
Ventilation Mode	V8	V8	V8	V8	V8	V8
Evacuation Mode	B	A	B	B	B	B

4.3.2. Example 2: Decision Analysis Based on Absolute Exposure Risk

(1) Case Setup

The room under study was 12 m long (X), 3.5 m high (Y), and 12 m wide (Z) (Figure 4.3.2-1). The contaminant source is assumed to be located at (X, Y, Z) = (2m, 8m, 0.1m), whose emission rate is 3g/s. The kind of contaminant is Chlorine Dioxide. In Figure 4.3.2-1, R1~R4 is the exhausts for normal ventilation, E1~E2 is the exhausts for emergency ventilation, CS is the contaminant source, P1~P4 are pillars.

(a) Three-dimensional sketch map.

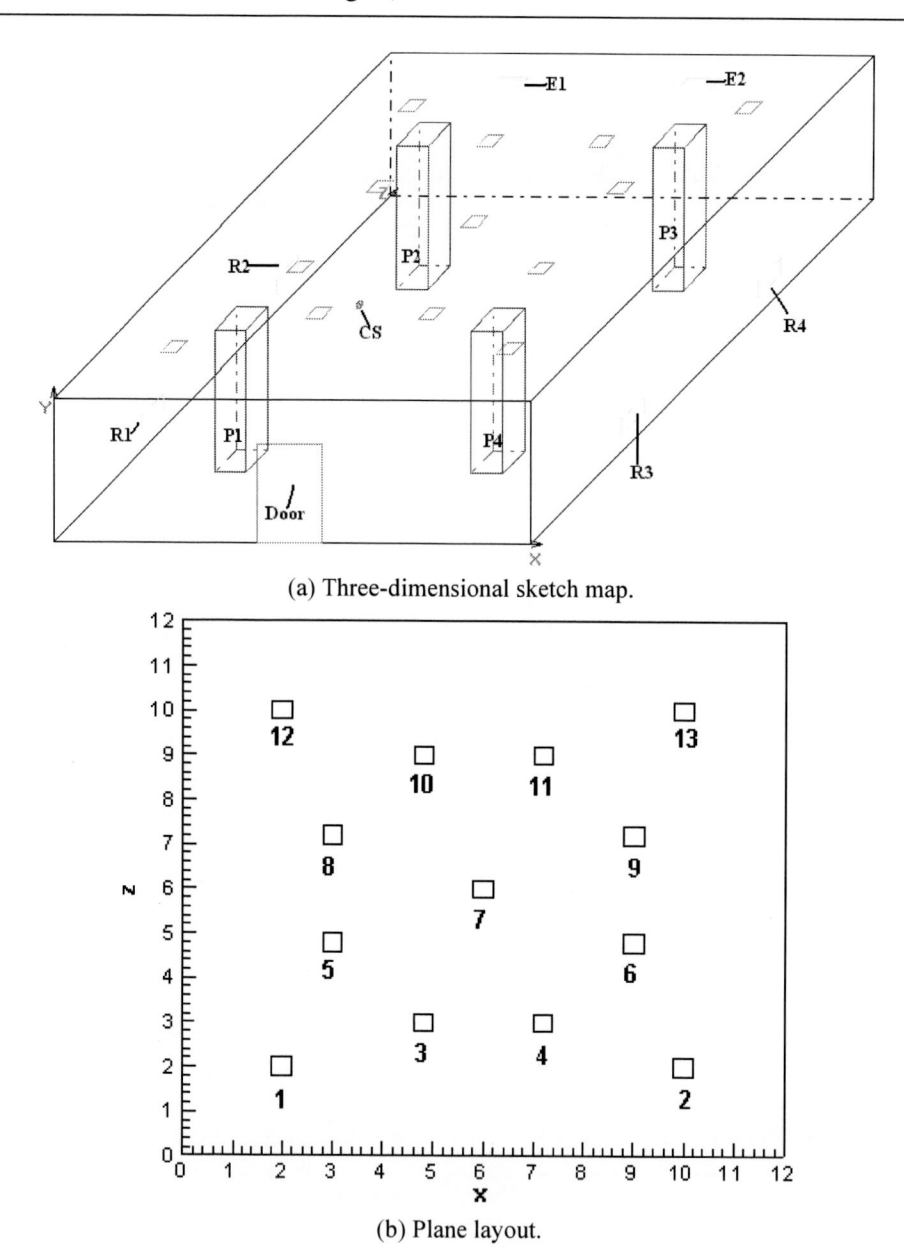

(b) Plane layout.

Figure 4.3.2-1. Schematic of the ventilation room.

The development process of emergency ventilation is referred to Figure 4.3.1-2. At time $t_0 = 0$, the contaminant source began to emit. At time $t_1 = 300s$, people began to evacuate, meanwhile the ventilation system switched to emergency mode. There were 80 persons stayed randomly in the room at time t_1. The exposure cells are divided in the height of respiration region (Y=1.4m~1.8m), whose size is (ΔX, ΔY, ΔZ) = (0.4m, 0.4m, 0.4m). The time step of evacuation is 0.5s. Table 4.3.2-1 shows the different kinds of ventilation modes. Case 0 is the normal mode. Case 1~ Case 6 are emergency modes.

Table 4.3.2-1. Emergency ventilation modes for the cases

Case Number	Openings in operation	Vertical air inlets velocity [m/s]	Vertical air outlets velocity [m/s]	Air Change Rate [ACH]
Case 0	O1-O13, R1-R4	0.4	——	6
Case 1	O1-O6, R2,R4	0.875	——	6
Case 2	O2,O6,O9,O13, R1,R2	1.3125	——	6
Case 3	O10-O13, R1-R4	1.3125	——	6
Case 4	E1,E2, door	——	2.625	12
Case 5	O1-O6, E1,E2, door	0.875	2.625	12
Case 6	O2,O6,O9,O13,E1,E2, door	1.3125	2.625	12

(2) Numerical Procedure

In order to analyze the dispersion of contaminant in the ventilation room, a well-validated CFD program, STACH-3 (Zhao et al. 2003b, Li and Yan 1995), is adopted to study the problems numerically.

An extended two-dimensional Cellular Automata (CA) model (Song et al. 2005) presented in the section 3.1.3 is adopted for modeling evacuation process. In this model, the occupants' evacuating characteristics involving suddenly released pollution during the event are included. It also considered the friction, repulsion and attraction of one person against another person or against building.

(3) Results and Discussion

The simulation result shows that, it spends 47 time steps that all the people evacuate out from the room. The evacuation time is 23.5s. Figure 4.3.2-2 (a)-(d) give the stages at the time-step of 0, 20, 30 and 40, respectively. The red blocks are the pillars location, which can not be occupied by any evacuating people. The green line shows the location of the door, the only exit of the room. In the available area, the blue boxes are the cells which are occupied by persons at this time, while the white ones are empty.

Table 4.3.2-2 gives the AEGLs results of Chlorine Dioxide (EPA. 2001).Figure 4.3.2-3 shows the absolute indices PIR for all the cases in the period of t_1-t_2. It is easy for us to find that Case 5 is the optimal mode based on the index PIR.

The below results indicate that the optimal modes based on different indices may be different. Therefore, we should make a choice between them according to the practical conditions and the aim of emergency ventilation. If it is hard to identify the source intensity with high accuracy in short time as presented in the section 2.3.3, EFCS3 may be a better choice which could be helpful for emergency ventilation aimed at minimizing the actual exposed concentration. If both the source location and intensity can be identified with high accuracy in short time, PIR may be a better choice which could be useful for emergency ventilation aimed at minimizing the average injured degree.

(a) Time step is 0

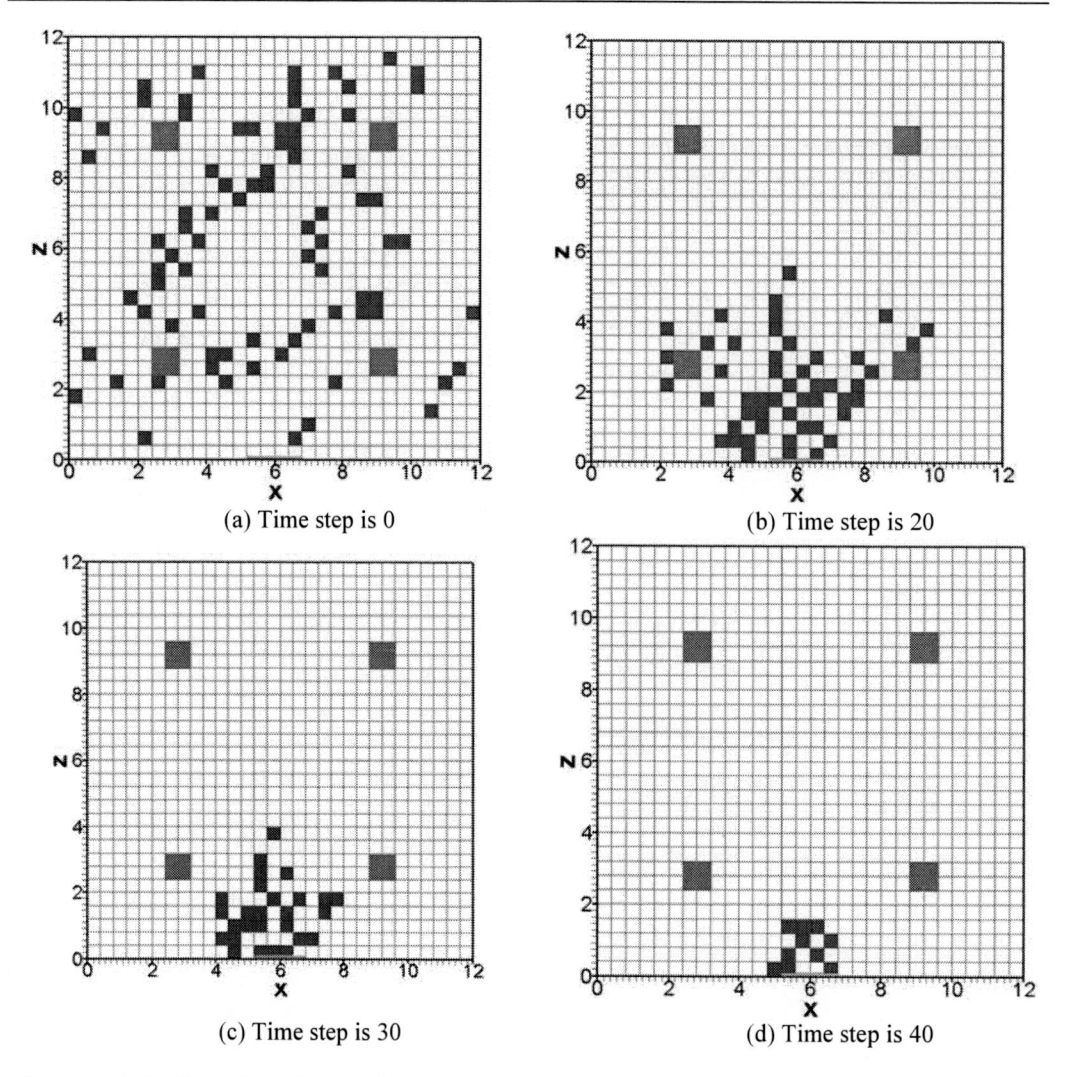

(b) Time step is 20

(c) Time step is 30

(d) Time step is 40

Figure 4.3.2-2. Simulation of evacuation.

Table 4.3.2-2. AEGLs results of Chlorine Dioxide (10-min)

Levels	AEGL-1	AEGL-2	AEGL-3
[mg/m^3]	0.41	3.9	8.3

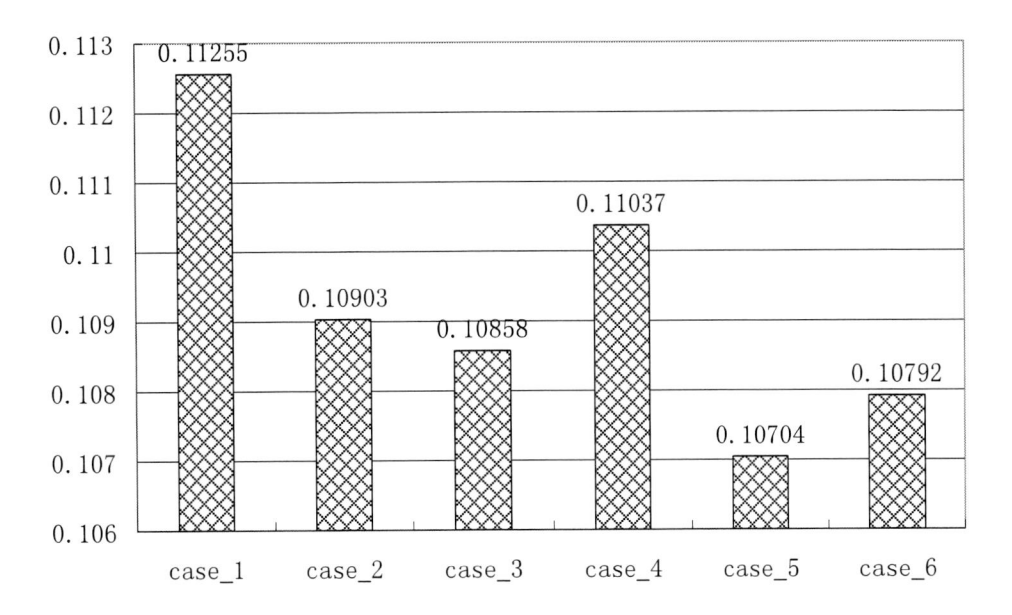

Figure 4.3.2-3. PIR for each case during the evacuation process.

Figure 4.3.2-4 shows the relative indices EFCS3 for all the cases. It is easy for us to find that Case 2 is the optimal mode based on the index EFCS3.

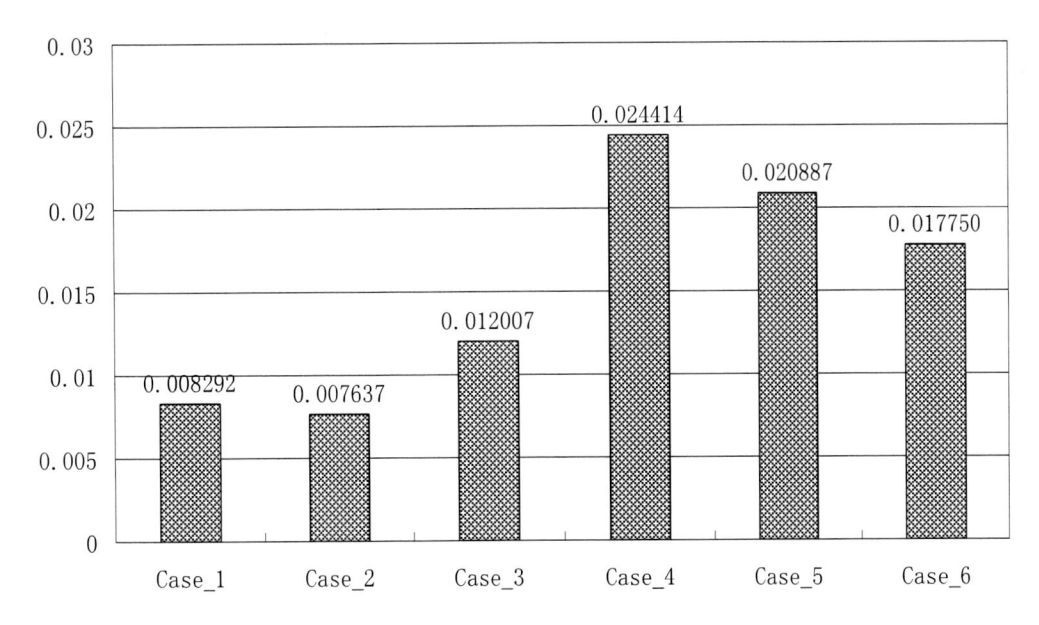

Figure 4.3.2-4. EFCS3 for each case during the evacuation process.

5. Emergency Ventilation System for Rescuing Hostages Held by Terrorists

5.1. Introduction

When anesthetic gas is supplied to building where hostages are held by terrorists, usually we have different options, including: (1) which inlet(s) to supply; (2) what kind of gas and concentration to supply; (3) how long to inject. All these options are closely related to the effect of emergency ventilation. A successful strategy is to incapacitate the terrorists as much as possible and hurt hostages as less as possible.

In order to be successful, we should know all the possible ways for ventilation, so that we can find the best inlet(s) to supply anesthetic gas into the building. We should also know the positions of hostages and terrorists, so that the gas can be supplied effectively to the zone where terrorists stand, rather than the zones where hostages stay. Although it is sometimes very difficult to know the exact positions of hostages and terrorists, we should do our best to get such kind of information to avoid treating all the zones equally.

Once getting the information about possible ventilation modes and the distribution of hostages and terrorists, we can simulate different cases with different kind of gas and concentration and different ventilation modes by CFD tools. After evaluating the effect of different cases, we can get the optimal strategy. This kind of method works well for different kinds of contaminant, including chemical gas, airborne particles and even bacteria. The only problem for this trial and error procedure is that we have too many cases to simulate, so that we may not have enough computing time before we provide results to decision-maker.

If the anesthetic gas can be treated as a passive contaminant, we can have an algorithm to get the optimal strategy in very short period based on the formula of contaminant dispersion, which will be convenient to the decision-making on-site. Therefore, the ventilation strategy for rescuing hostages based on the algorithm will be introduced in the following section in detail. Of course, if the anesthetic gas cannot be treated as passive contaminant, the above-mentioned trial and error procedure will be recommended and the evaluation system can be the same with the algorithm in the following section.

5.2. Strategy of Emergency Ventilation

For each ventilation mode, we can calculate the flow field and ASA of each supply air inlet to any point p in advance. Then the time-averaged contaminant concentration at any point p can be expressed with Eq. (2.2.2-4). The exposure can be calculated with time-averaged concentration by Eq. (3.2.3-2b). Then the population injury rate can be calculated by Eq. (3.2.3-7).

By substituting the occupied density with that of terrorists and hostages (with subscription t and h, respectively), the population injury rate for hostages and terrorists are calculated as follows:

$$\begin{cases} PIR_h(\tau) = \iiint\limits_{V_{room}} IR(x,y,z,\tau)D_h(x,y,z)dxdydz \\ PIR_t(\tau) = \iiint\limits_{V_{room}} IR(x,y,z,\tau)D_t(x,y,z)dxdydz \end{cases} \quad (5.2\text{-}1)$$

The most favorable ventilation strategy is to get a maximal exposure on hijackers but a minimal effect on civilian captives. However, such two criteria are always difficult to be satisfied simultaneously. Instead, compromises should be made between the above two aims. In practice, if the concentration at each inlet opening is between 0 and $C_{s,\,max}$, i.e., $0 \leq C_{s,i} \leq C_{s,max}$, there are three options for decision-maker (Li et al., 2005).

Option A

This option aims to reduce the impairment on hostages to as low as possible. A minimum $PIR_h(\tau)$ is preferred, and simultaneously, $PIR_t(\tau)$ is ensured to be above $L2$ thus the terrorists will be incapacitated. Such requirements are described in equation (5.2-2):

$$\begin{cases} \min & PIR_h(\tau) \\ \text{s.t.} & PIR_t(\tau) \geq L2 \quad , i = 1,...,M \\ & 0 \leq C_{s,i} \leq C_{s,max} \end{cases} \quad (5.2\text{-}2)$$

Option B

To protect hostages from severe injury, this option keep the innocents' injury rate below $L2$ while seeking the greatest toxic impact on terrorists, which can be described mathematically as follows:

$$\begin{cases} \max & PIR_t(\tau) \\ \text{s.t.} & PIR_h(\tau) \leq L2 \quad , i = 1,...,M \\ & 0 \leq C_{s,i} \leq C_{s,max} \end{cases} \quad (5.2\text{-}3)$$

Opition C

This option searches a maximum injury difference between hostages and terrorists while keeping the hostages from being incapacitated and subduing the criminals, which can be described mathematically as:

$$\begin{cases} \max & \Delta PIR(\tau) \\ \text{s.t.} & PIR_h(\tau) \leq L2 \\ & PIR_t(\tau) \geq L2 \quad , i = 1,...,M \\ & 0 \leq C_{s,i} \leq C_{s,max} \end{cases} \quad (5.2\text{-}4)$$

where $\Delta PIR(\tau) = PIR_t(\tau) - PIR_h(\tau)$.

The above-mentioned nonlinear programming mathematical model can be easily solved with MatLab 6.5 (MathWorks Inc., 2002). MatLab Optimization Toolbox employs sequential quadratic programming (SQP) algorithms and active-set methods to solve these nonlinear programming problems. The Principles of SQP can be found in textbooks on nonlinear programming (Nash, 1996; Rustem, 1998).

The solution of one ventilation mode is only a candidate for final optimization except that we have only one ventilation mode. After analyzing all the possible ventilation modes, we can select the best one from all the candidates for each option, which will be provided to decision-maker.

5.3. Demonstration Example of Emergency Ventilation

5.3.1. Description of Building

Figure 5.3.1-1 shows a room where the accident is assumed to happen (Li et al, 2005). The space dimensions are $X \times Y \times Z = 10.8$ m$\times$4.0 m$\times$10.8 m. Considering the central symmetry of the case, only a quarter of the entire room is considered, as shown in Figure 5.3.1-2. There are 4 grille diffusers (0.3 m$\times$0.3 m) uniformly distributed on the ceiling and 1 exhaust (0.9 m$\times$0.4 m) at the left and lowest corner. Air is supplied from all the intakes and exhausted from the outlet at the same speed of 0.7 m/s, resulting in a 7.8 h^{-1} air exchange rate. There is no air recirculation and no heat sources or sinks in the room. There are two blocks in Figure 5.3.1-2, which represents the zone of terrorists and hostages respectively. All the hostages are assumed to be in the center, and the terrorists are standing in the external part of the room.

An anesthetic agent, Methyl Mercaptan for instance, is supplied into the room from one or a combination of the four diffusers. AEGLs of the gas in 30 min are listed in Table 5.3.1-1. The injury degree value $L2$, equal to the clinical effect due to exposure level of AEGL2, is assumed to be 0.30 in this case, while the lethal damage $L3$ is assumed to be 0.99. The value of 200 mg/m^3 is adopted as the upper limitation of the agent concentration at each diffuser.

Table 5.3.1-1. AEGLs of Methyl Mercaptan in 30 mins (mg/m^3) [1]

Levels	AEGL-1	AEGL-2	AEGL-3
[mg/m^3]	1	14	61

Table 5.3.2-1. Optimization results in 1800s ($C_{s,max}$ = 200 mg/m^3)

Option	$C_{s,1}$	$C_{s,2}$	$C_{s,3}$	$C_{s,4}$	PIR_t	PIR_h
A	192	0	0	0	0.30	0.01
B	200	13	44	0	0.76	0.30
C	200	5.4	38	0	0.67	0.20

---

[1] Data from US EPA, "Acute Exposure Guideline Levels (AEGLs) Results" (January 17, 2001).

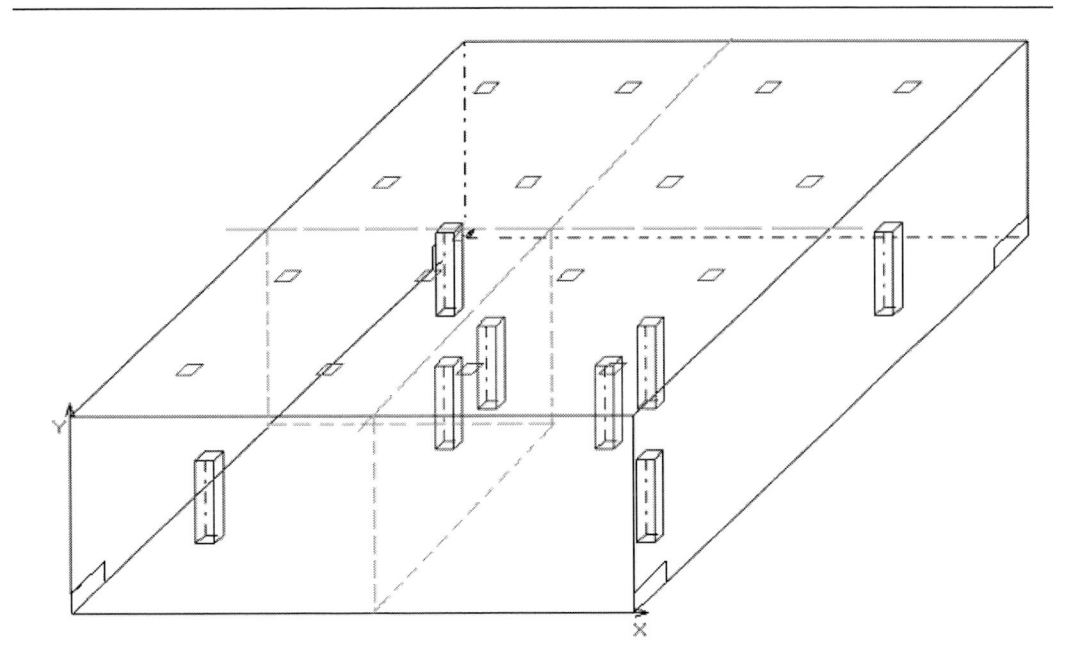

Figure 5.3.1-1. Illustration room where emergency occurs.

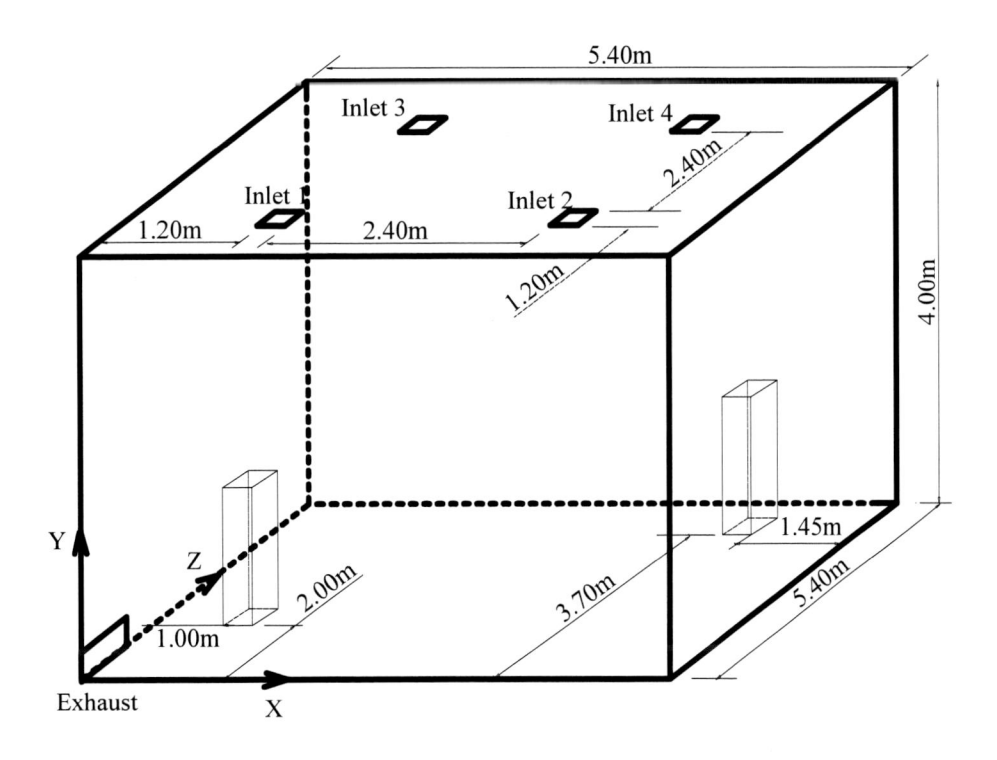

Figure 5.3.1-2. The computational domain.

5.3.2. Optimal Ventilation Strategy

Table 5.3.2-1 shows the optimal results for the three options in section 5.2. The time-averaged concentration in 30 min for three options are shown in Figure 5.3.2-1 (a), (b) and (c) respectively.

For *Option A*, it shows PIR_h is far below the threshold *L2* while PIR_t is 0.30. Figure 5.3.2-1(a) shows it is an over conservative consideration since $\overline{C}$ on some region occupied by the hijackers does not reach the anesthetic level (i.e., AEGL2).

For *Option B*, hostages' injury rate is just within the restriction of injury (i.e., no higher than *L2*=0.3), but PIR_t is 0.76 as shown in Table 5.3.2-1. Figure 5.3.2-1(b) proves that most terrorists are in a zone where $\overline{C}$ is much higher than AEGL2. However, the concentration in some area where innocents stay is also above AEGL2, implying the expense of the benefit.

If *Option C* is taken into account, PIR_t and PIR_h values have reached 0.67 and 0.20, respectively, leading to the largest difference. As anticipated, Figure 5.3.2-1 (c) reveals the resultant $\overline{C}$ around the hostages is quite low, comparing to almost all hijackers suffering an exposure above the threshold of AEGL2. Therefore, in this specific case *Option C* should be selected.

Table 5.3.2-1 also reveals a big difference of dosage concentrations from the four diffusers. Under all of the three conditions, Diffuser 1 is releasing the highest concentration while Diffuser 4 does not need to supply the agent, because Diffuser 1 is farthest from and Diffuser 4 is closest to the hostages. Diffusers 2 and 3 have low dosing rates under *Option B* and *C*. Under *Option A*, they should even not deliver the special gas.

If we supply anesthetic gas with the same concentration of 90 mg/m^3 from all diffusers, the distribution of time-averaged concentration in 30 min is shown in Figure 5.3.2-2. We can see all the terrorists will be killed while most hostages are also in lethal range. Therefore, to know the positions of terrorists and hostages and supply the anesthetic gas unevenly are much important in such kind emergency ventilation.

6. SUMMARY

Since the event of September 11, the threat of terrorism is frequently surrounding us. Emergency ventilation can decrease the loss of terrorist attack dramatically or even prevent us from being attacked. There are two kinds of roles for antiterrorist emergency ventilation system. One is to defend indoor environment against CBA attacks. The other is to supply calmative gas to incapacitate terrorists when they hijack hostages in public buildings. In the first case, the contaminant released suddenly should be detected online and the occupants should be evacuated with the help of emergency ventilation system so that they get least exposure to the contaminants before leaving the buildings. In the second case, the ways, concentrations and elapsed time to supply calmative gas will be optimized so that enough exposures will be to the terrorists and less exposures to the hostages.

(a) Option A

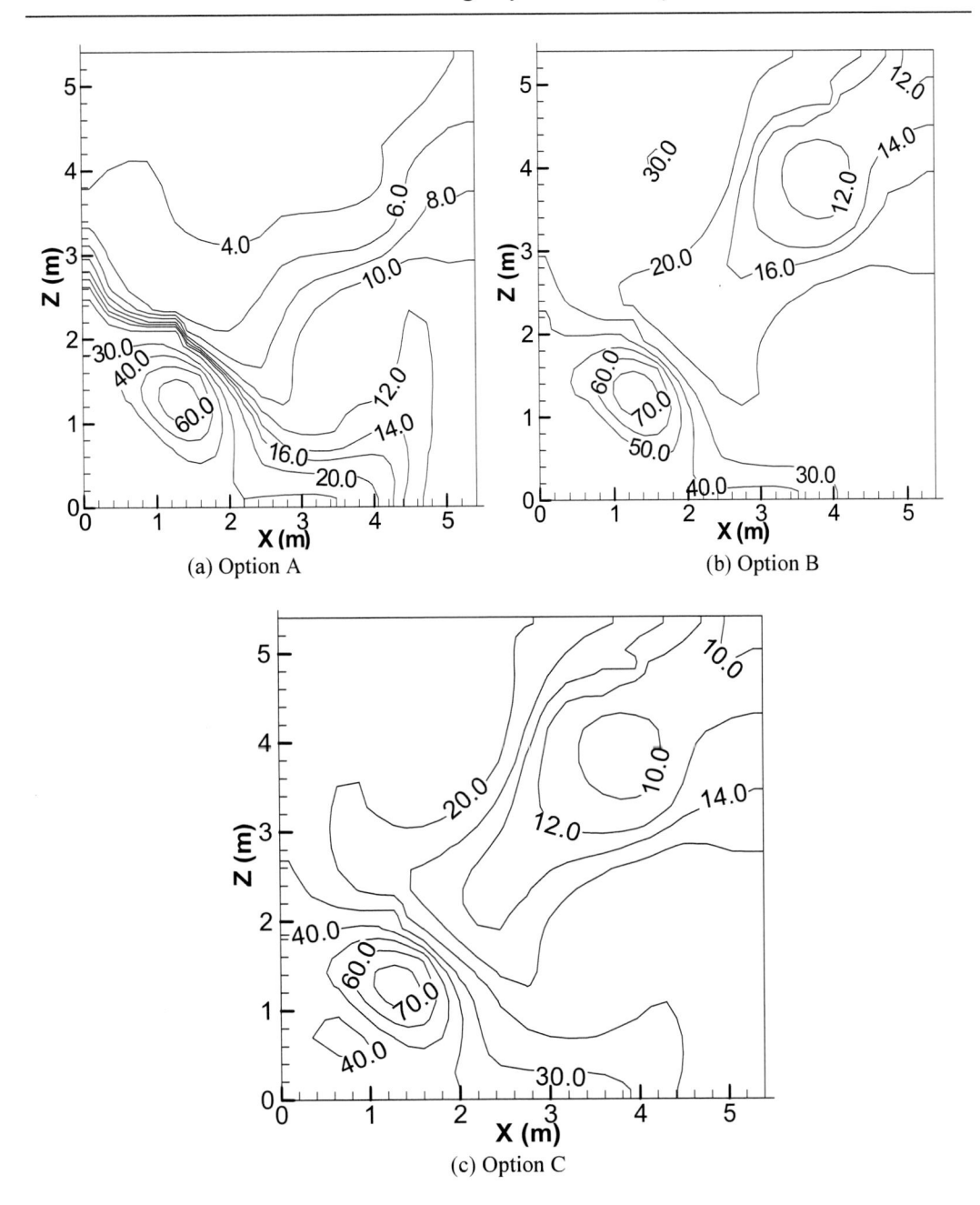

(b) Option B

(c) Option C

Figure 5.3.2-1. $\overline{C}$ in 30 min (mg/m^3, section y=1.6 m), resulted from different dosing strategies.

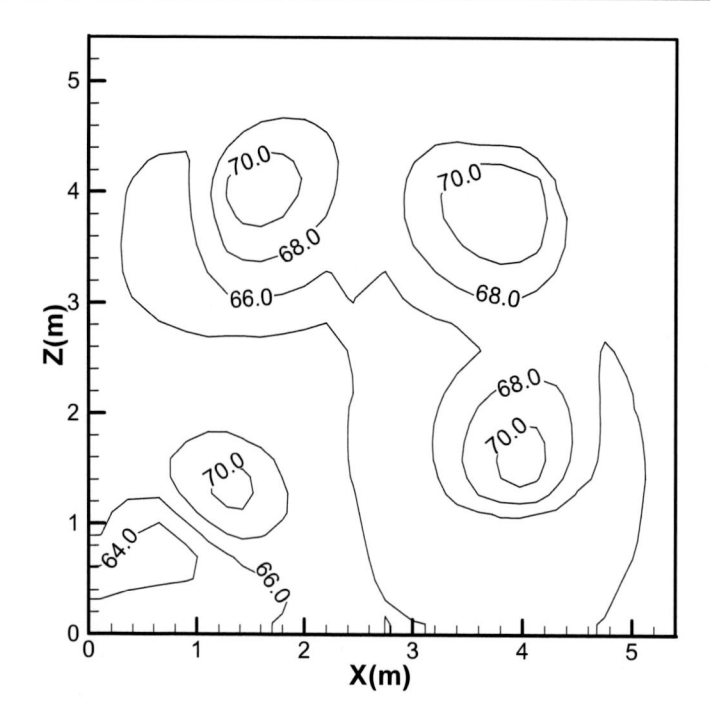

Figure 5.3.2-2. $\overline{C}$ in 30 min (mg/m^3, on the section $y=1.6$ m) when all diffusers are evenly dosing the gas ($C_{s,1} = C_{s,2} = C_{s,3} = C_{s,4}$ =90 mg/m^3).

In order to predict the dispersion of contaminant in buildings accurately, the CFD technique is introduced to predict the flow field and contaminant dispersion in the second part, which is important for two kinds of emergency ventilation systems. Since CFD will take long computing time to predict the dispersion of contaminant, an analytic modeling for contaminant dispersion is introduced then, which can be used for contaminant dispersion and source identification online.

The identification of contaminant source is important to the strategy of emergency ventilation when contaminant is released suddenly indoors. Therefore, the algorithm to identify the position and intensity of contaminant source with limited number of sensors is introduced and demonstrated. It is shown that we can identify the position and intensity of contaminant source even with only one sensor.

Since the evacuation process is important to the ventilation strategy when contaminant is released suddenly, the evacuation model and the exposure risk of occupants are introduced in section 3. The evacuation model and evaluation of exposure risk are the fundamentals for the first kind of emergency ventilation. The evaluation of exposure risk is also important for the strategy of second kind of emergency ventilation.

Both the dispersion model of contaminant and identification of contaminant source, and the evacuation model and evaluation of exposure risk are integrated in the emergency ventilation system against contaminant suddenly released in public buildings. Different kinds of decision methods are introduced. Examples are given to demonstrate how decisions are made when there is such kind of attack.

Both the dispersion model of contaminant and the evaluation of exposure risk are integrated in the emergency ventilation for rescuing hostages held by terrorists. Three options are provided for decision-making. The ventilation strategy is demonstrated in an illustration room when hostages are held by terrorists.

Although the emergency ventilation system, the algorithm of optimal strategy and method of decision are available now, there are still a lot of work to be done in the future, such as the influences of sensor accuracy on the identification of contaminant source, the time delay of identification to the strategy of ventilation and so on. And the most important thing to be done in the future is to have pilot project in real buildings.

ACKNOWLEDGEMENT

The research in the chapter is supported by National Natural Science Foundation of China (Grant No. 50578080)

REFERENCES

Ando, K.; Ota, H.; Oki, T. 1988. Forecasting the Flow of People. *Railway Research Review.* 945, 8-14.

Architectural Energy Corporation and Halton Company. 2004. CFD Validation with Full-Scale Mockup Final Test Report, D-2.4d.

Arvelo, J.; Brandt, A.; Roger, R. P.; et al. 2002. An enhancement multizone model and its application to optimum placement of CBW sensors. *ASHRAE Transaction.* 108, 818-825.

Bailey, D. M.; Chu, D.; Herron, D. L.; Schwenk, D. M.; Sohn, C. W. 2004. Protection of Department of Defense Facilities from Airborne CBR Threats: An Annotated Bibliography. Report: ERDC/CERL-SR-04-25. Sep, 105p

Barton, J., Leather, J. 1995. Passenger Terminal' 95. 71-77.

Bryan, R. B.; Jennifer, L. T.; Keith, G. C. 2004. Development of Evaluation Procedures for Local Exhaust Ventilation for United States Postal Service Mail-Processing Equipment. *Journal of Occupational and Environmental Hygiene.* 1, 423-429.

Buckmann L. T.; Leather J. A. 1994. *Traffic Engineering and Control.* 35, 373-377.

Burstedde C.; Klauck K.; Schadschneider A.; et al. 2001. Simulation of Pedestrian Dynamics Using a Two-dimensional Cellular Automaton. *Physica A.* 295, 507-525.

Cai H. 2006. Study on Key Issues of Emergency Ventilation to Control Indoor Contaminant Dispersion. Institute of mechanical engineering, *Ph.D. Dissertation,* Tongji University (Shanghai, P.R. China). 247 pages (In Chinese).

Cai H.; Long W. D.; Cheng B. Y.; Ma X. B. 2007a. Exposure cell: new concept for evaluating ventilation effectiveness and its applications. *Journal of Harbin Institute of Technology (New Series).* 14, 270-273.

Cai H.; Long W. D.; Cheng B. Y.; Ma X. B. 2007b. Efficiency factor indices for evaluating ventilation effectiveness based on spatial and temporal distribution of occupants and contaminants. *Journal of Harbin Institute of Technology (New Series).* 14, 213-216.

Cai H.; Long W. D.; Li X. T.; Du Y. X. 2007c. Decision analysis method of emergency ventilation to protect occupant from indoor contaminant by efficiency factor of contaminant source (EFCS). *The 22nd International Congress of Refrigeration 2007.* Beijing, China, Paper ID: ICR07-E1-1091

Chen, Q.; Xu, W. 1998. A zero-equation turbulence model for indoor air flow simulation. *Energy and Buildings.* 28, 137-144

Chen, Q. 2004. *Protecting buildings from chemical and biological warfare agent attacks– a long journey.* Editorial, HVAC&R Research. 10, 389-391.

Chen, X.; Zhao, B.; Li, X. T. 2005. Numerical investigation on the influence of contaminant source location, occupant distribution and air distribution on emergency ventilation strategy. *Indoor and Built Environment.* 14, 455-467.

Clemen, R. T. 1996. *Making hard decisions: An introduction to decision analysis,* 2d ed. Duxbury Press: Belmont, CA; 696.

EPA. 1997. National Advisory Committee for Acute Exposure Guideline Levels for Hazardous Substances; Notices. Federal Register Environmental Documents, Federal Register: October 30; 62: 58839-58851, *United States Environmental Protection Agency.*

EPA. 2000. National Advisory Committee for Acute Exposure Guideline Levels (AEGLs) for Hazardous Substances; Proposed AEGL Values. Federal Register: December 13; 65: 77866-77874, *United States Environmental Protection Agency.*

EPA. 2001. Proposed temporary Acute Exposure Guideline Levels (AEGLs) "PUBLIC DRAFT" Oak Ridge National Laboratory; Office of Pollution Prevention and Toxics, *United States Environmental Protection Agency.*

Fahy, R. F. 1996. *Enhancement of EXIT89 and analysis of World Trade Center Data.* NIST-GCR-95-684, Building and Fire Research Laboratory, NIST, USA.

FEMA. 2003. Reference Manual to Mitigate Potential Terrorist Attacks Against Buildings, FEMA 426, Federal Emergency Management Agency, http://www.fema.gov/fima/rmsp426.shtm.

Fluent Inc. 2002. *Airpak 2.1 User's Guide,* Fluent Inc.

Finney, D. J. 1971. *Probit Analysis.* Cambridge University Press: London.

Ghosh, B.; Fraser-Mitchell, J. 1999. Fire risk assessment: CRISP—a calculation tool. *Fire Safety Engineering.* 6, 11-13.

Goodwin, P.; Wright, G. 2004. *Decision analysis for management judgment,* 3rd ed.: Wiley, New York; 492.

Gwynne, S.; Galea, E. R.; Owen, M.; Lawrence, P. J.; Filippidis, L. 1999. A Review of the Methodologies Used in Evacuation Modeling. *Fire and Materials.* 23, 383-388.

Gwynne, S.; Galea, E. R.; Owen, M.; Lawrence P. J. 2002. An investigation of the aspects of occupant behaviour required for an evacuation modelling. In: P.R. DeCicco, Editor, *Evacuation from fires vol. II, Baywood Publishing Company:* Amityville, NY.

Haber, F. 1924. *Zur Geschichte des Gaskrieges. Fünf Vorträge aus den Jahren 1920-1923.* Springer-Verlag, Berlin (In German); 76-92.

HSE—Health Safety Executive. 1978. *Canvey report: an investigation of potential hazards from operation in the Canvey Island/Turrock area.* Stationery Office: London, UK.

Kato, S.; Murakami, S.; Kobayas, H. 1994. New Scales For Evaluating Ventilation Efficiency as Affected by Supply and Exhaust Openings Based on Spatial Distribution of Contaminant. *Proceedings of 12th International Symposium on Contamination Control.* The Japan Air Cleaning Association: 341-348.

Kerechanin, II C. W.; Cutchi,s P. N.; Vincent, J. A.; Smith, D. G.; Wenstrand, D. S. 2004. Development of Field Portable Ventilator Systems for Domestic and Military Emergency Medical Response. *Johns hopkings APL technical digest.* 25, 214-222.

Ketchell, N.; Cole, S. S.; Webber, D. M. 1993. *Engineering for Crowd Safety.* Elsevier Oxford: 361-370.

Ketchell, N. 1995. *Proceedings for the International Conference on Fire Science and Engineering.* ASIAFLAM' 95. Interscience. London; 499-505.

Kisko, T. M.; Francis, R. L. 1985. EVACNET+: a computer program to determine optimal building evacuation plans. *Fire Safety Journal.* 9, 211-220.

Kostreva, M. M.; Lancaster, L. C. 1998. A comparison of two methodologies in Hazard I fire egress analysis. *Fire Technology.* 34, 227-243.

Li, X. T.; Yan, Q. S. 1995. Field Model of Fires in Subway Tunnels. *The 2nd International Symposium on Heating, Ventilation Air Conditioning – HVAC'95.* Beijing, CN; 392-399.

Li, X. T.; Zhao, B. 2004. Accessibility: a new concept to evaluate the ventilation performance in a finite period of time. *Indoor and Built Environment.* 13, 287-293.

Li, X. T.; Yang, J. R.; Sun, W. 2005. Strategy to optimise building ventilation to aid rescue of hostages held by terrorists. *Indoor and Built Environment.* 14, 39-50.

Lo, S. M.; Fang, Z. 2000. A spatial-grid evacuation model for buildings. *Journal of Fire Science.* 18, 376-394.

Lo, S. M.; Fang, Z.; Lin, P.; et al. 2004. An evacuation model: the SGEM package. *Fire Safety Journal.* 39, 169-190.

MathWorks Inc. 2002. *Tutorial on Optimization Toolbox.* "Help" in MATLAB Version 6.5, Release 13, June.

Murakami, S. 1992. New scales for ventilation efficiency and their application based on numerical simulation of room airflow. *Proceedings of International symposium on room air convention and ventilation effectiveness.* University of Tokyo; 22-38.

Nash, S. 1996. *Linear and Nonlinear Programming.* McGraw-hill Companies, Inc.: USA.

NIOSH. 2002. *Guidance for Protecting Building Environments from Airborne Chemical, Biological, or Radiological Attacks.* Report: DHHS/PUB/NIOSH-2002-139, May, CD-ROM

Okasaki, S.; Matsushita, S. 1993. *Engineering for Crowd Safety.* 17-18, 271-280.

Owen, M.; Galea, E. R.; Lawrence, P. J. 1997. Advanced occupant behavioural features of the building EXODUS evacuation model. Fire Safety Science—In: *Proceedings of the fifth international symposium,* Melbourne, Australia; 795-806.

Ozel F. 1992. Simulation. 58, 377-384.

Patankar, S. V. 1980. *Numerical heat transfer and fluid flow.* Hemisphere Publishing Corporation: McGraw-Hill.

Poon, L. S.; Beck, V. R. 1994. *Proceedings of Fourth International Symposium on Fire Safety Science.* IAFSS. Ottawa; 681-692.

Poon, L. S. 1995. Proceedings of the International Conference on Fire Science and Engineering. *ASIAFLAM' 95. Interscience.* London; 163-174.

Pooransingh, S.; Hawkera, J. 2006. Are we prepared for a deliberate release of a biological agent? *Public Health.* 120, 613-617.

Purser, D. A. 1996. Behavioural impairment in smoke environment. Toxicology. 115, 25-40.

Reisser-Weston, E. 1996. *RINA, Int Conference of Escape, Fire and Rescue.* Royal Institute for Naval Architecture. London; 19/20.

Rijnmond Public Authority. 1982. *Risk analysis of six potentially hazardous industrial objects in the Rijnmond area, a pilot study.* Reidel Dordrecht, The Netherlands.

Rivera, A. F.; Char, D. M. 2004. Emergency department disaster preparedness: Are Regional efforts reaching local front lines? *Annals of Emergency Medicine.* 44, 94.

Rustem, B. 1998. A*lgorithms for Nonlinear Programming and Multiple-Objective Decisions.* John Wiley & Sons Ltd.: UK.

Sandberg, M. 1981. What is ventilation efficiency? *Building and Environment.* 16, 123-135

Sandberg, M. 1983. Ventilation efficiency as a guide to design. *ASHRAE Transaction.* 89, 455-479.

Sandberg, M.; Sjoberg, M. 1983. The use of moments for assessing air quality in ventilated rooms. *Building and Environment.* 18, 181-197.

Shestopal, V. O.; Grubits, S. J. 1994. *Proceedings of 4th International Symposium on Fire Safety Science.* IAFSS: Ottawa, 625-632.

Sime, J. D. 1994. Escape behaviour in fires and evacuations. P. Stallord and L. Johnston, Editors, *Design against fire: an introduction to fire safety engineering design.* E & FN SPON: London.

Sohn, M. D.; Reynolds, P.; Singh, N.; et al. 2002. Rapidly locating and characterizing pollutant releases in buildings. *Journal of Air & Waste Management Association.* 52, 1422-1432.

Song, W.; Yu, Y.; Fan, W.; Zhang, H. 2005. A cellular automata evacuation model considering friction and repulsion. *Science in China Series E Engineering & Materials Science.* 48, 403-413.

Speitel, L. C. 1996. Fractional effective dose model for post-crash aircraft survivability. *Toxicology.* 115, 167-177.

Still, G. K. 1993. *FIRE.* 84, 40-41.

Still, G. K. 1994. Paper 25, IMAS 94, Fire Safety on Ships. *Institute of Marine Engineers.* 26-27, 253.

Takahashi, K.; Tanaka, T.; Kose, S. 1989. *Proceedings of 2nd International Symposium on Fire Safety Science.* Hemisphere, London; 551-560.

Thompson, P. A.; Marchant, E. W. 1994. Simulex: Developing New Computer Modeling Techniques for Evaluation. *Fire Safety Science Proceedings of the Fourth International Symposium.* 613-624.

Thompson, P.; Marchant, E. 1995. *Fire Safety Journal.* 24, 131-148.

Thompson, P.; Wu.; Marchant, E. 1996. *Fire Engineers Journal.* 7-11.

Wang, P. 2005. *Research on the Performance-based Evacuation Model of Large Buildings. Master Dissertation,* Wuhan University (Wuhan, P.R. China). 93 pages (In Chinese).

Wax, P. M.; Becker, C. E.; Curry, S. C. 2003. Unexpected "Gas" Casualties in Moscow: A Medical Toxicology Perspective. *Annals of emergency medicine.* 41, 700-705.

Yang, J. R.; Li, X. T.; Zhao, B. 2004. Prediction of transient contaminant dispersion and ventilation performance using the concept of accessibility. *Energy and Buildings.* 36, 293-299.

Yang, L.; Fan, W.; Fang, W. 2003. Modeling Occupant Evacuation using Cellular Automata-Effect of Human Behavior and Building Characteristics on Evacuation. *Journal of Fire Science.* 21, 227-240.

Yang, L.; Zhao, D.; Li, J.; Fan, W.; Fang, W. 2004. Simulation of evacuation behaviors in fire using special grid. *Progress in Natural Science.* 14, 614-618.

Zhang T. F.; Chen Q. Y. 2007. Identification of contaminant sources in enclosed environments by inverse CFD modeling. *Indoor Air.* 17, 167-177.

Zhao, B.; Li, X. T.; Li, Y.; Yan, Q. S. 2000. Indoor and Outdoor Airflow Simulation by a Zero Equation Turbulence Model. *Proc 7th Intl Conf Air Distribution in Rooms – ROOMVENT' 2000.* Reading University, UK; 449-454.

Zhao, B.; Li, X. T.; Yan, Q. S. 2001. Simulation of Indoor Air Flow in Ventilated Room by Zero-equation Turbulence Model. *Journal of Tsinghua University (Science and Technology).* 41, 109-113 (in Chinese).

Zhao, B.; Li, X. T.; Lu, J. J. 2002. Numerical Simulation of Air Distribution in Chair Ventilated Room by Simplified Methodology. *ASHRAE Transaction.* 108, 1079-1083.

Zhao, B.; Cao, L.; Li, X. 2003a. Description of Perforated Panels in Simulation of Airflow Inside Clean Rooms. *Journal of Tsinghua University (Science and Technology).* 43, 690-692 (in Chinese).

Zhao, B.; Li, X. T.; Yan, Q. S. 2003b. A simplified system for indoor airflow simulation. *Building and Environment.* 38, 543-552.

Zhao, B.; Li, X. T.; Li, D. N.; Yang, J. R. 2003c. Revised air-exchange efficiency considering occupant distribution in ventilated rooms. *Journal of the Air and Waste Management Association.* 53, 759-763.

Zhao, B.; Li, X. T.; Chen, X.; Huang, D. T. 2004a. Determining ventilation strategy to defend indoor environment against contamination by integrated accessibility of contaminant source (IACS). *Building and environment.* 39, 1035-1042.

Zhao, B.; Cao, L.; Li, X.; Yang, X.; Huang, D. 2004b. Comparison of Indoor Environment of a Locally Concentrated Clean Room at Dynamic and Steady Status by Numerical Method. *Journal of IEST.* 47, 94-100.

In: Psychology of Decision Making
Editor: Paul M. Garrison

ISBN 978-1-60021-869-9
© Nova Science Publishers, Inc.

Chapter 2

DECISION-MAKING IN A STRUCTURED CONNECTIONIST AGENT ARCHITECTURE

Carter Wendelken
Helen Wills Neuroscience Institute, UC-Berkeley, Berkeley, CA, USA
Lokendra Shastri
International Computer Science Institute, Berkeley, CA, USA

ABSTRACT

To understand the mapping between networks of neurons and the mental constructs that underlie complex cognition and behavior is a central problem for the field of neurocomputing. The structured connectionist approach tackles this problem directly by investigating the relation between connectionist circuits and cognitive operations. One structured connectionist model, SHRUTI, has demonstrated how a system of simple, neuron-like elements can encode a large body of relational causal knowledge and provide a basis for rapid inference. The SHRUTI model explored the use of spreading activation across structured representations and temporal synchrony variable binding within a connectionist network. This article will describe the transformation of the SHRUTI model into a decision-making agent architecture. Key contributions of this effort include the development of a connectionist encoding of goals and utility and of connectionist mechanisms for cognitive control that support goal-oriented behavior. Specific connectionist circuits encode long-term goals or drives, associate value with possible events, and propagate utility from effects to possible causes. Together, these mechanisms support reactive planning and simple goal-driven decision-making. However, successful operation in more complex decision scenarios, such as those involving conflicting subgoals, requires top-down control mechanisms. Several such control mechanisms are described; it is then shown that each can be implemented via some combination of a small set of control primitives. Each of these control primitives -- including monitoring, filtering, selection, maintenance, organization, and manipulation – is implemented as a simple connectionist circuit.

INTRODUCTION

Consider what happens when we read a simple story such as the following:

"John fell in the hallway. Tom was cleaning it. He got hurt."

or hear a question such as:

"Where is the document that Mary handed you yesterday?"

or observe a scene involving:

- a soccer ball at your feet
- a red-jerseyed person rushing toward you
- a blue-jerseyed person running to your left

In the first example, a person quickly infers that Tom's cleaning of the hallway probably caused it to have a wet floor, and that John must have hurt himself by slipping on the wet hallway floor. In order to answer the question in the second example, one must access recent memories ("What document did Mary hand me yesterday?", " What did I do with it?") and also possibly perform inference ("If I gave it to the supervisor, what would he have done with it?"). For the third example, correct action requires inferring the intent of different players from their observed actions, based on experience in similar situations.

In all these cases, the ability to comprehend what we have read or heard or seen requires the capacity to combine the new information with a huge amount of existing knowledge and draw a large number of inferences rapidly and accurately. Specific memories, knowledge of causation, statistics of the environment, and knowledge about objects in the world must all be included in an episode of reasoning or decision-making. Yet people are capable of drawing inferences or making decisions rapidly, nearly spontaneously and without conscious effort, in many circumstances. This remarkable ability poses a significant challenge to the sciences of mind and brain: How can a system constructed from relatively simple and slow neuron-like elements represent a large body of knowledge and perform inference and decision-making with such speed?

To begin to address this question, a connectionist agent architecture, called SHRUTI-agent, has been developed. SHRUTI-agent is an extension of the SHRUTI model (Shastri and Ajjanagadde, 1993a), which demonstrated how a system constructed from simple neuron-like elements can represent large amounts of knowledge, in various forms, and perform inference using that knowledge rapidly and accurately. Major additions to the SHRUTI model include the capacity to represent and utilize reward and punishment (utility) and the ability to exert high-level control over reactive reasoning and decision processes. Following a brief introduction to the SHRUTI model, these additional capacities are described, demonstrated, and explored.

THE SHRUTI MODEL

SHRUTI is a connectionist model in which structured ensembles of nodes provide the basis for encoding various elements of knowledge -- such as types, relations, rules, and facts -- and in which inference involves spreading activation within and among these representations. The system supports encoding and manipulation of relational information, a capacity which is essential for dealing with large amounts of knowledge (Shastri and Ajjanagadde, 1993b). Evidential reasoning is central to the operation of the network, and it has been shown that the system performs well in the presence of uncertainty (Wendelken and Shastri, 2000). Importantly, the speed of inference in SHRUTI is independent of the size of the knowledge base, so the model is highly scalable.

Design of the SHRUTI Model

These properties of the SHRUTI model are determined to a large extent by two key design features: 1) the use of temporal synchrony variable binding, and 2) the use of focal clusters as the basic unit of organization. These two essential elements are described here.

Variable binding is achieved via temporal synchrony: For a system to deal effectively with relational representation and inference, a mechanism for dynamic variable binding – the capacity to temporarily associate items, such as relational role and the object that fills it -- is essential. In addition, variable binding can support creation of dynamic structures, representation of unique events, and grouping of features. The capacity to represent and manipulate variables can greatly enhance the combinatorial computational power of a system, and it is instrumental in modeling aspects of human cognition and language.

For symbolic computational models, variable binding is trivial; however, the need to manipulate variables within a connectionist network provides a significant challenge.

There are a number of proposals as to how this might be achieved, including conjunctive coding, use of tensor products (Smolensky, 1990) or holographic reduced representations (Plate, 1994), sign propagation or marker passing (Hendler, 1989; Lange and Dyer, 1989), and temporal synchrony.Temporal synchrony was proposed as a mechanism for perceptual binding by von der Malsburg (Malsburg, 1981), but its application to the problem of variable binding in complex inference originated in an early version of the SHRUTI model (Ajjanagadde and Shastri, 1989).

Temporal synchrony variable binding involves binding concepts together via synchronous firing of the nodes or neurons that represent them. The possible role of synchronization in neural representations has been suggested by several researchers (e.g. (Milner, 1974; Abeles, 1982; Crick, 1984), and a growing body of evidence supports the idea that temporal synchrony variable binding occurs in the brain (e.g. (Engel et al., 1991; Kreiter and Singer, 1996)). For reasons of its great practical utility and also in order to gain a stronger understanding of a likely mechanism of neural processing, the SHRUTI model utilizes temporal synchrony to achieve variable binding. While SHRUTI was the first detailed computational account of how temporal synchrony variable binding could be deployed on a large scale to solve complex cognitive problems, other models that rely on temporal synchrony have emerged in the past few years (e.g. (Park et al., 1995; Sougne, 1996; Hummel and Holyoak, 1997).

The focal cluster is the basic unit of organization: *Focal clusters* are the primary structured representation of the SHRUTI model. A focal cluster is a collection of nodes of varying functionality that all subserve a common representation. In neural terms, a focal cluster represents a collection of neurons, divided into a number of different functional classes, that are all involved in the representation of a particular concept. Predicate (relational) focal clusters were introduced in the earliest version of the SHRUTI model (Ajjanagadde and Shastri, 1989); entity and type focal clusters were described somewhat later (Shastri, 1999).

Each node in the implemented SHRUTI model stands in for a small cluster of neurons in the brain which are functionally integrated but possibly physically distributed. Nodes represent a highly abstract version of real neurons and neural clusters; they may contain limited state information and are allowed to combine their inputs in a variety of ways in order to determine their output. Nodes in SHRUTI are broadly divided into two classes: phasic ρ-nodes and non-phasic τ-nodes. Temporal synchrony variable binding is made possible by the presence of the phasic ρ-nodes. Phasic nodes fire rhythmically and have the capacity to synchronize their firing with that of the activity that drives them. In the implemented model, an active ρ-node spikes during the same phase in each cycle. The other major category of nodes, non-phasic τ-nodes, fire more or less continuously when active, outputting spike trains that fill every phase in a cycle. These include principally the $τ_{and}$ (temporal-and) nodes, which become active only when they receive uninterrupted spike trains, and $τ_{or}$ (temporal-or) nodes, which generate spike trains upon reception of sufficiently strong activity for at least one phase in a cycle. The τ-nodes produce a numerical output which is interpreted generically as strength of activation; in a neural realization of the model this could reflect proportion of active neurons in a cluster, mean or maximum firing rates, or some combination of these factors.

Major Structures and Mechanisms of SHRUTI

A key characteristic of SHRUTI is its use of structured representations, and the close relationship between representational structure and processing mechanisms. In this section, the most important structures of the SHRUTI model, and the mechanisms that operate on these structures, are presented. Structures include representations of entities and types, of relations, of long-term facts, and of rules; associated mechanisms include memory search.

Entities and Types: The simplest focal clusters in SHRUTI are those that represent unique entities.

The minimal representation of an individual, for example, *my-grandmother*, requires just two phasic nodes. Activity of the first, called the entity collector and labeled `+:my-grandmother`, indicates that *my-grandmother* plays a role in some current belief. Another node, the entity enabler labeled `?:my-grandmother`, is active whenever the concept *my-grandmother* is involved in some query. A link from collector to enabler allows for constant checking or querying of beliefs. On the surface, this model fits the extreme caricature of a localist representation. However, it is important first to note that SHRUTI nodes stand in for clusters of neurons and second to realize that the representation utilized here is just the minimal fraction, of a much richer representation, that is required for the computational purpose of the model. An expanded representation of the *my-grandmother* concept would include this focal cluster at its core, but would also involve connections to a wealth of other information.

Type focal clusters are similar to entity focal clusters, except that they are meant to represent classes of entities instead of individuals and thus they provide for the additional distinction between universal and existential quantification. Nodes are labeled +e, +v, ?e, and ?v, where e indicates existential quantification and v indicates universal quantification. Activity of +e:Person signifies that some particular person (though which one is not specified) is involved in a current thought, while activity of +v:Person indicates that something is believed about people in general. Activity of ?e:Person occurs when one is seeking a person as the filler of some role, while activity of ?v:Person is associated with a query about all people or person as a class.

Entity and type focal clusters exist as part of a connectionist type hierarchy. Connections within this hierarchy structure serve to expand the interpretation of a phase during an episode of reasoning, such that appropriate supertypes or subtypes become active along with the original type activity. For example, when there is a query about a particular entity (activity of ?:Tom, in Figure 1) these connections expand that into a query about all men (?v:Man) and then all people (?v:Person). This is correct and useful, since if something is known to be true for all people, then it certainly applies to Tom. Similarly, if we assert that something is true for all people (+v:Person), then it is clearly true for all men and also for Tom; the connections from the +v node of a supertype to the +v node of a subtype reflect this. There are also connections from type collectors to type enablers that result in an automatic querying of any type assertion.

Relational predicates: Arguably the most important variety of focal cluster in SHRUTI is the relational focal cluster. Also referred to here as a predicate focal cluster or just a predicate, the relational focal cluster is used to represent relational predicates and consists of a number of different node types. Chief among these are the positive collector, negative collector, and enabler (all τ_{and} nodes), and the phasic role nodes. Activity of the positive collector (+) of a predicate cluster indicates belief that the predicate is true. Negative collector (-) activity, on the other hand, indicates belief in the falsity of the predicate. These nodes are called collectors because they serve to collect evidence for and against the relational predicate. The enabler node (?) becomes active to indicate a querying of the relation; its activity "enables" a search for evidence and a checking of associated facts. Role node activity serves to bind type or entity role fillers with a relational role. Since both relational role nodes and type or entity nodes are phasic, they have the potential to fire in synchrony. When this happens, the synchronously active type or entity is considered to be dynamically bound to the role. In addition to the node types discussed here, predicate clusters may also have nodes serving other purposes such as conflict detection or, as will be described later, representation of utility.

In order to make an assertion or insert an observation into the system, it is necessary only to clamp the appropriate collector node, its role nodes, and type or entity role fillers. Observing "John buys a book" involves activation of +:buys, activation of the buys-buyer role in synchrony with +:John, and activation of the buys-object role in synchrony with

+e:Book (see Figure 1). Posing a query to the system is achieved by clamping the enabler along with roles and role-fillers. To ask "Who buys books?" requires that ?:buys be activated, and also buys-buyer in synchrony with ?e:Person and buys-object in synchrony with ?v:Books.

Long-term facts: We have shown how SHRUTI uses temporal synchrony along with its representation of relations and types to dynamically encode relational instances. However, in addition to dynamic encoding, static long-term encoding of relational instances is also important for any model of inference. Here, these sorts of memories are termed *long-term facts*. Long-term facts exist in SHRUTI as temporal pattern matching circuits associated with a particular relation. They are triggered by activity of the relation's enabler node, and if activity at the relation's role nodes matches the role-fillers that are associated with the fact, then the fact will become active and will in turn activate the appropriate collector node of the relational cluster.

Long-term facts can be divided into two basic types: episodic facts and taxon facts.

Episodic facts encode specific relational instances such as "John gave the book to Mary in the library on Tuesday" (i.e. `<give <giver=John> <recipient=Mary> <object=Book> <time=Tuesday> <location=Library> >`). These facts are sensitive to role mismatches, such that an episodic fact becomes active only if none of the predicate role nodes represent activity other than what is encoded in the fact. This allows for partial matches if some roles are unspecified, so the query "Did John give Mary something?" would be answered in the affirmative, but prevents activation of the fact if there is any mismatch, such that the query "Did John give Mary a book in the library on Wednesday?" would not activate the fact, even though it involves a greater number of role matches. Taxon facts are the repositories of statistical information about a predicate. For example, "People often give books to other people in libraries" or "Men sometimes give things to women" are possible taxon facts associated with the give relation. Although structurally similar to episodic facts, taxon facts are sensitive only to role matches. This insensitivity to mismatches allows them to generalize in a way that episodic facts cannot, but it means they can only record statistical regularities and not specific events.

Rules and causal inference: Inference occurs in this system as the rhythmic propagation of activity between focal clusters. Central to this is the encoding of causal rules. A *rule* in SHRUTI consists of a set of antecedent predicates and a set of consequent predicates bound together through a *rule mediator* focal cluster and a series of connections. Antecedent collectors send projections to the mediator collector which in turn projects to each of the consequent collectors (positive or negative depending on the rule). Thus, when there is a belief about the causal antecedent, this propagates through the rule structure to impact belief about the consequents or effects. Connections between enablers go in the opposite direction, from consequent to antecedent. Each consequent enabler projects to the mediator enabler, which projects in turn to each antecedent enabler. Because of these connections, a query about some consequent or effect results in a query about the antecedents or causes. In addition to its primary role of grouping inputs from antecedents and consequents, the rule mediator enforces type restrictions, prevents incongruous activity, and causes unbound roles to be instantiated. The links connecting each rule element (antecedent or consequent predicate) to the mediator are weighted, allowing for differential treatment of each element; evidence from multiple sources is combined via one of a limited set of evidence combination functions (Shastri and Wendelken, 1999).

An episode of reasoning in SHRUTI typically involves propagation of activity, in both the forward and backward directions, along multiple causal chains. Inputting a set of observations drives the system to both make predictions about the consequences of those observations and also to seek explanation for them.

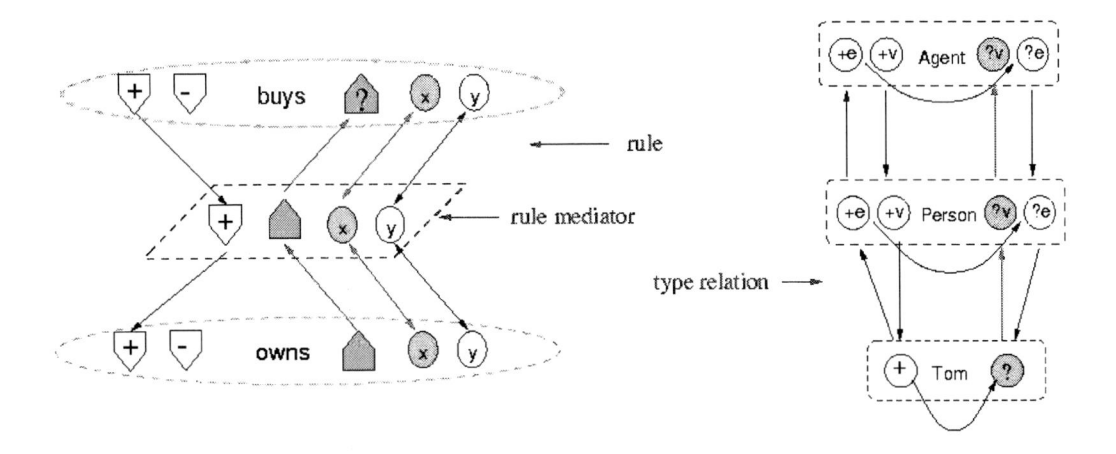

Figure 1. Depiction of a simple rule. The query "owns(Tom,x)?" results in a new query "buys(Tom,x)?".

DECISION-MAKING AND THE SHRUTI-AGENT

The SHRUTI model, described above, demonstrates how a connectionist network can represent and reason with large amounts of relational knowledge. However, it is not capable of using the encoded knowledge to make decisions or guide action. In order to do this, two additional components are required. First, the model must incorporate a representation of preferences, and second, it requires an appropriate representation of action. The decision-making agent architecture that expands on the underlying SHRUTI model and includes both of these elements is called the SHRUTI-agent. In this section, we describe how preference and action are respresented within the SHRUTI-agent architecture, and how these support decision-making.

A Connectionist Implementation of Utility

Of fundamental importance for any decision-making agent is having some basis to prefer one outcome over another. Such a capacity is not present in the SHRUTI model as it has been described so far. Therefore, an important part of transforming SHRUTI into a decision-making SHRUTI-agent architecture involves inserting a system of preferences into the model in a manner that is compatible with the existing connectionist structure.

The representation of utility in our connectionist architecture is analogous to its representation of belief. This consists primarily of a set of utility nodes associated with each relational focal cluster, reward facts denoting reward and punishment, value facts denoting learned utility values, probabilistically weighted utility-carrying connections between relations, and various modulatory mechanisms that affect the propagation of utility differently in different situations. Belief and utility in SHRUTI are tightly integrated, sharing much of the same structure, and are not separate modules in any conventional sense.

Utility nodes: The representation of a belief (relational instance) in SHRUTI is built around a relational focal cluster, which contains several different types of nodes including positive and negative collectors, an enabler, and role nodes. In order to incorporate utility into this representation, a set of utility nodes are introduced alongside these belief nodes. Through these utility nodes, reward and punishment come to be associated with relational instances. Four τ_{AND} utility nodes are includes as part of each relational instance. These are labeled u+, u-, n+, and n-, where "u" stands for positive utility (reward), "n" stands for negative utility (punishment), "+" indicates association with the truth of the relational instance (belief), and "-" indicates association with the falsity of the relational instance (disbelief). Thus, activity of u- signals that negative utility is associated with the truth of the relational instance, whereas activity of n+ signals that positive utility is associated with the falsity of the relational instance. In the example (Figure 2a), activation of eat:u+, along with synchronous activity of eat:x and Cake:+e, indicates that reward is currently associated with the eating of cake. (As a notational convenience, u+ and n+ are often grouped under the label $+, whereas u- and n- are grouped under the label $-)

Activation of a utility node can indicate that reward or punishment is currently being experienced, or that it is predicted or expected. In either case, it reflects not only reward or punishment that is directly associated with a particular relational instance (as, for example, satisfying a sweet tooth is associated with eating cake), but also sources of reward and punishment that are less directly related (such as potential weight gain). In this respect, the utility node is comparable to the value function in reinforcement learning (Sutton, 1984); however, utility node activity is transient and cannot by itself represent any permanent learned value associated with a relational instance (how this information is maintained will be described shortly). Instead, activity at a relational utility node reflects the combination of more permanent representations of value with the transient factors that make up current context.

Reward facts: Reward facts (R-facts) represent the source of reward and punishment in the system. Each reward fact designates a specific relational instance as a goal – something to be sought or avoided. Activation of a positive reward fact indicates the attainment (real or imagined) of some reward, while activation of a negative reward fact indicates the suffering (real or imagined) of some punishment. Like episodic facts in the belief system, reward facts are temporal pattern matching circuits that respond only when the specified set of role-fillers are active. In this case, activation of a relational collector along with synchronous activation of role nodes and appropriate type node role fillers leads to activation of an R-fact node for a matching R-fact. This in turn leads to activation of that relation's appropriate utility node.

Many different reward facts can be linked to a single relation; for example (see Figure 2) a relation like eat(x) might have associated with it positive reward facts such as eat(Cake) as well as negative reward (punishment) facts such as eat(Dirt).

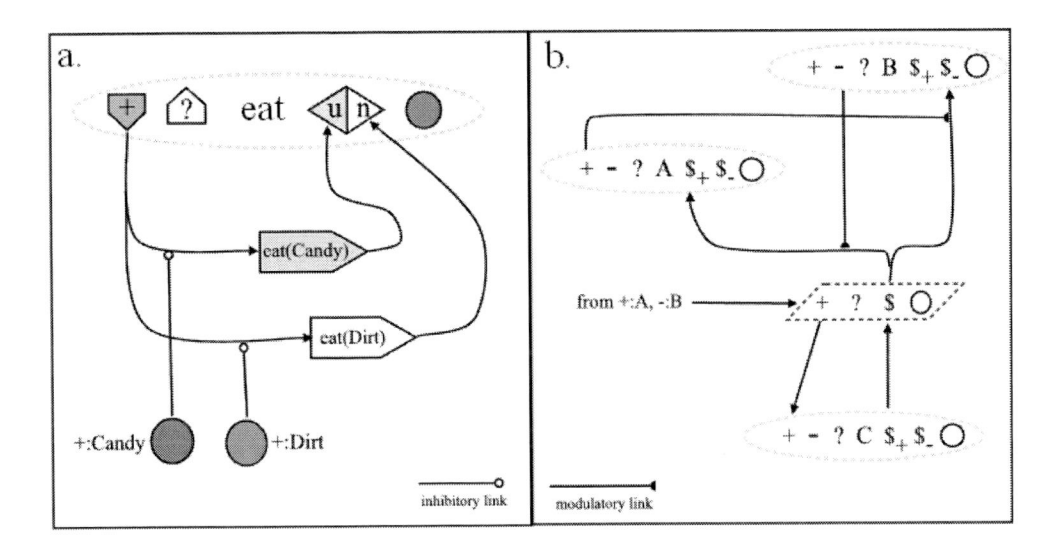

Figure 2. (a) Two reward facts for the relation eat(x). Negative weight indicates connection to a negative utility node. (b) A simple rule depicting the pathways along which utility propagates through a causal network.

Value facts: While relational utility nodes represent value estimates in the current context, and reward facts represent basic goals, the task of storing learned value estimates rests with the value facts (V-facts). Value facts are similar in form to reward facts, but instead of representing current reward, they represent predicted future reward. Like taxon-facts in the belief system, value facts hold a statistical summary of past activity. They too are associative, meaning that matching of relational activity to the fact is stronger with more role matches, but is not necessarily blocked by a single role mismatch; this helps with generalization of value to multiple related instances.

For both value facts and reward facts, utility values are stored as link weights (specifically, as the weight on the link leading from the fact node to the associated relational utility node).

A typical relation has many value facts associated with it, some very specific and some quite general. In this way, particularly important or salient items are explicitly encoded, whereas novel or less important items can fall back on more general representations. For the hypothetical agent for which eating cake is a paramount goal, find(Cake) should be a highly-rewarding value fact. Eating other things may still be beneficial, so the more general find(Food) may also appear as a weaker value fact; finding anything is more often good than bad, so even the most general value fact find(Thing) might appear in the agent's internal representation.

When the agent with these value facts happens upon a dollar bill, it will immediately perceive this as a positive situation according to the value of the find(Thing) value fact. If finding money turns out to be significantly more rewarding than finding that average-value random thing, then this should be learned and explicitly represented as a new value fact.

Communication of utilities: Links connect utility nodes of different relations in the same way that they connect belief nodes. These links run parallel to the belief system connections, but in the backward (consequent to antecedent) direction. Figure 2(b) provides a simple illustration of these connections: for the rule A & ~B ⇒ C, there are utility connections from the utility nodes of C, through the rule mediator, back to those of A and B. Weights on these connections are similar to the weights on the collector-collector links. Their purpose is to introduce probability into the calculations of value, such that the value estimate at some antecedent relation is based on both the value of its consequent (activity at its utility node) and the probability that it will be reached (weight on the connecting link). For the rule A ⇒ C (not depicted), where the utility node of C has a value of α, the utility node of A should obtain the value $\alpha \times P(C|A)$. This structure has the effect that assertion of a particular goal, via activation of a utility node, leads in the simplest case to assertion of its potential causes as sub-goals, via spreading activation backwards along the causal chain. Belief in some relation, represented as activation of a collector node, leads to internal reward or punishment (activation of a reward fact) or recognition that such reward or punishment is likely (activation of a value fact) if there is an intact causal chain leading from that relation to some goal relation.

Of course, the belief state of the system, represented in the activity of predicate collector nodes, must affect the propagation of utility. If satisfaction of two conditions is required in order to reach a desired goal, then the utility associated with one of the conditions depends on the state of the other. For example, in the rule above, if C is desired and A is true, then the full utility associated with C should be allowed to propagate to B. If however A is known to be false, then there is no benefit to achieving B, and so the propagation of utility from C to B should be blocked. If the status of A is uncertain, then this uncertainty should be reflected in the fraction of utility that is allowed to propagate from C to B. This effect is achieved via modulatory connections among rule antecedents, from collectors to utility nodes, that modulate incoming utility.

Simulation example: The encoding and propagation of utility in the network is illustrated here with a simple example. A screen capture from the simulator (Figure 3) shows a simple network representing the caveman's dilemma of whether to hunt or gather. Successful hunting yields the greatest reward (represented by the reward fact eat(Game)). Gathering, on the other hand, is more reliable, but only productive during the right season. We examine the propagation of beliefs and utilities around this simple network in detail. First, suppose that the caveman agent is hungry, and hence reward facts related to eating are fully active. Eating game or eating fruit are the current active goals of the system. Activity from the reward facts flows to multiple banks of the eat relation and from there back to kill(Game) and find(Fruit). The agent has realized that either killing game or finding fruit would be useful eventualities. Alongside the propagation of utility, a querying belief state is also being transmitted from relation to relation; this is represented in the activity of the enabler nodes. Since neither eventuality is thought to be true of the current world state, there is no competitive modulation of utility values; thus, kill(Game) has the full 0.8 value from the eat(Game) reward fact while find(Fruit) has the full 0.6 from eat(Fruit).

Utility value propagates further back to the hunt relation, this time modified by the uncertainty of hunting, such that hunt(Game) has associated with it a utility of 0.4. In order for gathering fruit to be perceived as useful, the agent must have some knowledge that the fruit is in season.

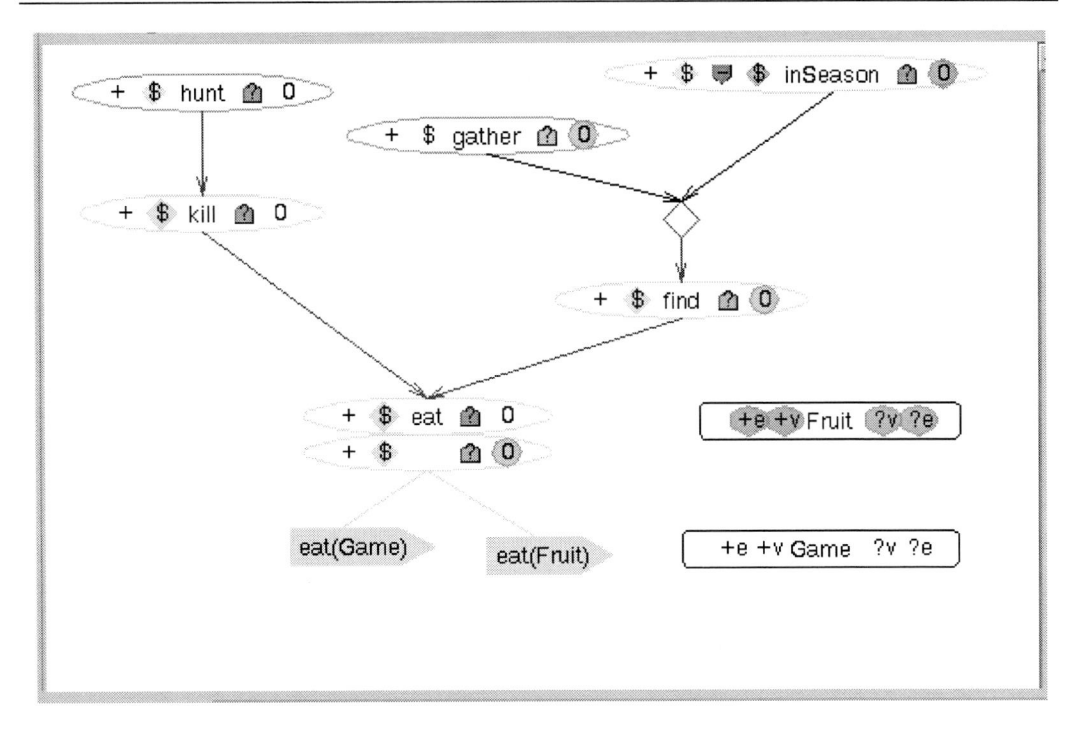

Figure 3. A captured moment from the simulation of the caveman scenario. Activity at the predicate collector -:inSeason blocks the propagation of utility to gather, resulting in a higher valuation of the hunt action.

Suppose first that the query inSeason(Fruit) is answered in the negative, either as a result of immediate knowledge of the agent or of further reasoning along paths not illustrated here. Then, according to the equation for distribution of utility values around an and-combination given above, and by means of a simple inhibitory mechanism, the flow of utility to the gather relation is blocked. Simlarly, If inSeason is uncertain, utility propagation to gather will be partially blocked. In either case, the hunt action, with a higher utility, will be favored.

This is the situation illustrated in Figure 3 and indicated by numeral 1 in Figure 4. If on the other hand the agent is reasonably certain that fruit is in season (numeral 2 in Figure 4 marks the point where +:inSeason becomes active), then sufficient utility will propagate from the find relation and gather will obtain a higher utility value than hunt (this occurrence is indicated by numeral 3 in Figure 4), marking gather as the preferred action.

Simple Decision-Making: Using Utilities to Select Actions

The target of any decision is a course of action. Thus, the effective representation of actions that an agent can perform is an essential component of any decision-making agent architecture. In this section we describe the representation of action within the SHRUTI-agent architecture, and how it is integrated with the representations of belief and utility.

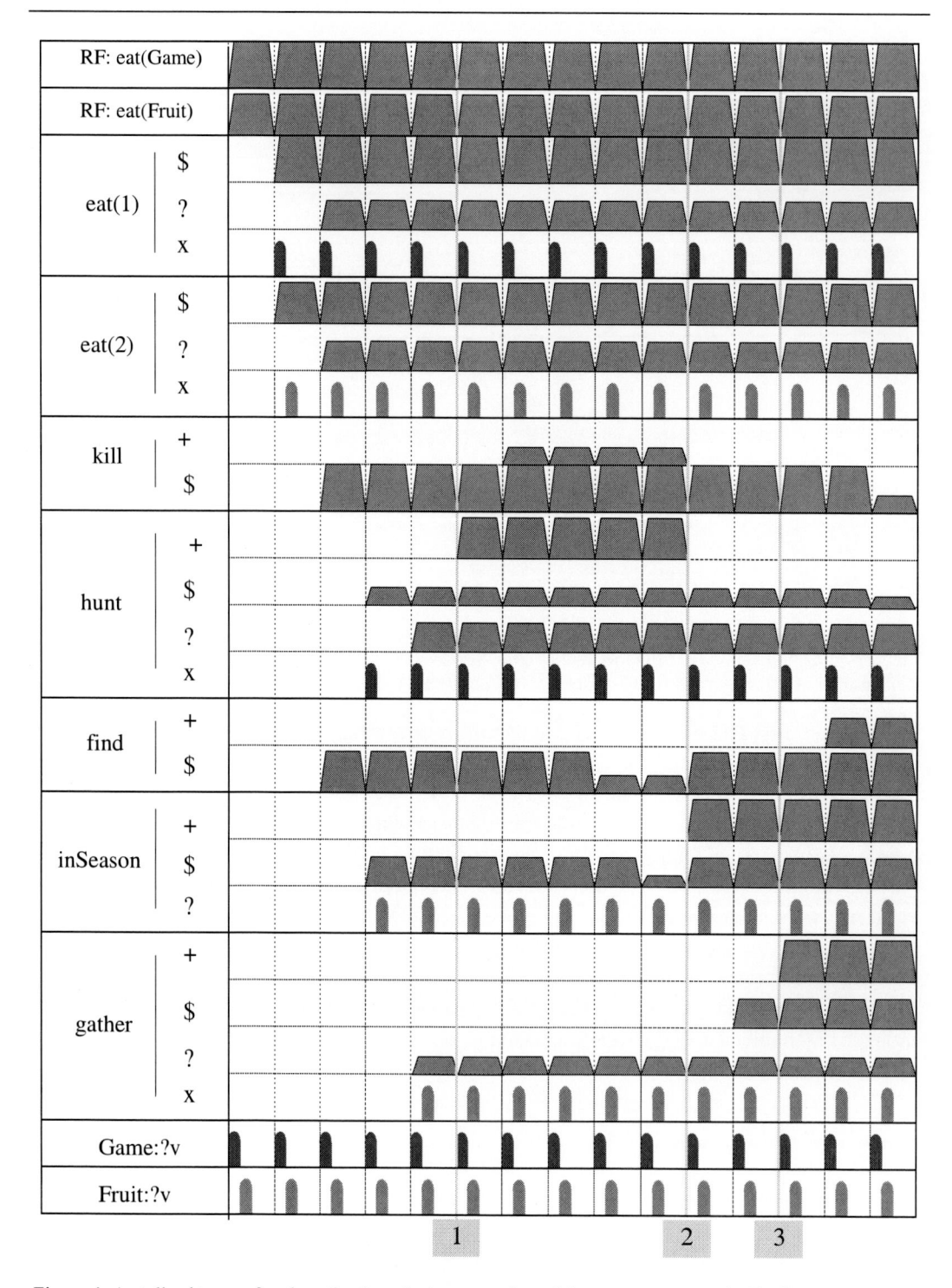

Figure 4. A stylized trace of node activations during execution of the caveman scenario. Each row represents a different node and each column represents a different cycle. Icon height represents activation strength while icon width represents duration of activity.

Representing action: On one level, actions are like any other relational predicates: they can be true (performed) or false (not performed), they can be relational, with roles and role-fillers (grab(Pencil) vs. grab(Pen)), and they can have utility associated with them. An action connects to the rest of shruti's representational machinery by means of an action focal cluster, which has an enabler, collectors, utility nodes, and role nodes just like other relational clusters. Action clusters may also include parameter nodes which can encode action characteristics (e.g. force-level) directly, via activation strength, instead of indirectly by means of temporal synchrony binding (such X-schema focal clusters are described in (Shastri et al., 1997)).

Activation of an action's positive collector indicates that the action is being or has been performed, actually or hypothetically (i.e. execution or simulation). The negative collector has little use in a representation of action and is thus excluded from the action focal cluster. Action simulation involves treating the action focal cluster as if it were a predicate focal cluster. The action collector node is activated, along with any associated role nodes and role-fillers, and the consequences of this activation are allowed to propagate throughout the network. This yields predictions about the results of action execution. Action execution relies more on interaction with the external environment than on the predictive ability of the network: network state must be reset based on external observations. In this case, action collector activation can be used as a signal to motor programs. More importantly, simulation accompanies execution, so that predictions can be compared with outcomes.

Whereas the activation of a standard predicate enabler signifies a request for explanation or indicates diagnostic support, activity of an action enabler indicates a request for hypothetical action (simulation). While activity of the action utility node indicates that an action is beneficial or harmful, activity of its enabler indicates just that the action is potentially relevant, and that simulation of the action is needed to determine its impact. In situations where utility cannot be readily determined, it can be very helpful to have a relevant subset of actions marked in this manner for further consideration. Unlike predicates, actions are not associated with prior probabilities, since it is up to the agent's decision making apparatus to decide whether or not they are made true in a particular situation. The action focal cluster is taken to represent the initiation of an action, not its successful completion. Thus, the probability of successful execution is incorporated into the link weights that connect the action cluster to its potential results. World state, or course, affects the likelihood of particular results: where an action is an antecedent in a causal rule, co-antecedent predicate clusters bring in relevant aspects of state.

Actions and utility: Activation of an action utility node is an indication that utility is being associated with the performance of the action. This can denote either reward for an action performed or potential reward if it were to be performed. Just as world state can affect probability of execution, the state in which an action is performed also has a significant effect on its utility. The importance of current world state is incorporated into the causal structure that connects an action to its associated rewards and punishments (represented as R-facts and V-facts attached to downstream predicates). Direct costs (and direct rewards, if applicable) may be associated with specific actions via R-facts attached to the action clusters..

Action focal clusters are given special treatment with regards to propagation of utility. Since the agent has complete control over whether or not an action is performed, activity level of an action collector does not modulate the utility values flowing to any sibling antecedents.

Instead, whenever an action is one of the antecedents of a rule, propagation of reward to the other antecedents is maximized, while propagation of punishment is minimized. This is because, at a high level, actions, unlike predicates, are under the direct control of the agent; it can always choose to act to maximize apparent reward, or to avoid action to minimize apparent punishment. With reference to the simple action-rule inReach(x)& grasp(x) => holding(x), if holding(Candy) is good, then inReach(Candy) can be just as good, since the grasp(Candy) action can always be attempted. If the agent prefers to avoid the eventuality holding(HotPotato), it can still be indifferent to inReach(HotPotato), since nothing will force it to perform the grasp action. In both these scenarios, there may be other reasons to desire or avoid the inReach(x) condition, but these would have to be expressed with additional rules.

From utilities and actions to decisions: With a mechanism for propagation of utility, and with a representation of available actions, a simple decision-making system can be instantiated. Just as reasoning within SHRUTI can be referred to as reflexive, because it occurs automatically as a response to input, so too can much of the decision-making of the SHRUTI-agent be labeled reflexive decision-making. Decision-making can occur more or less automatically when potential rewards or punishments are recognized as a result of observation or inference. This occurs whenever a predicate instance that has a utility fact associated with it becomes actively believed (or sometimes actively disbelieved). The utility fact also becomes active and starts the propagation of utility back through the causal chains that connect to it. When this utility reaches action clusters, decisions can potentially be made. In this approach however, only those rewards and punishments that are predicted as a result of observation or inference can impact the choice of action. Unless their simulation is a part of the inferential process, selected actions may have unpredicted negative consequences and unselected actions may have unpredicted positive consequences.

In order to ensure that the reflexive decision-making process takes a certain goal (rewarding or punishing circumstance) into account, the initial activation of the connectionist network must include activation of this goal. To activate a goal is to activate a relational utility node along with associated role nodes and role bindings. The activated goals can be statically defined utility facts or relational instances that are dynamically defined as goals for a particular scenario. Activation of all reward facts is a standard function of the system that puts it into an active decision-making state that takes all goals or drives into account. In some circumstances, activation of goals alone will lead to the association of utility with one or more actions. In most cases, it is also necessary to make a number of observations or assertions about the current world state. Regardless, once any actions have reward associated with them, the system is in a position to make some decision. Whether or not the system is actually driven to choose an action can depend on surpassing some threshold level of action utility node activation or on overcoming some threshold in the difference between two utility node activations. Better-quality decisions are achieved by incorporating more relevant goals and observations and by waiting for the network state to stabilize before looking at utilities; in this way all available information is brought to bear before any decision is made.

Some decision tasks require only selection of a single action or a sequence of independent actions. It is for these simple decisions that the sort of reflexive decision-making procedure described above is effective. As an example of a simple decision task, consider the caveman scenario presented previously (Figure 3). The situation involves a hypothetical caveman faced with the decision of whether to spend his day hunting for mammoth or gathering berries. This simple decision depends on the relative utility of the goals eat(Game) and eat(Fruit), the probabilities of obtaining each, and on the critical variable inSeason(Fruit). The network shown, or course, represents a vast simplification of the actual circumstances that would be involved in such a decision, but it is sufficient to illustrate the idea. Previously, we showed that utility propagates differently in different contexts; in this scenario, the propagation of utility to the action gather(Fruit) depends on the state of the predicate instance inSeason(Fruit). The decision-making mechanism that simply executes the action with highest associated utility is sufficient for this scenario. To the extent that inSeason(Fruit) is known to be false, utility is prevented from propagating to the gather(Fruit)action, and so the alternate action hunt(Mammoth) obtains a higher utility rating and would be chosen. If inSeason(Fruit) is believed to be true, then the higher probability that gathering berries will be successful, as opposed to mammoth hunting, outweighs the greater utility associated with eating mammoth meat, and so gather(Fruit) obtains the higher utility value of the two actions and would be chosen for execution.

Summary: Representing Utility and Action

Two essential steps in the transformation of the SHRUTI model of knowledge representation and inference into the SHRUTI-agent decision-making architecture are the incorporation of connectionist encodings of utility and of action. The addition of utility nodes, reward and value facts, and utility-carrying links in the causal network allows for propagation of utility from goals to subgoals, modulated by the belief state that is instantiated in the network. The inclusion of a representation of action then enables decision-making, as it allows for goals to drive choices between potential actions.

COMPLEX DECISION-MAKING AND COGNITIVE CONTROL

While the SHRUTI-agent architecture described above is capable of making decisions in many situations, there are many more complex decision scenarios in which the system proves inadequate. In this section, we discuss the limitations of the architecture as presented above and how these limitations can be addressed through the introduction of cognitive control.

Beyond Simple Decision-Making: the Importance of Control

The spreading activation mechanisms of the SHRUTI-agent architecture are sufficient to handle most simple inference and decision-making tasks. However, many complex decision-making scenarios do not lend themselves to easy solution by the connectionist mechanisms that have been described so far. Cognitive control, the capacity to pursue a cognitive goal despite the presence of obstacles to doing so, thus becomes an essential part of the full decision-making architecture.

The limitations of spreading activation: The implementation of decision-making via spreading activation in a connectionist network suffers from a number of limitations that are inherent to the basic spreading activation model. For instance, the mechanism of temporal-synchrony variable binding results in a soft bound on the number of entities that can be represented by the system. This means that an episode of complex decision-making, and complex inference in general, that involves a large number of entities must be broken down into simpler segments. The spreading activation mechanisms do not on their own produce this requisite segmentation. Also, in the SHRUTI model there is a high structural and computational cost associated with multiple instantiation of a single relation, and this means that the number of active instantiations of any given relation must be kept to a very low number during an episode of reasoning or decision-making. This too can necessitate breaking a complex episode into smaller elements. An expected limiting factor for any neural realization of the SHRUTI model is the noise inherent in the propagation of synchronous activity: as the depth of propagation increases, coherence decreases, and role bindings are eventually lost. When extensive propagation is required to solve a problem, some mechanism must cope with this potential loss of information. Finally, a particularly important limitation of the spreading activation model as it applies to sequential decision-making, and many other complex tasks, is its inability to maintain old activation patterns in the presence of new input. While the system can predict the consequences of a single action, it can fail to predict the result of a sequence of interdependent actions, since it is not possible to simultaneously instantiate the network with the conditions that hold prior to performance of the first action (necessary for predicting the consequences of the first action) and the conditions that hold prior to performance of the second (necessary in order to predict its consequences).

The limitations of the basic spreading activation model can be relevant to the understanding of human cognition. For example, the soft bound on the number of active entities has been calculated to be approximately 5-7 (based on realistic neural values of relevant parameters), providing a succinct explanation for observed bounds on working memory capacity (Shastri and Ajjanagadde, 1993a). But just as humans are able to solve very complex problems despite certain limitations of their cognitive apparatus, so too should the current system have the ability to work around many of the limitations described above. The capacity to focus on a problem or goal, overcoming obstacles along the way to its solution or realization, is generally referred to as cognitive control. Thus, the introduction of cognitive control into the SHRUTI-agent architecture is essential to support complex inference and decision-making.

Connectionism and cognitive control: A prerequisite to exploring how cognitive control can aid decision-making is to have a workable and sufficiently concrete definition of cognitive control. The concept of cognitive control has roots in psychology, neuroscience, and even philosophy. Here we present a working definition of cognitive control that is grounded in connectionist theory and the specifics of the SHRUTI model.

SHRUTI as described so far is primarily a model of *reflexive processing*, that is, processing that is very fast and is automatically triggered by appropriate input, almost like a reflex. This sort of processing occurs as spreading activation over a representational substrate, and it is tied very closely to the form and contents of that substrate. For example, type inference in SHRUTI occurs entirely as a result of activity of representational nodes in a connectionist type hierarchy. Causal inference occurs as spreading activation over a network of predicates and rules. Utility propagates from goal to subgoal by virtue of the interconnection pattern between utility nodes. All of these processes occur very quickly because they only require that information propagates some distance related to the depth of the connectionist network in order for results to be obtained. They occur automatically, insofar as an initial activation state is sufficient to set a chain of events in motion, without any further interference from outside the network.

Controlled processing can be defined as any processing that is not entirely reflexive in the manner described above. Controlled processing may include spreading activation as an important component, but it also includes the operation of some control mechanism or mechanisms, which have a very different character. Fundamentally, a control mechanism is characterized by the function it implements rather than by the content it represents. While reflexive processing is characterized by its dependence on a particular representational substrate, control mechanisms typically exhibit representational flexibility: a single control circuit might operate on a wide range of different content. All control mechanisms manipulate spreading activation in some manner. One mechanism might cause some process to repeat or iterate. Another might maintain activation that would otherwise decay. Still another may block or enhance activation of select nodes, node types, regions, or pathways

Controlled processing may appear quite complex, but it need not require a particularly complex central controller. Control mechanisms are just functional circuits, and these circuits are not necessarily any more complex than the representational circuits whose activity creates reflexive processing. The SHRUTI model demonstrates that much can be achieved without control mechanisms of any kind, so the requirement placed on cognitive control is to provide support to the reflexive processing apparatus, not to reinvent it. In the sections that follow, we will show that the addition of a few simple control mechanisms, each adding to the already significant capability of the underlying reflexive processing system, will prove adequate to deal with many complex decision-making tasks.

Cognitive Control for Decision-Making

As a first step towards understanding the nature and operation of cognitive control, specific decision-making failures that occur in the SHRUTI-agent model in the absence of control were considered and control processes to overcome these failures were developed. These control processes were developed initially as non-connectionist (algorithmic) procedures that manipulate the state of the connectionist network. Two such high-level control procedures are described in this section:

1. *Subgoal focus*: focusing on particular subgoals, to the exclusion of others.
2. *Hypothesis-testing*: evaluating action or predicate hypotheticals.

This is by no means a complete list of all the control processes that are compatible with SHRUTI or useful for complex cognition. Instead, the procedures described here are examples that address some of the most obvious limitations of the spreading activation model as it is applied to the task of decision-making. For each procedure, the limitations that are addressed, the algorithm that is implemented, and an example application are provided below. The translation of these high-level procedures into connectionist circuits will be addressed in the subsequent section.

Subgoal focus: The limitations that the SHRUTI architecture imposes -- on the number of entities that can be actively represented at one time and on the number of instantiations of a single predicate that can be simultaneously active -- make any mechanism that focuses activity just where it is needed particularly useful. In the decision-making domain, an ability to focus on particular subgoals, while ignoring others, makes it possible to cope with complex situations that might otherwise be unsolvable. A subgoal focus mechanism for SHRUTI operates as follows:

1. Monitor "complexity status" of ongoing propagation in the network (e.g. numbers of phases and banks in use); trigger step 2 when this is sufficiently high.
2. Select highest priority active goal (i.e. predicate instantiation with greatest magnitude utility) and block any other currently active goals.
3. Allow spreading activation to proceed. If utility is now associated with some action, then stop: only the selected subgoal influences the decision. Otherwise, unblock subgoals that are currently blocked, deactivate the current subgoal, and go to step 2.

A subgoal focus mechanism thus requires the ability to monitor complexity of ongoing propagation as well as the ability to selectively inhibit focal cluster activity. This mechanism can result in a degradation of decision quality, of course, since information not linked to the focused-on subgoal is excluded from consideration. However, this sacrifice may be necessary in some circumstances; it is better to find some useful action than to hold out for an optimal action and find nothing. Variations on the basic mechanism allow for focus to be given to several goals, instead of just one, or for the number of goals in focus to vary in proportion to the complexity status of ongoing propagation.

A minimal example of the basic subgoal focus mechanism in operation is illustrated in Figure 5. The network shown encodes a caveman's knowledge about methods of keeping warm. With the goal of being warm, being near a fire and being indoors are recognized as subgoals. If fire is found to not be available (indicated here by discovery of the fact ~near(Fire)), then spreading activation should still proceed along the alternate causal pathway and eventually uncover the action enter(Cave). However, if the maximum number of phases are already employed after near(Fire) becomes active (suppose for now that the maximum is one), then this cannot happen without some assistance. Fortunately, the failed attempt to instantiate a new phase triggers the subgoal focus mechanism. Two subgoals are currently active and so each in turn is inhibited for a period of time while results involving the other subgoal are obtained. When the near(Fire) subgoal is inhibited, propagation proceeds from the inside cluster, causes instantiation of a new role associated with the concept Cave, and ultimately leads to association of utility with the action enter(Cave).

Hypothesis testing: Complex decision problems often involve selecting a sequence of interrelated actions. Although testing many sequences until the best one or a satisfactory one is found is a possible approach, this can obviously be highly inefficient, and better approaches are available. Spreading activation within the SHRUTI-agent can fail to indicate in which order one needs to execute a sequence of actions, but still indicate which actions are relevant (by activating their enabler nodes). This happens frequently due to the fact that propagation of utility is more restricted by current beliefs than is propagation of query information. Consider a simple control process that becomes active whenever a goal is being sought but no actions appear useful. This "hypothesis-testing" procedure detects relevant actions and then selects one of them for simulated execution; typically, any action that is causally related to the goal would be marked by the network as relevant. If as a result of this simulation additional actions appear useful (via activity of their utility nodes), then it is likely that this chosen action was a good first step and it should be executed. If the simulation fails to reveal any likely second step, then a different relevant action is chosen for simulation. Consequences of the hypothesized action have a special status: since they may play a role in the propagation of utility to other actions, any action which negates one or more of them should be avoided. Temporary association of negative utility with the negation of each of these accomplishes this goal.

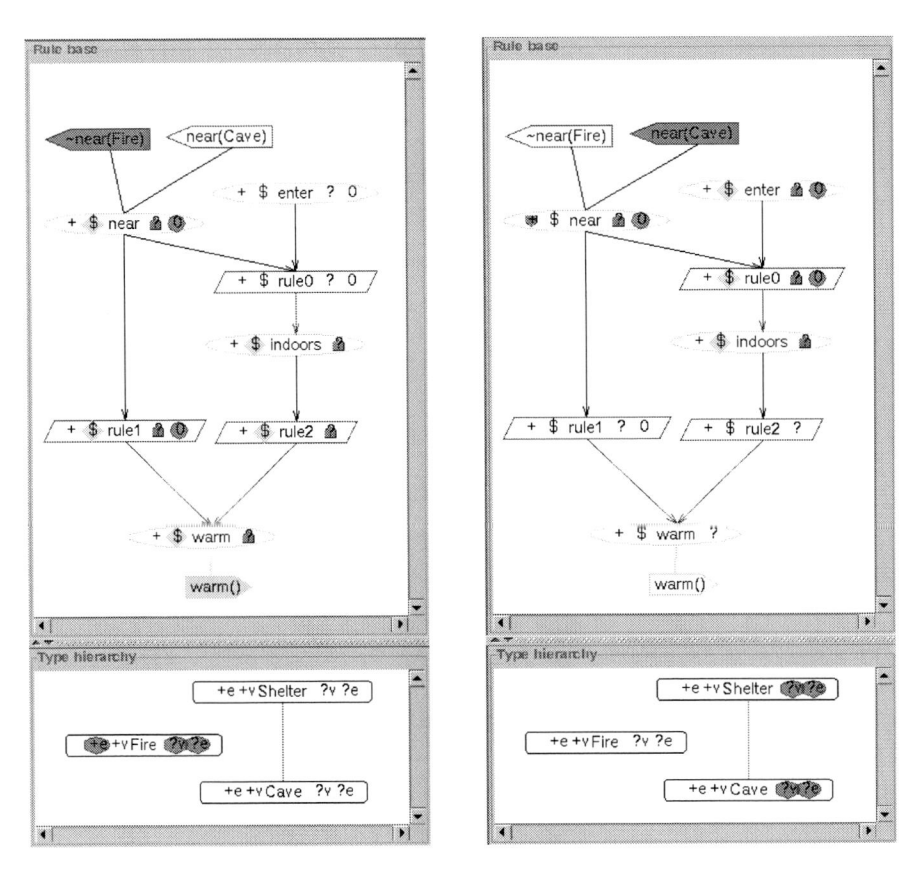

Figure 5. SHRUTI-agent Simulator instantiation of subgoal focusing, including snapshots at two different points during a simulation. On the left, competition for resources between multiple subgoals prevents propagation of activity to the enter(Cave) action. On the right, the near(Cave) subgoal is blocked by the control mechanism, allowing utility to proceed from the indoors subgoal to the enter(Cave) action.

In yet another caveman scenario (Figure 6), involving selection of three actions (tracking a Mammoth, fetching a spear, and throwing the spear at the Mammoth), this hypothesis-testing mechanism would recognize all three actions as relevant. (The pictured network of course represents a small fragment of the caveman's knowledge, most of which would not be marked as relevant to the goal at hand). Suppose that it first picked throw(Spear,Mammoth) for trial activation. Without either having the spear in hand or having found the prey, hypothesizing this action leads to no change in the network state and so clearly this is not a useful first action. If the system next chooses to simulate track(Mammoth), it will lead to a hypothesized world state where the prey has been found. It then considers the situation again in this context, marking found(Mammoth) as a situation that needs to be maintained (by associating negative utility with its negation). Having the spear now appears as a useful eventuality, but the fetch(Spear) action still does not because of negative utility propagating from found . Again no additional action is revealed as useful so the system starts over with another hypothesis, this time that get(Spear) should be performed first. When this is simulated, have(Spear) becomes active, allowing utility to propagate to found(Mammoth) and ultimately up to the track action. Since track(Mammoth) appears as a useful action after get(Spear) is hypothesized, the ordering of these first two actions is clear. Once these have been executed, then utility of the final action, throw(Spear,Mammoth), will also become apparent.

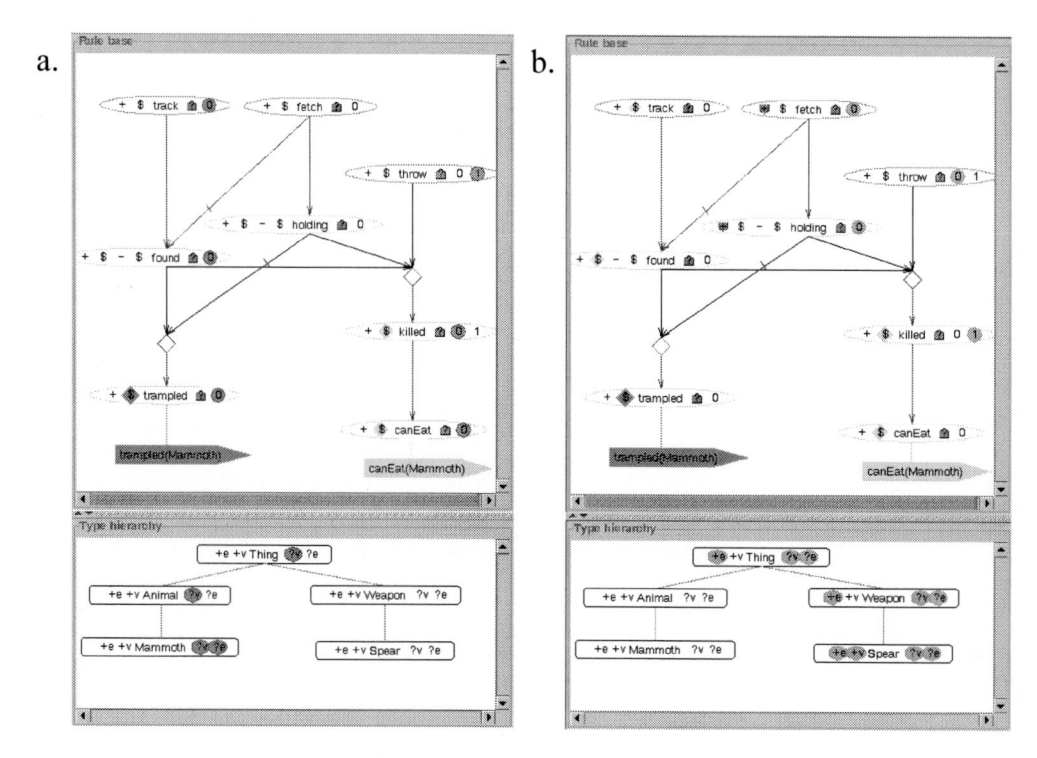

Figure 6. SHRUTI-agent Simulator instantiation of hypothesis-testing, including snapshots at two different points during a simulation. (a) Query activity reaches all three depicted actions, but utility fails to propagate to any of them. (b) Following simulated execution of the action fetch(Spear), utility propagates to track(Mammoth).

Connectionist Mechanisms for Cognitive Control

In evaluating the various control procedures developed to aid decision-making in SHRUTI , including the two procedures described above, it became clear that all make use of a limited set of basic capabilities, such as detecting particular local or global states, suppressing unwanted activity, or selecting one of a set of active nodes. These basic capabilities -- basic control mechanisms or control primitives – have simple connectionist implementations and form the building blocks of the more complex control procedures.

Control Primitives

The control primitives developed to support operation of complex control mechanisms in SHRUTI include the following:

Monitoring: Monitoring involves obtaining input from a set of targets and signaling whenever some specific property is satisfied by the input set. Detecting a simple property, such as all nodes firing above some threshold, can be achieved with a single monitor node; complex network states are more easily detected by a set of nodes or a circuit. Monitoring circuits are particularly useful for detecting properties that are not local to any one part of the network.

Conflict detection is one type of monitoring. A conflict node in SHRUTI obtains input from both positive and negative collector of a predicate focal cluster, and becomes active whenever the product of their activity is sufficiently high, signaling conflict at that predicate. At a higher level, another node receives input from many such conflict nodes and becomes active when conflict is found anywhere in the system (see Figure 7a). This activity has the potential to trigger mechanisms that manage or overcome conflict.

Filtering: Another basic aspect of control is the ability to filter, or selectively enhance or suppress activity in some part of the network. A filter operating on a SHRUTI network can suppress the activity of a set of goal representations (focal clusters). Another filter can enhance a set of queries. A third filter mechanism could entirely block the operation of one causal sub-network to prevent it from interfering with propagation in another.

Filters have a particularly simple connectionist implementation (see Figure 7b). Any node that has excitatory or inhibitory connections to a relatively large set of nodes, or one that has inhibitory projections to nodes in one set and excitatory projections to nodes in another, is effectively a simple filter. Appropriate combinations of simple filters produce useful complex filters that enhance certain aspects of a representation or computation and suppress others.

Selection: Another important capacity is the ability to select a node for further processing from some target set. The selection might be random or it might be based on activity level; choosing the most active node from a set would be a common task. Whatever selection strategy is chosen, the selection mechanism must have a way to impose its choice on subsequent processing.

A winner-take-all (WTA) network (Elias and Grossberg, 1975) is a kind of selection mechanism. In a WTA, a set of nodes with inhibitory interconnections compete until only one remains active. To serve as a control mechanism, a WTA can be connected to but physically distinct from the representations on which it operates. A gating mechanism allows activity to flow to the WTA structure and once the selection has been made, from there back to the source nodes (see Figure 7c). A more general purpose WTA mechanism can be constructed by combining the simple WTA controller with a filter. Each WTA node is then connected to many source nodes but the filter only allows one set to communicate with the WTA mechanism at any given time.

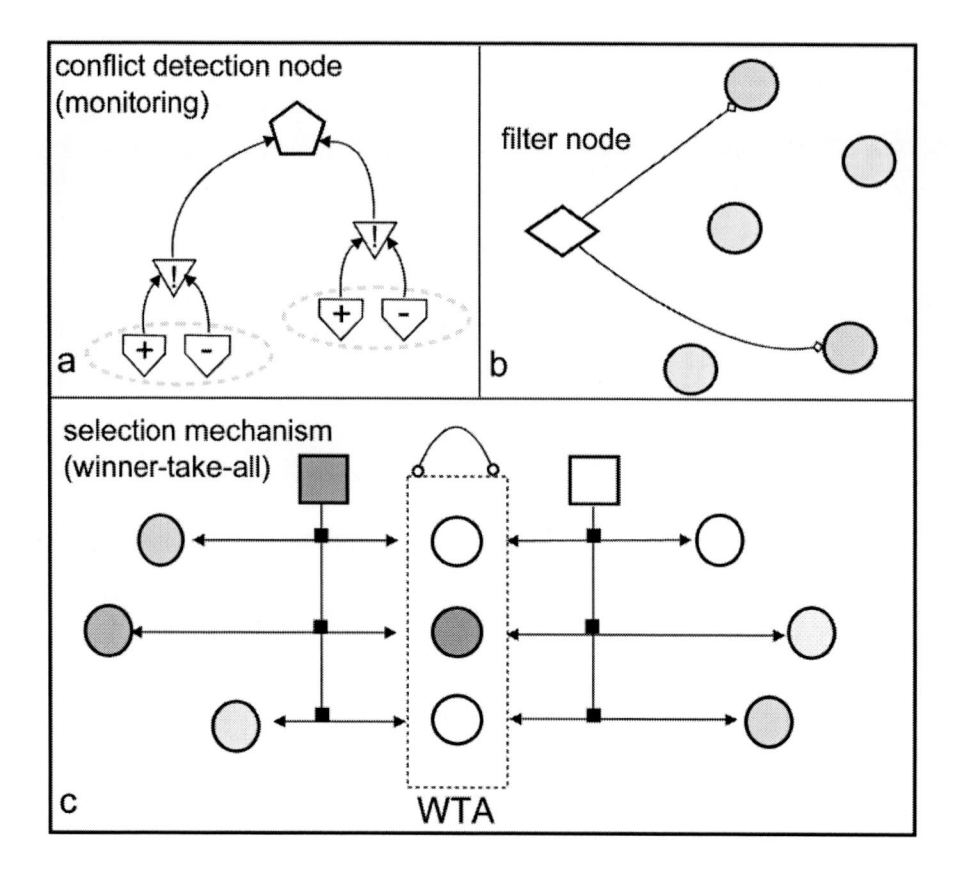

Figure 7. Connectionist implementation of control primitives, including (a) monitoring, (b) filtering, and (c) selection.

Maintenance: The nodes used in SHRUTI to represent types, entities, relations, and rules are active only in response to input, and their activity should ordinarily decay quickly when that input disappears. Sometimes it is useful to maintain activity at a node or set of nodes beyond its normal duration. Maintenance mechanisms accomplish this goal. Importantly, a maintenance mechanism does not create new activity at a node but instead sustains activity that was introduced from some other source.

Maintenance is achieved in SHRUTI with a very simple connectionist implementation, involving minimally a single link from a maintainer node to a target node. Maintainer nodes are activated (clamped) whenever there is a need to sustained activation. When inactive, the target node is not responsive to maintainer node activity. However, if the target node is active and at the same time input is obtained from the maintainer node, then the target node enters a new state in which it becomes responsive to maintainer activity, even in the absence of other input . The target node's level of activity while maintained corresponds to the activity level that it had prior to maintainer input. It returns to the original state when maintainer input disappears, with continued activation dependent on other input. Thus, while the maintainer node associated with some target node is active, any otherwise short-lived activity that the target node acquires will be sustained. Although maintenance has been described in terms of the interaction between two nodes, it is possible that a single maintainer node could be responsible for many target nodes, and also that a single target node could have multiple maintainers. Structured much like a filter mechanism, a maintainer circuit would be associated with a particular set of targets, possibly very many or a specific few. For example, one maintenance mechanism could maintain activity at all action focal clusters, while another might maintain activity at entity query nodes for entities that are subtypes of *Person*.

Organization and manipulation: The capacity to organize elements is critical for many tasks. Organization is related to maintenance, insofar as it is often useful to organize elements that are being maintained, and the structures involved in maintaining representations can be more accessible to an organizing controller than the representations themselves. Manipulation is in some sense an extension of organization, in that manipulation typically involves re-organization of maintained elements. This is potentially a very broad category of control mechanisms. Simple manipulation operators might be a circuit that causes an ordered set of maintained elements to shift forward one place, or one that causes an arbitrary shuffling of targets. Together, maintenance, organization, and manipulation mechanisms comprise what is commonly referred to as working memory. An account of how these components might be implemented in lateral prefrontal cortex is described in (Wendelken, 2002).

Realization of Complex Control Procedures Using Control Primitives

The complex control procedures described previously are realized in the SHRUTI-agent model as combinations of various connectionist control primitives. Details of this implementation are provided here.

Subgoal focus: Subgoal focus depends primarily on monitoring, filtering, and selection control primitives. A monitoring mechanism is required first to detect situations -- such as overuse of phases and predicate banks -- in which focusing on a subgoal might be useful. One implemented monitor circuit watches for inactive rule mediator role nodes, a sure sign of phase overuse. When the subgoal focus mechanism is activated, a winner-take-all mechanism connected to predicate utility nodes selects an appropriate subgoal. Focusing on a single subgoal essentially involves activating a filter that has a pre-wired association with that selected subgoal and inhibits collector and enabler nodes on unconnected causal pathways. To focus on distinct subgoals in sequence, an ordered selection mechanism that operates in essentially the same manner as that used for sequential action simulation is utilized. When the system operator selects a sequence of subgoals, this sequence is stored in the connectionist "sequencer" circuit and is accessed whenever there is a call to focus on a new subgoal.

Hypothesis-testing: The hypothesis-testing mechanism involves monitoring and selection. Monitoring first reveals when control should be applied; specifically it detects situations where goals are active but utility has failed to propagate sufficiently to relevant actions. An implemented monitor circuit consists of a node that receives input from reward facts and a second node that receives significantly delayed input from the first node as well as inhibitory input from action utility nodes. If the second node becomes active, this means that reward fact activity is not matched by action utility node activity, even after a significant delay period; this is exactly the situation that should trigger the hypothesis-testing mechanism. Once the hypothesis-testing mechanism has been activated, a selection mechanism takes over, selecting one action from the set of relevant actions (marked as such via enabler activity) for simulated execution. This selection involves interaction between predicate enablers and a winner-take-all circuit that causes the collector of the winning predicate to become active. Inference is allowed to proceed normally once the action cluster has been activated. When spreading activation has run its course, either the hypothesized action is identified as useful (due to detection of utility at another action) or another action is selected for simulation.

Summary: Complex Decision-Making and Cognitive Control

With an appropriate representation of action, in addition to the encoding of utility, the SHRUTI-agent system is capable of successful operation in simple decision-making scenarios. However, limitations of the basic spreading activation mechanisms put many complex decision tasks beyond the reach of the basic system. These limitations are overcome via the introduction of cognitive control. A range of control mechanisms allow for manipulation of spreading activation, and enable the SHRUTI-agent system to handle many complex decision problems that it would otherwise be unable to deal with effectively. The high-level control mechanisms useful for decision-making utilize a common set of simple control mechanisms or control primitives. These control primitives, including monitoring, filtering, selection, maintenance, organization, and manipulation, are all realized as connectionist circuitry.

SUMMARY AND CONCLUSION

In this chapter, we have shown how SHRUTI, a connectionist model of knowledge representation and inference, can be transformed into the SHRUTI-agent decision-making architecture. This transformation has involved the incorporation of compatible connectionist representations of utility and action into the SHRUTI model, as well as the introduction of connectionist mechanisms for cognitive control. We draw two main conclusions from this effort. First, utility and action can both be successfully represented using the same sorts of connectionist structures and mechanisms that support representation of facts and beliefs in SHRUTI. Second, cognitive control, which manipulates network state in various ways and can be used to support highly complex operations, need not have a particularly complex or centralized implementation. With a suitable underlying connectionist architecture, a small set of simple connectionist control mechanisms are can support highly complex episodes of reasoning and decision-making.

REFERENCES

Abeles M (1982) *Local Cortical Circuits: Studies of Brain Function*: Springer-Verlag.
Ajjanagadde V, Shastri L (1989) Efficient inference with multi-place predicates and variables in a connectionist system. In: *Proceedings of the Eleventh Conference of the Cognitive Science Society*, pp 396-403.
Crick F (1984) Function of the thalamic reticular complex: The searchlight hypothesis. *Proceedings of the National Academy of Sciences* 81:4586-4590.

Elias S, Grossberg S (1975) Pattern formation, contrast control, and oscillations in the short term memory of shunting on-center off-surround networks. *Biological Cybernetics* 20: 69-98.

Engel A, Konig P, Kreiter A, Singer W (1991) Interhemispheric synchronization of oscillatory neuronal responses in cat visual cortex. *Science* 252:1177-1179.

Hendler J (1989) Marker passing over microfeatures: Towards a hybrid symbolic/connectionist model. *Cognitive Science* 13:79-106.

Hummel J, Holyoak K (1997) Distributed representations of structure: a theory of analogical access and mapping. *Psychological Review* 104:427-466.

Kreiter A, Singer W (1996) Stimulus-dependent synchronization of neuronal responsed in the visual cortex of the awake macaque monkey. *Journal of Neuroscience* 16:2381-2396.

Lange T, Dyer M (1989) High-level inferencing in a connectionist network. *Connection Science* 1:181-217.

Malsburg Cvd (1981) *The correlation theory of brain function*. In. Gottingen Germany: Max-Planck Institute for Biophysical Chemistry.

Milner P (1974) A model for visual shape recognition. *Psychological Review* 81:521-535.

Park N, Robertson D, Stenning K (1995) An extension of the temporal synchrony approach to dynamic variable binding. *Knowledge-Based Systems* 8:345-358.

Plate T (1994) *Distributed Representations and Nested Compositional Structure*. In: University of Toronto.

Shastri L (1999) Advances in SHRUTI - a neurally motivated model of relational knowledge representation and rapid inference using temporal synchrony. *Applied Intelligence* 11.

Shastri L, Ajjanagadde V (1993a) From simple associations to systematic reasoning. *Behavioral and Brain Sciences* 16:417-494.

Shastri L, Ajjanagadde V (1993b) From simple associations to systematic reasoning. *Behavioral and Brain Sciences* 16:417-494.

Shastri L, Wendelken C (1999) Soft computing in SHRUTI. In: *Proceedings of the Third International Symposium on Soft Computing*, pp 741-747. Genova, Italy.

Shastri L, Grannes D, Narayanan S, Feldman J (1997) A Connectionist Encoding of Parameterized Schemas and Reactive Plans. In: *Hybrid Information Processing in Adaptive Autonomous Vehicles* (Kraetzschmar G, Palm G, eds): Springer-Verlag.

Smolensky P (1990) Tensor product variable binding and the representation of symbolic structures in connectionist systems. *Artificial Intelligence* 46.

Sougne J (1996) A connectionist model of reflective reasoning using temporal properties of nodes firing. In: *Proceedings of the 18th Conference of the Cognitive Science Society*. San Diego: Lawrence Erlbaum Associates.

Sutton R (1984) *Temporal Credit Assignment in Reinforcement Learning*, Ph.D. Thesis. In: University of Massachusetts, Amherst.

Wendelken C (2002) The role of mid-dorsolateral prefrontal cortex in working memory: a connectionist model. *Neurocomputing* 44-46:1009-1016.

Wendelken C, Shastri L (2000) Probabilistic inference and learning in a connectionist causal network. In: *Proceedings of the Second International Symposium on Neural Computation*.

In: Psychology of Decision Making
Editor: Paul M. Garrison

ISBN 978-1-60021-869-9
© Nova Science Publishers, Inc.

Chapter 3

COGNITIVE DYSFUNCTION IN COCAINE ABUSE: EVIDENCE FOR IMPAIRMENTS IN IMPULSE CONTROL AND DECISION-MAKING

Laurie M. Rilling1,† and Bryon Adinoff †,‡
†University of Texas Southwestern Medical Center, Dallas, TX, USA
‡VA North Texas Health Care System, Dallas, TX, USA

ABSTRACT

Cocaine is one of the most widely abused psychoactive substances in the United States, with an estimated 1.3 million Americans using the drug on a regular (at least monthly) basis. Even occasional cocaine use can result in serious medical complications, such as cardiac damage, vascular ischemia, respiratory failure, and persistent alterations in neural function. In this chapter, we will examine the most recent research on impulsivity and decision-making in cocaine use. First, we will present a brief overview of the cognitive processes affected by cocaine use. Next, we will review the relevant literature detailing the status of inhibitory control and decision-making in cocaine users, as well as their proposed neuroanatomical correlates. Finally, we will attempt to integrate these findings with the current view of cocaine addiction and relapse, with an emphasis on the role of impulsivity and decision-making in continued cocaine use despite the elevated risk of negative consequences.

Cocaine is one of the most widely abused psychoactive substances in the United States, with an estimated 1.3 million Americans using the drug on a regular (at least monthly) basis (Department of Health and Human Services, 1994). Even occasional cocaine use can result in serious medical complications, such as cardiac damage, vascular ischemia, respiratory failure, and persistent alterations in neural function (Bartzokis et al, 1999; Bolouri and Small, 2004; Frishman et al, 2003; Neiman, Haapaniemi, and Hillbom, 2000; Qureshi et al, 2001; Su et al.,

---

[1] Correspondence: Laurie M. Rilling, Ph.D., UT Southwestern Medical Center, 5323 Harry Hines Blvd., Dallas Texas 75390-8846; Telephone: (214) 648-4646; E-mail: laurie.rilling@utsouthwestern.edu

2003; Vallee et al., 2003; Velasquez, et al., 2004; Wilson and Saukkonen, 2004). The neurologic sequelae associated with these serious medical complications can include seizures, hypertensive encephalopathy, cerebral vasculitis, ischemic stroke and cerebral hemorrhage, and may result in severe and permanent cognitive disability in those who survive the acute phase of these potentially fatal conditions (Bolouri and Small, 2004; Keller and Chappell, 1997; Konzen et al., 1995; Nolte et al., 1996; Reeves, McWilliams, Fitz-Gerald, 1995; Strickland, Miller, Kowell, and Stein, 1998; Tolat, O'Dell, Golamco-Estrella, and Avella, 2000, Valee et al, 2003).

In addition to an acute medical event, alterations in neural structure, receptor action and cerebral blood flow occur with repeated exposure (Franklin et al, 2002; Matochik et al, 2003), leading to the persistent cognitive and functional declines that accompany the state of addiction (Ardila et al., 1991; Bolla, Cadet, and London, 1998; Franken, 2003; Di Sclafani et al., 2002; Strickland and Stein, 1995; see also Neiman, Haapaniemi, and Hillborn, 2000). Together, these neurophysiological and neurocognitive changes likely account for the reduced impulse control and poor decision-making that perpetuates the abuse and undermines attempts at prolonged abstinence.

In this chapter, we will examine the most recent research on impulsivity and decision-making in cocaine use. First, we will present a brief overview of the cognitive processes affected by cocaine use. Next, we will review the relevant literature detailing the status of inhibitory control and decision-making in cocaine users, as well as their proposed neuroanatomical correlates. Finally, we will attempt to integrate these findings with the current view of cocaine addiction and relapse, with an emphasis on the role of impulsivity and decision-making in continued cocaine use despite the elevated risk of negative consequences.

COCAINE USE AND COGNITIVE IMPAIRMENT

There is a growing body of evidence to support the relationship between chronic cocaine use and impaired neurocognitive functioning. Varying degrees of impairment have been reported in specific cognitive domains, including memory, verbal fluency, spatial relations, psychomotor speed, and grip strength (Hoff et al., 1996; Manschreck et al., 1990; O'Malley et al., 1990; Roberts and Bauer, 1993; Strickland and Stein, 1995). In contrast, several investigators have found that cocaine users demonstrate enhanced performance on select cognitive measures (Bauer, 1993; O'Malley et al., 1990, 1992; Sevy et al., 1990; Manschreck et al., 1990), but this likely reflects methodological differences among studies, such as sample characteristics, patterns of cocaine use, or the specific task employed. Despite these conflicting findings, two areas of cognition that appear to be consistently impaired are select aspects of attention and executive functioning, namely inhibitory control and decision-making.

COMPONENTS OF ATTENTION AND EXECUTIVE FUNCTIONS

The concept of attention is complex and engenders much debate among cognitive scientists. Several investigators have developed theoretical models of attention in which various cognitive mechanisms are identified as being responsible for the component processes of attentional function. For example, Shallice (1982) has proposed that two adaptive mechanisms underlie the process of attention: contention scheduling and supervisory attentional control. The first mechanism, *contention scheduling*, can be thought of as an automatic selection process which is elicited through external stimuli and involves little or no conscious awareness (e.g., bottom-up processing). It is ideal for handling routine behaviors which occur under well-known circumstances. In contrast, the second mechanism, *supervisory attentional control*, serves as a top-down process by which attention is modulated via inhibitory control over externally activated schemas held in working or short-term memory (see van Zomeren and Brouwer, 1994). This mechanism is similar to the *central executive* in the model of working memory proposed by Baddeley (1986). In the Baddeley model, the central executive modulates attention by exerting inhibitory control over a number of subsidiary *slave* systems (see van Zomeren and Brouwer, 1994 for a comprehensive review of attentional theories).

Although the supervisory attentional system (SAS) and central executive were conceptualized within the framework of attentional models, these complex attentional mechanisms are commonly associated with the cognitive construct of *executive functions*. This term refers set of higher-order cognitive processes involved in the monitoring and modulation of behavior. These include such functions as planning, organization, problem-solving and decision-making through the generation and implementation of strategies, the evaluation of behavioral outcomes, integration of feedback, and the consideration of response alternatives (Brandt and Blysma, 1993; Huber and Shuttlewoth, 1990). Both complex attentional mechanisms and executive functions have been neuroanatomically associated with distinct regions of the frontal cortex, as well as frontal-subcortical circuits (Salmon, Heindel, and Hamilton, 2001; Baddeley and Della Sala, 1998). This growing body of literature will be reviewed in greater detail in subsequent sections.

INHIBITORY CONTROL AND IMPULSIVITY IN COCAINE USE

The process of addiction is a complex phenomenon that involves reciprocal alterations in neurochemical and behavioral responses. Historically, the mesolimbic dopamine system and motivational processes have played a dominant role in the study of drug abuse and addiction (Taylor, 1985; Salamone et al., 1997; Adinoff et al., 2004). Increasingly, however, researchers interested in the effects of chronic drug abuse are turning their attention toward regions of the frontal cortex involved in inhibitory control (Ardila et al., 1991, Biggins et al. 1997; Fillmore, Rush, and Hays, 2002; Fuchs et al., 2004; Goldstein et al., 2001; Horner et al., 1996; Moeller et al., 2004; Volkow et al., 1996).

Evidence derived from the study of rodents and primates suggests that dysfunction of the frontostriatal system may be particularly important in the compulsive reward-seeking behavior observed in chronic drug abuse (Baylis and Gaffin, 1991; Butter, 1968; Dias et al.,

1996a, 1996b; Rosenkilde, 1979). Based upon these and other supporting studies (e.g., Weissenborn et al., 1997), Jentsch and Taylor (1999) have proposed a theoretical model which predicts that chronic drug use results in the disruption of normal frontostriatal function (specifically corticostriatal projections from the medial prefrontal cortex to the caudate nucleus and nucleus accumbens) which controls inhibitory modulation. Further, they propose that compulsive drug-seeking behaviors are perpetuated by the "functional synergism between impairments in inhibitory control and augmentations in conditioned reward (which) manifest as an overwhelming control of behavior by drugs and conditioned reinforcers," (p. 384). This model provides an excellent framework within which the emerging human data can be considered.

Inhibitory control serves as a top-down regulatory process through which a prepotent response can be suppressed or terminated. This control mechanism can be applied to both internal cognitive processes and overt behavioral actions. For example, in chronic cocaine use, the individual may be unable to suppress the recurrent thoughts of using cocaine, as well as the behavioral response triggered by cocaine-associated stimuli. Given the inherent difficulty in measuring internal thought processes, much of the research to date has focused on chronic cocaine use and its effect on impulsivity and behavioral inhibition.

Evidence from both animal and human research has consistently supported an association between long-term cocaine use and reduced behavioral inhibition (Ardila et al, 1991; Biggins et al, 1997; Butros et al., 1994, 1997; Fillmore, Rush, and Hays, 2002; Fuchs et al, 2994; Hester and Garavan, 2004; Horner et al, 1996; Volkow et al, 1996). Studies examining inhibitory function in humans have employed a variety of neuropsychological and cognitive paradigms, including traditional and computerized versions of the Stroop task (Stroop, 1935), continuous performance tasks, go/no-go tasks, and the stop-signal task. These tasks are commonly used to demonstrate impaired behavioral inhibition in non-substance abusing populations with impulse control disorders, such as Attention-Deficit-Hyperactivity Disorder (ADHD) and Oppositional/Defiant Disorder (e.g., Nigg, 1999; Oosterlaan and Sergeant, 1996; Schachar et al, 1995), as well as traumatic brain injury (Levin et al., 2004; O'Keeffe, et al., 2004; Whyte et al., 1998) and stroke (Reding et al., 1993).

Due to their excellent sensitivity, substance abuse investigators are increasingly utilizing these cognitive tasks to examine the role of behavioral inhibition in chronic drug abuse and addiction. In the stop-signal paradigm, response inhibition and execution are examined using a computerized choice reaction time (RT) task that requires the participant to respond or inhibit responding to a "go-signal" or a "stop-signal," respectively. Signals are presented at different ratios and the inter-stimulus-interval (ISI) may vary from 50 to 350 ms, with the probability of inhibiting decreasing in a linear fashion as the ISI increases (Fillmore et al, 2001, Fillmore and Vogel-Sprott, 1999, 2000). Response inhibition is measured by examining the number of successfully inhibited responses relative to the total number of stop-signals presented (i.e., probability of inhibition) and the estimated mean latency to inhibit a response (e.g., stop-signal RT; see Logan, 1994 for calculation details). Fillmore and colleagues (2002a, 2002b) employed the stop-signal task in a series of studies examining inhibitory control in adults with a history of chronic cocaine use. Results from these studies indicated that inhibitory control was reduced relative to non-cocaine using controls, both in terms of their ability to inhibit a response and the amount of time required to do so. Furthermore, inhibitory deficits were similar for chronic cocaine users who had used cocaine within one week of testing (Fillmore et al, 2002a) and those who received oral cocaine immediately prior to testing as part of a placebo-controlled inpatient design (Fillmore, Rush, and Hays, 2002b), independent of the inhibitory response latencies. Speed and accuracy performance to go-signals, as opposed to stop-signals, was unaffected in both cocaine groups. Taken together, these findings suggest that while cocaine has a negative effect on inhibitory control, it is not necessarily due to slowed inhibitory function but rather a disruption of the inhibitory process itself.

Similar to the stop-signal task, the go/no-go task requires the individual to inhibit a prepotent motor response to environmentally triggered stimuli (see Rubia et al, 2003 for a review of how these two tasks differ). Using a standard go/no-go paradigm, Kaufman and colleagues (2003) examined inhibitory control in sample of 13 active cocaine users with an average of 11 years of use. Compared to age-matched healthy controls, the cocaine users demonstrated significantly worse inhibitory control as measured by the number of commission errors (i.e., failure to inhibit a response to a non-target). . When this task was employed in conjunction with event-related functional magnetic imaging (fMRI), a neuroimaging technique used to assess brain function, cocaine users showed reduced activation following both successful STOPS and ERRORS in frontal and midline areas, including the anterior cingulate cortex (ACC) or Brodmann areas (BAs) 6 and 32. These areas are believed to be involved in error-detection and have been implicated in inhibitory dysfunction in other populations, such as schizophrenia (Carter et al, 2001) and obsessive-compulsive disorder (Ursu et al, 2001). Using a somewhat modified version of the go/no-go task, Hester and Garavan (2004) found that, relative to healthy controls, the magnitude of the cocaine users' inhibitory impairment tended to increase proportionally with the demand on executive (or inhibitory) control. Under even-related fMRI conditions, the inhibitory control deficit in cocaine users was associated with reduced activation in the ACC (BAs 32/34), pre-supplementary motor cortex (BA 6), and right superior frontal gyrus (BAs 10/9), relative to controls. Furthermore, unlike the controls, the cocaine users did not demonstrate any increased ACC activation in response to the increased executive demand; rather they exhibited an unexpected hyperactivation of the left cerebellum. This latter finding highlights the disruption of not only frontal cortical regions in chronic cocaine users, but perhaps the entire network of frontal-subcortical-cerebellar connections. Other brain regions that have been implicated in cocaine-related reductions in inhibitory control include the orbitofrontal cortex (Goldstein et al, 2001; Fuchs et al, 2004) and the anterior corpus callosum (Moeller et al, 2005).

In summary, the evidence supporting an association between chronic cocaine use and impaired inhibitory control is quite compelling, though admittedly still preliminary in nature. Replication of these results would provide additional support for this important link between impulsivity and the difficulties such individuals encounter when faced with the environmental triggers that entice them to use again. Moreover, although there is some evidence that ACC dysfunction may serve as the neural substrate for this impairment, the extent to which habitual cocaine use may disrupt other frontal, subcortical, and even cerebellar regions is yet to be determined. Clearly, this is an area of research that deserves continued attention from the scientific community.

COCAINE USE AND DECISION MAKING

One of the most difficult challenges substance abusers face when attempting to remain abstinent is resisting the urge to use when they encounter drug-related cues in the environment (Luborsky et al., 1995). In this situation, the individual is presented with the choice of whether they will resume their drug use or maintain their abstinence. This decision will undoubtedly be associated with positive and negative consequences, some of which will be short-lived and others which will be long-lasting. For those who have not developed a chemical addiction (or dependency), the decision to abstain from drug use in order to avoid potentially adverse consequences may seem relatively logical and straightforward. However, one of the hallmarks of addiction is the persistent use of chemical substances despite the likelihood of seriously negative long-term effects (Grant et al, 2000; WHO, 1992).

Individuals who engage in drug use are often described as "risk-takers" or "sensation seekers," both of which highlight the some of the variables involved in this decision-making process. For those who are able to postpone their response long enough to engage in the decision-making process (i.e., those with relatively preserved impulse control), they are compelled to engage in a spontaneous cost/benefit analysis. In other words, they must ask themselves, "What are the costs and benefits of returning to drug use versus maintaining abstinence?" This decision is highly influenced by multiple factors, including prior experiences, the expected rewards, and possible punishments. In the case of drug use, the reward typically involves a rapid transition from an unpleasant to a pleasant physiological (and perhaps psychological) state. Thus, the temptation of the immediate reward must be weighed against the reality of the delayed cost. There is a substantial scientific literature devoted to the study of decision-making in healthy individuals (see Tversky and Kahneman, 1981). The relationship between impaired decision-making and chronic cocaine use, however, is still somewhat preliminary and continues to be an area of intense study.

One of the most common paradigms used to examine human risk-taking and decision-making is the gambling task (GT). This measure was developed to assess behavioral patterns in the context of a reward-punishment situation and has proven to be quite sensitive to decision-making deficits in patients with ventromedial prefrontal cortex lesions (Bechara et al., 1994, 1999, 2000) as well as individuals with a history of chronic substance abuse (Grant et al., 2000; Petry et al., 1998; Mazas et al., 2000). In the computerized version of this task, subjects are required to choose between two options; one with the possibility of large immediate rewards and a risk of large punishments and a second with the possibility of small rewards and a risk of small punishments. Reward-punishment ratios are fixed so that the first option will result in a net loss and the second option will result in a net gain upon completion of the task. Optimal performance on this measure requires the subject to make conservative choices (e.g., smaller rewards) and delay the gratification achieved by receiving a larger payout until the end of the task.

There is a strong tendency, however, for humans (and animals) to "discount" delayed outcomes (Monterosso et al., 2001). As such, those who seek immediate gratification will more often choose a larger immediate reward despite the greater risk of long-term negative consequences. Indeed, findings from studies of drug-abusing individuals suggest that those who more steeply discount the future suffer from a kind of "temporal myopia," in which the overwhelming desire for immediate gratification interferes with their ability to contemplate future consequences (Bickle, Odum, & Madden, 1999; Kirby et al., 1999; Madden, Bickle, & Jacobs, 1999; Mitchell, 1999; Vuchinch & Simpson, 1998). This myopic perspective may predispose these individuals to problematic drug use even before they are exposed to their drug of choice (Bechara et l., 1994; Bickel & Marsch, 2001; Herrnstein & Prelec, 1992; Monterosso et al., 2001; Vuchinich & Tucker, 1988). It has also been suggested that chronic under-arousal in a subset of drug abusing individuals may serve to increase their tendency toward "risk-seeking" behavior. This phenomenon, combined with a myopic outlook, may elevate the risk of recurrent relapse following chemical dependency treatment (Bartzokis et al., 2000; Quay, 1965; Zuckerman, 1979, 1994). The interaction between perception of risk (e.g., risk-discounting) and the preference for risk (e.g., sensation-seeking) in the perpetuation of drug abuse has not been well studied however, and warrants further systematic examination.

Despite the controversies surrounding the role of risk-taking versus sensation-seeking, there is growing support in the scientific literature for an association between impaired decision-making and chronic drug abuse. Numerous studies have reported that drug-dependent individuals are impaired on the GT relative to matched controls (Bartzokis et al., 2000; Bechara et l., 2001; Ernst et al., 2003; Fishbein, 2000; Grant, Contoreggi & London, 2000; Mazas, Finn, & Steinmetz, 2000; Rotheram-Fuller, et al., 2004). For example, Grant and colleagues (2000) utilized the GT in conjunction with the Wisconsin Card Sorting Test (WCST) to examine decision-making in a group of active polysubstance abusers and drug-naïve controls. The majority of substance abusers acknowledged using cocaine (28/30 subjects) and over half endorsed using heroin (19/30 subjects). Most substance-abusing subjects also endorsed using marijuana, alcohol, and nicotine, while the only substance a majority of controls endorsed using was alcohol (16/24 subjects). After controlling for IQ differences, results indicated that drug abusers performed significantly worse than controls in terms of their net score on the GT, with almost 50% of the drug abusing subjects yielding net scores in the negative range as compared to only 8% of the controls. In a subsequent study, Ernst and colleagues (2003) examined GT performance over five blocks of 20-card choices and found that a similar sample of active substance abusers performed significantly worse than controls during the third block. The authors interpreted this finding as reflecting a critical "hunch" time-period when respondents should begin to internalize the reward/penalty differences between decks. Similar decision-making deficits have also been reported using a somewhat different version of the gambling task paradigm (Heyman & Dunn, 2002).

In contrast, several recent studies that examined cocaine-dependent individuals reported no differences in GT performance between these individuals and control subjects (Adinoff et al, 2003; Bolla et al., 2003; Tucker et al, 2004). Upon closer inspection, it appears that differences in methodology and sample characteristics may at least partially explain these conflicting findings. For example, subjects in the studies with negative findings consisted of patients who identified cocaine as their drug of choice, as opposed to individuals in the earlier described studies who acknowledged concurrent use of heroin and cocaine. In addition, studies with negative findings limited their sample to subjects who were abstinent for a specified period of time, many of whom were either enrolled in a residential chemical dependency treatment program or had recently completed such a program. This is in contrast to the "active" substance abusers who were included in the studies reporting group differences. Differences in gender distribution among patient and control samples may have also contributed to discrepant findings, as there is some evidence to suggest that males perform slightly better than females on gambling tasks (LeLand et al, 1998; Reavis et al., 1998). Finally, variability in the task parameters, administration procedures, and methods for computing primary outcome variables may also contribute to the inconsistencies among studies employing the GT.

Although the GT performance data reported in the literature thus far is equivocal at best, there is emerging evidence to support an association between cocaine use and alterations in brain function as measured by neuroimaging. Several recent studies have examined resting cerebral blood flow (rCBF) in cocaine-dependent individuals using single-photon emission computed tomography (SPECT) and positron emission tomography (PET), with a focus on frontal cortical regions believed to be involved in decision-making. One area of particular interest has been the orbitofrontal cortex (OFC). This brain region is an important part of the neural networks involved in positive reinforcement in primates (Rolls and Baylis, 1994) and has reciprocal connections with many brain regions that mediate the rewarding effects of cocaine in humans (Rolls, 2000; Volkow and Fowler, 2000). Damage to the OFC may produce changes in personality, social behavior, and judgment characterized by irresponsibility and repetition of inappropriate or self-destructive behaviors.

Studies using PET to examine the role of the OFC in drug addiction have revealed increases in activation in the OFC, anterior cingulate, right insular region, and the amygdala in response to cocaine-related cues (Bonson et al., 2002, Childress et al., 1999; Grant et al., 1996; Wang et al., 1999). Alterations in the striato-thalamo-orbitofrontal network have also been reported in association with cocaine addicted individuals' performance on tasks of impulsivity and conflict monitoring (Goldstein et al., 2001). Using PET to examine the neural activation patterns associated with decision-making, Bolla and colleagues (2003) found that cocaine abusers who were abstinent for an average of 24 days showed increased right OFC activation during the GT as compared to non-drug using controls. Moreover, they reported that the amount of cocaine used (grams/week) prior to their period of abstinence was negatively correlated with activation in the left OFC. Similar increases in rCBF have been found using SPECT in a sample of abstinent cocaine-dependent individuals (Tucker et al., 2004). Others have reported no association between OFC activation and GT performance in this population (Adinoff et al., 2003), but indicate a relative decrease in resting rCBF in cocaine-dependent subjects compared to controls (Adinoff et al., 2001, Volkow et. 1992). Other brain regions associated with GT performance in cocaine users include the ACC and the dorsolateral prefrontal cortex (DLPFC) (Adinoff et al, 2003; Bolla et al., 2003; Tucker et al., 2004). Taken together, these findings suggest that chronic cocaine users show persistent functional abnormalities in prefrontal regions involved in decision-making.

SUMMARY

Based on the currently available data, it is clear that cocaine use is associated with alterations in neural activation. How these changes are manifested in terms of cognitive dysfunction and treatment outcome, however, remains unclear. Historically, models of addiction have emphasized such constructs as incentive motivation and the subjective phenomenon of craving (Bindra, 1992; Cox and Klinger, 1988; Robinson and Berridge, 2000; Toates, 1994), with a focus on mesolimbic-dopamine system. In the field of addictions research, however, there is a growing interest in the role of cognitive factors and how they may influence the addictions process, as well as the likelihood of a successful treatment outcome. Studies thus far have provided preliminary data to support an association between cocaine use and impaired inhibitory control (i.e., impulsivity), with the ACC emerging as the likely neural substrate for the observed cognitive dysfunction. Evidence for a decision-making deficit in cocaine users is equivocal, but alterations in OFC activation, as well as the ACC and DLPC, suggest a disruption of frontal neural networks even in the absence of any overt performance decrement.

Despite these promising findings, the etiology of impaired "frontal" function and inhibitory control remains poorly delineated. For example, it is not known whether persons who engage in chronic cocaine use suffer from a preexisting neurocognitive impairment that places them at risk for addiction or whether the use of cocaine itself produces alterations in brain structure and function that ultimately result in the addiction despite an individuals' baseline susceptibility for developing such a disorder. It is likely that the truth lies somewhere between these two extremes. In other words, the majority of individuals who struggle with addiction likely carry an elevated premorbid risk due to impaired inhibitory function that is further exacerbated by alterations in neural function secondary to their prolonged use of the drug in question (e.g., cocaine). Beyond the etiology question lies a host of methodological issues that make interpretation of these intriguing findings even more challenging. Future studies would benefit from including greater detail regarding sample characteristics and drug use history (e.g., amount, duration, and method of use), as well as more comprehensive assessment of intellectual, neuropsychological, and psychosocial functioning. Such improvements in data collection and reporting would facilitate comparisons across studies and likely enhance our ability to isolate potentially critical cognitive mechanisms for successful treatment outcome. Given that prevention of relapse is a primary goal of treatment, there is clearly a need to better understand the role of impulsivity and decision-making in chronic drug use in order to tailor interventions to address these important factors.

REFERENCES

Adinoff, B., Devous, M. D., Cooper, D. B., et al. Resting regional cerebral blood flow and gambling task performance in cocaine-dependent subjects and healthy comparison subjects. *American Journal of Psychiatry* (2003) 160(10):1892-1894.

Ardila, A., Rosselli, M., and Strumwasser, S. Neuropsychological Deficits in Chronic Cocaine Abusers. *International Journal of Neuroscience* (1991) 57(1-2):73-79.

Baddeley, A., and Della Sala, S. Working Memory and Executive Control. In A. C. Roberts, T. W. Robbins, and L. Weiskrantz, eds., *The Prefrontal Cortex*. Oxford University Press, 1998.

Baddeley, A. D. *Working Memory*. Oxford University Press, 1986.

Bartzokis, G., Beckson, M., Hance, D. B., et al. Magnetic resonance imaging evidence of "silent" cerebrovascular toxicity in cocaine dependence. *Biological Psychiatry* (1999) 45(9):1203-1211.

Bartzokis, G., Lu, P. H., Beckson, M., et al. Abstinence from cocaine reduces high-risk responses on a gambling task. *Neuropsychopharmacology* (2000) 22(1):102-103.

Bauer, L. O. Eye-Movements in Recovering Substance-Abusers - a Prospective-Study. *Addictive Behaviors* (1993) 18(4):465-472.

Baylis, L. L., and Gaffan, D. Amygdalectomy and Ventromedial Prefrontal Ablation Produce Similar Deficits in Food Choice and in Simple Object Discrimination-Learning for an Unseen Reward. *Experimental Brain Research* (1991) 86(3):617-622.

Bechara, A., Damasio, A. R., Damasio, H., et al. Insensitivity to Future Consequences Following Damage to Human Prefrontal Cortex. *Cognition* (1994) 50(1-3):7-15.

Bechara, A., Damasio, H., and Damasio, A. R. Emotion, decision making and the orbitofrontal cortex. *Cerebral Cortex* (2000) 10(3):295-307.

Bechara, A., Damasio, H., Damasio, A. R., et al. Different contributions of the human amygdala and ventromedial prefrontal cortex to decision-making. *Journal of Neuroscience* (1999) 19(13):5473-5481.

Bechara, A., Dolan, S., Denburg, N., et al. Decision-malting deficits, linked to a dysfunctional ventromedial prefrontal cortex, revealed in alcohol and stimulant abusers. *Neuropsychologia* (2001) 39(4):376-389.

Bickel, W. K., and Marsch, L. A. Toward a behavioral economic understanding of drug dependence: delay discounting processes. *Addiction* (2001) 96(1):73-86.

Bickel, W. K., Odum, A. L., and Madden, G. J. Impulsivity and cigarette smoking: delay discounting in current, never, and ex-smokers. *Psychopharmacology* (1999) 146(4):447-454.

Biggins, C. A., MacKay, S., Clark, W., et al. Event-related potential evidence for frontal cortex effects of chronic cocaine dependence. *Biological Psychiatry* (1997) 42(6):472-485.

Bindra, D. Motivation, the Brain, and Psychological Theory. In S. Koch and D. Leary, eds., *A Century of Psychology as Science.* American Psychological Association, 1992.

Bolla, K. I., Cadet, J. L., and London, E. D. The neuropsychiatry of chronic cocaine abuse. *Journal of Neuropsychiatry & Clinical Neurosciences* (1998) 10(3):280-9.

Bolla, K. I., Eldreth, D. A., London, E. D., et al. Orbitofrontal cortex dysfunction in abstinent cocaine abusers performing a decision-making task. *Neuroimage* (2003) 19(3):1085-94.

Bolouri, M., and Small, G. Neuroimaging of hypoxia and cocaine-induced hippocampal stroke. *J Neuroimaging* (2004) 14(3):290-1.

Bonson, K., Grant, S., Contoreggi, C., et al. Neural systems and cue-induced cocaine craving. *Neuropsychopharmacology* (2002) 26:376-386.

Brandt, J., and Blysma, F. The neuropsychology of Huntington's disease. *Trends in Neurosciences* (1993) 9:118-120.

Butros, N., Uretsky, N., Bernston, G., et al. Effects of cocaine on sensory inhibition in rats: preliminary data. *Soc Biol Psychit* (1994) 36:242-248.

Butter, C. Perseveration in extinction and in discrimination reversal following selective frontal ablations in *Macaca mulatta. Psychiol Behav* (1968) 4:163-171.

Carter, C. S., MacDonald, A. W., Ross, L. L., et al. Anterior cingulate cortex activity and impaired self-monitoring of performance in patients with schizophrenia: An event-related fMRI study. *American Journal of Psychiatry* (2001) 158(9):1423-1428.

Childress, A. R., Mozley, P. D., McElgin, W., et al. Limbic activation during cue-induced cocaine craving. *American Journal of Psychiatry* (1999) 156(1):11-18.

Cox, W. M., and Klinger, E. A Motivational Model of Alcohol-Use. *Journal of Abnormal Psychology* (1988) 97(2):168-180.

Department of Health and Human Services. HHS releases 1993 household drug survery., *HHS News*, 1994.

Di Scalfani, V., Tolou-Shams, M., Price, L., et al. Neuropsychological performance of individuals dependent on crack-cocaine or crack-cocaine and alcohol, at 6 weeks and 6 months of abstinence. *Drug and Alcohol Dependence* (2002) 66:161-171.

Dias, R., Robbins, T. W., and Roberts, A. C. Dissociation in prefrontal cortex of affective and attentional shifts. *Nature* (1996a) 380(6569):69-72.

Dias, R., Robbins, T. W., and Roberts, A. C. Primate analogue of the Wisconsin Card Sorting Test: Effects of excitotoxic lesions of the prefrontal cortex in the marmoset. *Behavioral Neuroscience* (1996b) 110(5):872-886.

Ernst, M., Grant, S. J., London, E. D., et al. Decision making in adolescents with behavior disorders and adults with substance abuse. *American Journal of Psychiatry* (2003) 160(1):33-40.

Fillmore, M. T., and Rush, C. R. Alcohol effects on inhibitory and activational response strategies in the acquisition of alcohol and other reinforcers: Priming the motivation to drink. *Journal of Studies on Alcohol* (2001) 62(5):646-656.

Fillmore, M. T., and Rush, C. R. Impaired inhibitory control of behavior in chronic cocaine users. *Drug and Alcohol Dependence* (2002) 66(3):265-273.

Fillmore, M. T., Rush, C. R., and Hays, L. Acute effects of oral cocaine on inhibitory control of behavior in humans. *Drug and Alcohol Dependence* (2002) 67(2):157-167.

Fillmore, M. T., and Vogel-Sprott, M. An alcohol model of impaired inhibitory control and its treatment in humans. *Experimental and Clinical Psychopharmacology* (1999) 7(1):49-55.

Fillmore, M. T., and Vogel-Sprott, M. Response inhibition under alcohol: Effects of cognitive and motivational conflict. *Journal of Studies on Alcohol* (2000) 61(2):239-246.

Fishbein, D. Neuropsychological function, drug abuse, and violence - A conceptual framework. *Criminal Justice and Behavior* (2000) 27(2):139-159.

Franklin, T. R., Acton, P. D., Maldjian, J. A., et al. Decreased gray matter concentration in the insular, orbitofrontal, cingulate, and temporal cortices of cocaine patients. *Biological Psychiatry* (2002) 51(2):134-142.

Frishman, W., DelVecchio, A., Sanal, S., et al. Cardiovascular manifestations of substance abuse: part 2: alcohol, amphetamines, heroin, cannabis, and caffeine. *Heart Dis* (2003) 5(4):253-71.

Fuchs, R. A., Evans, K. A., Parker, M. C., et al. Differential involvement of the core and shell subregions of the nucleus accumbens in conditioned cue-induced reinstatement of cocaine seeking in rats. *Psychopharmacology* (2004) 176(3-4):459-465.

Goldstein, R. Z., Leskovjan, A. C., Hoff, A. L., et al. Severity of neuropsychological impairment in cocaine and alcohol addiction: association with metabolism in the prefrontal cortex. *Neuropsychologia* (2004) 42(11):1447-58.

Goldstein, R. Z., Volkow, N. D., Wang, G. J., et al. Addiction changes orbitofrontal gyrus function: involvement in response inhibition. *Neuroreport* (2001) 12(11):2595-2599.

Grant, S., Contoreggi, C., and London, E. D. Drug abusers show impaired performance in a laboratory test of decision making. *Neuropsychologia* (2000) 38(8):1180-1187.

Grant, S., London, E. D., Newlin, D. B., et al. Activation of memory circuits during cue-elicited cocaine craving. *Proceedings of the National Academy of Sciences of the United States of America* (1996) 93(21):12040-12045.

Herrstein, R., and Prelec, D. A theory of addiction. In G. Lowenstein and J. Elster, eds., *Choice over Time.* Russell Sage Press, 1992.

Hester, R., and Garavan, H. Executive dysfunction in cocaine addiction: Evidence for discordant frontal, cingulate, and cerebellar activity. *The Journal of Neuroscience* (2004) 24(49):11017-11022.

Heyman, G. M., and Dunn, B. Decision biases and persistent illicit drug use: an experimental study of distributed choice and addiction. *Drug and Alcohol Dependence* (2002) 67(2):193-203.

Hoff, A. L., Riordan, H., Morris, L., et al. Effects of crack cocaine on neurocognitive function. *Psychiatry Research* (1996) 60(2-3):167-176.

Horner, B., Scheibe, K., and Stine, S. Cocaine abuse and attention-deficit hyperactivity disorder: Implications of adult symptomatology. *Psychology of Addictive Behaviors* (1996) 10(1):55-60.

Huber, S., and Shuttleworth, E. Huntington's disease. In J. Cummings, ed., *Subcortical Dementia.* Oxford University Press, 1990.

Jentsch, J. D., and Taylor, J. R. Impulsivity resulting from frontostriatal dysfunction in drug abuse: implications for the control of behavior by reward-related stimuli. *Psychopharmacology* (1999) 146(4):373-390.

Kaufman, J. N., Ross, T. J., Stein, E. A., et al. Cingulate hypoactivity in cocaine users during a GO-NOGO task as revealed by event-related functional magnetic resonance imaging. *Journal of Neuroscience* (2003) 23(21):7839-7843.

Keller, T. M., and Chappell, E. T. Spontaneous acute subdural hematoma precipitated by cocaine abuse: Case report. *Surgical Neurology* (1997) 47(1):12-14.

Kirby, K., Petry, N., and Bickel, W. K. Heroin addicts have higher discount rates for delayed rewards than non-drug using controls. *J Exp Psychol* (1999) 128:78-87.

Konzen, J., Levine, S., and Garcia, J. Vasospasm and thrombus formation as possible mechanism of stroke related to alkaloidal cocaine. *Stroke* (1995) 26(6):1114-8.

LeLand, D., Richardson, J., Vankov, A., et al. Decision-making and associated ERPS in low- and high-dependence smokers performing the Iowa gambling task. *Society for Neuroscience Abstracts* (1998) 24:1175.

Levin, H. S., Hanten, G., Zhang, L. F., et al. Selective impairment of inhibition after TBI in children. *Journal of Clinical and Experimental Neuropsychology* (2004) 26(5):589-597.

Logan, G. On the ability to inhibit thought and action: a users' guide to the stop-signal paradigm. In D. Dagenbach and T. Carr, eds., *Inhibitory Processes in Attention, Memory, and Language.* Academic Press, 1994.

Luborsky, L., McKay, J., Mercer, D., et al. To use or refuse cocaine: The deciding factors. *J Substance Abuse* (1995) 7:293-310.

Madden, G. J., Bickel, W. K., and Jacobs, E. A. Discounting of delayed rewards in opioid-dependent outpatients: Exponential or hyperbolic discounting functions? *Experimental and Clinical Psychopharmacology* (1999) 7(3):284-293.

Manschreck, T. C., Schneyer, M. L., Weisstein, C. C., et al. Freebase Cocaine and Memory. *Comprehensive Psychiatry* (1990) 31(4):369-375.

Matochik, J. A., London, E. D., Eldreth, D. A., et al. Frontal cortical tissue composition in abstinent cocaine abusers: a magnetic resonance imaging study. *Neuroimage* (2003) 19(3):1095-1102.

Mazas, C. A., Finn, P. R., and Steinmetz, J. E. Decision-making biases, antisocial personality, and early-onset alcoholism. *Alcoholism-Clinical and Experimental Research* (2000) 24(7):1036-1040.

Mitchell, S. H. Measures of impulsivity in cigarette smokers and non-smokers. *Psychopharmacology* (1999) 146(4):455-464.

Mitchell, S. L., and Lawson, F. M. E. Decision-making for long-term tube-feeding in cognitively impaired elderly people. *Canadian Medical Association Journal* (1999) 160(12):1705-1709.

Moeller, F. G., Barratt, E. S., Fischer, C. J., et al. P300 event-related potential amplitude and impulsivity in cocaine-dependent subjects. *Neuropsychobiology* (2004) 50(2):167-173.

Moeller, F. G., Hasan, K. M., Steinberg, J. L., et al. Reduced anterior corpus callosum white matter integrity is related to increased impulsivity and reduced discriminability in cocaine-dependent subjects: Diffusion tensor imaging. *Neuropsychopharmacology* (2005) 30(3):610-617.

Monterosso, J., Ehrman, R., Napier, K. L., et al. Three decision-making tasks in cocaine-dependent patients: do they measure the same construct? *Addiction* (2001) 96(12):1825-1837.

Neimann, J., Haapanieme, H., and Hillbom, M. Neurological complications of drug abuse: pathophysiological mechanisms. *Eur J Neurol* (2000) 7(6):595-606.

Nigg, J. T. The ADHD response-inhibition deficit as measured by the stop task: Replication with DSM-IV combined type, extension, and qualification. *Journal of Abnormal Child Psychology* (1999) 27(5):393-402.

Nolte, K., Brass, L., and Fletterick, C. Intracranial hemorrhage associated with cocaine abuse: a prospective autopsy study. *Neurology* (1996) 46(5):1291-6.

O'Keeffe, F., Dockree, P., and Robertson, I. Poor insight in traumatic brain injury mediated by impaired error processing? Evidence from electrodermal activity. *Cognitive Brain Research* (2004) 22(1):101-112.

O'Malley, S., Adamse, M., Heaton, R., et al. Neuropsychological impairment in chronic cocaine abusers. *Am J Drug Alcohol Abuse* (1992) 18:131-144.

O'Malley, S., and Gawin, F. Abstinence symptomatology and neuropsychological impairment in chronic cocaine abusers. *NIDA Research Monographs* (1990) 101:179-190.

Oosterlaan, J., and Sergeant, J. A. Inhibition in ADHD, aggressive, and anxious children: A biologically based model of child psychopathology. *Journal of Abnormal Child Psychology* (1996) 24(1):19-36.

Petry, N. Substance abuse, pathological gambling, and impulsiveness. *Drug and Alcohol Dependence* (2001) 63:29-38.

Quay, H. Psychopathic personality as pathological stimulation seeking. *Am J Psychiatry* (1965) 122:180-183.

Qureshi, A. I., Suri, M. F. K., Guterman, L. R., et al. Cocaine use and the likelihood of nonfatal myocardial infarction and stroke - Data from the Third National Health and Nutrition Examination survey. *Circulation* (2001) 103(4):502-506.

Reavis, R., Overman, W., Hendrix, S., et al. Possible double dissociation of function between adult males and females in two brain system. *Society for Neuroscience Abstracts* (1998) 24:1177.

Reding, M., Gardner, C., Hainline, B., et al. Neuropsychiatric problems interfering with inpatient stroke rehabilitation. *J Neurol Rehab* (1993) 7(1):1-7.

Reeves, R. R., Mcwilliams, M. E., and Fitzgerald, M. Cocaine-Induced Ischemic Cerebral Infarction Mistaken for a Psychiatric Syndrome. *Southern Medical Journal* (1995) 88(3):352-354.

Roberts, L. A., and Bauer, L. O. Reaction-Time during Cocaine Versus Alcohol-Withdrawal - Longitudinal Measures of Visual and Auditory Suppression. *Psychiatry Research* (1993) 46(3):229-237.

Robinson, T. E., and Berridge, K. C. The psychology and neurobiology of addiction: an incentive-sensitization view. *Addiction* (2000) 95(8):S91-S117.

Rolls, E. T. The orbitofrontal cortex and reward. *Cerebral Cortex* (2000) 10(3):284-294.

Rolls, E. T., and Baylis, L. L. Gustatory, Olfactory, and Visual Convergence within the Primate Orbitofrontal Cortex. *Journal of Neuroscience* (1994) 14(9):5437-5452.

Rosenkilde, C. E. Functional-Heterogeneity of the Prefrontal Cortex in the Monkey - Review. *Behavioral and Neural Biology* (1979) 25(3):301-345.

Rotheram-Fuller, E., Shoptaw, S., Berman, S., et al. Impaired performance in a test of decision-making by opiate-dependent tobacco smokers. *Drug and Alcohol Dependence* (2004) 73:79-86.

Rubia, K., Smith, A. B., Brammer, M. J., et al. Right inferior prefrontal cortex mediates response inhibition while mesial prefrontal cortex is responsible for error detection. *Neuroimage* (2003) 20(1):351-358.

Salamone, J. D., Cousins, M. S., and Snyder, B. J. Behavioral functions of nucleus accumbens dopamine: Empirical and conceptual problems with the anhedonia hypothesis. *Neuroscience and Biobehavioral Reviews* (1997) 21(3):341-359.

Salmon, D., Heindel, W., and Hamilton, J. Cognitive Abilities Mediated by Frontal-Subcortical Circuits. In D. Lichter and J. Cummings, eds., *Frontal-Subcortical Circuits in Psychiatric and Neurologic Disorders*. The Guilford Press, 2001.

Schachar, R., Tannock, R., and Marriott, M. Deficient inhibitory control in attention deficit hyperactivity disorder. *J Abnorm Child Psychol* (1995) 23:411-437.

Sevy. (1990).

Sevy, S., Kay, S. R., Opler, L. A., et al. Significance of Cocaine History in Schizophrenia. *Journal of Nervous and Mental Disease* (1990) 178(10):642-648.

Shallice, T. Specific Impairments of Planning. *Philosophical Transactions of the Royal Society of London Series B-Biological Sciences* (1982) 298(1089):199-209.

Strickland, T. L., Miller, B. L., Kowell, A., et al. Neurobiology of cocaine-induced organic brain impairment: Contributions from functional neuroimaging. *Neuropsychology Review* (1998) 8(1):1-9.

Strickland, T. L., and Stein, R. Cocaine-Induced Cerebrovascular Impairment - Challenges to Neuropsychological Assessment. *Neuropsychology Review* (1995) 5(1):69-79.

Su, J., Li, J., Li, W., et al. Cocaine induces apoptosis in cerebral vascular muscle cells: potential roles in strokes and brain damage. *Eur J Pharmacol* (2003) 482(1-3):61-6.

Taylor, J. R. Neural mechanisms of the potentiation of conditioned reinforcement by psychomotor stimulant drugs, *Department of Experimental Psychology*. University of Cambridge, 1985.

Toates, F. Comparing Motivational Systems-An Incentive Motivation Perspective. In C. Legg and D. Booth, eds., *Appetite: Neural and Behavioural Bases*. Oxford University Press, 1994.

Tolat, R. D., O'Dell, M. W., Golamco-Estrella, S. P., et al. Cocaine-associated stroke: three cases and rehabilitation considerations. *Brain Injury* (2000) 14(4):383-391.

Tucker, K. A., Potenza, M. N., Beauvais, J. E., et al. Perfusion abnormalities and decision making in cocaine dependence. *Biological Psychiatry* (2004) 56(7):527-530.

Tversky, A., and Kahneman, D. The Framing of Decisions and the Psychology of Choice. *Science* (1981) 211(4481):453-458.

Ursu, S., van Veen, V., Siegle, G., et al. Executive control and self-evaluation in obsessive-compulsive disorder: an event-related fMRI study. Presented at conference, "Cognitive Neuroscience Society Meeting." New York, NY, 2001.

Vallee, J. N., Crozier, S., Guillevin, R., et al. Acute basilar artery occlusion treated by thromboaspiration in a cocaine and ecstasy abuser. *Neurology* (2003) 61(6):839-841.

van Zomeren, A., and Brouwer, W. *Clinical Neuropsychology of Attention.* Oxford University Press, 1994.

Velasquez, E., Anand, R., Newman, W., et al. Cardiovascular complications associated with cocaine use. *J La State Med Soc* (2004) 156(6):302-10.

Volkow, N. D., Ding, Y. S., Fowler, J. S., et al. Cocaine addiction: Hypothesis derived from imaging studies with PET. *Journal of Addictive Diseases* (1996) 15(4):55-71.

Volkow, N. D., Fowler, J. S., and Wang, G. J. Imaging studies on the role of dopamine in cocaine reinforcement and addiction in humans. *Journal of Psychopharmacology* (1999) 13(4):337-345.

Vuchinich, R. E., and Simpson, C. A. Hyperbolic temporal discounting in social drinkers and problem drinkers. *Experimental and Clinical Psychopharmacology* (1998) 6(3):292-305.

Wang, G. J., Volkow, N. D., Fowler, J. S., et al. Regional brain metabolic activation during craving elicited by recall of previous drug experiences. *Life Sciences* (1999) 64(9):775-784.

Weissenborn, R., Robbins, T. W., and Everitt, B. Effects of medial prefrontal or anterior cingulate cortex lesions on responding for cocaine under fixed-ratio and second-order schedules of reinforcement in rats. *Psychopharmacology* (1997) 134:242-257.

Whyte, J., Fleming, M., Polansky, M., et al. The effects of visual distraction following traumatic brain injury. *Journal of the International Neuropsychological Society* (1998) 4(2):127-136.

Wilson, K., and Saukkonen, J. Acute respiratory failure from abused substances. *J Intensive Care Med* (2004) 19(4):183-93.

World Health Organization. International statistical classification of diseases and related health problems (10th revision). 1992.

Zuckerman, M. *Sensation Seeking: Beyond the Optimal Level of Arousal.* Lawrence Erlbaum, 1979.

Zuckerman, M. *Behavioral Expressions and Biosocial Bases of Sensation Seeking.* Cambridge University Press, 1994.

In: Psychology of Decision Making
Editor: Paul M. Garrison

ISBN 978-1-60021-869-9
© Nova Science Publishers, Inc.

Chapter 4

EXPERT SYSTEMS, GIS, AND SPATIAL DECISION MAKING: CURRENT PRACTICES AND NEW TRENDS

Khalid Eldrandaly[*]
Assistant Professor of Computer Information Systems
Interim Head of Information Systems and Technology Department
College of Computers and Informatics
Zagazig University, Egypt

ABSTRACT

Spatial decision making is a routine activity that is common to individuals and to organizations. Spatial decision making problems are multi-facetted challenges. Not only do they often involve numerous technical requirements, but they may also contain economical, social, environmental and political dimensions that could have conflicting objectives. Solving these complex problems requires an integrative use of information, domain specific knowledge and effective means of communication. Although geographic information systems (GIS) and expert systems (ES) have played important roles in solving spatial decision problems, each of these tools has its own limitations in dealing with such problems. For instance, GIS is a great tool for handling physical suitability analysis. However, it has limited capabilities of incorporating the decision maker's preferences, experiences, intuitions, and judgments into the problem-solving process. Expert Systems, which is capable of addressing heuristic analysis, lacks the capabilities of handling spatial data/knowledge that are crucial to spatial analysis. The need for improvement of the performance of these tools in solving highly complex spatial decision-making problems has promoted the integration of GIS and ES. Numerous mechanisms enabling interoperability between GIS and ES have appeared over the years. Examples range from primitive solutions such as simple, loose coupling to much more sophisticated approaches, such as COM technology and Ontology. In this study, both primitive and advanced techniques for integrating GIS and ES are discussed.

---
[*] Khalid Eldrandaly: khalid_eldrandaly@yahoo.com

Keywords: Expert Systems, GIS, Spatial Decision Making, Systems Integration Techniques, Interoperability.

1. INTRODUCTION

Almost everything that happens, happens somewhere. Because location is so important, it is an issue in many of the problems society must solve (Longley et al. 2005). Spatial decision making is a routine activity that is common to individuals and to organizations. People make decisions influenced by location when they choose a store to shop, a route to drive, or a neighborhood for a place to live, to name but a few. Organizations are not much different in this respect. They take into account the realities of spatial organization when selecting a site, choosing a land development strategy, allocating resources for public health, and managing infrastructures for transportation or public utilities (Jankowski and Nyerges 2001). Spatial decision making is a highly complex process of choosing among alternatives to attain an objective or a set of objectives under constraints. It can be a structured process involving problems with standard solution procedures, or an unstructured process consisting of problems with no clear-cut solution procedures, or even semi-structured problems for which combinations of standard procedures and individual judgments have to be used to find a solution. All these processes generally involve voluminous spatial and aspatial information, structured and unstructured knowledge, and human valuation and judgment (Leung 1997). Spatial decision-making problems are multi-facetted challenges. Not only do they often involve numerous technical requirements, but they may also contain economical, social, environmental and political dimensions that could have conflicting objectives. Malczewski (1999) defined the main characteristics of spatial decision problems as follows:

1) A large number of decision alternatives.
2) The outcomes or consequences of the decision alternatives are spatially variable.
3) Each alternative is evaluated on the basis of multiple criteria.
4) Some of the criteria may be qualitative while others may be quantitative.
5) There are typically more than one decision maker (or interest group) involved in the decision-making process.
6) The decision makers have different preferences with respect to the relative importance of evaluation criteria and decision consequences.
7) The decisions are often surrounded by uncertainty.

Solving this complex type of decision problems usually requires an intelligent and integrative use of information, domain specific knowledge and effective means of communication (Leung 1997). Although geographic information systems (GIS) and expert systems (ES) have played important roles in solving spatial decision problems, each of these tools has its own limitations in dealing with such problems. For instance, GIS is a great tool for handling physical suitability analysis. However, it has limited capabilities of incorporating the decision maker's preferences and heuristics into the problem-solving process. ES, which is capable of addressing heuristic analysis, lacks the capabilities of handling spatial data/knowledge that are crucial to spatial analysis. The limitations inherent in both technologies have prompted a number of researchers and practitioners to suggest that the spatial decision-making process would be better served by the integration of both. Numerous mechanisms enabling interoperability between GIS and ES have appeared over the years. Examples range from primitive (although widely used) solutions such as simple, loose coupling to much more sophisticated approaches, such as COM technology. In the following sections, a brief description of GIS is presented, and the different techniques for integrating GIS and ES are discussed.

2. GEOGRAPHIC INFORMATION SYSTEMS

2.1. Brief History of GIS

The day-to-day necessity of dealing with space and spatial relationships represents one of the basic facets of human society. Geographic information systems evolved as a means of assembling and analyzing diverse spatial data. These systems evolved from centuries of mapmaking and the compilation of registers. The earliest known maps were drawn on parchment to show the gold mines at Coptes during the reign (1292- 1225 B.C.) of Rameses II of Egypt. At a later date, the Greeks acquired cartographic skills and compiled the realistic maps. The Greek mathematician, astronomer, and geographer Eratosthenes (ca. 276-194 B.C.) laid the foundations of the scientific cartography i.e., the science, art, and technology of making, using, and studying maps. The Arabs were the leading cartographers of the Middle Ages. The Arabian geographer Al-Idrisi made a map of the world in 1154. European cartography degenerated as the Roman Empire fell. Until the nineteenth century, geographical information was used mostly for trade and exploration by land and sea and for tax collection and military operations. New needs arose in step with evolving infrastructures, such as roads, railways, etc., because planning these facilities required information about the terrain beyond that commonly available. As planning advanced, specialized maps became more common. In 1838, the Irish government compiled a series of maps for the use of railway engineers, which may be regarded as the first manual geographic information system. By the late 1950s and early 1960s, second–generation computers using transistors became available and the first computerized geographic information system appeared. The first GIS was the Canada Geographic Information System (CGIS), designed in the mid 1960s as a computerized map measuring system. CGIS was developed by Roger Tomlinson and colleagues for Canadian land inventory. This project pioneered much technology and introduced the term GIS. The rapid development of powerful computers led to an increasing acceleration in the use of GIS. In the 1970s and 1980s, various systems evolved to replace manual cartographic computations. Workable production systems became available in the late 1970s. GIS really began to take off in the early 1980s, when the price of computing hardware had fallen to a level that could sustain a significant software industry and cost-effective applications. The market for GIS software continued to grow, computers continued to fall in price, and increase in power, and the software industry has been growing ever since (Clarke 2001;Bernhardsen 2002; Longley et al. 2005).

2.2. Definitions of GIS

Many definitions of GIS have been suggested over the years in different areas and disciplines. All GIS definitions recognize that spatial data are unique because geographic location is an important attribute of activities, policies, strategies, and plans. Following are some of these definitions:

Ducker (1979) defined GIS as " a special case of information systems where the database consists of observations on spatially distributed features, activities or events, which are definable in space as points, lines, or areas. A geographic information system manipulates data about these points, lines, and areas to retrieve data for ad hoc quires and analysis".

Star and Estes (1990) defined GIS as "an information system that is designed to work with data referenced by spatial or geographic coordinates. In other words, a GIS is both a database system with specific capabilities for spatially–referenced data, as well as a set of operations for working with the data".

Burrough and McDonnell (1998) defined GIS as "a powerful set of tools for storing and retrieving at will, transforming and displaying spatial data from the real world for a particular set of purposes".

Clarke (2001) defined GIS as "an automated system for the capture, storage, retrieval, analysis, and display of spatial data".

Davis (2001) defined GIS as "A computer–based technology and methodology for collecting, managing, analyzing, modeling, and presenting geographic data for a wide range of applications."

Worboys and Duckham (2004) defined GIS as "A computer-based information system that enables capture, modeling, storage, retrieval, sharing, manipulation, analysis, and presentation of geographically referenced data".

Whereas *Longley et al. (2005)* defined GIS as "A special class of information systems that keep track not only of events, activities, and things, but also of where these events, activities, and things happen or exist."

2.3. Major Components of GIS

Any functional GIS has six major components as shown in figure 1 (Zeiler 1999; Longley et al.2005). These components are:

1) *People* - People are the most important component of a GIS. People must develop the procedures and define the tasks the GIS will perform. People can often overcome shortfalls in other components of the GIS, but the opposite is not true. The best software and computers in the world cannot compensate for incompetence.
2) *Data* - Data, which are quite critical to GIS, contains both geographic and attribute data. The availability and accuracy of data affect the results of queries and analysis.
3) *Hardware* - Hardware is the devices that the user interacts directly in carrying out GIS operations, such as the computer, digitizer, plotter, etc. Hardware capabilities affect processing speed, ease of use, and the types of available output.
4) *Software* - This includes not only GIS software, but also various database, drawing, statistical, imaging, and other software programs.

5) *Procedures* - GIS analysis requires well-defined, consistent methods to produce correct and reproducible results.
6) *Network* - Network allows rapid communication and sharing digital information. The internet has proven very popular as a vehicle for delivering GIS applications.

Figure 1. Basic components of GIS (reproduced with permission, John Wiley and Sons, Ltd. Longley et al., "Geographic Information Systems and Science", 2nd edition, 2005).

2.4. GIS Data

The ability of GIS to handle and process geographically referenced data distinguishes GIS from other information systems. Geographically referenced data describe both the location and characteristics of spatial features on the earth's surface. GIS therefore involves two geographic data components: spatial data relate to the geometry of spatial features and attribute data give the information about the spatial features. A GIS organizes and stores information about the world as a collection of thematic layers that can be linked by geography. Each layer contains features having similar attributes, like streets or cities that are located within the same geographic extent. This simple but extremely powerful and versatile concept has proven invaluable for solving many real-world problems—from tracking delivery vehicles to recording details of planning applications to modeling global atmospheric circulation (Bolstad 2002). Data collection is one of the most time-consuming and expensive GIS activities. There are many diverse sources of geographic data and many methods available to enter them into a GIS such as digitizing and scanning of maps, image data, direct data entry using GPS and surveying instruments, and transfer of data from existing sources (Bernhardsen 2002; Bolstad 2002; Longley et al. 2005).

2.5. GIS Data Models

The real world is far too complex to model in its entirety within any information system, so only specific areas of interest should be selected for inclusion within a given GIS application. Once a particular application area has been chosen, the next task is to select those features which are relevant to the application and to capture information about their locations and characteristics. In order to bring the real world into GIS, one has to make use of simplified models of the real world. A geographic data model is a set of constructs for describing and representing selected aspects of the real world in a computer. There are two basic data models used in GIS; these models are (Zeiler 1999; Davis 2001; Bolstad 2002; Bernhardsen 2002; Longley et al. 2005):

Vector Data Model: The basis of the vector model is the assumption that the real world can be divided into clearly defined elements (features) each element consists of an identifiable object with its own geometry of points, lines, or areas. Vector data represents the shapes of features precisely and compactly as an ordered set of coordinates with associated attributes. Points (e.g., wells) are recorded as single coordinate pairs, lines (e.g., roads) as a series of ordered coordinate pairs, and polygons (e.g., census tracts) as one or more line segments that close to form a polygon area. Vector models are particularly useful for representing and storing discrete features such as buildings, pipes, or parcel boundaries.

Raster Data Model: In a raster model, the world is represented as a surface that is divided into a regular grid of cells. The x, y coordinate of at least one corner of the raster are known, so it can be located in geographic space. Raster models are useful for storing and analyzing data that is continuous across an area. Each cell contains a value that can represent membership in a class or a category, a measurement, or an interpreted value. Raster data includes images and grids. Images, such as an aerial photograph, a satellite image, or a scanned map, are often used for generating GIS data. Grids represent derived data and are often used for analysis and modeling. They can be created form sample points or by converting vector data. The smaller the cell size for the raster layer, the higher the resolution and the more detailed the map. Both vector and raster data models are shown in figure 2.

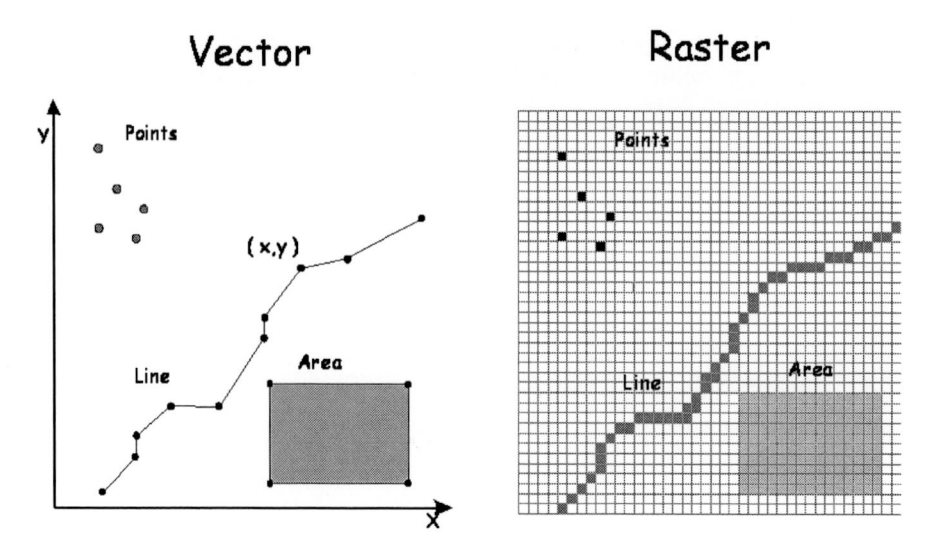

Figure 2. Vector and Raster Data Models (adapted from Bolstad 2002).

2.6. GIS Functions

Any geographic information system should be capable of six fundamental operations in order to be useful for finding solutions to real-world problems. A GIS should be able to capture, store, query, analyze, display, and output data (Zeiler 1999, Bolstad 2002).

Capturing data - Data describing geographic features is contained in a geographic database. The geographic database is an expensive and long-lived component of a GIS, thus data entry is an important consideration. A GIS must provide methods for entering geographic (coordinate) and tabular (attribute) data. The more input methods available, the more versatile the GIS.

Storing data - There are two basic models used for geographic data storage: vector and raster. A GIS should be able to store both types of geographic data.

Querying data - A GIS must provide tools for finding specific features based on their location or attributes. Queries, which are often created as logical statements or expressions, are used to select features on the map and their records in the database.

Analyzing data - Geographic analysis usually involves more than one geographic dataset and requires working through a series of steps to reach a final result. A GIS must be able to analyze the spatial relationships among multiple datasets to answer questions and solve problems. There are many types of geographic analysis. The two common types of geographic analysis are described below:

A. *Proximity analysis* - Proximity analysis uses the distance between features to answer questions like:

1) How many houses lie within 100 meters of this water main?
2) What is the total number of customers within 10 kilometers of this store?
3) What proportion of the alfalfa crop is within 500 meters of the well?

GIS technology often uses a process called buffering, defining a zone of a specified distance around features, to determine the proximity relationship between features.

B. *Overlay analysis* - The integration of different data layers involves a process called overlay. At its simplest, this could be a visual operation, but analytical operations require one or more data layers to be joined physically (i.e., combined into one layer in the database). Overlay analysis could be used to integrate data on soils, slope, and vegetation or land ownership data with tax assessment data.

Displaying data - A GIS also needs tools for displaying geographic features using a variety of symbology. For many types of geographic analysis operations, the end result is best visualized as a map, graph, or report.

Outputting data - Sharing the results of your geographic labor is one of the primary justifications for spending resources on a GIS. Taking displays created through a GIS (maps, graphs, and reports) and outputting them into a distributable format is a great way to do this. The more output options a GIS can offer, the greater the potential for reaching the right audience with the right information.

2.7. GIS Software

GIS software is constructed on the top of basic computer operating capabilities such as security, file management, peripheral drivers, printing, and display management to provide a controlled environment for geographic information collection, management, analysis, and interpretation. The GIS software employed in a GIS project has a controlling impact on the type of studies that can be undertaken and the results that can be obtained. There are also far reaching implications for user productivity and project costs. Today, there are many types of GIS software product to choose from and a number of ways to configure implementations. Longley et al. (2005) classify the main GIS software packages into four main types as follows:

Desktop GIS software: Desktop GIS software owes its origins to the personal computer and Microsoft Windows operating system and is considered the mainstream workhorses of GIS today. It provides personal productivity tools for a wide Variety of users across a broad cross section of industries. The desktop GIS software category includes a range of options from simple viewers (such as ESRI ArcReader, Intergraph GeoMedia Viewer and MapInfo ProViewer) to desktop mapping and GIS software systems (such as Autodesk Map 3D, ESRI ArcView, Intergraph GeoMedia, and MapInfo Professional), and at the high-end, full-featured professional editor/analysis systems (such as ESRI ArcGIS ArcInfo, Intergraph GeoMedia Professional, and GE Smallworld GIS). Desktop GIS software prices typically range from $1000- $20000 per user.

Server GIS: Server GIS runs on a computer server that can handle concurrent processing requests from a range of networked clients. Initially, it focused on display and query applications, but now offers mapping, routing, data publishing, and suitability mapping. Third generation server GIS offers complete GIS functionality in a multiuser server environment. Examples of server GIS include AutoDesk MapGuide, ESRI ArcGIS Server, GE Spatial Application Server, Intergraph GeoMedia Webmap, and MapInfo MapXtreme. The cost of server GIS products varies from around $5000-25000, for small to medium-sized systems, to well beyond for large multifunction, and multiuser systems.

Developer GIS: Developer GIS are toolkits of GIS functions (components) that a reasonably knowledgeable programmer can use to build a specific-purpose GIS application. They are of interest to developers because such components can be used to create highly customized and optimized applications that can either stand alone or can be embedded with other software systems. Examples of component GIS products include Blue Marble Geographics GeoObjects, ESRI ArcGIS Engine, and MapInfo MapX. Most of the developer GIS products from mainstream vendors are built on top of Microsoft's COM and .Net technology standards, but there are several cross platform choices (e.g., ESRI ArcGIS Engine) and several Java-based toolkits (e.g., ObjectFX Spatial FX). The typical cost for a developer GIS product is $1000 - $5000 for developer kit and $100-500 per deployed application.

Hand-held GIS: Hand-held GIS are lightweight systems designed for mobile and field use. A very recent development is the availability of hand-held software on high-end so-called 'smartphones' which can deal with comparatively large amounts of data and sophisticated applications. These systems usually operate in a mixed connected/disconnected environment and so can make active use of data and software applications held on the server and accessed over a wireless telephone network. Examples of Hand-held GIS include

Autodesk OmSite, ESRI ArcPad, and Intergraph Intelliwhere. Costs are typically around $400-$600.

3. GIS, EXPERT SYSTEMS AND SPATIAL DECISION MAKING

The ultimate aim of GIS is to support spatial decision-making. A GIS system typically has the following capabilities (Zhu and Healey 1992):

1. Describing spatial problems and their spatial relationships.
2. Storing and managing large quantities of complex and heterogeneous spatial data.
3. Using geographical data models for structuring the available information.
4. Providing spatial data handling and displaying facilities.

Malczewski (1999) analyzed the GIS capabilities for supporting spatial decisions in the context of Simon's decision making process framework which divides any decision making process into three major phases: *intelligence* (is there a problem or opportunity for change?), *design* (what are the alternatives?), and Choice (which alternative is best?). Malczewski mentioned the following conclusions:

1. Commercially available GIS systems tend to focus on supporting the first phase of the decision- making process through its ability to integrate, explore, and effectively present information in a comprehensive form to the decision makers,
2. These available GIS systems have limited capabilities of supporting the design and choice phases of the decision- making process, and
3. These systems provide a very static modeling environment and thus reduce their scope as decision support tools- especially in the context of problems involving collaborative decision-making.

Today, geographic information systems incorporate many state-of-the-art principles such as relational database management, powerful graphics algorithms, and elementary spatial operations such as proximity analysis, overlay analysis, interpolation, zoning and network analysis. However, the lack of analytical modeling functionality and the low level of intelligence in terms of knowledge representation and processing are widely recognized as major deficiencies of current systems (Fischer 1994).

Expert systems are fast becoming the leading edge of artificial intelligence (AI) technology because of the need for such systems in commercial and scientific enterprises and also because AI technology has evolved to the point where expert systems development has become well understood and feasible in many domains. An expert system is a computer program that embodies the expertise of one or more experts in some domain and applies this knowledge to make useful inferences for the user of the system (Hayes-Roth et al 1983). Firebaugh (1988) defined expert systems as" a class of computer programs that can advise, analyze, categorize, communicate, consult, design, diagnose, explain, explore, forecast, form concepts, identify, interpret, justify, learn, manage, monitor plan, present, retrieve, schedule, test, and tutor. They address problems normally thought to require human specialists for their solution." Expert systems (ES) perform decision-making tasks by reasoning using domain specific rules that have been judged by an expert in his domain to be true. They are best suited for ill-structured problems. The distinctive strength of ES can be summarized as (Jackson 1990):

1. Handling imprecise data, incomplete and inexact knowledge.
2. Exploiting knowledge at the right time.
3. Explaining and justifying the reasoning that lead to a conclusion.
4. Changing or expanding knowledge relatively easily.

There is ample scope for applying ES technology in decision making processes. For example, we may use knowledge representation techniques to characterize decision-making domains, use heuristic methods to generate and evaluate decision options, apply inference and reasoning to explain and justify decisions, etc.

Spatial decision making with expert systems began in the late of 1980s. Many expert systems have been developed to solve various site selection problems that are heavily dependent on human judgment and experience. These systems use symbolic knowledge to construct human understanding of problems in the area of site selection and evaluation. Because symbolic knowledge is not well suited to describe the spatial nature of site selection problems, expert systems lack a mechanism to derive solutions based on spatial knowledge (or knowledge about positional and topological characteristics) of different sites. Spatial knowledge is critical to spatial reasoning and decision making in many site selection applications (Jia 2000). Unfortunately, current expert systems can't handle spatial knowledge. They don't have an appropriate method to encode and represent the spatial nature of knowledge. Furthermore, they can't deal with locators, spatial relations, and spatial reference actions involved in spatial knowledge. Zhu and Healey (1992) asserted that expert systems technology alone does not adequately support spatial decision making because it has the following limitations:

1. Spatial decision making requires large volumes of spatial data. These data mainly reside in GIS and not in ES. ES lack facilities for handling large-scale data sets.
2. Expert systems are concentrated on symbolic reasoning and do not provide good arithmetic capabilities. Yet, arithmetic operations are required in spatial data handling.
3. Expert systems lack spatial data handling capabilities such as buffering and overlay which are unique and important to spatial analysis.
4. Expert systems do not provide facilities for spatial data representation and visualization.

Table 4.1 contrasts the strengths and weakness typically observed in expert systems and GIS .The advantages of integrating a GIS with an expert system have been recognized by a number of authors (Zhu and Healey 1992, Fischer 1994, Lilburne et al.1996, Moore 2000). Zhu and Healey (1992) argued that the integration of GIS and ES may avoid some of the limitations and difficulties existing in each of them and the spatial decision process can be made more effective within such integrated systems. They also mentioned that **a** conventional GIS is very suitable to well-structured spatial problem solving, while the integration of GIS and ES offers a best approach to solving ill-structured spatial problems and to providing knowledge of how to use and run the GIS. Lilburne et al. (1996) mentioned that domain knowledge represented in an expert system together with spatial data found in GIS can provide a decision support environment in which users are guided by the integrated system towards useful recommendations. Fischer (1994) asserted that there were no longer any questions that expert systems would be integral in building the next generation of intelligent GIS. Moore (2000) has noted that the reason why there is plenty of scope for use of expert systems in this subject area is that GIS without intelligence have a limited chance to effectively solve spatial decision support problems in a complex or imprecise environment.

Table 1. Comparison of some GIS and expert systems capabilities
(adapted from Lilburne et al.1996)

GIS	Expert Systems
Quantitative and Suited to structured problems	Qualitative and Suited to unstructured problems
Use geometric primitives, e.g., point, line, polygon	Use symbols
Integrate data	Integrate knowledge
Do not easily handle incomplete data	Handles incomplete data and knowledge
Spatially capable	No spatial capability
Cope with large volume of data	Do not cope well with lots of data
No explanation facility	Explanation facility
Can not represent and manage knowledge	Can represent and manage knowledge
No inference or reasoning capabilities	Have inference engines
Algorithmic	Opportunistic
Variety of output maps/graphics	No mapping capability
Can efficiently perform geometrical operations	Can not efficiently perform geometrical or arithmetical operations

4. INTEROPERABILITY AND SYSTEMS INTEGRATION TECHNIQUES

The concept of software interoperability is one of those buzzwords in the computer field that means different things to different people (Eddon and Eddon 1998). According to Goodchild et al. (1999) Interoperability means openness in the software industry, because open publication of internal data structures allows software users to use different software components from different developers to build their applications. It also means the ability to exchange data freely between systems, because each system would have knowledge of other systems' formats. Interoperability also means commonality in user interaction, as system designers build interfaces that can be customized to a look and feel similar to the user. Wegner (1996) defined interoperability as "is the ability of two or more software components to cooperate despite differences in language, interface, and execution platform". Interoperable systems are systems composed from autonomous, locally managed, heterogeneous components, which are required to cooperate to provide complex services (Finkelstein 1998). Although, Interoperability has been a basic requirement for modern information systems environment for over two decades (Sheth 1999), it is a recent research agenda element of geographic information science. To GIS users, interoperating GIS refers to the ability to exchange GIS data and functionality free among systems. Such interoperability can be achieved at three levels: technical (e.g. compatible data formats between systems), semantic (e.g. consistent meanings of data across systems), and institutional (e.g. legal and economic support for data sharing across organizations) (Goodchild et al. 1999). Major efforts in GIS interoperability are associated with organizations such as Open GIS Consortium and ISO/TC211 (Feng and Sorokine 2001). The development and deployment of successful interoperability strategies requires standardization that provides the lingua franca needed for the exchange and integration of information (Vckovski 1998). In the GIS community, the Open GIS Consortium has used the well known industry-wide specifications for exchanging data and functionality, such as COM (Component Object Model) by Microsoft and CORBA (Common Object Request Broker Architecture) by the Object Management Group, as the base standards to develop specifications for exchanging GIS data and functionality. Interoperability is sometimes distinguished from integration, but at other times the two terms are used almost interchangeably. Dictionary definitions suggest that any significant difference between them lies in the degree of coupling between the entities. Thus, an integrated system is sometimes considered to be more tightly coupled than a system composed of interoperable components. Yet even this distinction suggests that perspective is a key factor in discussing interoperability. Thus, when looked on from a distance, a system is perceived to be integrated, but from the perspective of its constituent elements, they are interoperating with each other. The issue of perspective is recursive, because the interoperable entities themselves may be an integration of other constituents. Thus, the relationship of the observer to the constituent makes a difference as to whether the appropriate term is integration or interoperability (Brownsword et al 2004). We shall not make any further distinction between these terms in the remainder of this study.

An extensive body of literature published since 1990 documents the need for additional GIS functionality (Lilburne 1996). To fulfill this need, researchers give considerable interest in integrating geographical information systems (GIS) with other specialist systems to meet the requirements of advanced applications. Also, the integration of GIS and other technologies such as expert systems will lead to new, richer approaches to problem solving (Abel and Kilby 1994). In the context of a particular problem, systems integration essentially seeks to fuse capabilities available in the individual systems and to provide some desired level of usability (Chou and Ding 1992). Abel and Kilby (1994) argued that the available GIS and modeling systems are complex systems which would be costly to re-implement or to re-modify and consequently, there is some value in determining the limits of possible integration using existing systems. They defined the system integration problem as "the problem which concerned with the coupling of pre-existing systems (the components of the integrated system) to fuse a desired set of capabilities with some targeted degree of usability of the integrated system. While the pre-existing systems (components) themselves are to be taken as not to be modified, systems integration typically involves the design of some specialist components linkage components to facilitate coupling. Identifying the types of the linkage components needed is then a core issue in the system integration problem." Coupling is a measure of the degree to which functions in one software package can be controlled directly from another. It refers to the physical and logical connection between software packages in the system implemented (Malczewski 1999). The degree of interoperability between an expert system and a GIS will affect the ability of an integrated system to model the complexity of the real world (Linlburne et al 1996). Numerous mechanisms enabling interoperability between GIS and ES have appeared over the years. Examples range from simple solutions such as, loose coupling techniques to much more sophisticated approaches, such as Component Object Model (COM) technology and Ontology.

4.1. Loose (Shallow) Coupling

In this approach GIS and ES support each other to solve specific problems through sharing data files written in ASCII or other standard file format by the use of file transfer utilities (Goodchild et al. 1992). Using this approach, the GIS serves as a preprocessor or postprocessor to the expert system and the expert systems could access to the data stored in the GIS or produced by the GIS. However, this approach does not provide the ES with the spatial data handling capabilities of the GIS. At this level of integration, each tool runs independently, the user interfaces continue to be separated, and there is no need to write extra software, only the file formats have to be adapted. However, manipulating the exchange files tends to be cumbersome and error prone (Fedra 1996, Jun 1997). In addition, the approach may not work if the data sets extracted from the GIS become too large to fit into the ES database (Zhu and Healey 1992).

The following paragraphs summarize some of the systems developed using this approach.

Kirkby (1996) used loose coupling to integrate a GIS with an expert system to identify and manage dry land salinization in South Australia. The developed system, Salt Manager, is a UNIX-based computer software that integrates "off the shelf" commercially available GIS (ARC/INFO), RDBMS (ORACLE), and ES (Harlequin Lisp works/ Knowledge Works Environment) Software. The communication between the RDBMS and both the ES and GIS is conducted via a standard interface file, while the communication between the GIS and ES is conducted via an ASCII text file.

Jun (1997) designed an expert geographic information system for industrial site selection by integrating GIS (ARC/INFO 7), expert system (CLIPS), and MCDM (AHP). The software integration between all the modules is based on loose coupling and is handled by the ASCII file transfer method.

Yialouris et al. (1997) followed loose coupling strategy to develop EXGIS, an integrated expert geographical information system for soil suitability and evaluation. EXGIS consists of two components: GIS (ARC/INFO) and Expert system shell. The expert system shell was implemented in CLIPPER because the files produced by it (dBase III+ files) can subsequently be processed by ARC/INFO.

4.2. Tight (Deep) Coupling

Tight (deep) integration means that one system provides a user interface for viewing and controlling the application, which may be built from several component programs (Pullar and Springer 2000). That is, tight coupling is to integrate ES with GIS using communication links in such a way that the GIS appears to the ES as an extension of its own facilities, or vice versa. One appears as the shell around the other. The system developed by this approach is called a "tight coupled standalone system". A "tight coupled standalone system" can be either a merged system with expert systems as a subsystem of GIS Functionality, or an embedded system, where existing GIS facilities are enhanced with expert system functionality. The second type of tight coupling is "expert command languages", where expert system reasoning is added to GIS macro or command languages (Zhu and Healey 1992). Compared with loose coupling, tight coupling is considered to be a more effective integration method as the decision problem can be modeled using generic tools on a single integrated database. However, the computations will not be optimal. Also, it sometimes causes serious problems due to the complicated communication between GIS macro language and the user-developed expert systems. The following paragraphs summarize some of the systems developed using this approach.

Kristijono (1997) followed a tight coupling strategy to develop a knowledge-based GIS for landscape suitability. The author used the available tools of ARC/INFO GIS to build his system entirely within the GIS environment The following ARC/INFO tools were used to design the system :(1) ARCEDIT environment, (2) a combination of the logical expressions and the commands of the ARCEDIT, and (3) the AML (ARC Macro Language) facilities. The first tool was used to perform as a rule editor, the second tools were used to transform the IF … THEN form of the production rules, and the third tool was used to control the whole operation of the entire transformed production rule.

Corner et al (2002) used tight coupling in developing EXPECTOR, a method of combining data and expert knowledge within a GIS to provide information on the occurrence of spatially distributed attributes. The method has been implemented as a stand-alone "Knowledge Editing" module coded in Visual Basic and interfaced with a GIS (ArcView) both to derive information about the input spatial data and to communicate back the results of its calculations. Total Probability Rule and Bayes Theorem were used as knowledge representation mechanism and as the inference engine. The data processing and combination phases are carried out in ArcView using routines written in Avenue (the ArcView scripting language).

Yang et al (2006) developed a GIS expert system for modeling distribution of matsutake mushrooms using tight coupling approach. The system was developed under ENVI-IDL environment and Bayesian theory was used as the inference engine

4.3. Client/Server

Client/server technology refers to the software that allows a process to receive messages from another process. These messages request services of the receiving system (the server). The service might be to perform a specified action or to return some information to the requesting system (the client). Both processes remain in memory concurrently, avoiding the loss of performance that occurs when loading a system into memory every time of one of its functions is required. There is no limit to the number of requests, nor are there any restrictions on the types of requests that can be made. In client/server integration approach GIS and ES communicate via a standard protocol such as DDE, OLE or PRC which enables them to send and receive messages from other concurrently running systems. Functionality is interleaved, dynamic and relatively full. Data may be transferred or shared and there may be one or two interfaces (Lilburne 1996). The following paragraphs summarize some of the systems developed using this approach.

Lilburne et al. (1996) used client/server technology in developing a spatial expert system shell (SES) that integrates two commercial products: the GIS ARC/INFO v7 and the expert system shell, Smart Elements. ARC/INFO v7 includes some commands which create a framework for client/server communication with another process. Once a connection has been initialized, messages can be sent between the processes. Smart Elements is a combination of a hybrid frame, rule-based expert system called Nexpert Object, and a GUI developer kit called Open Interface. It has an Application Programming Interface (API) which allows C routines to access Smart Elements functions. SES was developed on a Solaris SUN Workstation platform. Both ARC/INFO v7 and Smart Elements use Sun's ONCRPC client/server protocol. Smart Elements is the client and ARC/INFO is the server. A combination of C and ARC/INFO's macro language AML is used to develop the client/server interface between ARC/INFO and Smart Elements.

Jia (2000) developed a conceptual framework for integrating ES and GIS using Transmission Control Protocol/ Internet Protocol and Remote Procedure Calling technologies. A software system (called IntelliGIS) implementing the method has been developed. IntelliGIS was implemented by enhancing CLIPS (a rule and object-based expert system shell) with ARC/INFO GIS and the ES-GIS interface developed in the research. ARC/INFO performs as the GIS server and its Inter-Application Communications (IAC) function is used for developing the spatial reference engine because the IAC function allows direct "talk" between CLIPS and ARC/INFO, and it does not require text files for the talk. The ES-GIS interface used Transmission Control Protocol/Internet Protocol (TCP/IP) and Remote Procedure Calling technologies to integrate CLIPS and ARC/INFO.

Fedra and Winkelbauer (2002) developed a client/server DSS framework, RealTime eXPert System (RTXPS), which integrates a forward chaining expert system and a backward chaining system with simulation models and GIS for environmental and technological risk assessment. To integrate the various information resources in an operational decision support system, flexible client-server architecture is used, based on TCP/IP and the http protocol. The central system, which runs the RTXPS expert system as the overall framework is connected to a number of conceptual servers that provide high-performance computing and data acquisition tasks.

4.4. Component Object Model Technology (COM)

To achieve interoperability between the systems, one must proceed with the decomposition of the software system into small components that are available to other applications (Bian 2000). Leading commercial software vendors have adopted component-based software development (CBSD) approach in their software design. CBSD approach focuses on building large software systems by integrating previously existing software components as a way to reduce development costs, improve productivity, and provide controlled systems upgrade in the face of rapid technology evolution (Brown 2000). This approach, which is also called componentware, is a further development of the object oriented programming. It adds to the object oriented programming the concept of a highly reusable components. In CSBD, the notion of building a system by writing code has been replaced with building a system by assembling and integrating existing software components (Karlsson 1995). Brown (2000) defined a software component as "an independently deliverable piece of functionality providing access to its services through interfaces". A component is a reusable piece of software in binary form that can be plugged into other components from other vendors with relatively little effort (Eddon and Eddon 1998). A rather small group of objects is joined into the component with a well defined interface. Inside the component the objects can communicate with each other without any restrictions, but communication with the outside world is only possible through the component interface. A component acts like a black-box: the inner structure is hidden and protected from the outside world by the component interface (Rebolj and Sturm 1999). That is, with COM, applications interact with each other and with the system through collections of functions calls known as interfaces as shown in figure 3(a). An interface is a strongly typed contract between a software component and a client that describes the component's functionality to the client without describing the implementation at all (Eddon and Eddon 1998). Each component can act as both client and server as shown in figure 3(b). A server is a component that exposes interfaces and therefore a list of functions that a client can call (Lewis 1999). The main goal of the COM is to promote interoperability. COM supports interoperability by defining mechanisms that allow applications to connect (Eddon and Eddon 1998). COM specifies an object model and programming requirements that enable COM objects to interact with other COM objects. These objects can be within a single process, in other processes, or even on remote machines. They can be written in other languages and may have been developed in very different ways. COM allows these objects to be reused at a binary level, meaning that third party developers don't require access to source code, header files, or object libraries in order to extend the system (Zeiler 2001).

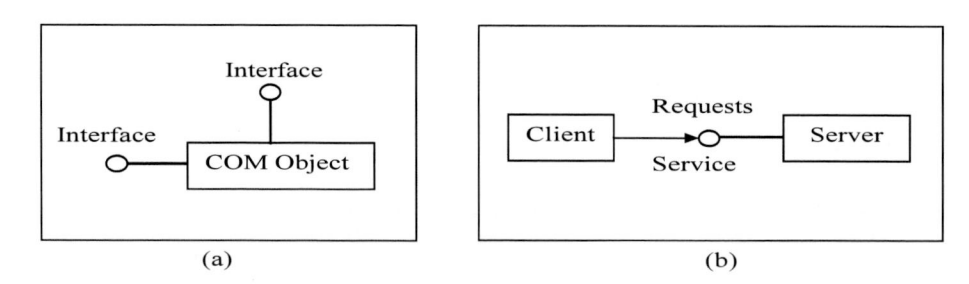

Figure 3. COM Architecture (adapted from Lewis 1999).

Leading commercial GIS software vendors have adopted component-based software development (CBSD) approach in their software design and choose COM as the component technology for their products. For example, ArcGIS Desktop (an integrated suite of professional GIS application) developed by Environmental systems Research Institute (ESRI), is based on a common modular component-based library of shared GIS software components called ArcObjects. ArcObjects includes a wide variety of programmable components which aggregate comprehensible GIS functionality for developers (Zeiler 2001). Also, Leading commercial ES software vendors have adopted COM technology in designing their software. Visual Rule Studio® (an object-oriented COM-compliant expert system development environment for windows) developed by RuleMachines is an example. Visual Rule Studio® solves the problem of software interoperability by allowing the developers to package rules into component reusable objects called RuleSets. By fully utilizing OLE and COM technologies, RuleSets act as COM automation servers, exposing RuleSet objects in a natural COM fashion to any COM compatible client. Visual Rule Studio installs as an integral part of MS Visual Basic 6.0, professional or enterprise editions, and appears within the visual Basic as an ActiveX Designer. RuleSets can be complied within Visual Basic .EXE, .OCX, or .DLL executables and used in any of the ways the developers normally use such executables (RuleMachines 2002). The following paragraphs summarize some of the systems developed using COM technology.

Eldrandaly et al (2003) used COM technology to develop an intelligent GIS-based spatial decision support system for industrial site selection. A prototype was developed using three COM-compliant commercially available software packages: Visual Rule Studio®, ArcGIS® 8.2, and Microsoft® Excel 2002. Visual Rule Studio® was used to develop the expert system component. ArcGIS® provided the GIS platform to manage the spatial data and conduct the required spatial analysis operations. Microsoft® Excel provided the tools to implement the AHP component. In addition, Microsoft® Visual Basic® 6.0 was used to provide the shell for the COM integration and to develop the system's user interface.

Tsamboulas and Mikroudis (2005) used COM technology in developing a DSS (TRANS-POL) for evaluating transportation polices and projects. It was developed using four COM-compliant commercially available software packages: Microsoft Visual Basic, Microsoft Access, ESRI MapObjects, and Amzi Prolog.

Eldrandaly (2006) developed a COM-based expert system to assist the GIS analysts in selecting suitable map projection for their application in ArcGIS software package. Visual Rule Studio® (an object-oriented COM-compliant expert system development environment for windows) was used to develop the expert system. The COM technology was used for integrating the expert system with ArcGIS® 9.0, a COM-complaint GIS software package. Its built in macro language, Visual Basic for Application (VBA), was used to develop the Map Projection application that implements the expert system using Automation Technology.

4.5. Ontology: A Promising Interoperability Approach

Ontologies are expected in various areas as promising tools to improve communication among people and to achieve interoperability among systems (Lee et al. 2006). Ontology for a philosopher is the science of beings, of what is, i.e., a particular system of categories that reflects a specific view of the world. For the Artificial Intelligence (AI) community, Ontology is an engineering artifact that describes a certain reality with a certain vocabulary, using a set of assumptions regarding the intended meaning of the vocabulary words (Fonseca et al. 2oo2). Ontology defines the terms and relationships among terms that represent an area of knowledge. In software engineering, computer-readable Ontologies are growing in importance for defining basic concepts within a domain. If multiple-domain applications are developed utilizing a shared Ontology, or if their distinct Ontologies can be related, then the applications can have a common understanding of data, and semantic interoperability is enhanced. In addition, Ontologies can be developed that relate information across domains, opening up new possibilities for interoperability (Carney et al. 2005). The importance of Ontologies in GIScience has been established over the past decade as scholars have demonstrated their value in multiple geospatial and reasoning contexts (Schuurman and

Leszczynski 2006). The use of Ontology, translated into an active information system component, leads to Ontology-Driven Information Systems and, in specific case of GIS, leads to what is called Ontology-Driven Geographic Information Systems- ODGIS (Fonseca et. al.2002). ODGIS are built using software components derived from various Ontologies. These software components are classes that can be used to develop new applications. Being Ontology-derived, these classes embed knowledge extracted from Ontologies (Fonseca et al. 2002). Ontologies aim at modeling and structuring domain knowledge and an Ontology development follows a cycle containing several phases, ranging from the requirements analysis and initial Ontology design to conceptual refinement, evaluation and evolution as shown in figure 4 (Linkova et. al. 2005). Software tools are available to accomplish most aspects of Ontology development. Today's most Ontology languages are based on the XML syntax such as OWL (Web Ontology Language). OWL (Linkova et. al. 2005) is a product of W3C (the World Wide Web Consortium) and is presented as an Ontology language for the semantic web. It allows representing not only concepts, taxonomies, binary relations, but also cardinalities, richer type definitions and other characteristics. Most of the Ontology languages are supported by tools such as the widely used Protégé system which provides OWL support. Protégé is a free, open-source platform that provides a growing user community with a suite of tools to construct domain models and knowledge-based applications with Ontologies. At its core, Protégé implements a rich set of knowledge-modeling structures and actions that support the creation, visualization, and manipulation of Ontologies in various representation formats. Protégé can be customized to provide domain-friendly support for creating knowledge models and entering data. Further, Protégé can be extended by way of a *plug-in architecture and a Java-based Application Programming Interface (API)* for building knowledge-based tools and applications. The Protégé platform supports two main ways of modeling Ontologies: The *Protégé-Frames editor* that enables users to build and populate Ontologies that are *frame-based*, in accordance with the *Open Knowledge Base Connectivity protocol (OKBC)* and The *Protégé-OWL editor* that enables users to build Ontologies for the *Semantic Web*(Protégé 2006). The following paragraphs describe one of the systems developed using Ontology.

Moore et al. (2001) established an ontological basis for geography and environmental science (feeding into coastal zone management), and GeoComputation from a holistic viewpoint. This Ontology serves as the foundation for the development of COAMES (COAstal Management Expert System), which uses the Dempster-Shafer theory of evidence to model holism. COAMES is an object-oriented expert system, consisting of a user interface, a database, an object-oriented knowledge base (incorporating both the expert's factual knowledge and the process knowledge embodied in models) and most importantly an inference engine. Within the inference engine are algorithms to calculate belief with uncertainty through the Dempster-Shafer Theory of Evidence. COAMES achieves technological holism, as it brings together expert systems and GIS, as well as remotely sensed data and GPS measurements.

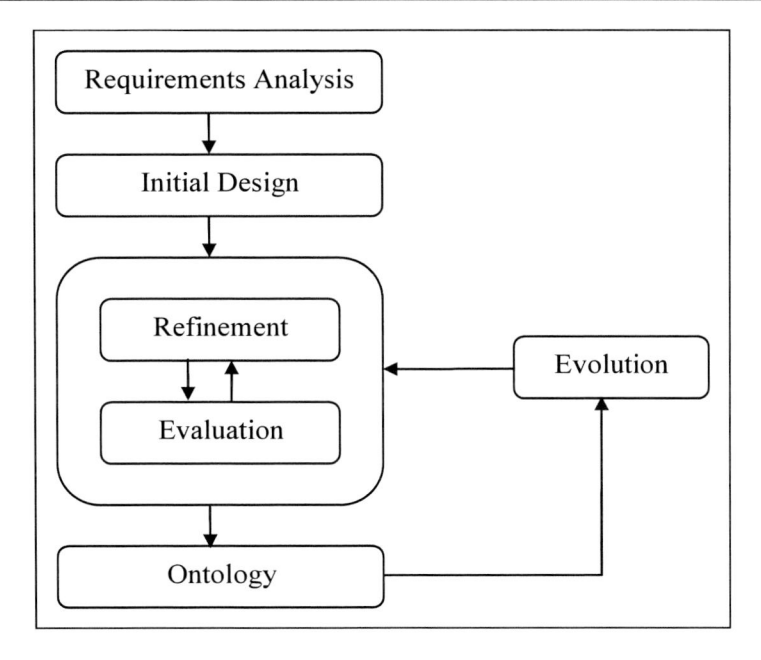

Figure 4. Ontology Lifecycle (adapted from Linkova et. al. 2005).

6. CONCLUSION

In this study, we have attempted to highlight the complexity of spatial decision making, system integration problems, and interoperability and to provide an overview of the different strategies for integrating GIS with Expert Systems. From the above discussion, it is clear that spatial decision making is a highly complex process and most spatial decision problems are complex and ill structured. GIS and ES are required for solving these problems but each of them has its own limitations and drawbacks in dealing with spatial decision making. The integration of these tools may avoid some of the limitations and difficulties existing in each of them and provide the decision maker with an efficient tool for solving these problems. The degree of interoperability between an expert system and a GIS will affect the ability of an integrated system to model the complexity of the real world. Numerous mechanisms enabling interoperability between GIS and ES have appeared over the years. Examples range from simple solutions such as, loose coupling techniques to much more sophisticated approaches, such as Component Object Model (COM) technology and Ontology. Although the simple techniques (loose and tight coupling) have achieved considerable success in integrating GIS and ES and they are still used now, these techniques have many drawbacks and limitations. These drawbacks can be eliminated or at least reduced by applying the recent approaches of software interoperability such to be COM technology and Ontology. Ontologies are expected as promising tools to achieve and open up new possibilities for software interoperability.

REFERENCES

Abel, D. and Kilby, P., 1994, The systems integration problem. *International Journal of Geographical Information Systems*, 8, pp.1-12.

Bernhardsen, T., 2002, *Geographic Information Systems: An Introduction* (New York: John Wiley and Sons).

Bolstad, P., 2002, *GIS Fundamentals* (Minnesota: Eider Press).

Bian, L., 2000, Component modeling for the spatial representation of wildlife movements. *Journal of environmental management*, 59, 235-245.

Brown, A., 2000, *Large – scale, component –based development* (New Jersey: Prentice Hall).

Brownsword, L., Carney, D., and Wrage, L., 2004, Current Perspectives on Interoperability, *Technical Report,* CMU/SEI-TR-009.

Burrough, P., and McDonnell, R., 1998, *Principles of Geographical Information Systems* (New York: Oxford University Press).

Carney, D., Fisher, D., and Place, D., 2005, Some Current Approaches to Interoperability, *Technical Report,* CMU/SEI-TN-033.

Chou, H. and Ding, Y., 1992, Methodology of integrating spatial analysis/modeling and GIS. In *Proceedings of 5th International Symposium on Spatial Data Handling* (South Carolina), pp.514-523.

Clarke, K., 2001, *Getting Started with Geographic Information Systems* (Upper Saddle River, NJ: Prentice-Hall).

Corner, R. and Hickey, R., 2002, Knowledge Based Soil Attribute Mapping in GIS: The Expector Method, *Transactions in GIS*, Vol.6, No.4, pp.383-402.

Davis, B., 2001, GIS: *A Visual Approach* (Canada: Onword Press).

Dueker, K., 1979, Land resource information system: a review of fifteen years' experience. *Geo-Processing*, 1, 105-128.

Eddon, G. and Eddon, H., 1998, *Programming Components with Microsoft Visual Basic 6.0*(Redmond: Microsoft press).

Eldrandaly, K., Eldin, N., and Sui, D., 2003, A COM-based Spatial Decision Support System for Industrial Site Selection, *JGIDA*, Vol.7, No.2, pp.72-92.

Eldrandaly, K. ,2006, A COM-based expert system for selecting map projection in ArcGIS, *Expert Systems with Applications*, Vol.31, pp.94-100.

Fedra, K., 1996, Distributed models and embedded GIS: integration strategies and case studies. In *GIS and Environmental Modeling: progress and research issues*, edited by Goodchild, Steyeart, and Parks (Fort Collins, GIS World Books), PP.413-417.

Fedra, K. and Winkelbauer, L. ,2002, A Hybrid Expert System, GIS, and Simulation Modeling for Environmental and Technological Risk Management, *Computer-Aided Civil and Infrastructure Engineering*, Vol.17, pp.131-146.

Feng,C., and Sorckine,A.,2001, Incorporating hydrologic semantic information for interoperable GIS with hydrologic model. In *Proceedings of the Ninth ACM International Symposium on Advances in Geographic Information Systems* (Atlanta), pp.59-63.

Finkelstein, A., 1998, Interoperable Systems: An introduction. In *Information Systems interoperability*, edited by Kramer, Papazoglou, and Schmidt (England: Research studies press), pp. 1-9.

Fischer, M.M., 1994, From conventional to knowledge-based geographic information systems, *Computers, Environment, and Urban Systems*, Vol.18, No.4, pp.233-242.

Firebaugh, M., 1988, *Artificial Intelligence: A knowledge-based Approach* (New York: Boyd and Fraser).

Fonseca, F., Egenhofer, M., Agouris, P., and Camara, G., 2002, Using Ontologies for Inegrated Geographic Information Systems, *Transactions in gis*, 6(3), 231-257.

Fonseca, F., Egenhofer, M., Davis,c., and Camara, G., 2002, Semantic Granularity in Ontology-Driven Geographic Information Systems, *AMAI annals of Mathematics and Artificial Intelligence*, 36(1-2), 121-151.

Goodchild, M., Haining, R., and Wise, S., 1992, Integrating GIS and spatial data analysis: problems and possibilities. *International Journal of Geographical Information Systems*, 6, 407-423.

Goodchild, M., Egenhofer, M., Fegeas, R., and Kottman, C.,1999, *Interoperating Geographic Information Systems* (Massachusetts: Kluwer Academic publishers).

Hayes-Roth, F., Waterman, D.A., and Lenat, D., 1983, *Building Expert Systems* (Reading: Addison-Wesley).

Jackson, P., 1990, *Introduction to Expert Systems*, Addison-Wesley.

Jankowski, P., and Nyerges, T., 2001, *Geographic Information Systems for Group Decision Making* (London: Taylor and Francis).

Jia, X., 2000, INTELLIGIS: Tool for representing and reasoning spatial knowledge. *Journal of computing in civil engineering*, 14, 51-59.

Jun, C., 1997, Incorporating decision preferences into an expert geographic information system for industrial site selection. PhD Dissertation, Texas AandM University, College Station, USA.

Karlsson, E.A., 1995, Software Reuse: A Holistic Approach (Chichester: John Wiley and sons).

Kirkby, S., 1996, Integrating a GIS with an expert system to identify and manage drayland salinization. *Applied Geography*, 16, 289-303.

Kristijono, A., 1997, Modeling a Knowledge–based Geographic Information System For Landscape Suitability: Siberut Island, Indonesia. PhD Dissertation, Texas AandM University, College Station, USA.

Lee, J., Chae, H., Kim, K., and Kim, C., 2006, An Ontology Architecture for Integration of Ontologies, In R.Mizoguch, Z.Shi, and F.Giunchiglia (Eds.): *ASWC-LCNS4185*, pp.205-211.

Leung, Y., 1997, *Intelligent Spatial Decision Support Systems* (Berlin: Springer).

Lewis, T., 1999, *VB COM* (UK: Wrox Press).

Lilburne, L., 1996, The Integration Challenges. In *Proceedings of the spatial information research center's 8th colloquium* (New Zealand), pp.85-94.

Lilburne, L., Benwell, G. and Buick, R., 1996, GIS, Expert Systems, and Interoperability. In *Proceedings of the 1st international conference in GeoComputation* (Leeds, UK), pp.527-541.

Linkova, Z., Nedbal, R, and Rimnac, M., 2005, Building Ontologies for GIS, *Technical Report No.932*, Institute of Computer Science, Academy of Sciences of the Czech Republic.

Longley, P., Goodchild, M., Maguire, D., and Rhind, D., 2005, *Geographic Information Systems and Science* (New York: Wiley).

Malczewski, J., 1999, *GIS and Multicriteria Decision Analysis* (New York: John Wiley and Sons).

McLeod, R. and Schell, G., 2001, *Management Information Systems* (Upper Saddle

Moore, T., 2000, Geospatial expert systems" In Openshaw, S. and Abrahart, R., *GeoComputation*, Taylorand Francis

Moore, A., Jones, A., Sims, P., and Blackwell, G., 2001, Integrated Coastal Zone Management's Holistic Agency: An Ontology of Geography and GeoComputation, *The 13th Annual Colloquium of the SIRC*, University of Otago, New Zealand.

Pullar, D. and Springer, D., 2000, Towards integrating GIS and catchment models. *Environmental Modeling and Software*, 15, 451- 459.

Rebolj, D., and Sturm, P., 1999, A GIS based component-oriented integrated system for estimation, visualization, and analysis of road traffic air pollution. *Environmental modeling and software*, 14, 531-539.

Protégé , 2006, Protégé OverView, http://protege.stanford.edu/overview/

RuleMachines, 2002, *Visual Rule Studio Developer's Guide (*Canada: OnDemandManuals).

Schuurman, N., and eszczynski, a., 2006, Ontology-Based Metadata, *Transactions in gis*, 10(5), 709-726.

Sheth, A., 1999, Changing focus on interoperability in information systems: from systems, syntax, structure to semantics. In *Interoperating Geographic Information Systems*, edited by Goodchild, Egenhofer, Fegeas, and Kottman, (Massachusetts: Kluwer Academic publishers).

Star, J., and Estes, J., 1990, *Geographic Information Systems: An Introduction* (Englewood Cliffs, NJ: Prentice Hall).

Vckovski, A., 1998, *Interoperable and distributed processing in GIS* (London: Taylor and Francis).

Wegener, P., 1996, Interoperability. *ACM Computing Surveys*, 28, 285-287.

Worboys, M., and Duckham, M., 2004, *GIS: A Computing Prespective*, CRC Press.

Yang, X., Skidmore, A., Melick, D., Zhou, Z., and Xu, J. ,2006, Mapping non-wood forest product (matsutake mushrooms) using logistic regression and a GIS expert system, *Economical Modeling*, doi:10.1016/j.ecolmodel.2006.04.001.

Yialouris, C., Kollias, V., Lorentzos, N., Kalivas, D., and Siderdis, A., 1997, An integrated expert geographical information system for soil suitability and soil evaluation. *Journal of Geographic Information and Decision Analysis*, 1, 90-100.

Zeiler, M., 1999, *Modeling Our World: The ESRI Guide to Geodatabase Design* (Redlands: ESRI Press).

Zeiler, M., 2001, *Exploring ArcObjects* (Redlands: ESRI Press).

Zhu, X. and Healy, R., 1992, Towards Intelligent Spatial Decision Support: Integrating Geographic Information Systems and Expert Systems. *GIS/LIS'92*, 2, 877-885.

In: Psychology of Decision Making
Editor: Paul M. Garrison

ISBN 978-1-60021-869-9
© Nova Science Publishers, Inc.

Chapter 5

DEVELOPMENT OF RESPONSE INHIBITION AND DECISION-MAKING ACROSS CHILDHOOD: A COGNITIVE NEUROSCIENCE PERSPECTIVE

Wery P. M. van den Wildenberg and Eveline A. Crone*

Department of Psychology, Universiteit van Amsterdam, the Netherlands
Laboratory of Neurobiology and Cognition, CNRS and Université de Provence, Marseille, France
Center for Mind and Brain, University of California, Davis, CA, USA

ABSTRACT

Recent advances within the field of neuroimaging and psychophysiological recording techniques have enabled the identification of key brain regions that contribute to developmental changes in cognitive control and decision-making. This chapter will focus on two influential paradigms in the field of experimental cognitive neuroscience that have contributed to our understanding of the nature of the increasing ability in children to control their own thoughts and actions as they grow older. The first section reviews the current cognitive developmental theories of behavioral inhibition. Response inhibition comes into play when prepotent, overlearned, or ongoing responses have to be suppressed in favor of executing an alternative response and is generally considered an important element of cognitive control and flexibility. These theories are supported by neuroimaging studies that identify the lateral prefrontal cortex as being relevant in tasks that require the on-line manipulation of information and the suppression of responses. The second part of this chapter provides an account of the development of cognitive processes involved in decision-making. Decision-making is required for a variety of behavior and often involves the consideration of multiple alternatives and reasoning about distant future consequences. According to the somatic-marker theory, the possible outcomes of a choice are mediated by emotions that are accompanied by anticipatory

---

* Correspondence can be addressed to the first author at the Department of Psychology, Universiteit van Amsterdam, Roetersstraat 15, 1018 WB, Amsterdam, the Netherlands (e-mail: *wery@dds.nl*)

somatic activity. The theory underlying emotional self-regulation assigns an important role to the ventromedial prefrontal cortex. Finally, the examination of developmental changes in cognitive control functions from the perspective of cognitive neuroscience has also led to better characterizations of behavioral deficits found in disordered child populations.

1. INTRODUCTION

Cognitive developmental theories have provided important insight into developmental changes in children's hypothetical thought, organizational strategies, and the emerging ability to introspect and self-monitor, which underlie age-related improvements in a broad range of intellectual and social behaviors. However, remarkably little is known about cognitive and neurophysiological dimensions of childhood and adolescent maturational processes. This issue is starting to be an important drive for recent progress in the field of developmental science. That is, we are now starting to examine developmental changes in cognitive control functions from the perspective of cognitive neuroscience. This chapter aims to provide an overview of recent advances in the study of cognitive development across childhood from a cognitive neuroscience perspective. We describe studies that were inspired by an understanding of neural systems contributing to the development of cognitive control and complex decision-making. This unified approach has the potential to move cognitive developmental theories toward incorporating the effects that neural system interactions have on reasoning, self-monitoring, and decision-making. Additionally, this unification may lead to integrating our understanding of normal cognitive functions with disordered processes, observed, for example, in children with impulse control disorders (e.g., Attention-Deficit Hyperactivity-Disorder; AD/HD), and may lead to better characterizations of behavioral deficits found in disordered child populations.

In this chapter, we argue that the prefrontal cortex is a key brain region contributing to developmental changes in cognitive control and decision-making. The frontal lobes comprise a substantial area of the human brain, and there is evidence that these regions have reached their maximum size in humans compared to other organisms, therefore allowing for a greater complexity in intellectual abilities (Grafman, 1994). Moreover, this region of the brain is proposed to be the latest to fully develop, reaching full maturation only in adolescence (Casey et al., 1997; Dempster, 1993; Stuss, 1992; van der Molen and Ridderinkhof, 1998).

Recently, many neuroimaging studies have investigated processes that are relevant for cognitive control functions in adults, such as inhibition, manipulating complex information in memory, reward processing, guessing, and planning. These functions can be broadly captured under the umbrella's *inhibitory control* (also referred to as 'cold cognition') and *affective decision-making* (also referred to as 'hot cognition'). These studies emphasize the importance of the prefrontal cortex in higher cognitive processing, and also point out that this region may be fractionated according to separate subprocesses, reflected in distinct neural connectivity between prefrontal and other brain regions. The lateral prefrontal cortex, for example, appears to be relevant in motoric response inhibition, manipulating information on-line, considering options, and updating performance outcomes (Fletcher, Frith, and Rugg, 1997; Goel and Dolan, 2000; Goldberg, Podell, Harner, Riggio, and Lovell, 1994; Robin and Holyoak, 1995). The ventromedial prefrontal cortex, in contrast, is presumed to be involved in best-guess estimations, and emotional experience associated with gains and losses (Breitner, Aharon, Kahneman, Dale, and Shizgal, 2001; Elliott, Rees, and Dolan, 1999; Knutson, Westdorp, Kaiser, and Hommer, 2000; Rogers, et al., 1999). Studies of humans with ventromedial brain injury and neuroimaging studies indicate that this region is highly relevant for processing many types of reward and punishment, and making rapid changes in behavior to accommodate to environmental change. Both the lateral and ventromedial prefrontal cortex are thought to have close connections with the anterior cingulate cortex, which is involved in conflict processing and outcome relevant processing (Botvinick, Nystrom, Fissell, Carter, and Cohen, 1999; Carter et al., 1998).

This fractionation should not be taken to suggest that separate regions carry out functions in isolation, but rather that different areas of the prefrontal cortex appear to be engaged in separable neural systems involved in separable cognitive functions, while interacting with many other brain areas. Within this context, the goal of this chapter is to describe recent advances made in the investigation of developmental changes in subprocesses that rely on lateral prefrontal cortex, subserving inhibitory control, and the ventromedial prefrontal cortex, subserving affective decision-making.

2. DEVELOPMENT OF RESPONSE INHIBITION

2.1 Inhibition in Developmental Theories

In accounting for cognitive development, traditional theories have emphasized the role of changes in the capacity to store and process information (e.g., Case, 1985; Halford, 1993; Pascual-Leone, 1970). More recently, the concept of *inhibition* emerged from the literature (Howe and Pasnak, 1993) as a key construct in explaining cognitive development (Bjorklund and Harnishfeger, 1995; Dempster, 1993; van den Wildenberg and van der Molen, 2004; van der Molen, 2000). Moreover, deficient inhibition is central to current theories of childhood psychopathology (e.g., Barkley, 1997; Gray, 1987; Quay, 1997). Inhibitory control is postulated as an important mechanism that comes into play when the selected action has to compete for activation with strong alternatives. The general concept of inhibition appears in many different guises and is measured in many different ways and in many different experimental paradigms. Therefore, we propose the following working definition throughout this chapter. Inhibition is described as: "the mechanism or set of processes that result in the containment of prepotent behavioral responses when such actions are reflex-like, premature, inappropriate, or incorrect" (according to Burle, Vidal, Tandonnet, and Hasbroucq, 2002).

Within the field of developmental psychology, the term inhibition covers a variety of constructs that can be broadly divided into two categories (e.g., Smith, 1992). One cluster of theories refers to a form of hierarchical control in which a lower force is controlled (e.g., activated or inhibited) by a higher force. This top-down form of cognitive control is also referred to as "deliberate inhibition" (Logan, 1994). This notion seems central to Dempster's theorizing that the resistance to interference contributes to diverse expressions of cognitive development (Dempster, 1993). His work is based on a synthesis of developmental research and neuropsychological research, both indicating that the frontal lobes are critically involved in interference-sensitive tasks. Dempster's *susceptibility to interference model* emphasizes active suppression as a key construct and stresses the role of cognitive control functions that rely on prefrontal parts of the brain. An example taken from the cluster of developmental theories that denote inhibition as the competitive interaction between two processes rather than active suppression is the *inefficient inhibition model* (Bjorklund and Harnishfeger, 1995). This theory holds that inhibitory processes become more efficient during childhood. As a result, less irrelevant information enters working memory, thereby increasing its functional capacity. Processing efficiency is conceptualized here in terms of activation speed and inhibition, and inhibitory control is exerted as a process blocking the spread of activation (see also Harnishfeger, 1995).

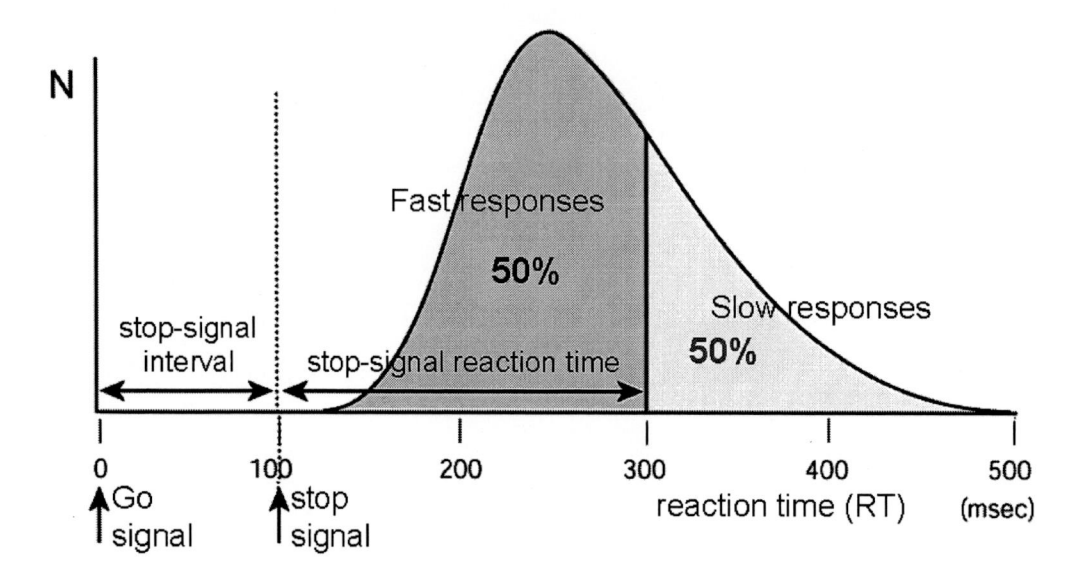

Figure 1. The estimation of stop-signal RT according to a race model (Logan and Cowan, 1984; Logan, 1994). The curve depicts the distribution of RTs on Go trials (trials without a stop signal) representing the finishing times of the response processes. Assuming independence of Go and stop processes, the finishing time of the stop process bisects the choice-RT distribution. Given that the button-press response could be withheld in 50% of all stop trials, stop-signal RT (200 ms) is calculated by subtracting mean stop-signal delay (100 ms) from the median choice RT (300 ms).

2.2 Measuring the Ability to Stop a Prepotent Motor Response: The Stop-Signal Paradigm

An influential paradigm that has been used successfully to investigate the development of inhibitory motor control is the *stop-signal procedure* (Lappin and Eriksen, 1966; Logan and Cowan, 1984; Ollman, 1973; for an overview see Logan, 1994). The stop-signal paradigm provides a useful tool to investigate the development of the covert cognitive processes that constitute inhibitory motor control. Conceptually, the type of inhibition manifested in the stop signal paradigm is one of several intentional acts of control that is required in many real-life situations, like stopping for a red traffic light, and that is exercised by a higher order executive system (e.g., Norman and Shallice, 1986). In the stop-signal paradigm, the participant usually performs a computerized choice reaction time (RT) task that requires the discrimination between two visual stimuli. For example, subjects may be instructed to press a response button with the left index finger to the presentation of a left-pointing arrow and to press another button with the right index finger to a right-pointing arrow. This primary RT task is referred to as the *Go task* and arrow signal are referred to as *Go signals*. During the execution of the Go task, a stop signal (usually a brief tone) is presented occasionally and unpredictably in a proportion, say 25%, of the trials. These trials are called *stop-signal trials*. The subject is instructed to put an effort into canceling his or her pending button-press response to the Go stimulus when faced with a stop signal. Usually, a staircase-tracking algorithm dynamically adjusts the timing of the stop-signal delay, that is, the interval between the presentation of the Go signal and the onset of the stop signal, working towards 50% successfully inhibited stop-signal trials (Levitt, 1971; Logan, Schachar, and Tannock, 1997). The advantage of the stop-signal paradigm is that it allows a precise measurement of the latency of the internally generated inhibitory process - *the stop-signal RT* - even though successful inhibition produces no overt behavior (see Figure 1).

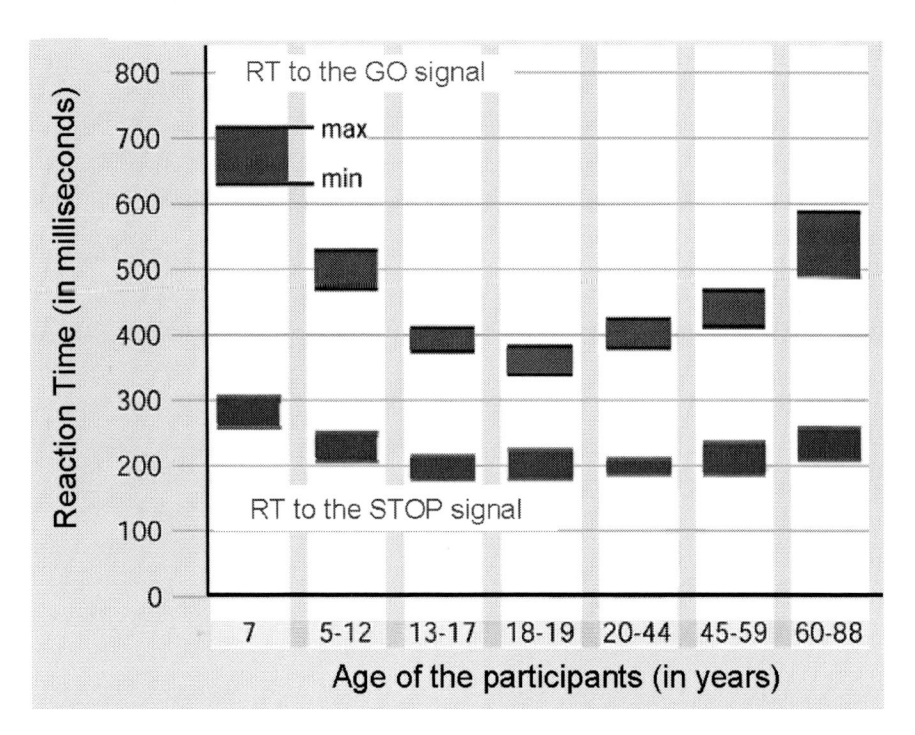

Figure 2. Depicted are the reaction times (RT) to the Go signal (upper area), representing the speed of executing a motor response, and the RT to the Stop signal (lower area), representing the time it takes to stop the motor response. As can be seen, the two cognitive processes follow distinct developmental trends. [Data reported by Williams et al., 1999].

2.2.1 Developmental Trends in Simple Inhibitory Control

The stop-signal RT as the dependent measure of inhibitory control has served developmental psychologists well. Developmental studies using the stop-signal paradigm have yielded evidence of age-related change in the speed of inhibitory processes. It has turned out that healthy young adults are able to stop whatever they are doing in about 200 to 250 ms, indicative of a very close control over their actions. Initially, studies that included children from different age groups failed to demonstrate clear systematic age-related changes in stop-signal inhibition (e.g., Band, van der Molen, Overtoom, and Verbaten, 2000; Jennings, van der Molen, Pelham, Brock, and Hoza, 1997; Oosterlaan, 1996; Schachar and Logan, 1990). However, Monte Carlo simulations suggested that these null findings can be explained through a lack of power, due to modest samples of subjects or insufficient experimental trials (Band, van der Molen, and Logan 2003).

More recent experimental studies were more successful in characterizing developmental changes in the ability to inhibit prepotent motor responses (e.g., Ridderinkhof, Band, and Logan, 1999; van den Wildenberg and van der Molen, 2004; Williams, Ponesse, Schachar, Logan, and Tannock, 1999). For example, Williams and colleagues (1999) used the stop task to examine the development of inhibitory control in a large sample that covered the life span. They reported a significant age-related change in stop-signal RT that decreased from 274 ms for 7-year-olds, and 223 ms for 10-year-olds, to 198 ms for 15-year olds, and 209 ms for young adults (see Figure 2). This significant developmental trend in stopping speed (i.e., the RT to stop signals) could be distinguished from the age-related change in response speed (i.e., the RT to Go signals), suggesting that different mechanisms are involved in stopping and executing a response (see also Ridderinkhof et al., 1999).

2.2.2 Developmental Trends in Selective Inhibitory Control

The studies described above measured children's ability to abort ongoing action in a non-selective manner, also indicated as *simple inhibition*. In the typical stop task, the execution of whatever motor response had to be aborted whenever a stop signal was presented. Modifications of the standard stop-signal paradigm were used to track the development of more subtle manifestations of stopping control, dubbed *selective inhibition* (Logan, 1994). For example, the stop process has been made more complex at the perceptual end by requiring discrimination between two or more stop signals. Bedard and colleagues were the first to examine the development of selective inhibition by manipulating the perceptual component of stop-signal processing by adding a second stop tone to the typical stop-signal task (Bedard et al., 2002). Their subjects, in the range of 6 to 82 years of age, were instructed to inhibit the planned motor response if presented with the valid stop signal (e.g., the high-pitched tone) but not to the invalid signal (e.g., the low-pitched tone). Again, like in the simple stopping experiments by Williams and colleagues (1999), there was a marked development throughout the life span in the execution of go responses. Specifically, response speed increased throughout childhood (see also Cerella and Hale, 1994; Kail, 1991; 1993). First, they observed that selective stopping gets faster with increasing age throughout childhood. That is, stop-signal RT speeded up from 456 ms in early childhood (6-8 years) and 336 ms in middle childhood (9-12 years) to 261 ms in adolescence (13-17 years) to 248 ms in young-adulthood (18-29 years). Again, the developmental trends in selective inhibitory control were unique and differed from the developmental trends in the ability to execute an overt response. Typically, selective stopping latencies are substantially longer than simple stopping latencies, because of the inclusion of the additional cognitive processing involved in the decision "to stop or not to stop".

2.2.3 Further Specification of Developmental Trends

Van den Wildenberg and van der Molen (2004) conducted a developmental experiment in which they directly compared selective inhibitory control as measured by the selective stop-signal task with simple (nonselective) inhibitory control. In the simple stop condition, a button-press response indicated by the direction of an arrow had to be stopped on some trials if both flanking squares turned red (see Figure 3). The selective stop condition differed from the selective stop task used by Bedard et al., who focused on perceptually defined selective inhibitory control that required discrimination between auditory tones. Instead, the task used by van den Wildenberg and van der Molen draws upon motor-based selective inhibitory control by requiring the selection of the appropriate motoric response. The stop signal in the selective condition required the inhibition of the response, but only if the stop signal was presented at the same side as the instructed response to the go signal (see Figure 3).

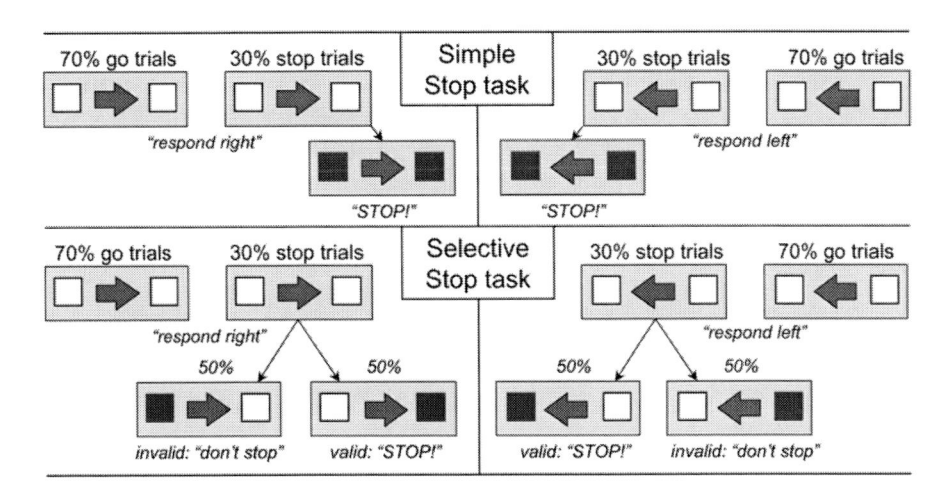

Figure 3. Schematic of the trial structures in the simple stop and the selective stop conditions used by van den Wildenberg and van der Molen (2004). The Go task in the simple and selective stop was to issue a button-press response with the hand indicated by the direction of the green arrow. In the simple stop task, participants were instructed to stop their response to the arrow if the two squares turned red. In the selective stop task, participants inhibited their response to valid stop signals but not to invalid stop signals (see text for further details).

First, their simple stop results replicated the findings reported in previous developmental studies showing that the speed of simple inhibition improved throughout childhood (Ridderinkhof et al., 1999; Williams et al., 1999). The speed of simple inhibition increased from 275 ms in 7-year-olds, to 248 ms in 10-year-olds, to 207 ms in young adults. Second, the results of the selective stopping task showed that the speed of selective inhibition increased with advancing age. Selective stop-signal RTs decreased from 327 ms in the 7-year-olds, to 300 ms in the 10-year-olds, to 237 ms in the young adult group. It should be noted that Bedard and colleagues (2002) found a larger change in stop-signal RTs between ages 7 and 9 to 12 years and found a smaller change between ages 9 to 12 and 22 years, precisely the opposite of the pattern observed by van den Wildenberg and van der Molen. The apparent discrepancy is most likely due to a difference in design. Bedard and colleagues manipulated perceptual processes related to selective inhibition, instructing participants to discriminate between two auditory stop signals. The relatively small difference in selective stopping speed that they observed between ages 9 to 12 and 22 years seems to suggest that inhibition processes drawing on perceptual processes reach mature levels during adolescence. In contrast, the experimental design employed in the current study focused on response-related processes involved in selective stopping, as participants were required to base their stopping response on the mapping between the stop signal and the go response. Apparently, inhibitory control drawing on response-related processes develops relatively late, that is, beyond adolescence. Third, and most importantly, analyses of shared variance indicated that, even after removing the age-related change in simple stopping speed, the developmental trend in selective stopping speed continued to explain a significant proportion of the variance. This finding suggests distinct developmental trends in the speed of selective stopping versus simple stopping.

2.2.4 Maturation of Neural Substrates Underlying Response Inhibition

Developmental neuroimaging studies suggest that similar brain circuitry is recruited in children and adults during performance of inhibition tasks, but the magnitude of activity is typically greater and more diffuse in children relative to adults (Casey, Davidson, and Rosen, 2002; see Casey, Giedd, and Thomas, 2000 for overviews). Casey et al. (1997) performed one of the first studies examining development of inhibitory control using fMRI. They found that inhibitory processes in a go/nogo task were associated with increased activation that was distributed across both dorsolateral and orbitofrontal cortices, and the volume of activation was significantly greater for children relative to adults. Similarly, Tamm, Menon, and Reiss (2002) found that performance on a go/nogo task was positively associated with age in the left interior frontal gyrus, insula, orbitofrontal gyrus, and negatively in the left middle/superior frontal gyri. These results suggest that children activate discrete regions of the prefrontal cortex more extensively than adults, whereas adults show increased focal activation in specific regions associated with response inhibition. Using an oculomotor response-suppression task, Luna et al. (2001) reported increased activation in frontal, parietal, striatal, and thalamic regions when inhibition was required, and prefrontal activation was more active in adolescents than in children or adults. These results were interpreted suggesting that efficient modulation of reflective acts might not be fully developed until adulthood.

2.3 The Ability to Resist Interfering Response Activation - Conflict Tasks

The above-mentioned studies focused on developmental changes in motor inhibition. Another aspect of the construct of inhibition comes into play in tasks that study interference control or response conflict; the so-called conflict tasks. For matters of clarity, we will refer to this inhibition of irrelevant information as interference suppression, to distinguish it from motor inhibition. Various experimental paradigms have been designed to investigate response suppression. For instance, suppression of irrelevant information is often thought to be invoked in conflict tasks, such as the Stoop task, the Simon task, and the Eriksen Flanker tasks (see Figure 4).

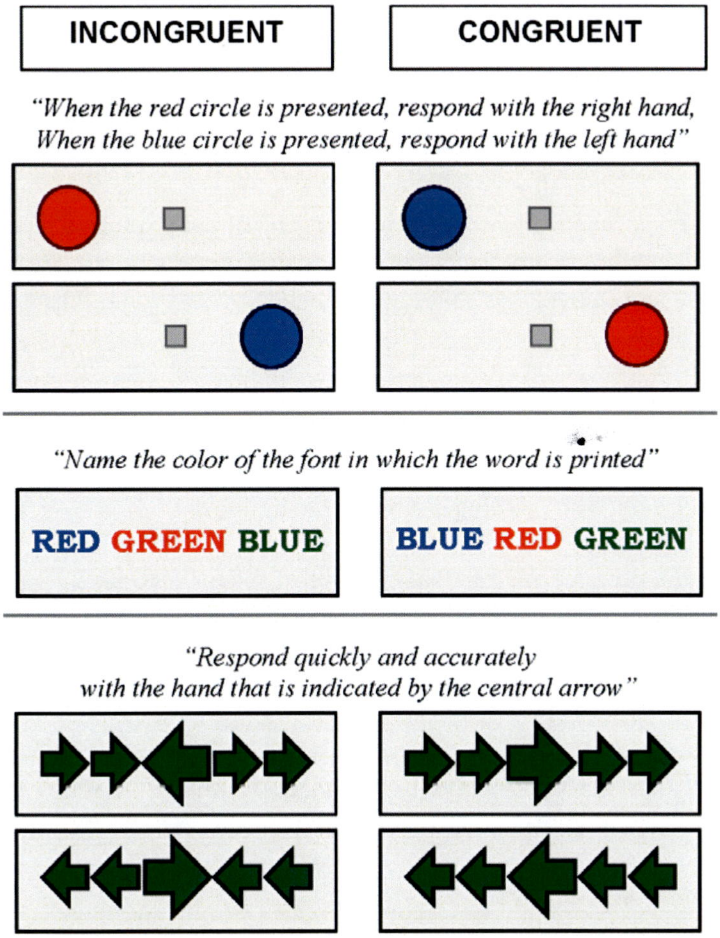

Figure 4. Signal displays in the Simon conflict task (upper display), the Stoop task (middle display), and the Eriksen flanker task (lower display). The dependent measure is the difference in RT between responses to incongruent trials (to the left) and congruent trials (to the right).

2.3.1. The Simon Conflict Task

The Simon task makes use of the general finding that, in choice reaction tasks, RT is shorter and error rate lower when the position of the signal corresponds to the position of the required response, even if the position of the stimulus is completely irrelevant for the task. For example, when subjects have to issue a right hand response to a green signal (and a left hand response to a red signal), RT is generally shorter on congruent trials with a red signal appearing on the right of fixation than on incongruent trials with a red signal appearing on the left (Figure 4, upper display). Although subjects are instructed to respond as a function of the stimulus color (relevant stimulus dimension), the position of the signal, entirely irrelevant, affects response speed. The RT difference between congruent and incongruent responses is often termed the Simon effect (Hedge and Marsh, 1975; see Simon, 1990 for a review). Developmental studies with the Simon task are scarce.

2.3.2 The Stroop Task

The Stroop task (Stroop, 1935) requires subjects to name the font color of color words (e.g., 'red') that are printed in an incongruent color ink (e.g., blue). Reading the word interferes with naming the color, inference that should be suppressed. This induces a conflict between the tendency to read the color word and the actual task of naming the color of the font (see Figure 4, middle display). This conflict is characterized by slower responses to incongruent color-ink words than to congruent or neutral color-ink words. Early behavioral studies indicated that Stroop interference declines during development, which could be taken to indicate maturation of cognitive control functions like the ability suppress processing of task-irrelevant information (Comalli, Wapner, and Werner, 1962; Daniel, Pelotte, and Lewis, 2000; Schiller, 1966).

Adleman et al. (2002) report a positive correlation between age and Stroop-related interference activation in the left lateral prefrontal cortex, the left anterior cingulate, and the left parietal and parieto-occipital cortices. A recent developmental study recorded brain activity during Stroop task performance in different age groups with a technique called functional near-infrared spectroscopy, or fNIRS (Schroeter, Zysset, Wahl, and von Cramon, 2004). Analyses of mean RT revealed that the ability to suppress the automatic tendency to read the color word improved gradually from childhood (aged 7-13) to adolescence (ranged 19-29 years old). This finding suggests that young children have more difficulty than young adults in suppressing response activation that comes from task-irrelevant information in the environment. This behavioral difference was further related to an increase in brain activation to Stroop interference that was most pronounced in the dorsolateral prefrontal cortex (Schroeter et al., 2004), suggesting that the development of interference control as measured by Stroop task relies on the development of frontal brain structures.

2.3.3 The Eriksen Flanker Task

Finally, in the Eriksen flanker task the designated response is indicated by one aspect of the stimulus display. Additionally, other aspects of the stimulus display may elicit competing response tendencies, even if these are to be ignored (Eriksen and Eriksen, 1974). The typical observation is that responses are slowed when to-be-ignored stimulus features are associated with the response opposite to (rather than the same response as) the response assigned to the target stimulus feature. For instance, in the arrow version of the Eriksen the subject's task is to execute a discriminative response according to the direction of a central target arrow, and to ignore flanking arrows (Figure 4, lower display). Responses are typically slowed in incongruent trials, that is, when the flanking arrows point in the direction opposite to, rather than in the same direction as the target arrow, as in congruent trials. Developmental studies by Ridderinkhof et al., (1999) and by Bunge, Dudukovic, Thomason, Vaidya, and Gabrieli (2002) used the Eriksen task and showed that children were more susceptible to interference from the environment than were adults. During task performance, Bunge and colleagues (2004) measured brain activity using functional Magnetic Resonance Imaging (fMRI). They showed that during interference suppression, 8-12-year-old children and adults both recruit the lateral prefrontal cortex. However, in adults this activation was associated with the right hemisphere, whereas in children activity was apparent in the left hemisphere. Both age groups exhibited brain-behavior correlations for homologous areas in the right and left hemisphere, respectively. A subset of children whose flanker-task performance was as good as adults (i.e., the best performers) still recruited left lateral prefrontal cortex, showing that this effect was not associated with performance differences, but rather reflects a qualitatively different recruitment of prefrontal cortex. These findings relate brain functions with cognitive abilities in children, indicating that the development of the ability to suppress interference is associated with differential recruitment of the prefrontal cortex (Dempster, 1993; Goldman-Rakic, 1987).

2.4 Deficient Inhibition and Childhood Pathology: AD/HD

As mentioned in the introduction, deficient inhibition is central in current theories of childhood psychopathology. This section focuses on attention deficit hyperactivity disorder (AD/HD), which is among the most prevalent and most extensively studied childhood pathologies. Mainstream theories of neurocognitive deficits associated with AD/HD currently focus on the role of impulsivity and response inhibition (e.g., Aron and Poldrack, 2005; Barkley, 1997; Nigg, 2001). A vast number of clinical applications of the stop-signal paradigm, described earlier, showed that children diagnosed with AD/HD exhibited slower stopping latencies than children diagnosed with other psychopathologies and normal control children (Jennings et al., 1997; Oosterlaan, Logan, and Sergeant, 1998; Oosterlaan and Sergeant, 1995; Overtoom et al., 2002; Schachar and Logan, 1990; for reviews of AD/HD studies with the stop-signal paradigm see Nigg, 2001). Next to distinguishing between groups like AD/HD versus non-pathological controls, stop-signal RT has been reported to discriminate AD/HD children tested under different conditions. Stopping latencies improved after administration of the stimulant drug *methylphenidate* (also known as Ritalin®) compared with administration of a placebo in children with AD/HD (Tannock, Schachar, Carr, Chajczyk, and Logan, 1989).

Ridderinkhof, Scheres, Oosterlaan, and Sergeant (2005) have presented an original approach to the study of cognitive deficits, particularly deficient response suppression, typically associated with AD/HD. They compared RT performance of children diagnosed with AD/HD with that of age-matched controls on an arrow version of the Eriksen flanker task. The principal distributional technique used is a graphical representation known as "the delta-plot", showing the magnitude of interference effects as a function of response speed (see also Ridderinkhof, van den Wildenberg, Wijnen, and Burle, 2004). In the Eriksen task, the interference effect is defined as the difference between RTs to incongruent and congruent trials. The slope of the delta plot visualizes the time-course of response suppression. The slopes between quintile points turn from positive to more negative relatively late when response suppression is relatively weak, and progressively earlier when the suppression is stronger. The delta plots obtained by Ridderinkhof et al. (2005) showed that in AD/HD, the slopes of especially the slower segments of delta plots for RT were more negative-going for controls than for children with AD/HD, suggesting that response inhibition in the latter group is slower to operate (see Figure 5). These observations are in line with current mainstream theories that hypothesized AD/HD to involve a response-inhibition deficit (e.g., Barkley 1997; Nigg, 2001).

Complementary to the above-mentioned behavioral studies, Casey et al. (1997) found that the volume of the right frontal cortex correlated with behavioral measures of response inhibition in AD/HD children. Recent imaging studies linked deficits in inhibitory motor control to significant reduction in the right inferior prefrontal cortex (Durston et al., 2004).

These fMRI studies are paralleled by studies using the electroencephalogram (EEG) to show that the amplitude of the N2, a component hypothesized to be a marker of behavioral inhibition, is significantly attenuated in AD/HD (Pliszka et al., 2000). Summarizing, several sources of evidence are consistent with the notion that deficits in response inhibition seen in AD/HD are related to functional and volumetric changes in the right inferior frontal cortex (see also Aron and Poldrack, 2005).

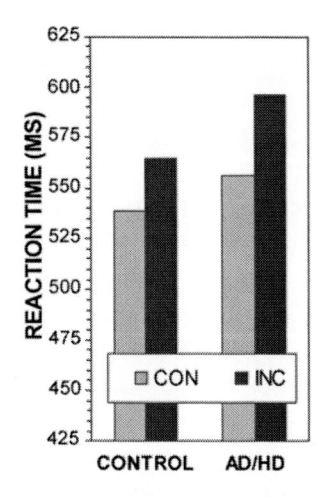

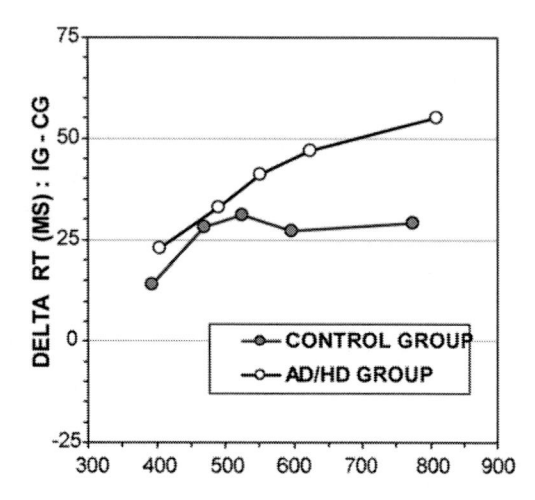

Figure 5. The left panel shows the overall RTs on congruent (CON) and incongruent (INC) task blocks for both AD/HD and control groups. The right panel displays the effect size (i.e., the magnitude of the flanker congruence effect) as a function of response speed as expressed in RT quintile score. Most importantly, the delta slopes diverge in the later segments of the RT distribution, with more-negative going slopes in the control group. This observation has been taken to suggest deficient suppression of activation elicited by irrelevant information in children with AD/HD. Note. Adopted from, and with kind permission from, K. R. Ridderinkhof (2005).

3. DEVELOPMENT OF DECISION-MAKING

3.1 The Somatic Marker Hypothesis

For a long time, developmental research of cognitive control functions only focused on 'cold cognition', including developmental changes in inhibitory control and working memory. Recently, however, there is an increased interest in developmental changes in affective decision-making processes in both infancy and childhood. These studies were inspired by Damasio's somatic marker hypothesis (1994), which is based on patient studies indicating that the ventromedial prefrontal cortex is important for forming relations between somatic responses associated with previously learned outcomes of situations and the reinstatement of these somatic states when a resembling decision has to be made. These associations hold the potential to reactivate an emotion by acting on the appropriate cortical or sub-cortical structures and become highly relevant in situations where future outcomes cannot be easily predicted on the basis of logical cost-benefit comparisons.

Given a certain situation, the ventromedial prefrontal cortex establishes a simple linkage between the aspects of the situation and the disposition for the type of emotion that in the past has been associated with the situation. The somatic markers normally help constrain the decision-making space by making that space manageable for logic-based cost-benefit analyses. Such constraints help an individual to decide efficiently in situations in which there is uncertainty about future outcomes. However, in the absence of somatic markers, options and outcomes become virtually equalized and the process of choosing will depend entirely on logic operations over many option-outcome pairs. This strategy is slow and may fail to take into account previous experience, and is often seen in ventromedial patients, who tend to engage in random and impulsive decision-making.

3.2 Measuring Decision-Making: The Iowa Card Gambling Task

The Iowa Card Gambling Task has been used as a test for assessing somatic markers that are experienced in real-life situations (Bechara, Damasio, Damasio, and Anderson, 1994). That is, the task resembles real-life in the way it factors reward, punishment, and uncertainty about future outcomes. The participant's task is to pick cards from four options; two options are followed by a high reward and, unpredictably, an even higher loss (disadvantageous options) and two other options are followed by a small reward but the unpredictable loss is also small (advantageous options). The participant should learn to differentiate between disadvantageous and advantageous choices. An important aspect of the task is that participants should use the outcome of their decisions to adjust their strategy. Interestingly, previous studies showed that besides immediate somatic responses following reward and loss, intact individuals develop anticipatory somatic "warning" markers preceding disadvantageous choices. This warning signal is missing for patients who have damage to the ventromedial prefrontal region (Bechara, Tranel, Damasio and Damasio, 1996).

3.2.1 Behavioral Studies

In a series of studies, Crone and colleagues (Crone, Vendel, and van der Molen, 2003; Crone and van der Molen, 2004; Crone, Bunge, Latenstein, and van der Molen, in press) showed that children's performance on a child version of the Iowa Gambling Task (the Hungry Donkey Task) resembled performance of patients with ventromedial prefrontal damage (see also Hooper, Luciana, Conklin, and Yarger, 2004; Overman, 2004). They examined children between the ages of 6 to 18 and consistently reported a pronounced developmental increase in the ability to learn to differentiate between disadvantageous and advantageous choices. Given that the task is complex, they considered the contribution of inductive reasoning, inhibitory control and working memory in the process of affective decision-making, but none of these functions could explain the developmental changes observed on the Hungry Donkey Task. Interestingly, however, in one study Crone et al. (in press) manipulated both the number of choice options as well as the frequency with which loss were given. The most important results from this study were that children as young as six years old were able to dissociate between disadvantageous and advantageous choices when the frequency with which delayed punishment was given was high, independent of whether the task included two or four response options. When the delayed punishment was infrequently given (but high in magnitude), children kept preferring the disadvantageous choices, also when there were only two choice options. Together, these results were interpreted to suggest that children's performance resembles that of patients with ventromedial prefrontal damage, and their decision-making impairment is most prominent when there is high uncertainty about future outcomes. This interpretation is consistent with Damasio's somatic marker hypothesis, suggesting that somatic markers are most relevant when the decision-making space is large. Similar results have been reported in studies focusing on 3-4-year olds and 3-6-year-olds (Garon and Moore, 2004; Kerr and Zelazo, 2004), suggesting that developmental changes in affective decision-making are already prominent during infancy.

3.2.2 Imaging Studies

To date, only two studies have examined the neural aspects of developmental changes in decision-making, and these studies both focused on changes during adolescence. May et al. (2004) reported that adolescents and adults recruit similar brain regions in a guessing game, including ventrolateral and medial prefrontal cortex. These regions were more active when participants received reward compared to punishment feedback. Bjork et al. (2004) reported similar findings, showing that adolescents and young adults do not differ in neural responses to positive and negative feedback. Interestingly, this study reported a strong relation between age and *anticipatory* neural activity in ventral striatum, insula, dorsal thalamus, and dorsal midbrain when participants prepared for a risky gamble. These results are largely consistent with the somatic marker hypothesis, which states that decision-making impairments in patients with ventromedial prefrontal damage are associated with reduced somatic activity when anticipating a risky decision, rather than deficient outcome processing. In an unpublished study, Crone et al. (2005) found that children and adolescents do not differ in autonomic activity (heart rate and skin conductance) when receiving punishment, but children showed reduced autonomic responses in preparation of a risky decision in comparison to adolescents. Thus, developmental changes in decision-making may be associated with reduced anticipatory warning signals before making a high-risk decision, as evidenced by reduced autonomic activity (Crone et al., 2005) and reduced neural activity in reward-associated brain regions (Bjork et al., 2004).

4. CONCLUSION

We examined two aspects of cognitive control development, inhibitory control, purportedly mediated by the lateral prefrontal cortex, and affective decision-making, purportedly mediated by the ventromedial prefrontal cortex. Both domains of control do not reach adult levels of performance until middle childhood, suggesting protracted maturation of brain regions associated with these functions.

Obviously, the parallelism proposed between brain maturation and developmental changes in performance on tasks presumed to rely on these regions can be readily criticized. For example, many studies do not measure direct brain activity, and the studies presented were largely cross-sectional. However, the perspectives derived from this research are supported by new approaches that were previously applicable only to adults and that have begun to be available for the study of how brain development and behavior change with growth and experience. Using functional MRI, researchers have become able to trace behavior-related changes in cortical areas (see Casey, 2002). By integrating these new noninvasive methods with techniques from developmental cognitive neuroscience, it is now possible to begin systematic research programs to directly test hypotheses of neurodevelopment.

One of the avenues taken in this chapter is to describe developmental changes in processes presumed to rely on prefrontal cortex in terms of the experimentally controlled subfunctions, instead of using complex neuropsychological tasks based on patient literature. Previous studies examining the development of prefrontal functioning typically used complex tasks (such as the Wisconsin Card Sorting Task) and used different measures to describe developmental changes. One of the major virtues of decomposing functions of the prefrontal cortex is that this method may allow assessment of each function in terms of its anatomical basis and psychophysiological manifestation. With the reviewed experimental paradigms as a basis, this future line of research is expected to increase our understanding of the development and functional role of cognitive control and decision-making systems and to identify the neural substrates potentially involved in pathophysiology of impulse disorders.

REFERENCES

Adleman, N. E., Menon, V., Blasey, C. M., White, C. D., Warsofsky, I. S., Glover, G. H., and Reiss, A. L. (2002). A developmental fMRI study of the stroop color-word test. *Neuroimage, 16*, 61-75.

Aron, A. R., and Poldrack, R. A. (in press). The cognitive neuroscience of response inhibition: Relevance for genetic research in Attention-Deficit/Hyperacitvity Disorder. *Biological Psychiatry*.

Band, G. P. H., van der Molen, M. W., and Logan, G. D. (2003). Horse-race model simulations of the stop-signal procedure. *Acta Psychologica, 112*, 105-142.

Band, G. P. H., van der Molen, M. W., Overtoom, C. C. E., and Verbaten, M. N. (2000). On the ability to activate and inhibit speeded responses. *Journal of Experimental Child Psychology, 75*, 263-290.

Barkley, R. A. (1997). Behavioral inhibitory control, sustained attention, and executive functions: Constructing a unifying theory of ADHD. *Psychological Bulletin, 121*, 65-94.

Bechara, A., Damasio, A. R., Damasio, H., and Anderson, S. W. (1994). Insensitivity to future consequences following damage to human prefrontal cortex. *Cognition, 50*, 7-15.

Bechara, A., Tranel, D., Damasio, H., and Damasio, A.R. (1996). Failure to respond autonomically to anticipated future outcomes following damage to the prefrontal cortex. *Cerebral Cortex, 6*, 215-225.

Bedard, A. C., Nichols, S., Barbosa, J. A., Schachar, R., Logan, G. D., and Tannock, R. (2002). The development of selective inhibitory control across the life span. *Developmental Neuropsychology, 21*, 93-111.

Bjork, J. M., Knutson, B., Fong, G. W., Caggiano, D. M., Bennett, S. M., and Hommer, D.W. (2004). Incentive-elicited brain activation in adolescents: Similarities and differences from young adults. *The Journal of Cognitive Neuroscience, 24*, 1793-1802.

Bjorklund, D. F., and Harnishfeger, K. (1995). The evolution of inhibition mechanisms and their role in human cognition and behavior. In F. N. Dempster and C. J. Brainerd (Eds.), *Interference and inhibition in cognition* (pp. 141-173). San Diego: Academic Press.

Botvinick, M., Nyström, L., Fissell, K., Carter, C. S., and Cohen, J. D. (1999). Conflict monitoring versus selection for action in anterior cingulate cortex. *Nature, 402*, 179-181.

Breitner, H. C., Aharon, I., Kahneman, D., Dale A., and Shizgal, P. (2001). Functional imaging of neural responses to expectancy and experience of monetary gains and losses. *Neuron, 30*, 619-639.

Bunge, S. A., Dudukovic, N. M., Thomason, M. E., Vaidya, C. J., and Gabrieli, J. D. E. (2004). Immature frontal lobe contributions to cognitive control in children: Evidence from fMRI. *Neuron, 33*, 1-20.

Burle, B., Vidal, F., Tandonnet, C., and Hasbroucq, T. (2004). Physiological evidence for response inhibition in choice reaction time tasks. *Brain and Cognition, 56*, 153-164.

Carter, C., Braver, T. S., Barch, D. M., Botvinick, M., Noll, D., and Cohen, J. D. (1998). Anterior cingulate cortex, error detection, and the on-line monitoring of performance. *Science, 280*, 747-749.

Case, R. (1985). *Intellectual development: Birth to adulthood.* New York: Academic Press.

Casey, B. J. (2002). Neuroscience-windows into the human brain. *Science, 298*, 1408-1409.

Casey, B. J., Davidson, M., and Rosen, B. (2002). Functional magnetic resonance imaging: Basic principles of and application to developmental science. *Developmental Science, 5*, 301-309.

Casey, B. J., Giedd, J. N., and Thomas, K. M. (2000) Structural and functional brain development and its relation to cognitive development. *Biological Psychology, 54*, 241-257.

Casey, B. J., Trainor, R. J., Orendi, J. L., Schubert, A. B., Nystrom, L. E., Giedd, J. N., Castellanos, F. X., Haxby, J. V., Noll, D. C., Cohen, J. D., Forman, S. D., Dahl, R. E., and Rapoport, J. L. (1997). A developmental functional MRI study of prefrontal activation during performance of a Go-No-Go task. *Journal of Cognitive Neuroscience, 9*, 835-847.

Cerella, J., and Hale, S. (1994). The rise and fall in information-processing rates over the life span. *Acta Psychologica, 86*, 109-197.

Comalli, P. E., Wapner, S., and Werner, H. (1962). Interference effects of Stroop color–word test in childhood, adulthood and aging. *Journal of Genetic Psychology, 100*, 47- 53.

Crone, E. A., Bunge, S. A., Bechara, A., and Van der Molen, M. W. (2005). Heart rate and skin conductance analysis of children's performance on the IOWA gambling task. Manuscript in preparation.

Crone, E. A., Bunge, S. A. Latenstein, H., and van der Molen, M. W. (2005). Developmental changes in decision-making reflects sensitivity to uncertainty, not task complexity. *Child Neuropsychology, 11*, 245-263.

Crone, E. A. and van der Molen, M. W. (2004). Developmental changes in real-life decision-making: Performance on a Gambling task previously shown to rely on ventromedial prefrontal cortex. *Developmental Neuropsychology, 25*, 251-279.

Crone, E. A., Vendel, I., and van der Molen, M. W. (2003). Decision-making in disinhibited adolescents and adults: Insensitivity to future consequences or driven by immediate reward? *Personality and Individual Differences, 34*, 1-17.

Damasio, A. R. (1994). *Descartes' error: Emotion, reason and the human brain.* New York: Grosset, Putnam.

Daniel, D. B., Pelotte, M., and Lewis, J. (2000). Lack of sex differences on the Stroop color–word test across three age groups. *Perceptual and Motor Skills, 90*, 483-484.

Dempster, F. N. (1993). Resistance to interference: Developmental changes in a basic processing mechanism. In M. L. Howe and R. Pasnak (Eds.), *Emerging themes in cognitive development, Vol. 1: Foundations* (pp. 3-27). New York: Springer.

Durston, S., Hulshoff Pol, H. E., Schnack, H. G., Buitelaar, J. K., Steenhuis, M. P., Minderaa, R. B., Kahn, R., and van Engeland, H. (2004). Magnetic resonance imaging of boys with attention-deficit/hyperactivity disorder and their unaffected siblings. *Journal of the American Academy of Child and Adolescent Psychiatry, 43*, 332-340.

Durston, S., Thomas, K. M., Yang, Y., Ulug, A. M., Zimmerman, R. D., and Casey, B. J. (2002). A neural basis for the development of inhibitory control. *Developmental Science, 5*, 9-16.

Elliott, R., Rees, G., and Dolan, R. (1999). Ventromedial prefrontal cortex mediates guessing. *Neuropsychologia, 37*, 403-411.

Eriksen, B. A., and Eriksen, C. W. (1974). Effects of noise letters upon the identification of a target letter in a nonsearch task. *Perception and Psychophysics, 16*, 143–149.

Fletcher, P. C., Frith, C. D., and Rugg, M. (1997). The functional neuroanatomy of episodic memory. *Trends in Neurosciences, 20*, 213-218.

Garon, N., and Moore, C. (2004). Complex decision-making in early childhood. *Brain and Cognition, 55*, 158-170.

Goel, V., and Dolan, R. (2000). Anatomical segregation of component processes in an inductive interference task. *Journal of Cognitive Neurosiences, 12*, 110-119.

Goldberg, E., Podell, K., Harner, R., Riggio, S., and Lovell, M. (1994). Cognitive bias, functional cortical geometry, and the frontal lobes: laterality, sex, and handedness. *Journal of Cognitive Neuroscience, 6*, 276-291.

Goldman-Rakic, P. S. (1987). Development of cortical circuitry and cognitive function. *Child Development, 58*, 601–622.

Grafman, J. (1994). Neuropsychology of the prefrontal cortex. In: D. W. Zaidel. (Ed.), *Neuropsychology* (pp. 159-181). San Diego, CA: Academic Press.

Gray, J. A. (1987). *The psychology of fear and stress* (2nd ed.). Cambridge, England: Cambridge University Press.

Halford, G. S. (1993). *Children's understanding: The development of mental models*. Hillsdale, NJ: Lawrence Erlbaum.

Harnishfeger, K. (1995). The development of cognitive inhibition: Theories, definitions, and research evidence. In F. N. Dempster and C. J. Brainerd (Eds.), *Interference and inhibition in cognition* (pp. 175-204). San Diego: Academic Press.

Hedge, A., and Marsh, N. W. A. (1975). The effect of irrelevant spatial correspondence on two choice response time. *Acta Psychologica, 39*, 427-739.

Hooper, C. J., Luciana, M., Conklin H. M., and Yarger, R. S. (2004). Adolescents' Performance on the Iowa Gambling Task: Implications for the Development of Decision Making and Ventromedial Prefrontal Cortex. *Developmental Psychology, 40*, 1148-1158.

Howe, M. L. and Pasnak, R. (Eds.). (1993). *Emerging themes in cognitive development Vol. 1: Foundations*. New York: Springer.

Jennings, J. R., van der Molen, M. W., Pelham, W., Brock, K., and Hoza, B. (1997). Inhibition in boys with attention deficit hyperactivity disorder as indexed by heart rate change. *Developmental Psychology, 33*, 308-318.

Kail, R. (1991). Developmental change in speed of processing during childhood and adolescence. *Psychological Bulletin, 109*, 490-501.

Kail, R. (1993). The role of a global mechanism in developmental change in speed of processing. In M. L. Howe and R. Pasnak (Eds.), *Emerging themes in cognitive development, Vol. 1: Foundations* (pp. 97-119). New York: Springer.

Kerr, A., and Zelazo, P. D. (2004). Development of 'hot' executive function: The children's gambling task. *Brain and Cognition, 55*, 148-157.

Knutson, B., Westdorp, A., Kaiser, E., and Hommer, D. FMRI visualization of brain activity during a monetary incentive delay task. *Neuroimage, 12*, 20-27.

Lappin, J. S., and Eriksen, C. W. (1966). Use of a delayed signal to stop a visual reaction–time response. *Journal of Experimental Psychology, 72*, 805-811.

Levitt, H. (1971). Transformed up–down methods in psychoacoustics. *Journal of the Acoustical Society of America, 49*, 467–477.

Logan, G. D. (1994). On the ability to inhibit thought and action: A users' guide to the stop signal paradigm. In D. Dagenbach and T. H. Carr (Eds.), *Inhibitory Processes in attention, memory and language* (pp. 189-239). San Diego: Academic Press.

Logan, G. D., and Cowan, W. B. (1984). On the ability to inhibit thought and action: A theory of an act of control. *Psychological Review, 91*, 295-327.

Logan, G. D., Schachar, R. J., and Tannock, R. (1997). Impulsivity and inhibitory control. *Psychological Science, 8*, 60–64.

Luna, B., Thulborn, K. R., Munoz, D. P., Merriam, E. P., Garver, K. E., Minshew, N. J., Keshavan, M. S., Genovese, C. R., Eddy, W. F., and Sweeney, J. A. (2001). Maturation of widely distributed brain function subserves cognitive development. *Neuroimage, 13*, 786-793.

May, J. C., Delgado, M. R., Dahl, R. E., Stenger, V. A., Ryan, N. D., Fiez, J. A., and Carter, C. S. (2004). Event-related functional magnetic resonance imaging of reward-related brain circuitry in children and adolescents. *Biological Psychiatry, 55*, 359-366.

Nigg, J. T. (2001). Is ADHD a disinhibitory disorder? *Psychological Bulletin, 127*, 571-598.

Norman, D. A., and Shallice, T. (1986). Attention to action. In R. J. Davidson, G. E. Schwartz, and D. Shapiro (Eds.), *Consciousness and self-regulation* (pp. 1-18). New York: Plenum Press.

Ollman, R. T. (1973). Simple reactions with random countermanding of the "go" signal. In S. Kornblum (Ed.), *Attention and Performance IV* (pp. 571-581). New York: Academic Press.

Oosterlaan, J. (1996). *Response inhibition in children with attention deficit hyperactivity and related disorders*. Unpublished doctoral dissertation, University of Amsterdam.

Oosterlaan, J., Logan, G. D., and Sergeant, J. A. (1998). Response inhibition in AD/HD, CD, comorbid AD/HD+CD, anxious, and control children: A meta-analysis of studies with the stop task. *Journal of Child Psychology and Psychiatry and Allied Disciplines, 39*, 411-425.

Oosterlaan, J., and Sergeant, J. A. (1998). Response inhibition and response re-engagement in attention-deficit/hyperactivity disorder, disruptive, anxious, and normal children. *Behavioural Brain Research, 94*, 33–43.

Overman, W. H. (2004). Sex differences in early childhood, adolescence and adulthood on cognitive tasks that rely on orbital prefrontal cortex. *Brain and Cognition, 55*, 134-147.

Overtoom, C. C. E., Kenemans, J.L., Verbaten, M. N., Kemmer, C., van der Molen, M. W., van Engeland, H., Buitelaar, J. K., and Koelega, H. S. (2002): Inhibition in children with attention-deficit/hyperactivity disorder: A psychophysiological study of the stop task. *Biological Psychiatry*, 51, 668-676.

Pascual-Leone, P. (1970). A mathematical model for the transition rule in Piaget's developmental stages. *Acta Psychologica*, 32, 301-345.

Pliszka, S. R., Liotti, M., and Woldorff, M. G. (2000). Inhibitory control in children with attention - deficit/hyperactivity disorder: Event-related potentials identify the processing component and timing of an impaired right-frontal response-inhibition mechanism. *Biological Psychiatry*, 48, 238-246.

Quay, H. C. (1997). Inhibitory control and attention-deficit/hyperactivity disorder. *Journal of Abnormal Child Psychology*, 25, 7-13.

Ridderinkhof, K. R., Band, G. P. H., and Logan, G. D. (1999). A study of adaptive behavior: Effects of age and irrelevant information on the ability to inhibit one's actions. *Acta Psychologica*, 101, 315-337.

Ridderinkhof, K. R., Scheres, A., Oosterlaan, J., and Sergeant, J. A. (in press). Delta plots in the study of individual differences: New tools reveal response inhibition deficits in AD/HD that are eliminated by methylphenidate treatment. *Journal of Abnormal Psychology*.

Ridderinkhof, K. R., van den Wildenberg, W. P. M., Wijnen, J., and Burle, B. (2004). Response inhibition in conflict tasks is revealed in delta plots. In M. I. Posner (Ed.), *Cognitive Neuroscience of Attention* (pp. 369-377). New York: Guilford Press.

Robin, N., and Holyoak, K. J. (1995). Relational complexity and the functions of the prefrontal cortex. In: M. S. Gazzaniga. (Ed.), *The cognitive neurosiences* (pp. 987-997). Cambridge, MA: MIT Press.

Rogers, D. R., Owen, A. M., Middleton, H. C., Williams, E. J., Pickard, J. D., Sahakian, B. J., and Robbins, T. W. (1999). Choosing between small, likely rewards and large, unlikely reward activates inferior and orbital prefrontal cortex. *The Journal of Neuroscience*, 19, 9029-9038.

Schachar, R. J., and Logan, G. D. (1990). Impulsivity and inhibitory control in normal development and childhood psychopathology. *Developmental Psychology*, 26, 710-720.

Schiller, P. H. (1966). Developmental study of color–word interference. *Journal of Experimental Psychology*, 72, 105-108.

Schroeter, M. L., Zysset, S., Wahl, M., and von Cramon, D. Y. (2004). Prefrontal activation due to Stroop interference increases during development - an event-related fNIRS study. *Neuroimage*, 23, 1317-1325.

Simon, J. R. (1990). The effect of an irrelevant directional cue on human information processing. In R. Proctor and T. Reeve (Eds.), *Stimulus-Response compatibility: An integrated perspective* (pp. 31-88). Amsterdam: North-Holland.

Smith, R. (1992). *Inhibition: History and meaning in the sciences of mind and brain*. London: Free Association Books.

Stroop, J.R. (1935). Studies of interference in serial verbal reactions. *Journal of Experimental Pychology*, 18, 643-662.

Stuss, D. T. (1992). Biological and psychological development of executive functions. *Brain and Cognition,* 20, 8-23.

Tamm, L., Menon, V., and Reiss, A. L. (2002). Maturation of brain function associated with response inhibition. *Journal of the American Academy of Child and Adolescent Psychiatry,* 41(10), 1231-1238.

Tannock, R., Schachar, R., Carr, R. P., Chajczyk, L., and Logan, G. D. (1989). Effects of methylphenidate on inhibitory control in hyperactive children. *Journal of Abnormal Child Psychology*, *17*, 473-491.

van den Wildenberg, W. P. M. and van der Molen, M. W. (2004). Developmental trends in simple and selective inhibition of compatible and incompatible responses. *Journal of Experimental Child Psychology*, *87*, 201-220.

van der Molen, M. W. (2000). Developmental changes in inhibitory processing: Evidence from psychophysiological measures. *Biological Psychology*, *54*, 207-239.

van der Molen, M. W., and Ridderinkhof, K. R. (1998). The growing and aging brain: Life-span changes in brain and cognitive functioning. In: A. Demetriou, W. Doise and C. van Lieshout (Eds.), *Life span developmental psychology* (pp. 35-99). New York: Wiley.

Williams, B. R., Ponesse, J. S., Schachar, R. J., Logan, G. D., and Tannock, R. (1999). Development of inhibitory control across the life-span. *Developmental Psychology*, *35*, 205-213.

Chapter 6

ENABLING PREGNANT WOMEN TO PARTICIPATE IN INFORMED DECISION-MAKING REGARDING THEIR LABOUR ANALGESIA

Camille Raynes-Greenow[1], Christine Roberts[1] and Natasha Nassar[2]

[1] The Kolling Institute of Medical Research
Northern Clinical School, The University of Sydney
[2] The Telethon Institute for Child Health Research
Centre for Child Health Research, The University of Western Australia

ABSTRACT

The pain of labour is a central part of women's experience of childbirth. Many factors are considered influential in determining women's experience of and her satisfaction with childbirth. Women's expectations of the duration and level of pain suffered, quality of her care-giver support, and involvement in labour decision making are the most commonly reported factors.[1]

Significantly, there have been more clinical trials of pharmacological pain relief during labour and childbirth than of any other intervention in the perinatal field[2] however to what degree this evidence is available or discussed with pregnant women before labour is unclear.

DECISION MAKING AND PAIN IN LABOUR

The importance of discussing women's preferences for labour pain relief and their hopes and expectations in terms of pharmacological pain relief before labour begins is well established although it may not be well practiced.[2, 3] Women report fear of pain in childbirth and often lack complete information on analgesic options prior to labour.[4] Epidural consent (covering only the procedure and complications) is obtained by the anaesthetist at the time of the procedure by which time most women are already distressed.[5.] There is some debate surrounding whether informed consent can truly be gained at that time.[6] Some clinical practice guidelines have acknowledged this and suggest asking each woman about her preferences before labour begins.[7] Further issues for women have become evident as a result of research which has shown that women wish to maintain personal control during labour and birth, participate fully in the experience, and are concerned about untoward effects of medications during labour.[8] Antepartum decisions about the use of pain relief are likely to be influenced by women's cultural background, friends, family, the media, literature and her antenatal caregivers.[9] Regardless of their plans most women want more detailed and specific information about pain relief in labour.[10]

PATIENT PARTICIPATION IN CLINICAL DECISION MAKING

Recently decision aids are emerging as an effective tool to assist practitioners and their patients in evidence-based decision making.[11] They assist consumers with informed decision making by presenting unbiased information which is based on current, high quality, quantitative research evidence, which can be tailored to an individuals personal preferences. Decision aids are "interventions designed to help people make specific and deliberative choices among options by providing (at minimum) information on the options and outcomes relevant to the person's health status".[11] They are non-directive in the sense that they do not aim to steer the user towards any one option, but rather to support decision making which is informed, consistent with personal values and acted upon.[12] There is a growing body of research in this area in regards to women and labour analgesia decision making and this will be the focus of this chapter.

PAIN IN LABOUR AND CHILDBIRTH

Childbirth is an important cultural event and has a significant social and emotional impact on the life of a woman and her family. It is also the most common reason for accessing health services,[13] and a major pain experience, and for most women the most extreme and memorable pain of their lives.[14] Managing women's labour and childbirth pain is an important element of childbirth preparation and also an important aspect of the care provided for labouring women. Many factors are considered influential in determining women's experience of and her satisfaction with childbirth. Satisfaction with the birth experience has been associated with a woman's preparation for childbirth, her confidence in her ability to handle labour, the physiological intensity of labour, and her role in decision making.[2, 5] Women's expectations of the duration and level of pain suffered, quality of her care-giver support, and involvement in labour decision–making are commonly reported factors.[13] The pain of labour in particular is a central part of women's experience of childbirth. Labour pain and pain relief choices have implications for not only women and their families as it impacts on women's health but also have important consequences on health services.[13]

Historically childbirth pain, and pain relief or amelioration has been subjected to different fashions. In recent years the view of childbirth and labour pain has been seen more dichotomously, and the gap between "natural childbirth" and "right to a pain free birth" has widened.[15] Childbirth pain is viewed as either an expected and normal part of life,[1] or to be avoided and be controlled. Some providers emphasize the advantages of pharmacological methods (pain control) and others focus on potential disadvantages, and unintended side-effects.[16] For example, the American College of Obstetricians and Gynecologists practice guidelines say "that there is no other circumstance in which it is considered acceptable for a person to experience untreated severe pain" and suggest labour pain should be treated upon maternal request [17], whereas the Royal College of Obstetricians and Gynaecologists recommend a framework that suggests "working" with the pain of normal childbirth.[4] Regardless of the view point, labour pain and analgesia are a constant feature of antenatal discussion groups.[4] Whether it is something to be avoided or employed, the experience of labour pain is acknowledged to be individual and a function of "women's emotional, motivational, cognitive, social and cultural circumstances".[15, pg S4]

Labour pain can be managed in many ways, but epidural analgesia is the most effective form of pain relief for labour.[15] In western countries most women use some methods of pain relief during labour whether it be pharmacological and or non-pharmacological analgesia. In the US the use of epidural analgesia is widespread, and approximately 50% or two million women receive an epidural for pain relief each year.[18] In 2005 in New South Wales, Australia (the most populous state of Australia) 96% of primiparas (women having their first baby) and 85% of multiparas (women having a subsequent baby) used some pharmacological analgesic agents for birth.[19] The use of epidural analgesia is influenced by factors at the patient level, the provider level, and at the institutional level.[16] For example in populations that have increased access and availability of epidurals the rate is strongly associated with this. In New South Wales, in hospitals with greater availability this rate could be as high as 74%. [20] Around the world other pharmacological methods of pain relief are also widely available and used. In New South Wales, for primiparas in 2005 this included 27% opioids and 52% nitrous oxide. [21]

Significantly, there have been more clinical trials of pharmacological pain relief during labour and childbirth than of any other intervention in the perinatal field.[2] There are however very limited examples of research translation of these clinical trials for pregnant women and to what degree this evidence is available or discussed with pregnant women before labour is unclear.

DECISION MAKING AND PAIN IN LABOUR

There is considerable evidence that women want to be involved in their pregnancy decision making, and that their level of involvement is related to their overall satisfaction with their care which in turn has been related to the quality of subsequent mothering.[22 - 26] Enabling women to make informed decisions for their pregnancy and labour care is therefore important, and relevant to health care providers, administrators and policy makers. However a study found that women's most important source of labour analgesia information was experiential information from their family and friends, and not with their antenatal care providers.[27]

The importance of discussing women's preferences for labour pain relief and their hopes and expectations before labour begins is well known although it may not be well practiced.[2, 3] Women report fear of pain in childbirth and often lack complete information on analgesic options prior to labour.[4, 27] For example the Royal Australian and New Zealand College of Obstetricians and Gynaecologists brochure on 'Epidural and Spinal Anaesthesia' reports the advantages of epidurals but does not mention any possible adverse outcomes or complications.[28] While written informed consent is required for epidural analgesia, it is not required for other analgesic options. Further, the epidural consent (covering only the procedure and complications) is obtained by the anaesthetist at the time of the procedure - by which time most women are already distressed. [5.] There is some debate if informed consent can truly be gained at that time and whether it is ethical.[6] Some clinical practice guidelines have acknowledged this and suggest asking each woman about her preferences before labour begins.[7] Further issues for women have become evident as a result of research which has shown that women wish to maintain personal control during labour and birth, participate fully in the experience, and are concerned about untoward effects of medications during labour.[29] Antepartum decisions to use pain relief is likely influenced by women's cultural background, friends, family, the media, literature and her antenatal caregivers.[9] Specifically a survey of Australian women found that antepartum information about analgesia was most commonly derived from hearsay and least commonly from health professionals.[26] Ranta found that prior to birth 82% of women wish to see how labour progresses and only want analgesia when pain becomes severe or intolerable, [30] however definite plans for analgesia are strongly associated with use. One study found that 96% of women who definitely planned to have an epidural, received one.[9] Regardless of their plans most women want more detailed and specific information about pain relief in labour.[10]

PATIENT PARTICIPATION IN CLINICAL DECISION MAKING

Making evidence-based decisions in clinical practice is not always straightforward: patients and their healthcare providers must often weigh up the evidence between several comparable options, and the evidence for some treatments may be inconclusive. O'Connor suggests that to be useful the information needs to be tailored to each patient's clinical context and personal preferences.[31] The (Australian) National Health and Medical Research Council states that good medical decision making should take into account the best available evidence, along with patients' preferences and values.[32] And a paper arising from a symposium on the nature and management of labour pain writes "We are obligated to inform women ... so they can make truly informed decisions about the use of pain relief in labor".[33] However, finding effective and efficient mechanisms for doing this in the clinical setting is a challenge.

DECISION AIDS TO SUPPORT DECISION MAKING

The first efforts to provide information to patients were through leaflets and brochures. However these often become outdated and or inaccurate, omit relevant data, fail to give a balanced view and ignore uncertainties and scientific controversies.[34-36] Conversely, decision aids have been shown as an effective tool to assist practitioners and their patients in evidence-based decision making.[37] They assist health consumers with informed decision making by presenting unbiased information which is based on current, high quality, quantitative research evidence, which can be tailored to an individuals personal preferences.

Decision aids are "interventions designed to help people make specific and deliberative choices among options by providing (at minimum) information on the options and outcomes relevant to the person's health status".[37] Decision aids differ from usual health education materials because of their detailed, specific, and personalised focus on options and outcomes for the purpose of preparing people for decision making. In contrast, health education materials are broader in perspective, helping people to understand their diagnosis, treatment, and management in general terms, but not necessarily helping them to make a specific, personal, choice between options.[11] Decision aids are non-directive in the sense that they do not aim to steer the user towards any one option, but rather to support decision making which is informed, consistent with personal values and acted upon.[38] Decision aids have been found to improve patient knowledge and create more realistic expectations, to reduce decisional conflict (uncertainty about the course of action) and to stimulate patients to be more active in decision making without increasing anxiety.[12]

DECISION AID FORMATS

There is a wide variety of formats for decision aids. A Cochrane systematic review of decision aids identified 221 aids, for screening or treatment decisions, using an array of presentation designs. The traditional format of an aid is a booklet style, with or without the an audio guide, however formats include video presentations, brochures, analytical hierarchal processing via personal computers, poster board cards and on-line presentations.[11] Despite the evaluation of decision aids in clinical settings the style and presentation format has not be properly evaluated. The results of a randomised controlled trial evaluating two formats will provide the first evidence of the benefit or otherwise of using an audio guided book compared to a stand alone book.[39]

DECISION AID COMPONENTS

Regardless of the format there are common components included in decision aids. All decision aids include; information about the clinical problem, the management options, the probability of these options, examples of other people making the decision, and guidance in the steps of decision making. They may also include a values clarification exercise, which helps the user consider the outcomes in accordance to how important each outcome is to the user.[40] An important difference between decision aids and other patient information are that they are tailored as much as possible to the individual considering the options.[38] The probabilistic information are obtained from the highest quality research evidence available. These probabilities are presented in styles that are specifically designed to assist consumers understand complex risk data using graphics such as the 100 faces™ (Ottawa Health

Research Institute) diagrams (with the number of shaded faces representing the probability of each outcome occurring) and indicate via a rating system (such as gold, silver or bronze medal) the quality of evidence supporting each probability estimate. These pictorial designs have been shown to be acceptable to women and helpful to understanding risk data.[41]

DECISION AIDS FOR PREGNANCY AND CONSUMER PARTICIPATION

Although there are many decision aids that have been developed and evaluated for a variety of health conditions there are only a few decision aids developed for pregnancy and birth issues. [39, 42-45] However this is an area in which consumers are known to want to actively participate in decision making.[46] A survey of 790 Australian women reported a tenfold increase in dissatisfaction among those who did not have an active say in decisions about pregnancy care.[46] Similarly in the UK, women rated the explanation of procedures, including the risks, before they are carried out and involvement in decision making as most important in satisfaction with care.[47] A recommendation from a US survey suggested that women, caregivers and administrators need access to results of the best available research about the effectiveness and possible side-effects of both pain medications and drug-free measures for labour pain relief, and further stated that women need full and complete information about these matters well in advance of labour and again during labour.[48] It is increasingly evident that the provision of patient and provider information alone, even if evidence-based, is not sufficient to influence health outcomes and behaviour.[49] It is only when mechanisms are provided that tailor this information to the individual patient that health outcomes, related to treatment decisions, are positively effected.[50]

Importantly satisfaction with childbirth is not necessarily contingent upon the absence of pain.[30] Many women are willing to experience pain in childbirth but do not want pain to overwhelm them. The Royal College of Obstetrics and Gynaecology makes the following evidence-based recommendations [51], midwives must involve women in decisions about analgesia and recognise the value of promoting personal control, maternity services should ensure access to written and verbal information on pain relief and should support women in their choices for pain relief, maternity services should respect women's wishes to have some control over their pain relief and there should be improved public information and data on labour pain and analgesia.

INTRAPARTUM LABOUR ANALGESIA
EVIDENCE OF EFFECTIVENESS FOR PHARMACOLOGICAL ANALGESIA

There is a myriad of evidence assessing the effectiveness and outcomes of analgesia for labour. Randomised controlled trials have shown epidural analgesia provides the most efficacious pain relief for labour, but this must be balanced by the increase in risk of adverse consequences[33]. For epidural analgesia the immediate outcomes can include prolonged labour, restricted mobility, use of oxytocin augmentation, unsatisfactory analgesia, dural-puncture headache, hypotension, nausea and vomiting, fever, intermediate localised backache, shivering, pruritis and urinary retention and an increased incidence of instrumental delivery.[48, 49] The consequences of instrumental delivery in the longer term can include increased risk of continuing perineal pain, short-term urinary incontinence, and sexual problems.[50] Although not as effective for labour pain relief as epidural, randomised trials show inhalational analgesia (e.g. 50% nitrous oxide in oxygen) and systemic opioid analgesics (e.g. pethidine) can provide modest benefit to some patients during labour or supplement an unsatisfactory epidural, however also have increased risks, although different to epidural analgesia.[52] These risks include nausea, vomiting and dizziness, and additionally opioid side-effects may include hypotension, delayed stomach emptying and respiratory depression in the baby.[51] Although the risks and benefits of these analgesics are well studied they may not be fully understood by women who are choosing these options for labour pain relief.

EVIDENCE OF EFFECTIVENESS FOR NON-PHARMACOLOGICAL ANALGESIA

Non-pharmacological analgesic options has also been widely investigated and often have less adverse consequences, and considerable numbers of women prefer to avoid the pharmacological methods if possible.[29] Non-pharmacological methods of pain relief include maternal movement and position changes, superficial heat and cold, immersion in water, massage, acupuncture, acupressure, transcutaneous electrical nerve stimulation (TENS), aromatherapy, attention focusing, hypnosis, music or audio analgesia and continuous caregiver support. Most of these methods have been assessed in randomised trials.[53] The results vary with regard to the effectiveness of the pain relief they provide however they are well liked by women and have few side effects.

Although there is a large amount of information of the effectiveness and outcomes of labour analgesia the availability of this evidence for women who are known to be interested in making informed decisions is limited.

FACILITATING LABOUR ANALGESIA DECISION MAKING SUITABILITY FOR A DECISION AID

Eddy 1992, suggests that when a clinical decision is modifiable by patients' values and preferences then it fulfils the criteria in which patients would benefit from a decision aid.[54] The management of pain in labour meets Eddy's criteria for a decision aid as the outcomes for analgesia options and women's preferences for the relative value of benefits compared to risks are variable. For such a clinical decision, a decision aid would be expected to improve patient knowledge and create realistic expectations, to reduce decisional conflict and to stimulate patients to be more active in decision making without increasing anxiety.[54]

The availability of good evidence for labour analgesia coupled with the desire of women to participate in their decision making suggests that a decision aid may be an ideal tool for women choosing between a range of options for the management of labour pain. Such a tool may also benefit antenatal care-providers who are interested in practicing shared decision making. Ideally any such tool would need to present pain management in a positive and flexible way, acknowledging the unpredictability of events around childbirth, and would encourage flexibility in choices and create awareness of the unpredictability of childbirth that may change the appropriateness of some options. The success of decision aids thus far in a variety of health settings is encouraging and results of trials conducted in the perinatal setting [43, 45, 55] also suggest that a decision aid will be well received and useful for pregnant women interested in making informed decisions regarding labour analgesia. There is currently a trial of a decision aid for labour analgesia recently completed[39], and another in development.[56] The results of these will be an important step for enabling pregnant women to participate in informed decision-making regarding their labour analgesia.

REFERENCES

[1] McLachlan, H. and U. Waldenstrom, *Childbirth experiences in Australia of women born in Turkey, Vietnam and Australia.* Birth, 2005. 32(4).
[2] Dickersin, K., *Pharmacological control of pain during labour*, in *Effective care in pregnancy and childbirth*, I. Chalmers, M. Enkin, and M.J.N. Keirse, Editors. 1989, Oxford University Press: Oxford. p. 913-945.
[3] Enkin, M., Keirse, M.J.N.C., Neilson, J., Crowther, C., Duley, L., Hodnott, E., Hofmeyr, J., *Control of pain in labor*, in *A guide to effective care in pregnancy and childbirth*. 2000, Oxford Medical Publications: Oxford. p. 314-331.
[4] Leap, N., *Pain in labour: towards a midwifery perspective.* MIDIRS Midwifery Digest, 2000. 10(1): p. 49-53.
[5] Swan, H.D. and D.C. Borshoff, *Informed consent--recall of risk information following epidural analgesia in labour.* Anaesthesia and Intensive Care, 1994. 22(2): p. 139-41.
[6] Siddiqui Meraj N, et al., *Does labor pain and labor epidural analgesia impair decison capabilities of paturients.* The Internet Journal of Anesthesiology, 2005. 10(1).
[7] National Collaborating Centre for Women's and Children' Health, *Antenatal care: routine care for the healthy pregnant woman Royal College of Obstetrician and Gynaecologists.* Commissioned by the National Institute for Clinical Excellence (UK). 2003.
[8] Simkin, P. and O.H. M., *Nonpharmacologic relief of pain during labor: Systematic review of five methods.* Am J Obstet Gynecol, 2002. 186(Suppl 5): p. S131 - S159.
[9] Goldberg, A.B., A. Cohen, and E. Lieberman, *Nulliparas' preferences for epidural analgesia: their effects on actual use in labor.* Birth, 1999. 26(3): p. 139-43.
[10] Stewart, A., et al., *Assessment of the effect upon maternal knowledge of an information leaflet about pain relief in labour.* Anaesthesia, 2003. 58(10): p. p1015-9.
[11] O'Connor, A., et al., *Decision aids for people facing health treatment ot screening decisions.* In: The Cochrane Library, Issue 1. Oxford: Update Software., 2004.
[12] O'Connor, A., et al., *Decision aids for patients facing health treatment or screening decisions: systematic review.* BMJ, 1999. 319(7212): p. 731-4.
[13] Hodnett, E.D.R.N.P., *Pain and women's satisfaction with the experience of childbirth: A systematic review.* American Journal of Obstetrics and Gynecology May, 2002. 186(5)): p. S160-S172.

[14] Niven, C. and T. Murphy-Black, *Memory of labour pain: A review of the literature.* Birth, 2000. 27: p. 244-254.
[15] Caton, D., et al., *The nature and management of labor pain.* American Journal of Obstetrics and Gynecology, 2002. 186(5 Suppl): p. S1-15.
[16] Rust, G., et al., *Racial and ethnic disparities in the provision of epidural analgesia to Georgia Medicaid beneficiaries during labor and delivery.* Am J Obstet Gynecol, 2004. 191(2): p. 456-462.
[17] American College of Obstetricians and Gynecologists, *ACOG practice bulletin no. 36. Clinical management Guidelines for Obstetrician-Gynaecologists.* Obstetric Analgesia and Anesthesia, 2002. 100(1).
[18] Hawkins, J.L., B.R. Beatty, and C.P. Gibbs, *Update on anaethesia practices in the US*, in *Society for Anesthesia and Perinatology.* 1999.
[19] NSW Department of Health, *NSW Mothers and Babies 1998*, in *NSW Public Health Bulletin.* 2000, NSW Department of Health: Sydney.
[20] NSW Department of Health, *NSW Mothers and Babies 2000*, in *NSW Public Health Bulletin Supplement.* 2001, NSW Department of Health: Sydney.
[21] Laws P.J, et al., *Australia' mothers and babies 2005*, in *Perinatal Statistics series. no.20 Cat.no.PER 40.* 2007, AIHW National Perinatal Statistics Unit: Sydney.
[22] Brown, J.B., et al., *Women's decision-making about their health care: views over the life cycle.* Patient Education and Counseling, 2002. 48: p. 225-231.
[23] Fenwick J, et al., *The childbirth expectations of a self-selecetd cohort of Western Australian women.* Midwifery, 2005. 21(1): p. 23-35.
[24] Gibbins J and Thomson A.M, *Women's expectations and expereinces of childbirth.* Midwifery, 2001. 17(4): p. 302-13.
[25] Mackay, M.C., *Women's evaluation of the labour and delivery experience.* Nursing Connections, 1998. 11(3): p. 19-32.
[26] Paech, M.J. and L.C. Gurrin, *A survey of parturients using epidural analgesia during labour. Considerations relevant to antenatal educators.* Australian and New Zealand Journal of Obstetrics and Gynaecology, 1999. 39(1): p. 21-5.
[27] Raynes-Greenow, C.H., et al., *Knowledge and decision-making for labour analgesia of Australian primiparous women.* Midwifery, 2007. 23(2): p. 139-145.
[28] Royal Australian and New Zealand College of Obstetricians and Gynaecologists. *Epidural and spinal anasthesia. Patient information pamphlet.* 1998 [cited 1998 Feb]; Available from: http://www.ranzcog.edu.au.
[29] Simkin, P., *Non-pharmacological methods of pain relief during labour*, in *Effective care in pregnancy and childbirth*, I. Chalmers, M. Enkin, and M.J.N. Keirse, Editors. 1989, Oxford University Press: Oxford. p. 1182-1195.
[30] Ranta, P., et al., *Maternal expectations and experiences of labour pain--options of 1091 Finnish parturients.* Acta Anaesthesiologica Scandinavica, 1995. 39(1): p. 60-6.
[31] O'Connor, A., et al., *Decision aids for people facing health treatment or screening decisions.* Cochrane Library, Issue 4., 2002.
[32] National Health and Medical Research Council, *A Guide to the Development, Implementation and Evaluation of Clinical Practice Guidelines.* 1999.
[33] Lieberman, E. and C. O'Donoghue, *Unintended effects of epidural analgesia during labor: a systematic review.* American Journal of Obstetrics and Gynecology., 2002. 186(5 Suppl Nature): p. S31-68.

[34] Coulter, A., *Evidence based patient information. is important, so there needs to be a national strategy to ensure it.* BMJ, 1998. 317(7153): p. 225-6.

[35] Coulter, A., V. Entwistle, and D. Gilbert, *Sharing decisions with patients: is the information good enough?* BMJ, 1999. 318(7179): p. 318-22.

[36] Paech, M.J., R. Godkin, and S. Webster, *Complications of obstetric epidural analgesia and anaesthesia: a prospective analysis of 10 995 cases.* International Journal of Anesthesia, 1998. 7: p. 5-11.

[37] O'Connor, A. and A. Edwards, *The role of decision aids in promoting evidence-based patient choice*, in *Evidence based patient choice*, A. Edwards and G. Elwyn, Editors. 2001, Oxford University Press: Oxford.

[38] O'Connor, A.M., et al., *Decision aids for patients considering options affecting cancer outcomes: evidence of efficacy and policy implications.* Journal of the National Cancer Institute. Monographs, 1999(25): p. 67-80.

[39] Roberts, C., et al., *Protocol for a randomised controlled trial of a decision aid for the management of pain in labour and childbirth [ISRCTN52287533].* BMC Pregnancy and Childbirth, 2004. 4(1): p. 24.

[40] O'Connor, A., et al., *Decision aids for people facing health treatment or screening decisions.* Cochrane Library, Issue 4., 2001.

[41] Nassar, N., et al., *Development and pilot-testing of a decision aid for women with a breech-presenting baby.* Midwifery, 2007. 23(1):38-47.

[42] Karraz, M.A., *Ambulatory epidural anesthesia and the duration of labor.* Int J Gynaecol Obstet, 2003. 80(2): p. 117-22.

[43] Nassar, N., et al., *Evaluation of a decision aid for women with breech presentation at term: a randomised controlled trial [ISRCTN14570598].* BJOG: An International Journal of Obstetrics and Gynaecology, 2007. 114(3): p. 325–333.

[44] O'Cathain, A., et al., *Use of evidence based leaflets to promote informed choice in maternity care: randomised controlled trial in everyday practice.* British Medical Journal, 2002. 324(7338): p. 643-647.

[45] Montgomery, A.A., et al., *Two decision aids for mode of delivery among women with previous caesarean section: randomsied controlled trial.* BMJ, 2007. 334 (7607): p. 1305-1312.

[46] Brown, S. and J. Lumley, *Satisfaction with care in labor and birth: a survey of 790 Australian women.* Birth, 1994. 21(1): p. 4-13.

[47] Drew, N., P. Salmon, and L. Webb, *Mothers', midwives' and obstetricians' views on the features of obstetric care which influence satisfaction with childbirth.* Br J Obstet Gynaecol, 1989. 96(9): p. 1084-8.

[48] Association, M.C., *Recommendations from Listening to Mothers: The First U.S Survey of Women's Childbearing Experiences. .* Birth, 2004. 31: p. 61-65.

[49] Bekker, H., et al., *Informed decision making: an annotated bibliography and systematic review.* Health Technology Assessment, 1999. 3(1): p. 1-156.

[50] Edwards, A., et al., *The effectiveness of one-to-one risk communication interventions in health care: a systematic review.* Medical Decision Making, 2000. 20(3): p. 290-7.

[51] Royal College of Obstetricians and Gynaecologists. *Recommendations arising from the 41st Study Group on Pain in Obstetrics and Gynaecology.* 2002 [cited 2nd of Jan]; Available from: http://www.rcog.org.uk/study/rec_41st.htm.

[52] American College of Obstetricians and Gynecologists, *ACOG committee opinion. Mode of term singleton breech delivery. Number 265, December 2001. American College of Obstetricians and Gynecologists.* International Journal of Gynaecology and Obstetrics., 2002. 77(1): p. 65-6.

[53] Smith, C.A., et al., *Complementary and alternative therapies for pain management in labour. Cochrane Database of Systematic Reviews* 2006, Issue 4.

[54] Eddy, D.M., *A manual for assessing health practices and designing practice policies: the explicit approach.* 1992, Philadelphia: American College of Physicians.

[55] Shorten, A., et al., *Making choices for childbirth: development and testing of a decision-aid for women who have experienced previous caesarean.* Patient Education and Counseling, 2004. 52(3): p. 307-313.

[56] Personal communication via email. Between Dr. W .Otten and Dr. C. Raynes-Greenow, (Author). Sydney December 2007.

In: Psychology of Decision Making
Editor: Paul M. Garrison

ISBN 978-1-60021-869-9
© Nova Science Publishers, Inc.

Chapter 7

ADOLESCENT DECISION-MAKING ABOUT SUBSTANCE USE: A VIDEO-BASED ASSESSMENT

Kristen G. Anderson[1,*] *and Sara J. Parent*[2]

[1]University of California, San Diego, Departments of Psychology & Psychiatry CA, USA
[2]University of California, San Diego, Department of Psychology CA, USA

ABSTRACT

Adolescence is a period characterized by rapid cognitive and social change. As youth move through adolescence, they are faced with a myriad of decisions regarding risky behavior, including substance involvement. Given the importance of the social sphere for teens, these decisions are often influenced by peers. There is a growing body of research into the processes underlying adolescent decision-making regarding alcohol and drug use. However, few process-oriented assessment approaches have been developed to understand how youth make these decisions in the moment. This chapter briefly reviews the literature on adolescent decision-making regarding alcohol and drugs, presents a social-information processing model for adolescent substance use, and describes the development of a novel video-based approach to assessing adolescent decision-making. This assessment integrates methods traditionally used in the educational setting as well as those developed for clinical populations of youth. Preliminary data from the development phase of the assessment will be presented. The implications for adolescent research in risk taking, substance involvement and intervention with youth will be discussed.

INTRODUCTION

Adolescence is a period of rapid biological, cognitive and social change, initiated by the biological transition of puberty and culminating with the cognitive development necessary to

---

[*] Correspondence to: Kristen G. Anderson, Ph.D., Reed College, Department of Psychology, 3203 S.E. Woodstock Avenue, Portland, Oregon 97202, Kristen.Anderson@reed.edu

make adult decisions (S.A. Brown, personal communication, November 29, 2006). Throughout this period, adolescents are faced with the challenges of identity development, growing independence from parents, and navigating an increasingly complex social sphere (Graber & Brooks-Gunn, 2002). Youth decisions regarding the use of alcohol and other drugs take place within the shifting landscape of adolescent development (Brown, Anderson, Ramo & Tomlinson, 2005). The purpose of this chapter is to outline the developmental processes of adolescence that influence substance use decision-making, present a model of social-information processing regarding alcohol and other drug involvement, and describe the development of a novel process-oriented procedure for assessing adolescent substance use decision-making.

ADOLESCENT DEVELOPMENT AND DECISION-MAKING

Adolescent development represents a complex interplay of biological, cognitive, emotional, and psychosocial changes (Brown, Anderson, Ramo & Tomlinson, 2005). The biological changes of puberty, i.e., rapid increases in size, hormonal changes, and the development of secondary sexual characteristics, influence gender-based conceptions of self and identity (Brookes-Gunn & Reiter, 1990). As a function of neuromaturation during this period, teens increase their ability to inhibit, control and modulate behavior. The prefrontal cortex becomes more efficient and better able to communicate with other brain structures throughout adolescence and into adulthood allowing for higher level abstract thinking and improved executive functioning (Giedd et al., 1999). Compared to adults, adolescents are less able to delay gratification, use forethought, spontaneously generate consequences for their actions, and learn from negative outcomes (Reyna & Farley, 2006). Emotionally, adolescents tend to experience greater negative affect, but are less able to regulate and cope with these feelings than adults. In the context of increasing psychosical demands (e.g., greater independence from parents, increasing peer influence, instigation of sexual relationships, and greater academic expectations), youth are disadvantaged by their lack of experience and poorer emotional regulation abilities when coping with stress (Tate et al., 2007). As teens mature, their primary social influences move away from their parents to peers as a normative transition towards greater autonomy (Zimmer-Gembeck & Collins, 2006). When youth are unable to adequately meet the specific challenges associated with adolescence, psychopathology may develop (Rekers, 1992).

Adult decision-making is predicated on the ability to adequately understand available behavioral choices and predict potential consequences for our actions. In adolescence, youth decision-making is influenced by their level of cognitive development. Research suggests that youth are generally more impulsive and tend to focus on immediate rewards for behavior in comparison to adults (Reyna & Farley, 2006). While adults certainly evidence faulty decision-making at times and may evidence personality traits (i.e., impulsivity, sensation seeking) that predispose them to risk-taking, adolescence seems to be developmental period associated with a greater likelihood for risky decision-making than adulthood (Reyna & Farley, 2006). As youth transition into more adult roles, they are required to make important decisions with regard to the future, i.e., going to college, initiation of sexual activity, and substance involvement (Brown et al., 2005) at a time when their ability to recognize the long term consequences of these choices are immature (Reyna & Farley, 2006).

ADOLESCENCE AND SUBSTANCE USE

The majority of youth make their first decisions about recreational alcohol and drug use during the adolescent period. Data from the Monitoring the Future study (Johnston, O'Malley, Bachman, & Schulenberg, 2006) indicates that three quarters of US high school students have tried alcohol by 12th grade and over half report being drunk in their lifetime. In terms of substance involvement, more than half of high school seniors report lifetime illicit substance use with slightly over a quarter reporting substance use other than marijuana (Johnston et al., 2006). By contrast, only 20 percent of 8th graders have tried alcohol and 16 percent marijuana, suggesting that mid-adolescence is an important period in decision-making about substance use (Johnston et al., 2006).

While not all youth who use alcohol and other drugs progress to dependence, a significant proportion of teens meet criteria for a substance use disorder. In the US, it has been estimated that 9.7% of youth (15 - 24 years) suffer from alcohol use disorders and 6.2% from other drug use disorders (Warner, Canino & Colon, 2001). For those youth who do receive treatment for substance use disorders (the vast majority with these disorders do not obtain treatment; SAMHSA, 2002), anywhere from a third to three quarters of adolescents relapse to alcohol or other drugs during the first year post-treatment (Brown, Mott & Myers, 1990; Cornelius, Clark, Bukstein & Salloum, 2005) and many return to problematic substance use (Tomlinson, Brown & Abrantes, 2004). From a developmental perspective, relapse to substance use exposes youth to a myriad of risks associated with poor developmental outcomes in a number of important domains including health, interpersonal, occupational and educational (Anderson, Ramo, Cumins & Brown, 2007; Brown & Tapert, 2004).

Consistent with the growing influence of social networks and peers, youth tend to drink alcohol or use drugs with friends. Research into situational precursors of alcohol and drug relapse among teens after treatment suggest that youth most commonly use in small groups of 3 to 4 youth in the afternoon or evening, at home or in a friend's home, when socializing (Anderson, Frissell & Brown, in press; Brown, Vik & Creamer, 1989). In unpublished data from community samples, young adolescents also evidence a similar pattern in early use situations (Anderson & Brown, 2007). The decision-making literature suggests that youth abilities to make rational decisions are likely disadvantaged in social situations involving peers (Reyna & Farley, 2006). As such, understanding youth decisions regarding alcohol and other drugs should be considered within the social milieu.

Many theories and models have been posited to explain how youth first use alcohol and other substances and return to substance use after treatment (Connors, Maisto, & Donovan, 1996; Schulenburg, Maggs, Steinman, & Zucker, 2001). A comprehensive review of these models far exceeds the scope of this chapter. However, these models often present the distal and proximal predictors of alcohol and other drug use initiation (Ellickson & Hays, 1992; McGue, Iacono, Legrand, & Elkins, 2001), problematic use (Deas & Upadhyaya, 2003; Willoughby, Chalmers, & Busseri, 2004) and relapse (Anderson, Ramo, Cumins & Brown, in press; Rohde & Andrews, 2006). Adolescent and adult relapse models have been presented that outline the multiple influences impacting decisions to use in high-risk situations (Brown & Ramo, 2006; Witkiewitz & Marlatt, 2004). However, missing from the literature is a process-oriented model that depicts the social cognitive processes underlying adolescent choices to use or not use alcohol or drugs in social situations.

SOCIAL INFORMATION PROCESSING MODEL FOR ADOLESCENT SUBSTANCE USE

One potential explanatory model is the Social Information Processing (SIP; Crick & Dodge, 1994) model which uses an information processing approach to examine decision-making in social situations. Social information processing models describe a sequence of cognitive events related to encoding environmental cues, creating mental representations of these cues, making associations to emotional states and goals, generating and evaluating response options, and decision-making (Dodge, Lochman, Laird, & Zelli, 2002). Developed to explain the linkage between cognition and behavior in children in the midst of challenging social situations, the social information processing framework has recently been integrated into a developmentally-focused cognitive behavioral model of substance use relapse for youth (Brown & Ramo, 2006). Our goal here is to provide a general framework to understand how social-information processing could impact "in the moment" decisions by adolescents to use alcohol or drugs in the social milieu, across the range of situations from initiation to hazardous use to relapse for youth post-treatment.

At the individual level, the SIP model describes a sequence of information processing underlying adolescent decisions to drink or use other drugs. In the encoding phase (see figure 1), youth identify the salient internal and external cues within the social context. Internal affective cues (e.g., anxiety, depression, anger), prevalent among those with substance use problems (Tomlinson, Brown & Abrantes, 2004) may bias the encoding of information within the social milieu (Crick & Dodge, 1994). Cue reactivity, or conditioned responses to environmental stimuli associated with alcohol and other illicit substances, has been implicated in the process of substance use relapse (Niaura et al., 1988). Teens with alcohol use disorders have been shown to have substantially greater brain activation to alcohol-related cues than controls (Tapert et al., 2003) and recent theoretical work suggests that enhanced attentional focus on drug cues might trigger both explicit and implicit processing of drug-related cognitions (e.g., expectancies and intrusive thoughts; Franken, 2003). Additionally, personality traits associated with alcohol and other drug use (e.g., disinhibition, impulsivity) might bias youth encoding of situationally-specific cues associated with drinking and drug use (Anderson, Smith, & Fischer, 2003).

The stored database of information regarding past experience with alcohol, whether direct or modeled is believed to influence all aspects of social-information processing to a greater or lesser degree. When youth interpret cues from the social environment (Phase 2), it is believed that learning in similar situations has a significant impact on information processing (Crick & Dodge, 1994). For example, expectancies, in the form of probabilistic, if-then relationships, are learned and held in memory to influence an individual's future behavior (Goldman, Brown, Christiansen & Smith, 1991; Miller, Smith, & Goldman, 1990). In the literature, outcome expectancies have held a central role in explanations for initiation of drinking in adolescence (Smith, Goldman, Greenbaum, & Christiansen, 1995), the progression and maintenance of substance use over time (Brown, 1993; Sher, Walitzer, Wood, & Brent, 1991) and have often been shown to mediate the influence of more distal risk factors (e.g., personality, family history; Anderson, Smith & Fischer, 2003; Sher et al., 1991). In addition, investigations have found that implicit cognitions, below the level of conscious processing, are also predictive of substance use (Stacy, 1997).

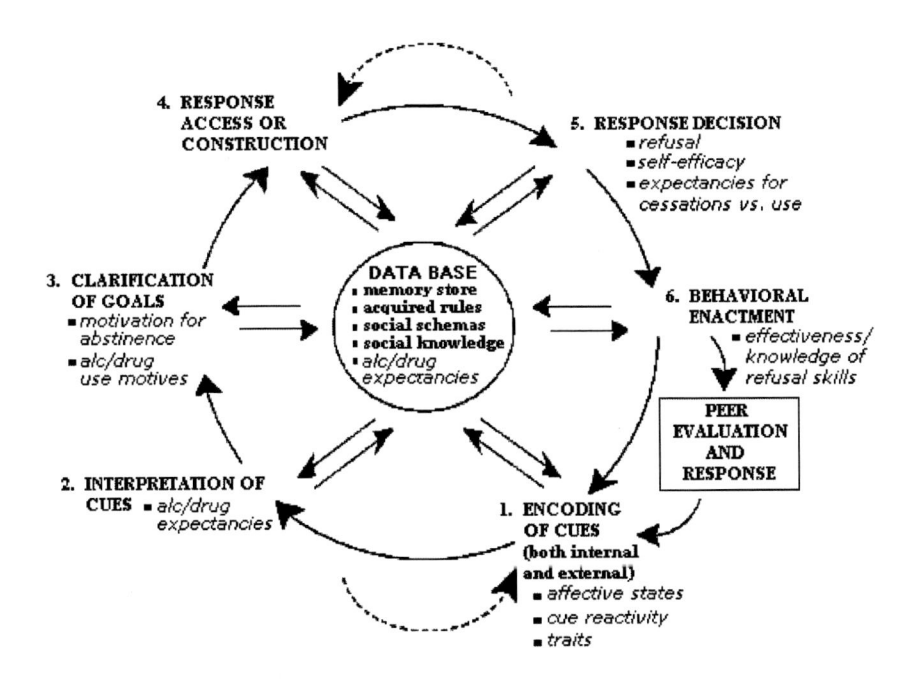

Figure 1: Crick, N. R., & Dodge, K. A. (1994). A review and reformulation of social information-processing mechanisms in children's social adjustment. *Psychological Bulletin, 155*(1), p. 76. American Psychological Association. Adapted with permission.

When clarifying goals (Phase 3), youth identify what they would like to happen in a given situation. In relation to alcohol and other drug use, motivation determines to a great degree what outcome is preferred. For youth with a high motivation for abstinence, engaging socially with peers without using substances might be their desired outcome (Metrik et al., 2003). However, competing motives might impact decision-making. Using Cooper's model of motivations for drinking (Cooper, Russell, Skinner, & Windle, 1992), individuals are believed to use substances on the basis of three potential motives: coping, social or enhancement. For youth facing social situations where alcohol and drugs are available, these motives might conflict with their motivation for abstinence, leading to difficulties in identifying situationally specific goals (i.e., a motivation to abstain or use moderately versus a motivation for social conformity).

Consistent with the view presented above for cue interpretation, it is believed that the learning history of individuals influences their ability to access potential response choices and make decisions regarding alcohol use (Phase 4- response access and Phase 5- behavioral choice). For youth with substantial substance use histories, their memory network regarding substance use, biased towards more positive expectancies for the effects of substances as well as exposure to more models of past use, make them more susceptible to say "yes" when making the choice between using and not using alcohol or other drugs. Decisions to use or not use in high-risk situations are a function of their self-efficacy to refuse (Marlatt & Gordon, 1980). Recent investigations have examined use and cessation patterns integrating social-cognition from this perspective for adolescents and adults. Metrik and colleagues (2003) examined beliefs about abstinence from alcohol use from the social information processing perspective in adolescents. In adolescents, youth expectations for the consequences of reducing or stopping drinking were clustered in global and peer social domains, both predictive of youth decisions to reduce or stop drinking. Further, Schuckit et al. (2005) examined how level of response to alcohol could influence alcohol outcomes for adolescents integrating social information processing. It was found that a model that integrated family history of alcoholism, level of response to alcohol, and expectancies for drinking predicted alcohol use in adolescents. In terms of youth abilities to refuse substances (Phase 6), research on adolescents continues to explore the assertion that youth who drink have demonstrable social skill and coping skill deficits. Refusal skills have been the focus of many substance use interventions in school-aged children and community youth (Silverman, 1990). From the SIP perspective, we might expect youth in social situations geared toward drinking and drug use to demonstrate impaired ability to refuse direct or repeated alcohol or drug offers as a functioning of their use histories; youth with substance use disorders would be seen as having the greatest level of impairment.

As stated at the outset, the model presented above is stated in generic terms. Specific types of substance use decisions, whether to initiate use or relapse after abstinence, might highlight deficits at different phases of social information processing (e.g., cue reactivity impacting encoding for substance use disordered youth). Future investigations from this theoretical framework with different samples of youth will elucidate the specific mechanisms relating to use patterns and social information processing.

VIDEO-BASED ASSESSMENT OF SOCIAL INFORMATION PROCESSING

While the SIP model for substance use is consistent with the literature on substance use and social information processing, a missing link in validating this perspective is a method for assessing youth decision-making regarding alcohol and drug use in the moment. Our goal was to develop an in vivo assessment of the cognitive processes underlying adolescent decisions regarding alcohol and other drug use in a safe, controlled environment. To do so, we have integrated two existing procedures for assessing cognitions in the moment as well as social information processing: the Articulated Thoughts in Simulated Situations paradigm (ATSS; Davison, Robins & Johnson, 1983) and a video-based method for assessing social-information processing (Dodge & Price, 1994).

The ATSS is a method of cognitive assessment using a think-aloud approach. Think-alouds are commonly used in classroom settings, and are useful in evaluating both the products and processes of cognition as they occur. In the ATSS paradigm, participants are presented with simulated social situations and asked to report, either verbally or in writing, on their thoughts while the situations are taking place. Past research has validated this procedure for assessing cognitions associated with anxiety and depression (Davison et al., 1991; White et al., 1992), 1992), cognitive changes due to therapeutic intervention (Davison et al., 1991), and investigations of the SIP model with adolescent aggression (DiLiberto, Katz, Beauchamp & Howells, 2002). Research into cognitions associated with smoking cessation and relapse based on a cognitive behavioral model of relapse suggest that the ATSS procedure is a useful adjunct to traditional self-report measures (Haaga, 1989; Haaga & Stewart, 1992).

Several key structural elements of the ATTS paradigm make it an appropriate assessment model for evaluating the SIP model for substance use. First, the ATTS paradigm asks participants to report on all cognitions associated with the presented situations in an open-ended format rather than limiting participants to predetermined alternatives that may or may not represent their actual thoughts or feelings. Second, this paradigm allows for near-concurrent cognitive assessment in situations with a high degree of specificity and complexity. Third, this approach is ideal for assessing cognitions related to substance use for youth, since it is possible to elicit a variety of responses without exposing youth to the risk associated with in-vivo situations involving alcohol or other illicit substances. Finally, the ATSS paradigm allows for the use of multiple think-aloud procedures and technologies to assess online cognitions in response to prerecorded presentations (Davison, Vogel, & Coffman, 1997).

Dodge and Price (1994) developed a comprehensive assessment of social-information processing using video-based stimuli. In their method, children were presented with a series of video depictions of social situations involving peer group entry and peer provocations. Children's social information processing was assessed by a structured interview geared towards understanding all phases of the SIP model. The SIP interview is a particularly effective measure of how individuals encode, represent and process new social cues as it provides real time assessment of the controlled and automatic components of SIP (Coie & Dodge, 1998). By assessing children's cognitions across a number of different scenarios, estimates of reliability can be made of the content elicited at each stage of processing as well as allowing for associations with other measures, both concurrently and prospectively (Dodge & Price, 1994).

VIDEO CONTENT AND ASSESSMENT

There are numerous challenges in developing a video-based procedure. Like all laboratory measures, a balance must be achieved between adequate scientific rigor and external validity. While the use of visual stimuli can have great impact, it also raises considerable design challenges including how issues such as age, gender, race and cohort that can influence the final product. In this project, the goal of the video taped scenes was to have the greatest applicability to the largest number of youth. For that reason, actors chosen for the film were selected to include both girls and boys, fit within the age range in which SUD treatment is most common (ages 15-17; Brown, 1993) and represent the largest racial groups represented within the US (i.e., Caucasian, African-American, Hispanic-American). While the inclusion of both boys and girls and multiple ethnicities within one situation might influence the cognitions accessed within these situations, this strategy seems the most appropriate way to develop an assessment protocol that maximizes generalizability and decreases bias against a particular group.

Due to the higher base rates for alcohol and marijuana use in adolescent populations (Johnston et al., 2006), the use of these two substances in social situations were the focus of the video. Based on prior research (Anderson, Frissell, & Brown, in press; Brown, Vik & Creamer, 1989), teens with SUDs most commonly return to use in situations when they are with peers and socializing is the primary activity. As such, the scenes were constructed to include four youth socializing at a friend's home in the afternoon or early evening. The overall context for the film was based on the vignette presented in the Adolescent Relapse Coping Questionnaire (Myers & Brown, 1995), a reliable and validated instrument to assess adolescent coping beliefs when faced with situations providing temptations for alcohol and other drug use. In the current measure, adolescents are presented with the scenario, "You arrive at a friend's house in the evening. There are a few other people there; everyone is sitting around talking, drinking and using drugs. When you first sit down, you are offered drugs and something to drink." The video was filmed from the participant's point of view. Adolescents have the opportunity to interact with four teens (2 males, 2 females) in two types of social groupings (participant and individual vs. participant and group) with two types of offers (substance related vs. non substance related). For example, one scene begins with the participant/camera walking into a kitchen where a boy and girl are speaking. The actors include the participant in the social interaction. At the end of the dialogue, one of the actors in the scene make an offer to the participant of either an alcoholic beverage (e.g., can of beer), marijuana (e.g., joint), non-alcoholic beverage (e.g., soda), or food (e.g., chips).

The sequence of the assessment is described in figure 2. Prior to the evaluation phase of the assessment, participants view two training scenes (i.e., a social interactions without an offer) to orient participants to the think-aloud procedure. The administrator provides feedback to the participant regarding their performance and models a think-aloud if necessary. Based on past research with this paradigm, statements such as, "Rather than say what you would think if you were in this situation, try to actually believe that you are in the situation and then say whatever is going through your mind" are used as feedback in the training phase (Davidson, 1997, p. 30). The purpose of these training scenes is to ensure that youth understand the ATSS task and are able to provide sufficient content for analysis.

After training, all participants are shown a cue reactivity scene. In this scene, participants "open" a door, via camera shot, to a home and enter a living room (i.e., common area with a sofa, chairs and tables). In order to assess cue reactivity, the room contains an equal number of objects rated by teens as clearly marijuana-related (e.g., rolling papers and lighter, alcohol bottle), alcohol-related (e.g., can of beer, bottle of hard liquor), and related to eating or drinking non-alcoholic beverages (e.g., bag of chips, soda). In addition, a set of items are included within the scene that have ambiguous meaning and can be associated with alcohol or drug use, but less directly (e.g., tonic water, incense). The cue scene assesses the participant's ability to identify substance related cues within the environment as well as initiate behavioral decision–making without social cues (e.g., choose to leave the home upon seeing alcohol and drugs are present).

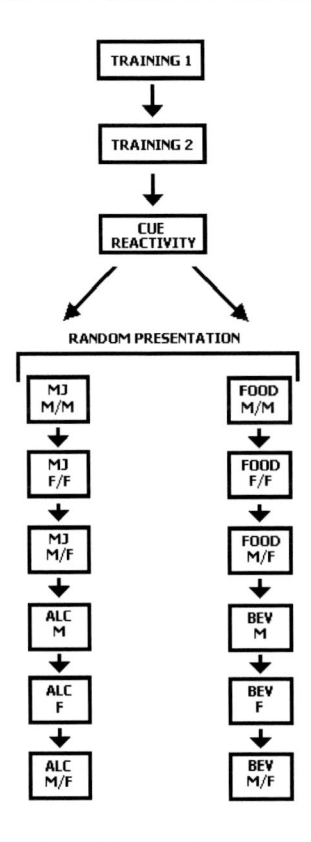

Figure 2. Sequence of the video-based social information processing assessment. M= male; F=female; ALC=alcohol offer; MJ = marijuana offer; BEV= non-alcoholic beverage offer; FOOD= food offer.

After the cue reactivity assessment, youth are presented with the remaining social interactions in randomized order. Immediately after each segment, participants are cued by the computer to complete a think-aloud. In addition to the unstructured elicitation of the ATSS procedure, a structured interview evaluating the six phases of social information processing is conducted for each scene viewed. The interview assesses the six SIP domains: encoding, interpretation, goal clarification, response access, response decision, and behavioral enactment as they relate to each social interaction (Coie & Dodge, 1998; Dodge & Price, 1994). For Phase 1, participants are asked to "Describe what happened in this situation" in order to assess the salient cues for them within the scene. "What kind of situation are you in? What are they asking you to do? How intent are they (the actors) in getting you to accept their offer?" examines youth interpretation of the social cues presented (Phase 2). Adolescent goals within the situation (Phase 3) are identified by asking, "What do you have happen? Why?" In order to generate a list of response options (Phase 4), participants are asked, "What will you do?" "Do you think it would work?" provides the adolescent's evaluation of their chosen response. The question "Why?" is geared to elicit self-efficacy statements and outcome experiences. Finally, behavioral enactment (Phase 6) is evaluated when youth are asked to demonstrate the quality of their response via a role play. The interviewer asks youth to, "Pretend I am someone in the scene. Show me what you would do." By integrating the SIP assessment methodology with the ATSS paradigm, a more complete understanding of the effects of risk situations on youth cognitions is provided.

VIDEO DEVELOPMENT

Given our goal of designing a visual stimulus for use with adolescents, realism and timeliness were major concerns during the development phase. Two strategies were used to maximize realism: conducting focus groups of youth with a diversity of substance use and treatment histories and collaboration with a professional film company. First, we will review the findings of the focus group phase of development. The overarching aim of the youth focus groups was to develop realistic social scenarios involving the choice to use alcohol or marijuana. Particular attention was given to clothing, language and use patterns in order to maximize the video procedures utility across time and geographic location.

Participants

29 adolescents (17 boys; 12 girls) age 15 to 17 participated in four, two hour focus groups. Youth identified themselves as Caucasian (79.3%), Hispanic-American (13.8%), and Multiracial (6.9%). Adolescents were recruited from public schools, both regular and alternative, in Southern California participating in longitudinal research on substance use in teens (Brown & D'Amico, 2001). At lunch, research assistants distributed fliers with the contact number for the study. 46 youth expressed interest in participating in the project. Of those who provided contact information, 29 were between the ages of 15 and 17, had a lifetime and 12-month history of alcohol or marijuana use within target ranges, and attended the focus group. About one third of participants ($n = 9$), all from alternative schools, had a history of treatment for substance use problems. Treated youth had participated in outpatient treatment for substance use including group ($n = 8$), individual ($n = 3$) and family therapy ($n = 1$). 56% also had participated in a sobriety support group provided by the schools. The average duration of treatment was 39.6 treatment sessions ($sd = 61.0$) with all but two participants receiving treatment in the past six months.

There was a diversity of alcohol and marijuana use patterns within this sample. On average, youth from the regular education setting had used alcohol 11.0 times ($sd = 6.7$) and marijuana 3.9 times ($sd = 5.6$) in their lifetime with 5.8 alcohol use ($sd = 4.0$) and 3.3 marijuana use episodes ($sd = 4.9$) in the past year. Participants from the alternative school setting, but without history of substance abuse treatment, had an average lifetime alcohol involvement of 36.8 episodes ($sd = 20.4$), lifetime marijuana use of 78.8 episodes ($sd = 110.6$), and average past year alcohol episodes averaging 14.1 times ($sd = 13.1$) and 26.9 for marijuana ($sd = 40.6$). Youth with substance abuse treatment history used alcohol on average 106.7 times ($sd = 86.5$) and marijuana 79.9 times ($sd = 79.9$) in their lifetime. Treated youth had average past year rates of 42.9 episodes ($sd = 38.8$) for alcohol and 45.0 ($sd = 65.2$) for marijuana. Alcohol use frequencies, at both time points, was significantly different by group (lifetime: $F[2, 28] = 9.9, p = .001$; 12-month: $F[2, 28] = 7.2, p = .003$). A priori contrasts were conducted to test for differences between the alternative school groups (treated vs. non-treated) and the non-treated groups (regular education vs. alternative). Planned comparisons suggested that lifetime alcohol use rates were significantly different between treated youth and youth in alternative schools without SUD treatment histories, $t(26) = 2.4, p = .04$, as well as the alternative school youth without treatment and regular education students, $t(26) = 3.5, p$

= .009. For marijuana, the three groups only differed from each other for lifetime marijuana use rates, $F(2, 28) = 4.1$, $p = .03$, with non-significant differences for past year use, $F(2, 28) = 2.6$, $p = .10$. Contrasts for past year alcohol and marijuana involvement were non-significant.

Measures

Stimulus rating form. A ten item stimulus rating form was developed to assess whether the focus group participants accurately identified sixty photographed images of objects from the following categories: 1.) alcohol and alcohol-related (e.g. beer, wine, liquor, shot glass), 2.) marijuana and related objects (e.g., joint, rolling papers), 3.) non-alcoholic beverages (e.g., soda, juice, cup), and 4.) food (e.g., chips, candy, plate). Included within this set were items that had more tangential relation to substance use like incense, psychedelic posters, etc. Of interest to this investigation, six questions, rated 1 (not at all) – 7 (very much), were asked to assess the object's relation to alcohol, drugs, eating, alcohol use, drug use, and likelihood of seeing the object at a party.

Actor ratings. An audition was held prior to the focus groups to narrow the number of prospective actors, recruited from acting and modeling agencies in Southern California. Approximately 30 actors were invited to audition for the research and production staff after a careful review of photographs for age appropriateness and demographic characteristics. Audition tapes for 18 actors (9 boys, 9 girls) were compiled for examination by the focus groups. Participants rated actors on attractiveness (1 = not at all attractive, 9 = very attractive), likelihood of seeing the actor "at your school" (1 = not likely, 9 = very likely), and whether the actor was someone the participant would "like to hang out with" (1 = not at all, 9 = very much).

Script rating form. A script rating form was developed to assess participants' perceptions of the realism and risk level of the scenes depicted in the video. 14 scripts were written by a professional screen writer to depict common conversations between adolescents while socializing casually (e.g., school, sports, movies, music). Two questions were selected from the ARCQ (Myers & Brown, 1995; Items 1 & 3): whether the participants were ever in a "similar situation" (1 = never, 6 = ten or more times), and how much the scene made participants "want to drink or use" (1 = not at all, 9= very much) to assist in rating the scripts. The participants also assessed the realism of the scenes (1 = not realistic, 9 = very realistic).

Focus group discussions. Focus group sessions were digitally recorded and participants were encouraged to volunteer their opinions of the scripts as well as the actors. The transcripts made from these taped sessions provided qualitative data coded and categorized by the PI and the research assistant.

Procedures

Four, two- hour long focus group sessions of 5 to 9 adolescents were conducted after school. All facilitators were trained by the Principal Investigator on the focus group protocol. Participants were informed that the focus group sessions would be digitally recorded and that the content of the discussion would be transcribed. Only participants with signed consent forms for participation were allowed to enter the focus group room. After issues surrounding confidentiality and audio recording were discussed, adolescent assent forms were collected, recording commenced and participants were given the stimulus rating form to complete.

Facilitators read the scripts for the scenes to the group and presented photos and audition tapes of the prospective actors. Individually, focus group members completed the script and actor rating forms in balanced order by focus group session. In addition to these pencil and paper measures, participants were asked to discuss scenarios and actors with each other according to certain criteria (e.g. realism, likeability and risk levels). Using the funnel approach, two research assistants facilitated the focus group discussion. At the end of the session, rating forms were collected, participants were debriefed, and paid $25.00 for their participation.

After initial approval of the project, the IRB was provided with study materials throughout the development process to allow them to evaluate the proposed film and express concerns as appropriate. The board was provided with images of all of the potential objects to be used in the video before focus groups were held and story boards and scripts before filming.

Results

Cluster analysis (SPSS 14.0) was used to select the alcohol, marijuana, food and non-alcoholic beverages to be used in taping. Data from the image rating form was collapsed across participants for the six questions related to the attributes of the object (alcohol-, drug-, eating-like; alcohol use and drug use relation; likelihood of seeing at a party). A hierarchical cluster analysis using Ward's method of clustering and squared Euclidian distance using standardized values to estimate similarity was used (Hair, Anderson, Tatham & Black, 1992). Two, three and four cluster solutions were extracted. The agglomeration coefficient showed the largest percent change (95.6%) from a 2 to 3 cluster solution. Examination of the icicle plot and tree diagram suggested that the three cluster solution provided the best approximation of the clustering of objects needed for the cue reactivity phase. Cluster one consisted of alcoholic beverages, cluster two marijuana and marijuana smoking paraphernalia, and cluster three included food and non-alcoholic beverages. In the second step, the clusters were redrawn separating the sample by treatment history to insure that the variability between these solutions was acceptable for the purposes of the project. While differences emerged among the distances between some objects within classes for each group, the overall hierarchical clustering was unchanged. As such, the total sample results were used to select objects for filming.

Mean values for the actor and script ratings were computed. The top four actors (2 boys, 2 girls) were cast on the basis of their conjoint ratings on likelihood of "hanging out" with them (range: 5.3 - 6.5), likelihood of seeing them at school (range: 6.0 - 7.0) and attractiveness (range: 4.9 - 7.3). The most highly rated actors were able to fulfill goal of casting youth representing Caucasian, African-American and Hispanic-American racial/ethnic groups.

Transcripts of the focus groups, particularly in the area of script modification, were broken into interpretable units by the PI and examined for emergent themes by the authors

(Glaser & Strauss, 1967). Focus group feedback was used to modify the content and wording of scripts to increase realism. The scripts were modified on the basis of feedback after each focus group. Realism ratings, collapsed across the 14 scripts (two training plus 12 social scenes), progressed from a mean of 5.46 (sd = 2.3) to 6.8 (sd = 1.8), falling within the realistic range. ANOVAs were conducted for each scene and suggested that realism maintained a high level or increased across iterations of the scripts with F values ranging from .09 to 12.95, p values from .91 to .0001, respectively. Across scenes and samples, the modal rating of the number of times youth had experienced these types of situations was 3 to 5 occasions. In support our goal to develop scripts that had appropriate social content without directly relating to alcohol or drug use, youth rated their subjective craving, or "how much do you want to drink or use in this situation," at a mean of 2.9 (sd = 2.7) across samples.

Filming and Post-production

The video stimulus was produced in conjunction with the video production group at a local public television station in Southern California. The video production team provided all technical aspects of the production including casting professional actors, writing and revising scripts, scouting and procuring the location, providing media for focus groups, and all staff and equipment for video taping and editing. While the research team provided the scientific guidelines for the video, the film professionals ensured that a realistic film was produced. After the selection of stimulus objects, scripts and actors via focus group data, care was taken to choose locations (i.e., moderate SES home, not clearly located in Southern California) and wardrobe (e.g., avoiding too loose or too tight clothing) that would be acceptable to youth in various geographic areas, demographic groups, and across time. As our goal was for the social situation and offer to be the central focus of each scene, every effort was made to avoid implied content surrounding dating or sex (e.g., a male-female dyad interacting in a bedroom or making plans to go to an event together) or aggression (e.g., exerting any pressure to accept an offer). Scripts for each scene and the type of offers (alcohol, marijuana, food, drink) were randomly assigned to each constellation of actors (e.g., solo scene, balanced dyads by gender). The actor making the offer was randomly assigned initially and balanced across scenes so that no actor was consistently identified with a making a particular type of offer (i.e., alcohol, marijuana, food or non-alcoholic beverage).

Filming was conducted with research staff (PI and research assistants) and the production company (producer/director, camera operators, wardrobe/makeup and production assistant). Post-production editing was completed at the television station with the producer, editorial staff and PI. In all aspects of the filming, the PI held responsibility for maintaining scientific rigor while the production team was responsible for creating a visually stimulating but realistic product.

CONCLUSION

The goal of this project was to develop a novel, video-based procedure to assess social information processing in youth during alcohol and drug use situations. To our knowledge, no other project of this scope has been undertaken before. To that end, two existing methods for assessing cognitions were integrated (ATSS and SIP video-based methods). Extensive work was conducted, based on empirical evidence from the literature and focus groups, to create a video stimulus that was realistic and developmentally appropriate. The benefit of this approach is the ability to assess information processing underlying substance use decision-making without exposing youth to risks associated with in-vivo situations involving alcohol or other drugs. In addition, the use of a professional video development team produced a visual stimulus that was realistic. However, the development of this measure was time consuming and expensive. It required extensive collaboration with institutional officials, funding agencies, consultants and contractors. We believe the time and money required to develop this assessment was well spent. Adolescents are savvy consumers of popular culture (e.g., film, music, computer games); any procedures using these modalities must be seen by youth as realistic, professional and respectful of their sophistication in this realm.

The development phase of this project was only the first step in creating a reliable and valid instrument for assessment. The purpose of this chapter was to outline the steps involved in creating a video-based assessment of substance use decision-making in youth based on a strong theoretical and empirical foundation. However, demonstrating reliability and validity is a long process. Pilot work is underway to examine the effectiveness of this procedure to describe social information processing for youth with and without substance use disorders. Pilot testing will evaluate the social information processing of 15 to 17 year olds after treatment for substance use disorders in comparison to peers with extensive alcohol and marijuana use histories but no treatment experience. This initial study will allow us to estimate the reliability of the content elicited across each scene as well as examine relations among social information processing components. Preliminary estimates of convergent validity will be determined through correlations with existing measures of craving, coping, self-efficacy, outcome expectancies, and motivation for abstinence. Finally, construct validity of the SIP model for substance use will be determined by examining the relations between model components through structural equation modeling.

Future investigations are planned to examine the ability of this procedure to predict future alcohol and drug use in diverse samples of adolescents. Based on the theory outlined above, we would expect that certain aspects of the model may be more salient to decision-making for youth early in their substance use histories (e.g., Phase 3 - social conformity goals) than for youth exhibiting substance use dependence (e.g., Phase 1 - cue reactivity). Additionally, various forms of psychopathology, such as social anxiety or conduct problems, might suggest differential attention to (Phase 1) or interpretation of (Phase 2) social and substance-related cues in these scenes. This paradigm has sufficient flexibility to allow for the examination of many different influences on adolescent decision-making regarding alcohol and drug use.

We feel this procedure has great potential for use in assessment as well as a starting point for intervention for teens. However, the clinical utility of this procedure must be established. How well can practitioners use this assessment to identify youth at risk for poor substance use decision-making? Can social information processing surrounding alcohol and drug use be modified through intervention? These types of questions can be answered only through the application of this procedure across settings and populations. Developing a greater understanding of the processes underlying adolescent decision-making regarding alcohol and drug use affords us the opportunity to develop more effective prevention and intervention programs for youth (Brown & Ramo, 2006).

Author Note

Kristen G. Anderson, Ph.D., University of California, San Diego, Departments of Psychology and Psychiatry; Sara J. Parent, University of California, San Diego, Department of Psychology. This research was funded by the National Institute of Drug Abuse (R21 DA 019960-01; K. Anderson, PI). Dr. Anderson is now at Reed College in Portland, OR.

The authors would like to thank the participants, research staff, Craig Bentley and KPBS Video Production Services for their work on this project. We would also like to thank Dr. Sandra Brown (UCSD) for her mentorship through the development and implementation of this project as well as Drs. Joseph Price (SDSU) and Michael Dougherty (University of Maryland, College Park) for their consultation on this project.

References

Anderson, K.G. & Brown, S.A. (2007). [Social-information processing and alcohol use in middle school students]. Unpublished raw data.

Anderson, K.G., Frissell, K.C., & Brown, S.A. (in press). Contexts of post-treatment use for substance abusing adolescents with comorbid psychopathology. *Journal of Child and Adolescent Substance Abuse*.

Anderson, K.G., Ramo, D.E., Schulte, M.T., Cummins, K., & Brown, S.A. (2007). Substance use treatment outcomes for youth: Integrating personal and environmental predictors. *Drug and Alcohol Dependence, 88*, 42-48.

Anderson, K.G., Ramo, D.E., Schulte, M.T., Cummins, K., & Brown, S.A. (in press). Impact of relapse predictors on psychosocial functioning of SUD youth one year after treatment. *Substance Abuse*.

Anderson, K.G., Smith, G.T., & Fischer, S. (2003). Women and expectancies: Personality and learning implications. *Journal of Studies on Alcohol, 64*(3), 384-392.

Brooks-Gunn, J. & Reiter, E.O. (1990). The role of pubertal processes. In S.S. Feldman & G.R. Elliott (Eds.), *At the Threshold: The Developing Adolescent* (pp. 16-53). Cambridge: Harvard University Press.

Brown, S.A. (1993). Recovery patterns in adolescent substance abuse. In J.S. Baer, G.A. Marlatt, R.J. McMahon (Eds.) *Addictive Behaviors Across a Lifespan: Prevention, Treatment and Policy Issues* (pp. 161-183). Beverly Hills, CA: Sage Publications, Inc.

Brown, S.A., Anderson, K.G., Ramo, D.E., & Tomlinson, K.L. (2005). Treatment of adolescent alcohol-related problems: A transitional perspective. In M. Galanter (Ed.), *Recent Developments in Alcoholism (Vol. 17)*. New York: Kluwer Academic/Plenum Publishers.

Brown, S.A. & D'Amico, E.J. (2001). Outcomes of alcohol treatment for adolescents. In M. Galanter (Ed.), *Recent Developments in Alcoholism, Volume 15: Service Research in the Era of Managed Care*. (pp. 289-311). New York, NY: Plenum.

Brown, S.A., Mott, M.A., & Myers, M.G. (1990). Adolescent alcohol and drug treatment outcome. In R.R. Watson (Ed.), *Drug and Alcohol Abuse Prevention. Drug and Alcohol Abuse Reviews*. (pp. 373-403). Totowa, NJ, US: Humana Press.

Brown, S.A. & Ramo, D.E. (2006). Clinical course of youth following treatment for alcohol and drug problems. In H. A. Liddle & C. L. Rowe (Eds.), *Adolescent Substance Abuse: Research and Clinical Advances* (pp. 79-103). New York, NY: Cambridge University Press.

Brown, S.A. & Tapert, S.F. (2004). Adolescence and the trajectory of alcohol use: Basic to clinical studies. *Annals of the New York Academy of Sciences, 1021*, 234-244.

Brown, S.A., Vik, P.W., & Creamer, V.A. (1989). Characteristics of relapse following adolescent substance abuse treatment. *Addictive Behaviors, 14*(3), 291-300.

Coie, J.D., & Dodge, K.A. (1998). Aggression and antisocial behavior. In W. Daman & N. Eisenberg (Eds.), *Handbook of Child Psychology: Social, Emotional, and Personality Development* (pp. 779-862). New York: John Wiley & Sons, Inc.

Connors, G. J., Maisto, S. A., & Donovan, D. M. (1996). Section I. theoretical perspectives on relapse: Conceptualizations of relapse: A summary of psychological and psychobiological models. *Addiction, 91*, S5-S13.

Cooper, M.L., Russell, M., Skinner, J.B., & Windle, M. (1992). Development and validation of a three-dimensional measure of drinking motives. *Psychological Assessment, 4*(2), 123-132.

Cornelius, J.R., Clark, D.B., Bukstein, O.G., & Salloum, I.M. (2005). Treatment of co-occurring alcohol, drug, and psychiatric disorders. In M. Galanter, (Ed.), *Alcohol Problems in Adolescents and Young Adults: Epidemiology, Neurobiology, and Treatment.* (pp. 349-365). New York: Springer Science & Business Media.

Crick, N.R., & Dodge, K.A. (1994). A review and reformulation of social information-processing mechanisms in children's social adjustment. *Psychological Bulletin, 115*(1), 74-101.

Davison, G.C., Robins, C., & Johnston, M. (1983). Articulated thoughts during simulated situations: A paradigm for studying cognition in emotion and behavior. *Cognitive Therapy and Research, 7*, 17-40.

Davison, G.C., Vogel, R.S., & Coffman, S.G. (1997). Think-aloud approaches to cognitive assessment and the articulated thoughts in simulated situations paradigm. *Journal of Consulting and Clinical Psychology, 65*(6), 950-958.

Davison, G.C., Williams, M.E., Nezami, E. Bice, T.L., & DeQuattro, V.L. (1991) Relaxation, reduction in angry thoughts, and improvements in borderline hypertension. *Journal of Behavioral Medicine, 14*, 453-469.

Deas, D. & Upadhyaya, H. (2003). Crossing the line: When does teen substance use become abuse or dependence? *Current Psychiatry Online*, 2(7). Retrieved January 19, 2005, from http://www.currentpsychiatry.com/2003_07/0703_substance.asp.

DiLiberto, L., Katz, R.C., Beauchamp, K.L., & Howells, G.N. (2002). Using articulated thoughts in simulated situations to assess cognitive activity in aggressive and nonaggressive adolescents. *Journal of Child and Family Studies, 11*(2), 179-189.

Dodge, K.A., Lochman, J.E., Laird, R., & Zelli, A. (2002). Multidimensional latent construct analysis of children's social information processing patterns: correlations with aggressive behavior problems. *Psychological Assessment, 14*(1), 60-73.

Dodge, K.A., & Price, J.M. (1994). On the relation between social information processing and socially competent behavior in early school-aged children. *Child Development, 65*(6), 1385-1397.

Ellickson, P.L. & Hays, R.D. (1992). On becoming involved with drugs: Modeling adolescent drug use over time. *Health Psychology, 11*(6), 377-385.

Franken, I.H. (2003). Drug craving and addiction: Integrating psychological and neuropsychopharmacological approaches. *Progress in Neuro-Psychopharmacology & Biological Psychiatry, 27,* 563-579.

Giedd, J. N., Blumenthal, J., Jeffries, N. O., Castellanos, F. X., Liu, H., Zijdenbos, A., et al. (1999). Brain development during childhood and adolescence: A longitudinal MRI study. *Nature Neuroscience*, 2, 861-863.

Glaser, B.G. & Strauss, A.L. (1967). The discovery of Grounded Theory: Strategies for qualitative research. New York: Aldine de Gruyter.

Goldman, M.S., Brown, S.A., Christiansen, B.A., & Smith, G.T. (1991). Alcoholism and memory: Broadening the scope of alcohol-expectancy research. *Psychological Bulletin, 10*(1), 137-146.

Graber, J.A., & Brooks-Gunn, J. (2002). Adolescent girls' sexual development. In Wingood & DiClemente (Eds.), *Handbook of Women's Sexual and Reproductive Health* (pp. 21 - 42). New York: Kluwer Academic/Plenum Publishers.

Haaga, D.A. (1989). Articulated thoughts and endorsement procedures for cognitive assessment in the prediction of smoking relapse. *Journal of Consulting and Clinical Psychology, 1*(2), 112-117.

Haaga, D.A. & Stewart, B.L. (1992). Self-efficacy for recovery from a lapse after smoking cessation. *Journal of Consulting and Clinical Psychology, 60*(1), 24-28.

Hair, J.F., Anderson, R.E., Tatham, R.L., & Black, W.C. (1992). Cluster analysis. *Multivariate Data Analysis with Readings* (pp. 265-291). New York: Macmillan Publishing Company.

Johnston, L. D., O'Malley, P. M., Bachman, J. G., & Schulenberg, J. E. (2006). *Monitoring the Future national results on adolescent drug use: Overview of key findings, 2005.* (NIH Publication No. 06-5882) Bethesda, MD: National Institute on Drug Abuse.

Marlatt, G.A. & Gordon, J.R. (1980). Determinants of relapse: Implications for the maintenance of behavior change. In P. Davidson & S. Davidson (Eds.), *Behavioral medicine: Changing health lifestyle* (pp. 410-452). New York: Brunner Mazel.

McGue, M., Iacono, W.G., Legrand, L.N., & Elkins, I. (2001). Origins and consequences of age at first drink: Associations with substance-use disorders, disinhibitory behavior and psychopathology, and P3 amplitude. *Alcoholism: Clinical and Experimental Research, 25*(8), 1156-1165.

Metrik, J., Frissell, K.C., McCarthy, D.M., D'Amico, E.J., & Brown, S.A. (2003). Strategies for reduction and cessation of alcohol use: Adolescent preferences. *Alcoholism: Clinical and Experimental Research, 27*(1), 74-80.

Miller, P.M., Smith, G.T., & Goldman, M.S. (1990). Emergence of alcohol expectancies in childhood: A possible critical period. *Journal of Studies on Alcohol, 51*(4), 343-349.

Myers, M.G. & Brown, S.A. (1995). The Adolescent Relapse Coping Questionnaire: Psychometric validation. *Journal of Studies on Alcohol, 57*(1), 40-46.

Niaura, R.S., Rohsenow, D.J., Binkoff, J.A., Monti, P.M. Pedraza, M. & Abrams, D.B. (1988). Relevance of cue reactivity to understanding alcohol and smoking relapse. *Journal of Abnormal Psychology, 97*(2), 133-152.

Rekers, G.A. (1992). Development of problems of puberty and sex roles in adolescence. In C.E. Walker, & M.C. Roberts (Eds.), *Handbook of Clinical Child Psychology* (pp. 674-691). New York: John Wiley & Sons, Inc.

Reyna, V.F. & Farley, F. (2006). Risk and rationality in adolescent decision making: Implications for theory, practice, and public policy. *Psychological Science in the Public Interest, 7*(1), 1-44.

Rohde, P. & Andrews, J. A. (2006). Substance use disorders. In C. A. Essau, (Ed.), *Child and adolescent psychopathology: Theoretical and clinical implications* (pp. 184-220). New York: Routledge/Taylor & Francis Group.

Schuckit, M.A., Smith, T.L., Danko, G.P., Anderson, K.G., Brown, S.A., Kuperman, S., Kramer, J., Hesselbrock, V., & Bucholz K. (2005). Evaluation of a level of response to alcohol-based structural equation model in adolescents. *Journal of Studies on Alcohol, 66*, 174-184.

Schulenberg, J., Maggs. J.L., Steinman K, J., & Zucker R, A. (2001). Taking the long view on substance abuse etiology and intervention during adolescence. In P. M. Monti, S. M. Colby & T. A. O'Leary (Eds.), *Adolescent, alcohol and substance abuse: Reaching teens through brief interventions* (pp.19-57). New York: Guilford Press.

Sher, K.J., Walitzer, K.S., Wood, P.K., & Brent, E.E. (1991). Characteristics of children of alcoholics: Putative risk factors, substance use and abuse, and psychopathology. *Journal of Abnormal Psychology, 100*(4), 427-448.

Silverman, W.H. (1990). Intervention strategies for the prevention of adolescent substance abuse. *Journal of Adolescent Chemical Dependency, 1*(2), 25-34.

Smith, G.T., Goldman, M.S., Greenbaum, P.E., & Christiansen, B.A. (1995). Expectancy for social facilitation from drinking: The divergent paths of high-expectancy and low-expectancy adolescents. *Journal of Abnormal Psychology, 104*(1), 32-40.

Stacy, A.W. (1997). Memory activation and expectancy as prospective predictors of alcohol and marijuana use. *Journal of Abnormal Psychology, 106*(1), 61-73.

Tapert, S.F., Cheung, E.H., Brown, G.G., Frank, L.R., Paulus, M.P., Schweinsburg, A.D., et al. (2003). Neural response to alcohol stimuli in adolescents with alcohol use disorder. *Archives of General Psychiatry, 60*, 727-735.

Tate, S.R., Patterson, K.A., Nagel, B.J., Anderson, K.G., & Brown, S.A.(in press). Addiction and Stress in Adolescents. In al'Absi (Ed.), *Stress and Addiction: Biological and Psychological Mechanisms.* New York: Elsevier Press.

Tomlinson, K.L., Brown, S.A., & Abrantes, A. (2004). Psychiatric comorbidity and substance use treatment outcomes of adolescents. *Psychology of Addictive Behaviors, 18*, 160-169.

Warner, L.A., Canino, G., & Colón, H.M. (2001). Prevalence and correlates of substance use disorders among older adolescents in Puerto Rico and the United States: a cross-cultural comparison. *Drug and Alcohol Dependence, 63*, 229-243.

White, J.A., Davison, G.C., Haaga, D.A.F., & White, K.L. (1992). Cognitive bias in the articulated thoughts of depressed and nondepressed psychiatric patients. *Journal of Nervous and Mental Disease, 180*, 77-81.

Willoughby, T., Chalmers, H., & Busseri, M.A. (2004). Where is the syndrome? Examining co-occurrence among multiple problem behaviors in adolescence. *Journal of Consulting and Clinical Psychology, 72*(6), 1022-1-37.

Witkiewitz, K. & Marlatt, G.A. (2004). Relapse prevention for alcohol and drug problems: That was Zen, this is Tao. *American Psychologist, 59*(4), 224-235.

Zimmer-Gembeck, M.J. & Collins, W.A. (2006). Autonomy development during adolescence. In G.R. Adams & M.D. Berzonsky (Eds.), *Blackwell Handbook of Adolescence* (pp. 175-204). Malden, MA: Blackwell Publishing.

In: Psychology of Decision Making
Editor: Paul M. Garrison

ISBN 978-1-60021-869-9
© Nova Science Publishers, Inc.

Chapter 8

INTERPROFESSIONAL DECISION MAKING IN ELDERLY CARE: MORALITY, CRITERIA AND HELP ALLOCATION

Pirjo Nikander
Department of Sociology and Social Psychology,
33014 University of Tampere, Finland

INTRODUCTION

Talk and interaction between health and social care professionals form one central arena where statutory decisions concerning the care of elderly people are made. Cooperative work between members of different professional groups in meetings, or in teams is also a practical arena where various agreed upon policies and principles of elderly care are turned into practice through talk. In this chapter, I analyze interprofessional meetings as a practical site for decision making over service and help allocation to elderly people and their carers. I attempt to lay out for view some characteristics of professional deliberation and decision making. Discursive analysis of professional-professional interaction and talk is seen here as a powerful means of studying help allocation, and the unfolding of institutional criteria and morality.

The interdisciplinary field of discourse studies has in recent years produced an ample supply of work on institutional and lay caring relations. The existing literature already provides information on the construction of elderly identities (Paoletti 1998; see also Nikander 2002), on the discursive construction of frailty (Taylor 1992), of caring relations and the professionals' role as part of the care arrangements (e.g. Grainger 1993), on intergenerational relations (e.g. Cicirelli 1993), and on professional construction of client or patient cases (e.g. Nikander 2003, 2005).

Empirical research on professional or institutional discourses in elderly care falls roughly into three distinctive areas of interest (c.f. Linell 1998). Perhaps most prominently, research has focused on professional – lay discourse i.e., on encounters involving the co-presence of doctors and elderly patients (e.g. Coupland and Coupland 1998, 1999), elderly mental patients and attorneys (Holstein 1990), or for instance district nurses and patients (Leppänen 1998). A second area of research gives discourse *within* specific professional groups centre focus. Analysis of nurses' actions within a medical unit may for instance tease out specifics of how this professional group constitutes patient classes or patient types as part of their own everyday ordering work (Latimer 1997). Third, discursive analysis on care and caring relations has also been concerned with interprofessional discourse, i.e., encounters, cooperation and joint decision-making *between* individuals from different professional groups. Research in this area varies from managerial interests (e.g. Dockrell and Wilson 1995) to a focus on professional roles and narratives (Housley 2003), and joint professional categorization work (e.g. Nikander 2003, 2005). It is this area of research that this chapter also hopes to contribute to.

In terms of its methodological stance, the current chapter draws on prior work on discourse analysis, categorization in institutional settings as well as work that analyses categorization in talk more broadly (e.g. Antaki and Widdicombe 1998; Baker 1997; Boden 1994; Hester and Eglin 1993; Housley 2003; Nikander 2000, 2002). It provides numerous illustrations and detailed analyses of professional care allocation. Doing this, the chapter hopefully shows how the criteria and morality of decision making are jointly constructed in interaction, and how the responsibilities of professionals as well as the rights and responsibilities of elderly clients and of their carers are discursively carved and talked into being in institutional meeting talk. Special focus in the chapter will be given to the ways in which professionals use *imageries and ideals concerning the caring relationship and the life course* as part of their descriptive work.

In the remaining sections of this chapter I will first introduce the data and the institutional setting in which they were collected. Following this, I will then move to the analysis of two elderly client cases and provide several data excerpts on both. To conclude, I will briefly discuss possible benefits and practical implications of discursive analyses of professional argumentation.

THE MEETINGS DATA: INFORMAL HOME CARE ALLOWANCE

In the Finnish care system, the state and municipalities are to a large degree responsible for arranging social and health services for the elderly. To date, public funds have secured the services provided, and citizens have received them either against a moderate fee or for free (Anttonen and Sipilä 2000). More recently a variety of market-based service systems are also available and there is an increasing tendency towards supporting informal care at home (Vaarama and Kautto 1999).

The data and analysis in this chapter elucidate the practical institutional work whereby decisions about care allocation are reached. The data originate from a wider research project titled *Constructing Age, Health and Competence: Argumentation and Rhetoric in Institutional and Personal Discourse*. In the course of this project, 42 hours of video taped materials were collected from two types of interprofessional meetings in the Finnish social and health care.

1. Meetings making decisions over informal home care allowances for the elderly (15 meetings)

2. Meetings making decisions over long-term nursing home placements (15 meetings) [1]

Given the shared interest in family care giving in the chapters of this book, I focus here only on the first of the meeting types mentioned above. In the course of this chapter, I attempt to provide one concrete example of how formal – in this case financial support – is allocated to people who take care of elderly relatives living at home, and how members of interprofessional teams argue for, and advocate specific decisions to be taken.

The meetings making decisions on informal home care allowance are attended by (community) nurses, members of home help teams (home helpers, home helpers in charge, and head of home help), a medical doctor and a secretary. The participants not only represent a mix of professionals from both the social and the health sector, they are also somewhat differently positioned in the professional power hierarchy. Consequently interprofessional encounters like these are often also about displaying professional knowledge, power and competence and, at least potentially, saturated with boundary marking between professional tribes (see Housley 2003; Nikander 2005).

The meetings in focus are task-oriented. The practical business for the participants is to go through applications sent in by elderly people who currently still live at home and are cared for by a family member or an outside lay carer. According to the Finnish elderly care system, carers are eligible to apply for financial support when taking care of elderly relatives in their homes. Finland has a long tradition of supporting informal care which is also seen as an effective means of saving in the costs of long-term institutional care. This form of financial support becomes available once a year, and carers who have received it previously need to re-apply yearly. Carers are normally family members or relatives of the elderly client, but also so called outside carers with no relative status are eligible. The amount given to caregivers varies from two hundred to a thousand Euros, and the benefit is considered taxable income. This means that in addition to its financial importance, the benefit also carries symbolic meanings to caregivers: it says that that their caring work is officially acknowledged and appreciated as paid work. The funds available, and the monthly sums allocated to support informal elderly home care vary regionally within Finland. As a rule, however, funds are insufficient, and typically run out midway to the year. This means that despite the cost-effectiveness of this form of allowance, in practice the majority of informal care by relatives happens without such outside recognition and direct financial support.

The elderly client or the carer is not present in the meetings. Instead the absent client's case is presented to the meeting via textual documentation and through the detail that members of the interprofessional team take up and describe as relevant (see also Nikander 2003). Participants in the meetings have a pile of applications in front of them and they present client cases and follow the flow of the meeting using these textual materials. Each application also includes a doctor's certificate detailing the elderly person's medical status. Documentary realities and paper work (Atkinson and Coffey 1997) on client cases as well as discussion and development on the basis of these documents thus form the basis on which the meeting interaction in question unfolds.

---

[1] The project was funded by the Academy of Finland. The meetings were video taped and the researcher was not present in the meetings. The data were then transcribed into text. Both meeting types were video taped routinely in the course of one year.

Additional information on the elderly persons and their carers is available to the meeting as one member of the team always makes a home visit before a decision for or against financial support can be made. As the data excerpts in this chapter show in detail, home visits provide first-hand detailed information on the housing, caring and family circumstances of the elderly person, on how well both the carer and the cared for are coping, and on whether any significant change has happened that favours the possible earlier care benefit to go up this year.

One further detail is perhaps worth mentioning here. Despite being task-oriented, the informal home care allowance meetings discuss issues to do with the well-being and coping of their elderly clientele more generally. The discussion is rife with longer and detailed narratives about carers and the elderly clients themselves. The interprofessional team also discusses issues that have to do with the wider mix of formal and informal eldercare: the number of home help visits and short term admissions, meal services, housing and family arrangements and special aids. They also discuss forms of support to the carer: trips to day centres that allow time off, and care vouchers that allow for holidays from the caring relationship. Discussions also cover wider moral and ethical issues concerning the whole decision making process. During all this, speakers often move between their own professional perspective and financial imperatives and the concrete life situation, worries and perspectives of their clients. In the previous chapter, Sand pointed out that decision about terms of employment of kin care providers can often completely differ, depending on the municipality, since they depend on individual civil servants' assessment. In this chapter we can observe this type of decision making process in its making. That is, institutions are seen at work, through the analysis of actual instances of institutional interaction.

In sum then, the meeting data in this chapter illuminate some of the core elements and key questions topical to all ageing societies (e.g. Walker 1995; Gilleard and Higgs 1998). What constitutes a proper mix between professional care and informal care given by family members and relatives? How should we define and demarcate the rights, obligations and responsibilities of elderly citizens and their relatives on the one hand, and of the official system of health and social care on the other? Can ageing societies find better means of supporting good quality home care in ways that secure the well-being and coping of all involved? As I am about to show in more detail, these are questions that professionals in the meetings data in focus also tackle and seek to resolve.

PRACTICES OF INSTITUTIONAL DECISION MAKING: DATA ANALYSES

The excerpts chosen for analysis in this chapter, deal with two client cases discussed in the same three-hour long meeting. The meeting was attended by nine professionals: four community nurses, two home care workers, the head of home help, a medical doctor and a secretary. The number of client cases in the whole meeting was 31. The interaction during the decision making phase of informal home care allowance meetings routinely consists of case or client presentations. The professional most familiar with the elderly client's history and current situation normally takes these longer turns of talk. The same professional has often also made the home visit required before a decision on a potential allowance can be made.

The first excerpt is an example of a case presentation that was made 31 minutes into the meeting in question. In it, one of the home-helpers describes a female elderly client who lives at home cared for by her daughter who visits daily. The case description below includes many elements typical to client description in this meeting type. The transcription symbols used in the excerpts can be found at the end of this chapter.

Excerpt One: Mother and daughter I (HCA4, 31:35-36.32)
Speakers: HH = home helper, HHH = head of home help, S = Secretary,
? = unidentified speaker

```
01 HH:      Then the next one is this (0.8) ((last name-middle name-first name))
02          (3.8) ((hands the doctor's certificate over to the doctor sitting next to her))
03 HH:      I went there yesterday (8.0)
04 HH:      Lives there in ((name of town district)) (0.5)
05          in a flat with all modern conveniences and the house has
06          a lift fortunately so (.) this lady moves about (1.5.) poorly (1.5)
07          Here the (.) carer is the daughter ((first name + last name))
08          and she was present there yesterday (1.0) also and-a
09          (2.8.)
10 HH:      Here the (.) situation has remained er approximately the same
((meeting jointly discuses the client's medical condition and physical aids in use))
11 HH:      ((the daughter)) terribly actively wants to keep her mother
12          (0.2) [keep her in good shape and the mother
13 HHH:            [mmm
14 HH:      wants to ⌊keep herself in ⌊shape
15 S:             [mm:   [yes sure she herself wants that [too
16 HH:                                                   [yes
17 HH:      heh but this lady still needs help in getting dressed like she
18          no longer (.) is able to deal with poppers or zippers and all these so
19          and needs help showering and meals the daughter takes care of
20          and then she (.) eats unassisted (0.8) with the other hand
21          and ((the daughter)) takes care of clothes maintenance
22          and shopping and (1.0) the length of care is roughly
23          two to four hours a day and (1.5.)
24          wants to live at home (0.8) and at this stage they don't want any
25          short term admissions or anything (.) nor care vouchers, nor anything
26          else like this cause the lady said that she is so happy here at ho(h)me
27 ?:       mmm
28 HH:      and-a (.) and she still has a social network so a group of friends
29          that visit her there (.) and-a
30          So they've had this lowest rate and they said that for them it is
31          quite (1.5) all right and then if there's some quite radical [change
32 S:                                                                    [mm
33 HH:      then they'll get in touch and we can have another look at the situation
```

The home helper moves the meeting forward by mentioning the next client and by identifying her by her last, middle, and first name. The mentioning of the name in this order (usually in the form last name – first name) follows the documentary format on the application forms everyone in the meeting has in front of them. Having identified the client, the home-helper then opens the file, and hands the medical documentation on the client to the doctor sitting next to her. By this simple move that often follows the introduction of a new case, the home-helper simultaneously demarcates medical knowledge and the physical status of the client as something belonging to the doctor's professional area of expertise.

In what follows, the home-helper then moves to list specifics of the client in question. In the beginning of the client description that lasts five minutes in all, the home helper delivers detail about the client's living arrangements (lines 4-6), her physical state (*moves about (1.5) poorly*, line 6) She also makes reference to the fact that she has made the home visit the day before (line 3), and that the daughter of the elderly client, who is also the carer, has been present during the visit. On line ten we learn that the situation within the past year has not changed significantly. This indicates implicitly that the elderly client is already within this particular form of support, i.e., she has previously already received the informal home care allowance. In case of such 'old cases', the task for the meeting is to check whether any significant change has occurred in the medical status of the cared for, and whether the amount of care needed per day has risen to a degree that favors the amount to be raised.

Despite the no change –status of the elderly lady in question (line 10), the home-helper nonetheless continues to describe the caring relationship between her and her daughter in some considerable detail. This is in line with the how such seemingly 'routine' cases are treated in the data more generally. After jointly discussing the medical status of the client and the level of physical aids provided by the home help team (discussion omitted from excerpt), the home helper and the secretary of the meeting in co-operation make reference to the committed nature of both mother and daughter alike: they both do their best to keep the elderly lady in good shape (lines 11-16). The home-helper also points out that despite these active efforts and the ideal initiative shown by both, the elderly lady still needs help with daily chores. She also outlines the detail of acts that go into the caring relationship (lines 17-23: dressing, showering, clothes, shopping). On line 23, the home-helper then summarizes the care with quantification: two to four hours of care work per day. This type of quantification is crucial information for the meeting to reach a decision on the exact level of support and the sum of money to be allocated.

From line 24 the home-helper then moves to summarize the opinions and viewpoints of the elderly client herself. Stating that the daughter and her mother do not want short-term hospital admissions nor care vouchers[2], she simultaneously makes clear that she, as the professional has made clear all the options open to her clients. Note, how she also resorts to active voicing (Wooffitt 1992) when describing the elderly lady's own wishes. On line 27 she reports the words of the elderly client herself, and does it in a way that repeats her own exact words "h*appy* h*ere* at ho(h)me" (here instead of there). This direct active voicing that repeats the words as they were uttered the day before adds to the factuality and authenticity of the report delivered. The wishes to continue living at home are then further fleshed out and supported with detail about the client's wide network of friends that still visit her there. The excerpt then closes with the statement of both the mother's and the daughter's wishes of maintaining the home care allowance at its current level.

What we have here then is an account of a fairly well-functioning caring relationship. The elderly person's home is depicted as the ideal place that allows the maintenance of

---

[2] Care vouchers are part of the municipal means of supporting informal home care. Using service vouchers granted to them, family carers can buy necessary services from private service providers and take some time off.

ongoing friendships in familiar surroundings. What I find particularly noteworthy in excerpt one is the agency attached to both the carer and the cared for. They are both depicted as responsible, as good and devoted people who do their own share. Both mother and daughter want to do their utmost to keep the mother in good shape, *but* (line 17) help from the daughter is still crucial. This raises two further analytic points. First, describing the current devoted activity of the carer and the cared for, the home-helper also evokes moral notions concerning the responsibilities of elders and of their formal and informal carers. The home-helper's account also makes available the possible trajectory that, should the best efforts of the mother and daughter fail (*radical change* line 32), potential next steps then need to be taken by us, the professionals.

In excerpt two, moral and ideal notions of devoted care by the daughter become even more pronounced as the case description unfolds further.

Excerpt Two: Mother and devoted daughter (HCA4, 32:15-36.32)

```
01 HH:     ((talking about the mother)) [She] copes on her own while the daughter
02   goes to work at this moment (.) she's she works at the town library
03   (0.8) in some library she's at work sort of 50 percent
04   (1.8.)
05 HH:     But the daughter said that a realistic time for the mother to stay on her own
06   is (0.8) something like eight hours but she still needs to phone up several
07   times in between (1.0) what with the recent tendency to fall she's now
08   taken up work half time
09   (1.5)
10 S:      yes
11 HH:     so
12   (0.5)
13 HH:     they do want to do a great deal for the (0.8) mother (0.2) I mean
14   with the daughter also like sacrificing for her mother
15 All:    mm, yes
16 HH:     a part of her work too but I mean they said that they understand
17   that there are lots of applicants and they'd like this (.) lowest level
```

In excerpt two, the daughter is depicted as someone who is willing to sacrifice a part of her life in order to take care of the mother (line 14), while not demanding full financial compensation for the caring. Both daughter and mother are described as people who understand the institutional scarcity involved and as people who therefore are ready to settle for less.

Of all excerpts, one and two seem to construct something of a moral balance between the actions of the client and her daughter on the one hand and the public professional eldercare on the other. This public–private divide is also placed on a continuum where the situation and the efforts of all involved today are depicted, while potential changes along the caring trajectory are suspended to the background. Therefore, should changes despite all the moral and ideal devotion depicted occur, we, as the professional providers of care should be prepared to act accordingly.

Life Course Ideals and Cultural Imagery as Part of Decision Making Talk

In the two excerpts shown so far, we already saw how professionals evoked notions of good and devoted family care. In what follows, I would like to provide further examples of how notions of ideal circumstances and surroundings for ageing well, as well as moral notions of devoted care by family members are brought to bear and used in support of decision making.

The interaction I chose to present concerns a case marked as exceptional by the meeting participants. This time the caring relationship consists of two brothers living together. This is a case where an elderly male carer is actively involved in the daily care of his own brother. In addition, as the excerpts below show, he is also partly responsible for another brother of his who is in long-term institutional care.

Male caregivers are not a rarity in the data as a whole. However, care provided by one brother to another is fairly rare, and also discursively marked as such in the excerpts below. Excerpt 3 begins 40 minutes into the meeting. The professional describing the case is the same speaker as in excerpts one and two. She again starts by identifying by name both the carer and the cared for, and by stating that a home visit has been done the day before. After this, however, she immediately moves to what can be analyzed as moral talk about the caring relationship in question. This time, the description also builds on some interesting discursive detail that evokes cultural ideals of good ageing as well as positive life course imagery.

Excerpt Three: The brothers (HCA4, 0:40-0:53)
Speakers: HH = home helper, S = secretary
Pseudonyms: Roundhill = a hospital

```
01 HH:      <Then there's> er ((last name + first name)) I went there yesterday and-a
02  (3.5)
03 HH:      hh and here the carer is the brother ((last name + first name))
04  (1.8)
05 HH:      It was a such a (1.8.) an extremely good feeling to
06  to make the (0.2) home visit because just how ((name of the carer))
07  had taken it to his heart to care after these brothers
08  He's had £several brothers in his care£ and now
09  one of them has gotten a place in Roundhill
10  (0.2)
11 S:       yes
12 HH:      a permanent [placement and
13 S:                   [he has
14  (1.0)
15 HH:      and (0.8) it's with such joy and with a sincere heart
16  he does this
17  (1.5)
18 HH:      So this ((name of the cared for)) has er (1.8) turned eighty hh
19  said he just (0.2) er (1.0) in September turned eighty and
20  (.) has lived all his life in the same house and was born in it
21  and lived in it all his life this house that's not quite well-equipped
```

```
22   so there's no .hh (0.4) no Sauna or any other proper bath facilities
23   a sort of olden times house in ((name of town region))
24   (1.5)
25   and er so (2.2) this ((name of carer)) takes care of all shopping
26   handles all (.) all money matters and shopping and (0.4) takes
27   care of meals. He is (2.2) a good cook has become a good cook
28   in the course of all these years, takes care of the dishes and
29   cares for the clothes of this ((name of the cared for)) a:nd (0.8)
30   the cleaning and (0.8) helps him get dressed and (1.0)
31   washed up. Cares for him during the night if needed but he
32   says that luckily t-this ((cared for)) sleeps well at night
```

In the excerpt the home-helper clearly sets out to depict the carer as someone fully and admirably devoted to the caring of his brothers. The attributes attached to him evoke notions of genuineness and of honesty: he has taken it to his heart to care for his brothers (line 7) and does this with joy and sincerity (line 15). The home-helper also describes her own feelings when coming face-to-face with such an ideal caring relationship (line 5)[3].

As the case description continues, we learn that the existence of such a devoted carer also ensures ideal surroundings for the ageing 80-year-old brother. Secured by the care by his (presumably somewhat younger) brother, he is able to continue living in the house of his childhood where he has lived all his life. In the home-helper's narration, the notion of continuity and the romantic, and in many ways old fashioned idea of living in the same house throughout one's entire life course also clearly surmount small deficiencies in the housing arrangements of the brothers (line 21-23). In all, the case is constructed as something of a nostalgic and rare glimpse into a way of living and to a form of devoted care that is about to become extinct. Moral, emotional and nostalgic overtones, in other words, clearly mark the case description.

The meeting still needs to deal with the practical question of whether and how much economic support is to be given to these brothers. In the next excerpt, the home-helper starts by pointing out that the applicants have received a modest amount so far, and that the brother in charge of the care giving has implied that the benefit should perhaps be revised.

Excerpt Four: The brothers II (HCA4, 0:43:08-0:53)
Speakers: HH = home helper, S = secretary, HHH = head of home help

```
01 HH:      they've had this lowest er this (.) I mean this (0.2) .thh
02          ((the carer)) suggested that couldn't he like get a little bit more
03          than the lowest rate cause (0.2) everything (0.2)
04          he never sees any of that money himself
05          like he's done a lot of wo(h)rk for the society
06          £having taken [care of all
07 S:                     [he has
08 HH: his brothe(h)rs
09 ?:        that's right
10 HHH: >What< about the leg sore on ((the cared for)) at the moment
11     like how many medical home visits do they get nowadays?
```

---

[3] For a detailed analysis of emotion evocation and emotion categories in meeting talk, see Nikander forth.

The home-helper (on line 2) makes reference to the wishes of the carer and describes how, probably due to taxation, he hardly sees any of the money currently granted to them. She then goes on to argue for a raise in the allowance due to the long-term nature and the cost-effectiveness of the care given. In this context it is not quite clear whether the home-helper is quoting the words of the carer himself, or whether "the work for society" argument is something she herself is advocating. The laughter tokens and the smiley voice might suggest that she is in fact quoting the carer's words and marking them as delicate or as a fitting argument made by the carer. Despite the agreement by the meeting secretary, other members of the meeting do not join in or express their opinion on the home-helpers indirect suggestion. Instead, the head of home help changes the course of the discussion by asking a specific question on the elderly brother's health (*>what< about the leg sore*, line 10). Note how the temporal marking in the question (*nowadays*, line 11) infers that she too has access to specific information on these two brothers and their care history. The head of home help, in other words, also has a platform from which to participate in the discussion. By asking a direct question she also marks the case description as lacking in some crucial detail, and as incomplete.

It is only later in the discussion over the two brothers' case that the team comes back to the question of whether the allowance should remain on its current level or whether it should be raised. In excerpt five, the question is raised by the home-helper in charge who asks the team's and the case presenter's views on the matter. Instead of providing an answer the home helper continues by providing additional information on the case.

Excerpt five: The brothers III (HCA4, 45.00-)
Speakers: HHC = Home helper in charge, HH = home-helper, S = secretary

```
01 HHC: So what are we going to thin- (0.2) decide what do all you think
02      (.)
03      or what do you yourself (0.5) think about this
((addressing the home-helper who is the case presenter))
04 HH:      then this ((carer)) also asked me to say (.) inform the meeting that he also .hh
05      (.) continuing (.) like this brotherhood and brotherly love (.) in a way
06      er so (.) he like (.) now that the othe- this other brother is there in Roundhill
07 S:       mm
08      (0.8)
09 HH:      then every other weekend cause he misses home so much
10 HHC: but the task [here is to
11 HH:             [and he then every other weekend brings him home and-a
12      takes care of them both he heh he
13      ((general laughter, talk and nodding))
14 S:       That's lovely
15      ((general laughter and talk))
16 HH:      £so I mean brotherly love like that I haven't come across£
17      for a few years (.) not like what you can see in that house
18 S:       (( )) but then surely the carer too (0.2) is tired
19 HH:      that's right
20 ??       mm[m
21 HH:        [yes that is what I told him too that he should think about that other
22      day in the day centre in Roundhill that they've been offered
```

((a few lines omitted))
23 HH: They've received the lowest rate before (0.2) but this ((*carer*))
24   just said that couldn't it be raised somewhat and I said that
25   I can always take the message but like I cannot ((*talk cut off*))

The home helper in charge directs the question concerning the amount of the allowance first to the whole meeting but then addresses the case presented directly (*what do you (0.5) yourself think about this*, line 3). The case presenter is reluctant to move to the decision phase, and instead, quoting the caring brother, proceeds to present further information to the meeting. What follows is further evidence on the devoted nature of the carer who, out of brotherly love, also takes his other brother out of the hospital and thus takes care of two of his brothers for shorter periods of time.

The home-helper's turns here clearly advocate a specific outcome. She continues her narrative despite the interruption on line 10 and manages to get a general, understanding and sympathetic reaction from the meeting participants (*that's lovely*, line 14). On lines 16-17 she sums up the case in a way that marks the caring relationship between the three brothers as one of a kind and exceptional. In her case description the "house of brotherly love" seems to encapsulate or turn into something of a metaphor of rare and devoted care. Discursively constructing the case as special, as something that she, as a professional, has not come across for years (lines 16-17), the speaker simultaneously advocates a specific favourable decision to be taken. Note also that towards the end of the excerpt the case presenter pronouncedly distances herself from any direct advocate work. She positions herself as simply an even-handed messenger who passes on the wishes of the client to the meeting and leaves it at that (lines 23-25).

In sum, the two cases presented above bring forth three interesting discursive phenomena. First, I have been focusing on how notions of ideal circumstances for ageing as well as positive (romantic) life course imagery are evoked when describing elderly clients and their carers. Second, I have attempted to show how such imagery trades in and calls into being moral and emotional notions of both formal and informal care and responsibility. Third, the excerpts also showed how professionals when presenting and describing their clients, walk a discursive tight rope between advocacy and notions of neutral descriptive institutional work. In both of the cases shown here, and despite the advocacy work done by one of the members, the team decided to keep the informal home care allowance at its current level.

Conclusion

In this chapter, the analytic focus has been on the local decision making level and on the logic and argumentation via which practical decisions about elderly care are made. This type of decision making takes place in the delicate area where the strengths, coping and abilities of individual elderly people and their carers must be appreciated and supported to the full. Simultaneously, a crucial part of any professional deliberation includes the capability of making well-informed and ethical decisions about the timing, form and level of outside support. As we have seen, interprofessional deliberation and joint decision making evoke notions of justice and morality and make use of imagery concerning the life course and "good ageing" as part of the argumentation. It seems then that professional decision-making hardly ever escapes more general ideals, and moral notions about the responsibilities of 'us' as professionals vis-à-vis those of the relatives or the elderly clients themselves. Decision making practice also trades in and discursively establishes distinct characteristics for what constitutes good and devoted care, and what the life circumstances of individual elders should ideally look like.

In sum, the key message in this chapter has been that institutional decision making over home care services consists of more than mere rational people-processing. Close discursive analyses of professional argumentation, categorization and decision making reveal the reflexive, sensitive practices whereby the morality, criteria and ethical basis of care and support allocation are negotiated. The complexity and conflicting demands under which professionals work within elderly care is hardly going to become easier in ageing societies. Therefore, close discursive analyses of professional everyday practices today, be it in meetings, by the bed side or in the cabinets of policy making may, in part, help us better understand the dynamics, ethics and challenges of elderly care tomorrow.

Practical Considerations and Recommendations:

1. Close analysis of institutional interaction lays out for view the day-to-day logic and argumentation of professional deliberation and decision making.
2. The training and schooling of elderly care professionals could make better use of discursive studies and analysis on professional practice.
3. Work arrangements and time budgeting within elderly care should enable and support professionals' joint reflection and analysis of their work and decision making practices.
4. Forming and maintaining an outspoken set of criteria on the local level helps professionals work and makes the processes of decision making accessible and transparent to all involved.
5. Analysis and awareness of shared ideals, morality and criteria helps prepare for the ongoing changes and challenges within elderly care.

References

Antaki, C. and Widdicombe, S. (eds) (1998): *Identities in Talk*. London: Sage.
Anttonen, A. and Sipilä, J. (2000): Suomalaista sosiaalipolitiikkaa [Social Policy in Finland]. Tampere, Vastapaino.
Atkinson, P. and Coffey, A. (1997): Analysing Documentary Realities. In D. Silverman (Ed.): *Qualitative Research. Theory, Method and Practice*. pp. 45-62 London, Sage.
Baker, C.D. (1997) 'Ticketing rules: Categorization and moral ordering in a school staff meeting.' In S. Hester and P. Eglin (eds) *Culture in Action: Studies in Membership Categorisation Analysis*. pp. 77-98. Lanham, Maryland: International Institute for Ethnomethodology and Conversation Analysis and University Press of America.
Boden, D. (1994): *The Business of Talk: Organizations in Action*. Cambridge, Polity Press.

Cicirelli, V.G. (1993): Intergenerational communication in the mother-daughter dyad regarding caregiving decisions. In Coupland, N. and Nussbaum, J.F. (Eds.): *Discourse and Lifespan Identity*. (pp. 215-236) Newbury Park, CA: Sage.

Coupland, N. and Coupland, J. (1998): Reshaping lives: Constitutive identity work in geriatric medical consultations. *Text*, 18(2): 159-189.

Coupland, N. and Coupland, J. (1999): Ageing, ageism and anti-ageism. Moral stance in geriatric medical discourse. In Hamilton, H.E. (Ed.): *Language and Communication in Old Age. Multidisciplinary Perspectives.* (pp. 177-208.) New York: Garland.

Dockrell, J. and Wilson, G. (1995) 'Management issues in interprofessional work with older people.' In K. Soothill, L. Mackay and C. Webb (eds) *Interprofessional Relations in Health Care*. pp. 281-296 London: Edward Arnold.

Gilleard, C. and Higgs, P. (1998): Old People as Users and Consumers of Healthcare: A third age rhetoric for a fourth age reality? *Ageing and Society* 18, 233-248.

Grainger, K. (1993): That's a lovely bath dear: Reality construction in the discourse of elderly care. *Journal of Aging Studies*, 7(3): 247-262.

Hester, S. and Eglin, P. (eds) (1997): *Culture in Action: Studies in Membership Categorisation Analysis*. Lanham, Maryland: International Institute for Ethnomethodology and Conversation Analysis and University Press of America.

Holstein, J.A. (1990): The discourse of age in involuntary commitment proceedings. *Journal of Aging Studies*, 4(2): 111-130.

Housley, W. (2003): *Interaction in Multidisciplinary Teams*. Cardiff Papers in Qualitative Research, Hants, Ashgate.

Latimer, J. (1997): Giving patients a Future: The constituting of classes in an acute medical unit. *Sociology of Health and Illness* 9(2), 160-185.

Leppänen, V. (1998): *Structures of District Nurse – Patient Interaction*. Lund Dissertations in Sociology, University of Lund.

Linell, P. (1998): Discourse Across Boundaries: On recontextualizations and the blending of voices in professional discourse. *Text* 18(2), 143-157.

Nikander, P. (2000): 'Old' vs. 'Little Girl': A discursive approach to age categorisation and morality. *Journal of Aging Studies*, 14(4): 335-358.

Nikander, P. (2002). *Age in Action: Membership work and stage of life categories in talk*. Helsinki, Finnish Academy of Science and Letters.

Nikander, P. (2003). The Absent Client: Case description and decision-making in multi-professional meetings. Interactions, identities and practices. In Hall, C., Juhila, K., Parton, N. and Pösö T. (Eds.) *Constructing clienthood in social work and human services*. (pp. 112-128) London: Jessica Kingsley.

Nikander, P (2005): *Managing Scarcity: Joint decision making in interprofessional meetings*. In Heinonen, T. and Metteri, A. (Eds.): Social Work in Health and Mental Health: issues, Developments and Actions. pp.273-299. Toronto, Canadian Scholar's Press.

Nikander, P. (forth): Emotion Categories in Meeting Talk. In A. Hepburn. and S. Wiggins (Eds.): *Discursive Research in Practise. New Approaches to Psychology and Interaction.* Cambridge University Press, Cambridge.

Paoletti, I. (1998): *Being an Older Woman: A Study in the Social Production of Identity.* Everyday Communication: Case Studies of Behavior in Context Series. Mahwah, NJ: Lawrence Erlbaum Associates.

Taylor, B.C. (1992): Elderly identity in conversation: Producing frailty. *Communication Research*, 19(4): 493-515.

Vaarama, M. and Kautto, M. (1999): Social Protection for the Elderly in Finland. Saarijärvi, Gummerus.

Walker, A. (1995): The family and the mixed economy of care. In I. Allen and E. Perkins, *The future of family care for older people*. pp. 22-35. London: HMSO.

Wooffitt, R. (1992): *Telling Tales of the Unexpected: The Organization of Factual Discourse.* London: Harvester Wheatsheaf.

In: Psychology of Decision Making
Editor: Paul M. Garrison

ISBN 978-1-60021-869-9
© Nova Science Publishers, Inc.

Chapter 9

ANALYSING THE EFFECTS OF MORTALITY SALIENCE ON PREJUDICE AND DECISION-TAKING

Agustin Echebarria- Echabe[*] and Francisco J. Valencia Gárate

Department of Social Psychology. Psychology faculty. The University of the Basque Country. Tolosa avenue, 70. San Sebastian 20009. Spain

ABSTRACT

Recently (Echebarria & Fernandez, 2006) we carried out a quasi-experimental study on the effects of the terrorist attacks against the railways in Madrid and found that these attacks provoked a generalized prejudice directed not only against groups regarded as the responsible of the attacks but also against other non-related group (Jews). A generalized displacement toward more conservative values and political options was also found. Here we present two follow-up experimental studies designed to analyse the socio-psychological processes that might underlie these changes. The first study manipulated, through pictures, the salience of death- related thoughts without involving any personal or group based threat. The generalized increment of prejudices and group bias are reproduced but only at an implicit level. The second study proved that mortality salience affects how social dilemmas are approached. Participants assigned to the mortality salient condition approached a health related dilemma in terms of losses, independently of how it was experimentally framed. In contrast, control participants shifted their choices in function of the experimental manipulation. We discuss the implications of these results in terms of understanding the effects of terrorism from the Terror Management Theory.

The Terror Management Theory (TMT) (Greenberg, Pyszczynski, & Solomon, 1986; Landau, Johns, Greenberg, Pyszczynski, Martens, Goldenberg, & Solomon, 2004) is based on the work of Ernest Becker (1973) and suggests that the awareness of mortality facilitates the social construction of, and continuing investment in, a cultural worldview that protects people

---

[*] E-mail: pspeteta@ss.ehu.es

from death-related fears by presenting a meaningful and orderly world and standard of value by which one´s own life is perceived as significant and enduring.

The TMT proposes that one distinctive human characteristic is that the phylogenetic development of the brain, together with the development of symbolic communication systems and culture, has made possible the emergence of self-consciousness. Perhaps the human being is the only animal that is conscious of the finite duration of life. Thus, two conflicting forces are in permanent struggle: the survival instinct, present in all animals, and the consciousness of the finite nature of life. This consciousness raises feelings of existential anxiety that can be coped with by means of two resources: self-esteem and adherence to the group's cultural values and world-views.

There is ample evidence that the salience of mortality awareness has a variety of effects: increasing desire to have children (Wisman & Goldenberg, 2005); derogation of deviant ingroup members (See & Petty, 2006); increment of pro-social behaviours but only on behalf of ingroup members (Jonas, Schimel, Greenberg, & Pyszczynski, 2002; van den Bos, Poortvliet, Maas, Miedema, & van den Ham, 2005); strong attachment to ingroups and derogation of outgroups (Arndt, Schimel, Greenberg, Pyzczynski, & Solomon, 2002; Dechesne, Janssen, & van Knippenberg, 2000); negative evaluation of wilderness (Koole & Van den Berg, 2005); intensification of beliefs in supernatural agents (angels, demons, etc.) (Norenzayan & Hansen, 2006); attachment to ingroup values and worldviews (Cozzolino, Staples, Meyers, & Samboceti, 2004) and derogation of alternative worldviews (Schmeichel & Martens, 2005); promotion of affiliation (Wisman & Koole, 2003); increment of prejudice against older people (Martens, Greenberg, Schimel, & Landau, 2004); preference for information that supports one's own choices and decisions (Jonas, Greenberg, & Frey, 2003); or preference for simple knowledge structures (for example adherence to explanations presenting the world as fair) (Landau, Johns, Greenberg, Pyzczynski, Martens, Goldenberg, & Solomon, 2004).

More interesting for our interests, TMT has been used as a theoretical approach to understand the effects of terrorism. For example, Landau and colleagues (2004) proposed that the 9/11 terrorist attacks increased the accessibility of death-related thoughts leading to positive attitudes toward Bush and his counter-terrorism policies. In the same way, Pyszczynski and colleagues (2006) proved that making mortality salient increased Iranian students support of martyrdom attacks against US forces and conservative American students' support for massive attacks in Iraq. It is hypothesized that terrorism directly arouses existential anxiety by reminding us of the frail nature of our lives.

Recently we (Echebarria & Fernandez, 2006) published a study of the effects that Islamic terrorist attacks in Madrid (11 March, 2004) had on general attitudes of the Spanish population. It must be remembered that these attacks (there were three coordinated attacks) targeted the railways system, causing two hundred deaths and hundreds of injuries. In a quasi-experimental design we were able to collect data about conservatism, liberalism, authoritarianism, political orientation, and prejudice just before and after the attacks. We found a generalized tendency to increase the adherence to conservative values, a displacement towards more conservative ideological positions, a stronger authoritarianism, as well as an increment of prejudice not only directed against Arabs, but also extended against another group, Jews. However, the nature of the study left open a number of questions about the underlying psychosocial processes involved in these changes. It is be possible that the processes described by the TMT were not responsible for these changes and another more parsimonious explanation could shed light on the situation. Hewstone, Rubin, & Willis (2002) stated that one of the common criticisms of TMT is that the effects of mortality salience (death-related thoughts) can be reinterpreted as the effects of self-relevant threats in general. Namely, it could be hypothesized that the attacks roused feelings of threat against the ingroup. It is well known in the literature that attacks against ingroup members enhance a number of changes within and between groups (Sherif, 1966; Sherif, Harvey, White, Hood, & Sherif, 1961;Tajfel, 1978, 1981). Groups that feel they are under threat increase the attachment to previous group values and beliefs, increase cohesion, and develop prejudices against outgroups. And all these changes can occur without the participation of death-related thoughts. In fact, Hart, Shaver, & Goldenberg (2005) proved that the same effects of mortality salience could be found as a result of attachment threats (imagine a romantic break-up) or threats against ingroup worldviews without directly involving mortality questions.

Given the impossibility of researching into the role played by death- related thoughts we decided to designed two laboratory studies to look into these issues.

The first study aimed to determine whether the increasing prejudice found in our study can be explained by the death-related thoughts alone without involving any reference to one's own death or group threat. The second study was oriented towards establishing whether the conservative changes induced by mortality awareness are part of a more general change in the way social dilemmas are approached.

STUDY 1

Sample and Procedure

A hundred and fifteen undergraduate students enrolled in an introductory course of social psychology participated in this study. As happens in this kind of sample most of them were women (100). They were informed that the study was designed to collect data about a number of topics studied by social psychology in order to use the data in the practical sessions of the course. The experiment was carried out in three phases.

The first phase manipulated the salience of death- related thoughts. Students were randomly assigned to two groups: mortality versus control group. The mortality salience was manipulated through an aesthetic task. Two pictures were printed in a booklet. In the mortality condition the two pictures were taken from the tenebrist pictorical movement (see annex). This was a counter-reform picture school developed in the 17th century with numerous references to themes related to death and strong contrasts between light and shadow. Participants assigned to the control condition were exposed to two bright abstract pictures from the 20th century (see annex). Participants were asked to concentrate on the pictures and list in a free format all the thoughts that came into their minds while observing the pictures. This thought- listing variable was introduced to check the effectiveness of the experimental manipulation and analyse the role played by death- related thoughts.

In the second phase participants communicated the extent to which they felt joy, fear, anxiety, anguish, and anger (1 = not at all and 5 = a lot). Moreover, they completed several tasks that evaluated visual accuracy and mathematical thinking. These were introduced as filler tasks.

Anti-Arab prejudice was measured in the third phase. Firstly, participants responded to the paper-and-pencil version of the IAT (Implicit Association Task) created by Lowery, Hardin and Sinclair (2001). In the centre of the page 36 word-pairs are presented in each condition. Each pair shows a name in capital letters and just below a word. The task is presented as a categorization task. Subjects have to decide if each name is a Spanish or an Arab name and if the word printed below has positive or negative connotations. Categorization conditions are printed on the top of each page. For instance on the right appear the heading "ARAB- positive" and on the left "SPANISH- negative". Participants have to make a mark on the left of a "NAME- word" each time an "Arab-name/ positive-word" is found. Each time a "Basque- name/ negative-word" is found participants have to make a mark on the right. Pairs that do not correspond to any of the two categorization conditions should be left unmarked. Participants were instructed to work quickly for 20 seconds in each trial. Four trials (36 pairs and 20 seconds for each one) were completed. The first was a training task. Women's and men's names were paired with 36 words with positive (18) and negative (18) connotations. The instruction was to find Women's-name and positive words and men's-names and negative words pairs. The second was also a trial reversing the instruction: Man name- positive words and Women- name and negative word. The third and forth were critical trials. Here, Spanish and Arab names were paired with positive and negative words. The instruction of the third task was to find out "Arab-name/positive word" and "Spanish-name/negative word" pairs. The instruction was reversed in the fourth trial (Arab-name/negative word/ Spanish-name- positive word" pairs). Average trial response latencies were calculated by dividing the number of correct answers within each trial by 20 (seconds). The final IAT score was assessed by the difference in the average number of correct responses on the critical prejudice-congruent (Arab-negative/ Spanish-positive) trial versus average number of correct responses on the critical prejudice incongruent (Arab-positive/ Spanish-negative) trial.

The IAT was followed by two explicit measures of Anti-Arab prejudice. The first was an adaptation of McConahay's (1986) Modern Racism scale (the alpha reliability coefficient in our study was = 0.79) and the second was the Echebarria and Fernandez (in press) Anti-Arab prejudice scale (alpha = 0.91).

Results

The effect of the mortality manipulation was checked. Participants assigned to the death-thoughts inducing condition reported more death-related thoughts ($X = 1.46$, $SD = .97$) than participants placed in the control condition ($X = 0.13$, $SD = 0.34$) ($F(1,113) = 90.69$, $p \leq .001$). The correlation between the experimental manipulation and the number of death-related thoughts was very strong $(r = .67)$.

Also preliminarily to the main analysis, correlations between the explicit and implicit measures of prejudice were computed. The correlation between the two explicit measures was high ($r = 0.99$, $p \leq .001$). By contrast, the correlations between the Modern racism ($r = 0.11$, p = .223) and the Anti-Arab $(r = 0.16$, $p = .10)$ scales and the IAT were not significant. This goes in the well-established direction of independence between explicit and implicit prejudices.

Differences were analysed between implicit and explicit anti-Arab prejudice of participants assigned to the mortality versus control conditions. There were no differences in the Modern Racism ($F(1,113) = 0.43$, $p = .523$) and the Anti-Arab ($F(1,113) = 0.15$, $p = .696$) scales. In contrast, the mortality manipulation had a significant effect on the implicit measure of prejudice (IAT) ($F(1,113) = 40.61$, $p \leq .001$). IAT scores were higher in the mortality ($X = 0.11$, $SD = .14$) than the control ($F(1, 113) = -0.05$, $SD = .12$) condition. We must remember than higher scores means more efficient performance on the prejudice-congruent than on the prejudice-incongruent trials.

The feelings aroused by the mortality manipulation were also analysed. Emotions were not affected by the experimental manipulation. Thus, it seems that it was death thoughts induced by the manipulation, and not feelings of fear, that were responsible for the increasing implicit anti-Arab prejudice.

In our previous study (Echebarria & Fernandez, 2006) we found that the terrorist attacks provoked a generalized prejudice extended to groups no directly involved in the attacks. We tried to analyse whether our manipulation also affected gender bias. Taking the training trials, an IAT score was computed based on prejudices against men. The reason for this choice was that 100 out of the 115 participants were women. The IAT resulted from subtracting the number of correct answers in the incongruent condition (women-name-negative word/ men-name –positive word) from the number of correct answers in the congruent condition (women-name/positive word/ men-name/negative word) and dividing the total by 20. The manipulation had also a significant effect in this index ($F(1, 108) = 4.26$, $p = .04$). Women in the mortality condition had higher scores than those assigned to the control condition ($X = .05$, $SD = .008$ versus $X = .01$, $SD = .008$). In other words, although lower than in the Arab case, the mortality condition also led an increment of group bias amongst our female participants.

Discussion

The attacks against the railway in Madrid provoked a generalized increment of explicit prejudices against Arabs and Jews. But we could not explore the psycho-social factors underlying these changes. At least three factors could be responsible for them: death-related thoughts induced by the exposition to the images broadcast by the mass media, feelings of fear, or a perception of threat against the ingroup. Our laboratory study provides some tentative answers to this question. Here, we used a completely new method to induce death-related thoughts without involving any direct threat either against personal or social identities. The dominant method to induce mortality salience involves thinking of one's own death. Thus, the effects of death-related thoughts and threats against personal identity are confounded. In other words, the traditional findings of studies based on the TMT could be explained as the results of responses against personal or group threats, without recurring to death-related thoughts or consciousness of mortality. In this line, Hart, Shaver and Goldenberg (2005) show that the same effects caused by the dominant manipulation of TMT (thinking of one's own immediate death) could be induced by other threats against personal identity (thinking about divorce or separation from a romantic partner), without making any reference to death. In our study about the effect of terrorist attacks and in the classical manipulation of the TMT there are explicit threats against individual or social identities. One effect of these threats is the increment of explicit prejudice and group bias. In this study we avoided any explicit personal threats and tried to induce only death-related thoughts. The result was that the manipulation increased implicit but not explicit anti- Arab prejudice. Moreover, these attitude changes were also extended to attitudes towards gender groups.

These results point out the complexity of the socio-psychological processes that underlie at least the changes found in the manipulations of TMT. We speculate that there are two independent processes working in this setting: one is related to the induction of death-related thoughts, and the other is related to threats against some component of the global self (either the personal and/ or the social identity). In the extent to which these two processes are independent, each one could have different effects on group bias and prejudice. Personal or group threats can explain overt and explicit changes while death- related thoughts could explain implicit changes. More research is necessary to disentangle the diversity of processes involved.

Mortality Salience and Decision-taking

As mentioned above, the second aim of this paper was to enquire into the socio-psychological processes responsible for the effects of mortality salience on general ideological positions, namely the tendency to endorse more conservative values and positions after exposure to factors that enhance the salience of mortality. We hypothesised that the ideological changes observed in our previous study (Echebarria & Fernández, 2006) might be a specific example of a more general tendency to adopt preventive and conservative decisions in all kinds of social dilemmas including issues not directly related to politics. We combined the TMT theory and the studies of Kahneman and Tversky (1979; Tversky & Kahneman, 1981) on the use of heuristic rules in decision-taking contexts.

We must remember that these authors formalised decision strategies known long ago as common sense or folk psychology. There are longstanding proverbs in Spanish and English folk knowledge that make recommendations about how to behave in decision-making situations. The first one ("de perdidos al río" or "when there is nothing to lose, throw caution to the wind") explains how to take decisions in loss-framed contexts. It recommends that when all is lost it is time to take risky and uncertain decisions. In loss situations the risky and uncertain decisions may help to reduce and/ or avoid losses. Kahneman and Tversky (1979) formalised this rule. They stated that social dilemmas framed in term of losses push us to assume risky and uncertain decisions (here presented in probabilistic terms). Coming back to common-sense knowledge, the second proverb says that it is better to secure what has been won than to risk it by trying to win more ("más vale pájaro en mano que cientos volando" or "a bird in the hand is worth two in the bush"). This means that when a social dilemma is framed is terms of gains or benefits, people adopt a conservative decision strategy, holding what has been won and not risking losing it all by trying to win more. According to the authors, although people like to win, they fear losing more. There is an asymmetry between the impact that wins and losses have, the impact of losses is stronger than that of wins. The biggest intuition of these authors was to prove that the use of these heuristic rules was not exclusive to ordinary people but was present in the professional decisions taken by economists (Fennema & Wakker, 1997), physicians (Levin & Chapman, 1990, 1993), or public health designers (Quattrone & Tversky, 1988).

How can mortality salience affect decisions in dilemma situations? We think that mortality salience and death-related thoughts put people in a pessimistic, negative, or loss-framed state of mind. Social dilemmas in general are regarded in terms of risk of losing. This means that if a social dilemma is framed in term of losses, both subjects exposed to a mortality salience manipulation and control subjects will adopt the same strategy (risky or uncertain alternatives). In contrast, if a social dilemma is framed in terms of gains, both groups will choose different alternatives. Control subjects would be sensitive to the change in the way the social dilemma is framed (win) and shift their strategies, opting for certainty and security. In contrast, people submitted to the salience mortality manipulation, to the extent that it induces a negative or loss- focused state of mind, should be relatively insensitive to the shift in the way the dilemma is framed and should continue to adopt strategies typical of loss-framed social dilemmas.

STUDY 2

Procedure

A 2 (salient mortality versus control) by 2 (losses versus wins framed dilemmas) experimental study was designed to test the above-mentioned hypothesis. The dependent variable was the preference for either (a) a health programme that specifies the exact number (certain alternative) of people that will survive or die (depending on how the dilemma is framed), r (b) a health programme that presents the expected efficiency in probabilistic terms (probabilistic or uncertain alternative).

Sixty-seven university undergraduate students participated in this study.

The study was carried out in three apparently unrelated phases.

The first was presented as a study about personality evaluation. Here, the mortality salience manipulation was introduced. The classical mortality salience manipulation was used in this study. Participants in the mortality salience conditions were asked to think about their own death and (a) write down all they would think and feel in the process of dying and (a) what would happen to their body after death. Subjects assigned to the control condition were asked to imagine they had a ad toothache and explain what their thoughts and feelings would be.

All the participants filled the Positive and Negative Affect Schedule (PANAS) (Watson, Clark, & Tellegen, 1988). This served as a filler task typically introduced after the mortality salience manipulation and before measuring its effects on the dependent variables.

The Social dilemmas were introduced in the third phase. This was an adaptation of the Tversky and Kahneman (1981) study f the Asian bird flu (aviar fever). This phase was presented as a study on strategies used in decision-making situations. Participants were asked to imagine that "a mortal variant of the Asian bird flu (aviar fever) that affects humans will reach our country. Epidemiologists calculate that 600 people will be infected. The public health minister has summoned the most prestigious specialists in this type of disease. Two alternative programs have been proposed". In the *loss-framed condition,* participants were informed that if the first program (program a) is implemented 400 of the infected patients will die (certainty option); while if the second program (program b) is implemented the 66.6 % of infected patients will die (probabilistic or uncertain option). In the *benefit-framed condition*, participants were informed that if the first program (program a) is implemented 200 infected-patients will survive (certainty option) whereas if the second program (program b) is implemented 33.3 % of infected persons will survive (probabilistic option). Participants were asked to choose between option "a" or "b". This was the dependent variable measured at a categorical level. It is important to note that in both the experimental conditions the effect of implementing the programs was the same: 400 patients will die and 200 patients will survive.

Results

Given the nature of our dependent variable the correlation between the two options is perfect (r = -1.00). Thus, we decided to transform this variable into a dummy variable with option-b (probabilistic or uncertain) as "1" and option-a (secure or certain) as "0". The reason for taking that decision was that option-b reflects decisions taken under a "loss-framed" or negative state of mind. It must be remembered that we speculated that the mortality salience was expected to create a similar state of mind.

An ANOVA was performed with the dummy-variable as the dependent variable and mortality salience (one's own death versus toothache) and the framing (loss versus benefit) manipulations as independent variables. The framing main effect (F (1,63) = 18.51, $p \leq .001$) and the framing by mortality salience interaction effect (F (1,63) = 3.70, p = .05) were significant (mortality main effect, F (1,63) = 0.33, p = .571). Means and standard deviation are printed in table 1.

It is important to remember that the means represent the percentage of participants in each condition that chose the probabilistic or uncertain option (1- means represents the percentage of participants that chose the other option).

The framing main effect reproduced the heuristic decision rules predicted by Kahneman and Tversky (1979). When the dilemma is framed in terms of loss, the large majority of participants decided to adopt the uncertain, probabilistic, or risky option (M = 0.75, SD = .43) whereas when the dilemma is framed in terms of gains or benefit, the majority chose the secure or certain option (M = 0.71, SD = .46).

Post-hoc contrasts were carried out in order to analyse in depth the effects of the mortality by the framing interaction. Firstly, a comparison between participants assigned to the mortality salience condition indicates that they were not affected by the framing manipulation (F (1,34) = 2.56, p = .12). They seemed to have been quite insensitive to the framing manipulation. Even in the win or benefit framing condition almost half of them chose the uncertain or probabilistic option. In contrast, control participants (toothache) were deeply influenced by the framing manipulation (F (1,29) = 24.11, $p \leq .001$). The majority of control-subjects assigned to the benefit condition chose the secure or certain option (1 – 0.17 = 0.83) while the large majority of those assigned to the loss condition opted for the probabilistic or uncertain option.

Table 1. ANOVA. Means and standard deviations

Variables	M	SD
Mortality Condition		
Loss-Framing	0.70	.47
Benefit-Framing	0.44	.51
Toothache Condition		
Loss-Framing	0.85	.37
Benefit-Framing	0.17	.38

Discussion

This second study was designed to address the question of whether the conservative value and political changes observed as a consequence of making mortality salient was a particular example of a more general change in the way that social dilemmas are approached. Taking the Kahneman and Tversky (1979; Tversky & Kahneman, 1981) heuristic rules as indices of a more general way to approach social problems we found that mortality salience predisposed subjects to the adoption of alternatives that reflect a negative or pessimistic approach to social problems (loss- framed situations). Participants submitted to a salient mortality manipulation were insensitive to the way the health dilemma was framed. They chose in a higher percentage strategies usually used in loss- conditions. This was not the case for control-participants, who shifted their preferences depending on how the problems were framed.

CONCLUSION

We have presented two follow-up studies designed to respond to some questions that remained open after our previous study about the effects of the terrorist attacks against the railways in Madrid. One of the more influential current theories used to understand the effect of terrorism is the Terror Management Theory (TMT) (Greenberg, Pyszczynski, & Solomon, 1986; Landau, Johns, Greenberg, Pyszczynski, Martens, Goldenberg, & Solomon, 2004). In short, it has been proposed that terrorism raises feelings of existential anxiety because it reminds people of the limited nature of their own existence. However, there are some unanswered questions due in part to the way in which mortality salience is manipulated. We think that there are several socio-psychological processes underlying the effects observed by the method used almost exclusively in the laboratories: asking participants to imagine their own death. We think that at least three different processes are involved in this: real threat against our personal identity; the cognitive process of thinking about death-related issues; and the fear aroused by the manipulation. There is some experimental evidence that indicates that some of these processes may explain the typical results found by the TMT. Hart, Shaver, & Goldenberg (2005) found that threats against personal self-regard not involving death-related thoughts (romantic break-ups) produce similar effects. Hewstone, Rubin, and Willis (2002) stated that the effects of TMT could be due to threats against personal and social identities. It is important to clarify the role played by these factors, because each one may affect different variables.

Our first study analysed the effects on prejudice of inducing death-related thoughts without involving a direct personal threat (observing pictures displaying death-related topics). We found that these death-related thoughts increased prejudice against Arabs and enhanced gender group bias but only at an implicit level. These changes were not reflected at an overt or explicit level. This induces us to speculate that some kind of personal or group threat should be added to death-related thoughts to translate inner changes into an overt rejection of outgroups.

The second study showed that the conservative value and political changes induced by the salience of mortality ay be a particular example of a more general change in the way people address social dilemmas. Mortality salience seems to induce a negative or pessimistic state of mind. We found that subjects under a mortality salience manipulation adopted decision-making rules that reflect an approach to social dilemmas framed in term of losses.

We think that TMT will continue to represent one of the more fruitful theoretical approaches to the understanding of the effects of terrorism in the population. Nevertheless some data indicates that the underlying processes may be more numerous that previously supposed. This is why we think that more experimental and correlational studies are needed to disentangle the complexity of processes involved in this experience.

ANNEX

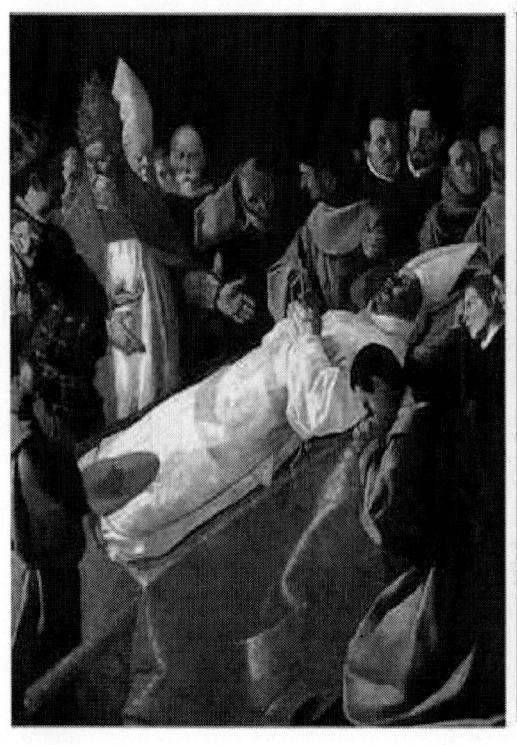

Mortality condition.

Control condition.

REFERENCES

Arndt, J., Greenberg, J., Schimel J., Pyzczynski, T., & Solomon, S. (2002). To belong or not to belong that is the question: Terror management and identification with ender and ethnicity. *Journal of Personality and Social psychology 3*, 26-43.

Becker, E. (1973). *The denial of death*. New York: Academic Press.

Cozzolino P. J., Staples, A. D., Meyers L. S., & Samboceti, J. (2004). Greed, death, and values: From error management to transcendence management theory. *Personality and Social Psychology Bulletin, 30*, 278-292.

Dechesne, M., Janssen, J., & van Knipenberg, A. (2000). Derogation and distancing as terror management strategies: The moderating role of need for closure and permeability of group boundaries. *Journal of Personality and Social Psychology, 79*, 923-932.

Echebarria, A. & Fernandez, E. (2006). Effects of terrorism on attitudes and ideological orientation. *European Journal of Social psychology, 36*, 259-265.

Echebarria, A. & Fernández, E. (in press). A new scale of Anti-Arab prejudice: Reliability and validity evidence. *Journal of Applied Social Psychology*.

Fennema, H. & Wakker, D. (1997). Original and cumulative prospect theory: A discussion of empirical differences. *Journal of behavioural Decision Making, 10*, 53-64.

Friedman, R. & Arndt, J. (2005). Reexploring the connection between terror management theory and dissonance theory. *Personality and Social Psychology Bulletin, 31*, 1217-1225.

Greenberg, J., Pyzczynski, T., & Solomon, S. (1986). The causes and consequences of a need for self-esteem: A terror management theory. In R. F. Baumeister (Ed.), *Public self and private self* (pp. 189-212). New York: Springer-Verlag.

Hart, J., Shaver, P. R., & Goldenberg, J. L. (2005). Attachment, self-esteem, worldviews, and terror management: Evidence for a tripartite security system. *Journal of Personality and Social Psychology, 88*, 999-1013.

Hewstone, M., Rubin, M., & Willis, H. (2002). Intergroup bias. *Annual Review of Psychology, 53*, 575-604.

Jonas, E., Greenberg, J., & Frey, D. (2003). Connecting terror management and dissonance theory: Evidence that mortality salience increases the preference for supporting information after decisions. *Personality and Social Psychology Bulletin, 29*, 1181-1189.

Jonas, E., Schimel, J., Greenberg, J., & Pyczynski, T. (2002). The scrooge effect: Evidence that mortality salience increases prosocial attitudes and behavior. *Personality and Social Psychology Bulletin, 8*, 42-1335.

Kahneman, D. & Tversky, A. (1979). Prospect theory: An analysis of decisions under risk. *Economatrica, 47*, 313-327.

Koole S. L. & Van en Berg, A. (2005). Lost in wilderness: Terror management , action orientation and nature evaluation. *Journal of Personality and Social Psychology, 8*, 1014-1028.

Landau, M. J., Solomon, S., Greenberg, J., Cohen, F., Pyzczynski, T., Arndt, J., Miller, C. H., Ogilvie, D., & Cook, A. (2004). Deliver Us from evil: The effects of mortality salience and reminders of 9/11 on support for president George W. Bush. *Personality and Social Psychology Bulletin, 30*, 1136-1150.

Landau, M. J., Johns, M., Greenberg, J., Pyzczynski, T., Martens, A., Goldenberg, J. L., & Solomon, S. (2004). A function of form: Terror management and structuring the social world. *Journal of Personality and Social Psychology, 87*, 190-210.

Levin, J.P. & Chapman, P. P. (1990). Risk taking, frame of reference, and characterization of victims groups in AIDS treatment decisions. *Journal of experimental Social Psychology, 26*, 421-434.

Levin, J. P. & Chapman, P. P. (1993). Risky decision making and allocation of resources for leukemis and AIDS programs. *Health Psychology, 12*, 110-117.

Lowery, B. S., Hardin, C. D., & Sinclair, S. (2001). Social influence effect on automatic racial prejudice. *Journal of Personality and Social Psychology, 81*, 842-855.

McConahay, J. (1986). Modern racism, ambivalence, and the modern racism scale. In J. F. Dovidio & S. L. Gaertner (Eds.), *Prejudice, discrimination, and racism* (pp. 91-126). San Diego: Academic Press.

Martens, A., Greenberg, J., Schimel, J., & Landau, M. J. (2004). Ageism and death: Effects of mortality salience and perceived similarity to elders on reaction to elderly people. *Personality and Social Psychology Bulletin, 30*, 1524-1536.

Noreayan, A. & Hansen, I. G. (2006). Belief in supernatural agents in he face of death. *Personality and Social Psychology Bulletin 32*, 174187.

Pyzczynski, T., Abdollahi, A., Solomon, S., Greenberg, J., Cohen, F., & Weise, D. (2006). Mortality salience, martyrdom, and military might: The great Satan versus the axis of evil. *Personality and Social Psychology Bulletin, 32*, 525-537.

Qattrone, G. A. & Tversky, A. (1988). Contrasting rational and psychological analyses of political choice. *American Political Science Review, 82*, 719-736.

Schmeichel, B. J. & Martens, A. (2005). Self-affirmation and mortality salience: Affirming values reduces worldview defense and death-thought accessibility. *Personality and Social Psychology Bulletin, 31*, 658-667.

See, Y., M. & Petty, R. E. (2006). Effects of mortality salience on evaluation of ingroup and outgroup sources: The impact of pro- versus counterattitudinal positions. *Personality and Social Psychology Bulletin, 32*, 405-416.

Sherif, M. (1966). *Group conflict and cooperation.* London: Routledge and Kegan Paul Ltd.

Sherif, M., Harvey, O. J., White, B. J., Hood, W. R., & Sherif, C. W. (1961). *Intergroup conflict and cooperation. The Robber's cave experiment.* Norman, Okñahome: University Book Exchange.

Tajfel, H. (1978). *Differentiation between social groups.* London: Academic Press.

Tajfel, H. (1981). *Human groups & social categories.* Cambridge: Cambridge University Press.

Tversky, A. & Kahneman, D. (1981). The framing of decisions and the psychology of choice. *Science, 211*, 453-458.

Van Des Bos, K, Pootvliet, P. M., Maas, M., Miedema, J., & van den Ham, E. J. (2005). An enquiry concerning the principles of cultural norms nd values: The impact of uncertainty and mortality salience on reactions to violations and bolstering of cultural worldviews. *Journal of Experimental Social Psychology, 41*, 91-113.

Watson, D., Clark, L. A., & Tellegen, A. (1988). Development and validation of brief measures of positive and negative affect: The PANAS scale. *Journal of Personality and Social Psychology, 54*, 1063-1070.

Wisman, A. & Koole S. L. (2003). Hiding in the crowd: Can mortality salience promote affiliation with others who oppose one's woldviews? *Journal of Personality and Social Psychology, 84*, 11-526.

Wisman, A. & Goldenberg, J. L. (2005). From the rave o the cradle: Evidence hat mortality salience engenders a desire of offspring. *Journal of Personality and Social Psychology 9*, 46-61.

INDEX

A

ablations, 116
abnormalities, 114, 121
abstinence, 108, 112, 114, 117, 181, 182, 190
academic, 178
ACC, 111, 114, 115
access, 82, 105, 135, 137, 138, 170, 181, 185, 206
accessibility, 10, 16, 21, 22, 25, 78, 79, 212, 222
accounting, 147
accuracy, 7, 17, 19, 27, 28, 32, 33, 38, 43, 65, 75, 111, 126, 213
ACE, 6
ACE inhibitors, 6
ACM, 142, 144
ACS, 14, 16, 17, 22, 23, 24
activation, viii, 81, 83, 84, 85, 86, 88, 90, 92, 93, 94, 95, 96, 97, 98, 99, 102, 104, 111, 114, 116, 121, 147, 148, 152, 154, 156, 159, 160, 163, 180, 194
activation state, 97
active type, 85
activity level, 93, 101, 102
acupuncture, 171
acute, 2, 6, 15, 49, 108, 118, 209
Acute respiratory failure, 121
ad hoc, 126
adaptation, 214, 217
addiction, viii, 107, 108, 109, 110, 112, 114, 115, 117, 118, 120, 121, 193
adenosine, 2
adenosine triphosphate, 2
ADHD, 110, 119, 159, 162
adiabatic, 23, 29
adjustment, 181, 192
administration, 114, 155
administrators, 167, 170

adolescence, x, 146, 150, 151, 154, 158, 161, 162, 177, 178, 179, 181, 193, 194, 195
adolescent, 146
adolescents, 117, 152, 158, 159, 160, 162, 178, 179, 180, 182, 184, 186, 187, 190, 191, 192, 194
adult, 118, 119, 151, 158, 178, 179
adulthood, 150, 152, 160, 162, 178
adults, 110, 117, 146, 149, 150, 151, 152, 154, 158, 159, 160, 178, 182
advances, ix, 145, 146, 147
advocacy, 207
African-American, 183, 188
afternoon, 179, 184
Ag, 143
age, 3, 4, 15, 111, 146, 149, 150, 151, 152, 154, 155, 158, 160, 163, 183, 186, 187, 193, 209
ageing, 200, 204, 205, 207, 208
agent, vii, viii, 9, 14, 16, 17, 49, 50, 51, 70, 72, 76, 77, 81, 82, 87, 89, 90, 91, 93, 94, 95, 96, 97, 98, 99, 100, 103, 104
agents, 212, 222
age-related, 146, 149, 150, 152
aggression, 183, 189
aggressive behavior, 192
aging, 160, 164
aid, 17, 77, 96, 100, 169, 171, 174, 175
AIDS, 222
air, 10, 11, 12, 15, 16, 17, 18, 19, 20, 21, 22, 23, 29, 30, 31, 52, 58, 59, 60, 61, 65, 68, 70, 76, 77, 78, 79, 144
air pollution, 144
air quality, 78
airborne particles, 68
aircraft, 78
alcohol, x, 113, 116, 117, 177, 178, 179, 180, 181, 182, 183, 184, 185, 186, 187, 188, 189, 190, 191, 192, 193, 194

alcohol use, 179, 180, 181, 186, 187, 188, 191, 192, 193, 194
alcoholics, 194
alcoholism, 119, 182
alfalfa, 129
algorithm, viii, 2, 9, 21, 24, 68, 74, 75, 97, 149
alpha, 214
alternative, vii, ix, 11, 12, 42, 52, 53, 54, 55, 56, 57, 61, 62, 63, 124, 131, 145, 175, 186, 212, 217
alternatives, ix, 52, 53, 55, 56, 57, 62, 63, 109, 124, 131, 145, 147, 183, 217, 219
alters, 43
ambivalence, 222
amelioration, 166
American Psychological Association, 116, 181
AML, 136, 137
amphetamines, 117
amplitude, 119, 156, 193
Amsterdam, 145, 162, 163
amygdala, 114, 116
anaesthesia, 174
analgesia, 166, 167, 168, 170, 171, 172, 173, 174
analgesic, 165, 167, 168, 171
analgesic agent, 167
analgesics, 171
analysts, 139
anger, 180, 213
angina, 4
angiography, 2, 5, 6, 7
angiotensin, 3
angiotensin converting enzyme, 3
anhedonia, 120
animals, 112, 212
ANOVA, 218, 219
ANS, 21
antecedents, 86, 90, 93
anterior, 147, 154, 160
anterior cingulate cortex, 111, 121, 147, 160
anthrax, 15
antisocial, 119, 192
antisocial behavior, 192
antisocial personality, 119
anxiety, 169, 171, 180, 182, 190, 212, 213, 219
API, 137, 140
APL, 77
apoptosis, 120
application, 39, 46, 51, 52, 75, 77, 83, 97, 128, 130, 135, 138, 139, 160, 190, 199, 201
Arabs, 125, 212, 215, 220
ARC, 135, 136, 137
argument, x, 57, 198, 206, 207, 208
arithmetic, 27, 132
arousal, 113

arteriography, 7
artery, vii, 1, 2, 4, 5, 6, 7, 121
artificial, 43, 131
artificial intelligence, (AI), 43, 131, 139
Asian, 217
assessment, x, 2, 5, 6, 7, 76, 115, 129, 137, 159, 177, 182, 183, 184, 185, 190, 192, 193, 200
association, 110, 111, 113, 114, 115, 117
associations, 105, 156, 180, 183
assumptions, 24, 31, 139
asymmetry, 216
atherosclerosis, 5, 7
attachment, 212, 213
attacks, vii, x, 9, 14, 15, 16, 72, 76, 211, 212, 215
attention, 108, 109, 111, 118, 120, 155, 159, 161, 162, 163, 171, 186, 190
attention deficit hyperactivity disorder, 155, 161
Attention Deficit Hyperactivity Disorder (ADHD), 155, 161, 162
attenuated, 156
attitudes, 212, 216, 221, 222
attorneys, 198
attractiveness, 187, 188
audio, 169, 171, 188
audition, 187, 188
Australia, 77, 135, 165, 167, 172
authenticity, 202
authoritarianism, 212
automata, viii, 9, 78
automation, 139
autonomic, 158
autonomic activity, 158
autonomous, 105, 133
autonomy, 178
autopsy, 119
availability, 126, 130, 167, 171
averaging, 186
awareness, 109, 172, 208, 211, 212, 213
axis of evil, 222

B

babies, 173
bacteria, 68
banks, 90, 98, 103
base rate, 184
base rates, 184
basilar artery, 121
Bayesian, 24, 136
Bayesian theory, 136
beer, 184, 187

Index

behavior, viii, ix, x, 39, 40, 61, 81, 109, 113, 114, 117, 118, 145, 147, 149, 154, 158, 159, 163, 177, 178, 180, 192, 193, 222
behaviors, 146
Beijing, 9, 76, 77
beliefs, 84, 90, 98, 104, 182, 184, 212, 213
benefits, x, 112, 171, 198, 216
beverages, 184, 187, 188
bias, x, 161, 180, 183, 194, 211, 215, 216, 220, 221
binding, viii, 81, 83, 84, 93, 96, 105
bindings, 94, 96
biological, vii, 9, 14, 15, 16, 17, 76, 77, 177, 178
biologically, 119
bioterrorism, 15
bird flu, 217
birth, 166, 167, 168, 170, 174
black, 138
black-box, 138
blocking, 148
blocks, 65, 70, 91, 113, 156
blood, 7, 108, 114, 115
blood flow, 7, 108, 114, 115
body, 108, 109
borderline, 192
bottleneck, 41
bottom-up, 109
boundary conditions, 19, 20, 21, 22
bounds, 96
boys, 161, 183, 186, 187, 188
brain, ix, 82, 83, 84, 105, 110, 111, 114, 115, 119, 120, 121, 145, 146, 147, 148, 152, 154, 158, 159, 160, 162, 163, 164, 178, 180, 212
brain activity, 154, 158, 162
brain damage, 120
brain development, 158, 160
brain functions, 155
brain injury, 110, 119, 121, 147
brain structure, 115, 154, 178
breech delivery, 175
British, 174
brothers, 204, 205, 206, 207
building blocks, 100
buildings, vii, 9, 15, 16, 17, 18, 19, 20, 24, 39, 72, 74, 75, 76, 77, 78, 128
business, 199
buyer, 85
bypass, vii, 1, 5, 7
bypass graft, 5

C

CA model, 42, 43, 45, 46
cabinets, 208
CAD, 14, 40
caesarean section, 174
caffeine, 117
California, 145, 177, 186, 187, 189, 191
Canada, 125, 142, 144
cancer, 174
candidates, 70
cannabis, 117
capacity, 82, 83, 84, 87, 95, 96, 101, 103, 147, 148
capital, 214
cardiac catheterization, 2
caregiver, 171
caregivers, 166, 168, 170, 199, 204
caregiving, 209
Cartesian coordinates, 47
case study, 33
cast, 188
casting, 188, 189
categorization, x, 198, 208, 214
catheter, 2, 6
catheterization, 2
Caucasian, 183, 186, 188
causal antecedent, 86
causal inference, 86
causation, 82
cave, 223
CBF, 114
cell, 10, 11, 12, 43, 47, 48, 49, 75, 128
central executive, 109
centralized, 104
cerebellum, 111
cerebral blood flow, 108, 114, 115
cerebral hemorrhage, 108
cerebrovascular, 115
certainty, 52, 56, 57, 61, 62, 63, 217
certificate, 199, 201
CFD, vii, 9, 14, 16, 17, 18, 19, 20, 21, 22, 24, 25, 31, 32, 33, 61, 65, 68, 74, 75, 79
Chalmers, 172, 173, 179, 194
Chechen rebels, 15
chemical, vii, 9, 14, 15, 16, 17, 19, 21, 50, 51, 52, 68, 76, 112, 113
CHF, 4
childbirth, ix, 165, 166, 167, 168, 170, 172, 173, 174, 175
childhood, 146, 147, 148, 150, 151, 154, 155, 156, 158, 160, 161, 162, 163, 193, 205
children, ix, 118, 119, 145, 146, 149, 152, 154, 155, 156, 157, 158, 160, 162, 163, 164, 180, 182, 183, 192, 194, 212
China, 9, 75, 76, 78
Chinese, 75, 78, 79

chronic, 4, 108, 109, 110, 111, 112, 113, 114, 115, 116, 117, 119
cigarette smoke, 119
cigarette smokers, 119
cigarette smoking, 116
circulation, 127
citizens, 198, 200
civil engineering, 143
civil servant, 200
civil servants, 200
civilian, 16, 69
classes, 84, 85, 140, 188, 198, 209
classical, 46, 215, 217
classification, 52, 121
classified, 52
classroom, 182
classroom settings, 182
cleaning, 82, 205
clients, x, 130, 198, 200, 202, 207, 208
clinical, ix, x, 4, 6, 51, 70, 155, 165, 166, 167, 168, 169, 171, 177, 190, 192, 194
clinical trial, ix, 165, 167
clinical trials, ix, 165, 167
closure, 221
clothing, 186, 189
cluster analysis, 188
cluster of differentiation (CD), 162
clustering, 188
clusters, 83, 84, 85, 86, 93, 94, 101, 103, 188
Co, 172
coastal zone, 140
cocaine, viii, 107, 108, 110, 111, 112, 113, 114, 115, 116, 117, 118, 119, 120, 121
cocaine abuse, 114, 116, 118, 119
cocaine use, viii, 107, 108, 110, 111, 112, 114, 115, 117, 118, 121
Cochrane Database of Systematic Reviews, 175
coding, 83
cognition, viii, 81, 97, 108, 159, 161, 180, 182, 192
cognitive, viii, ix, x, 81, 83, 95, 96, 97, 104, 107, 108, 109, 110, 114, 115, 117, 145, 146, 147, 148, 149, 150, 154, 155, 156, 158, 159, 160, 161, 162, 163, 164, 167, 177, 178, 180, 182, 183, 192, 193, 219
cognitive abilities, 155
cognitive activity, 192
cognitive deficits, 155
cognitive development, ix, 145, 146, 147, 160, 161, 162, 177, 178
cognitive domains, 108
cognitive dysfunction, 114
cognitive function, 146, 147, 161, 164
cognitive functioning, 164

cognitive functions, 146, 147
cognitive process, viii, ix, 107, 108, 109, 110, 145, 146, 148, 149, 150, 180, 182, 219
cognitive processes, ix, 145, 148, 149
cognitive processing, 146, 150
cognitive tasks, 110, 162
coherence, 96
cohesion, 213
cohort, 173, 183
Cold War, 14
collaboration, 186, 190
commercial, 15, 20, 21, 31, 61, 131, 137, 138
commitment, 209
communication, ix, 123, 124, 127, 135, 137, 138, 139, 174, 175, 178, 209, 212
communication systems, 212
community, 111, 134, 139, 179, 182, 199, 200
comorbidity, 194
compatibility, 163
compensation, 203
competence, 199
competition, 27, 99
competitive, 148
compilation, 125
complex, 146, 150, 157, 159
complex behaviors, 40
complex systems, 134
complexity, 52, 98, 135, 141, 146, 160, 163, 183, 208, 216, 220
complications, viii, 107, 119, 121, 165, 168
components, 12, 19, 23, 40, 42, 87, 103, 126, 127, 130, 133, 134, 135, 137, 138, 140, 169, 183, 190
composition, 118
computation, 18, 40, 101
computational fluid dynamics, vii, 9, 14
computed tomography, 114
computer, 18, 33, 39, 77, 126, 128, 130, 131, 133, 135, 139, 185, 190
computer software, 135
computers, 123, 125, 126, 143
computing, 16, 17, 18, 19, 68, 74, 105, 114, 125, 137, 143
concentration, 10, 12, 18, 19, 21, 22, 23, 24, 25, 31, 48, 49, 50, 51, 61, 65, 68, 69, 70, 72, 117
concept, 147
concrete, 96, 199, 200
conditioned response, 180
conduct problems, 190
confidence, 166
confidentiality, 188
configuration, 39
conflict, 11, 12, 44, 85, 101, 114, 117, 147, 152, 153, 154, 163, 169, 171, 181, 222, 223

Index

conformity, 181, 190
congestive heart failure, vii, 1, 4
Congress, 76
congruence, 156
connectionist, viii, 81, 82, 83, 85, 87, 94, 95, 96, 97, 100, 101, 102, 103, 104, 105
connectivity, 42, 146
conscious awareness, 109
consciousness, 212, 215
consent, 165, 168, 172, 187
consequences, ix, 145, 159, 160
conservation, 19
constraints, 124, 157
construct validity, 190
construction, 197, 209
consultants, 190
consumers, 166, 169, 170, 190
contaminant, vii, viii, 9, 10, 11, 12, 15, 16, 17, 18, 19, 20, 21, 22, 23, 24, 25, 27, 28, 29, 31, 35, 36, 37, 48, 49, 50, 51, 52, 54, 55, 56, 57, 58, 59, 61, 63, 64, 65, 68, 72, 74, 75, 76, 78, 79
contaminants, 15, 48, 55, 72, 75
contamination, 15, 16, 63, 79
context, 112, 147
continuing, 171, 206, 211
continuity, 39, 40, 205
contractors, 190
control, viii, ix, x, 11, 13, 16, 24, 25, 26, 27, 28, 52, 53, 54, 55, 81, 82, 93, 95, 96, 97, 98, 99, 100, 101, 102, 103, 104, 105, 107, 108, 109, 110, 111, 112, 113, 115, 117, 118, 120, 121, 136, 145, 146, 147, 148, 149, 150, 152, 154, 155, 156, 157, 158, 159, 160, 161, 162, 163, 164, 167, 170, 172, 178, 211, 213, 214, 215, 217, 218, 219
control condition, 213, 214, 215, 217
control group, 156, 213
controlled, 111, 130, 134, 137, 147, 159, 167, 169, 170, 174, 182, 183
controlled trials, 170
convergence, 19
coping, 184, 193, 200, 207
CORBA, 134
coronary angioplasty, 4, 6
coronary arteries, 7
coronary artery disease, vii, 1, 2, 6, 7
corpus callosum, 111, 119
correlation, 105, 154, 214, 218
correlations, 154, 190, 192, 214
cortex, ix, 105, 109, 110, 111, 112, 114, 116, 117, 120, 121, 146, 147, 152, 154, 156, 158, 159, 160, 161, 162, 163, 178
cortical, 111, 114, 118, 156, 158, 161
cost-effective, 125, 199, 206

costs, 93, 112, 130, 137, 199
counter-terror, 212
coupling, ix, 123, 125, 134, 135, 136, 141
covering, 165, 168
Cp, 10, 22
crack, 117, 118
craving, 114, 116, 117, 121, 189, 190, 193
CRC, 144
creativity, 53
criminals, 69
critical period, 193
cross-cultural, 194
cross-cultural comparison, 194
cross-sectional, 158
cues, 112, 114, 180, 183, 184, 185, 190
cultural, vii, 166, 167, 168, 204, 211, 212, 223
cultural factors, vii
cultural norms, 223
cultural values, 212
culture, 190, 212
customers, 129
cybernetics, 105
Czech Republic, 143

D

daily care, 204
Dallas, 107
damage, viii, 107, 120, 157, 158, 159
danger, 43, 50, 51
data analysis, 143
data collection, 115
data processing, 136
data set, 132, 135
data structure, 133
database, 126, 129, 131, 135, 136, 140, 180
database management, 131
dating, 189
death, x, 211, 212, 213, 214, 215, 216, 217, 218, 219, 220, 221, 222
deaths, 212
decay, 97, 102
decentralized, 42
decision, ix, 145, 146, 147, 150, 156, 157, 158, 159, 160, 161
decision makers, 52, 58, 124, 131
decision making, vii, viii, ix, x, 1, 2, 5, 52, 93, 116, 117, 121, 123, 124, 131, 132, 141, 165, 166, 167, 168, 169, 170, 171, 174, 194, 197, 198, 200, 204, 207, 208, 209, 222
decision support systems, 143
decision support tool, 131
decision task, 94, 104

decision-making, ix, 145, 146, 147, 156, 157, 158, 159, 160, 161
decision-making process, 58, 94, 112, 124, 125, 156
decisions, vii, x, 7, 39, 52, 63, 74, 76, 82, 87, 94, 95, 124, 131, 132, 157, 166, 167, 168, 169, 170, 171, 172, 173, 174, 177, 178, 179, 180, 181, 182, 197, 198, 199, 207, 209, 212, 216, 217, 218, 222, 223
decomposition, 137
defense, 222
deficit, 111, 115, 118, 119, 120, 155, 161, 162, 163
deficits, ix, 110, 112, 113, 116, 146, 155, 163, 182
definition, 22, 25, 49, 54, 55, 96, 147
degradation, 98
degree, ix, 11, 12, 13, 32, 33, 45, 51, 52, 55, 65, 70, 134, 141, 165, 167, 180, 181, 183, 198, 202
delivery, 127, 171, 173, 174
delta, 155, 156, 163
demand, 111
demographic, 187, 189
demographic characteristics, 187
denial, 221
density, 10, 11, 13, 19, 40, 41, 47, 50, 68
Department of Defense, 75
Department of Health and Human Services, 107, 117
dependent, 149, 153
dependent variable, 13, 19, 217, 218
depressed, 4, 194
depression, 171, 180, 182
designers, 133, 216
desire, 94, 112, 171, 212, 223
detection, 2, 17, 85, 101, 104, 111, 120
deterministic, 26, 32, 33
development, ix, 145, 146, 147, 148, 150, 152, 154, 155, 156, 158, 159, 160, 161, 162, 163, 164
developmental change, ix, 145, 146, 147, 150, 152, 156, 157, 158, 159, 162
developmental process, 178
developmental psychology, 147, 164
developmental theories, ix, 145, 146, 148
deviation, 50
diabetes, 3
diagnostic, 16, 93
differences, 155, 159, 160, 162, 163
differential equations, 19, 40, 42
differential treatment, 86
diffusion, 21
dimensions, 146
disability, 108
disaster, 15, 78
discount rate, 118
discounting, 113, 116, 118, 121
discourse, x, 197, 198, 209
discretization, 39

discrimination, 116, 149, 150, 151, 222
diseases, 121
disinhibition, 180
disorder, 111, 115, 118, 120, 121, 155, 161, 162, 163, 179, 194
dispersion, vii, 9, 10, 15, 16, 17, 18, 19, 20, 21, 23, 24, 31, 55, 56, 61, 65, 68, 74, 78
displacement, x, 211, 212
disposition, 156
dissatisfaction, 170
dissociation, 119
distal, vii, 1, 2, 4, 179, 181
distraction, 121
distribution, viii, 9, 16, 17, 18, 19, 23, 24, 40, 46, 47, 49, 51, 52, 53, 55, 56, 61, 68, 72, 75, 76, 79, 91, 113, 136, 148, 156
diversity, 186, 216
divorce, 215
dizziness, 171
doctor, 199, 200, 201, 202
doctors, 197
domain specific knowledge, ix, 123, 124
dopamine, 109, 114, 120, 121
dorsal, 158
dorsolateral prefrontal cortex, 105, 114, 154
dosage, 72
dosing, 72, 73, 74
drinking, 180, 181, 182, 184, 192, 194
drive, 146
drug, 155
drug abuse, 109, 110, 113, 117, 118, 119
drug abusers, 113
drug addict, 114
drug addiction, 114
drug dependence, 116
drug treatment, 191
drug use, x, 110, 112, 113, 115, 118, 177, 179, 180, 181, 182, 184, 187, 188, 189, 190, 193
drug-related, 112, 180
drugs, x, 110, 120, 177, 178, 179, 180, 181, 182, 184, 187, 190, 193
dry, 135
DSM-IV, 119
DSS, 137, 139
duration, ix, 32, 33, 49, 92, 102, 115, 165, 166, 174, 186, 212
dysfunctional, 116

E

earth, 127
eating, 88, 89, 90, 95, 184, 187, 188
economic, 116, 134, 205

economy, 210
ecstasy, 121
education, 169, 173, 175, 186
educators, 173
EEG, 156
efficacy, 174, 182, 185, 190, 193
efficiency, 148
Egypt, 123, 125
elderly, x, 119, 197, 198, 199, 200, 201, 202, 204, 206, 207, 208, 209, 222
elders, 203, 208, 222
electrical, 171
electroencephalogram (EEG), 156
email, 175
e-mail, 145
emergence, 43
emergency response, 61
emission, 22, 49, 63, 114
emotion, 156, 192, 205
emotional, ix, 146, 147, 166, 167, 178, 180, 205, 207
emotional experience, 147
emotional state, 180
emotions, ix, 145
employment, 200
encephalopathy, 108
encoding, viii, 81, 83, 86, 90, 104, 105, 180, 182, 185
endurance, 45
energy, 11, 19
engagement, 6, 162
engineering, 19, 49, 75, 78, 139
engines, 133
England, 142, 161
English, 216
enhancement, 76
enlargement, 5, 7
enterprise, 139
environment, vii, 9, 15, 16, 43, 72, 77, 79, 82, 112, 130, 131, 133, 134, 136, 138, 139, 154, 180, 182, 184
environmental, ix, 39, 52, 111, 123, 124, 137, 140, 142, 147, 180, 191
environmental change, 147
environmental factors, 39
environmental predictors, 191
Environmental Protection Agency (EPA), 14, 50, 65, 70, 76
environmental stimuli, 180
episodic, 86, 88, 161
episodic memory, 161
equipment, 15, 52, 189
error detection, 120, 160
error management, 221

ethical, 168, 200, 207, 208
ethical issues, 200
ethics, vii, 208
ethnic groups, 188
ethnicity, 221
etiology, 115, 194
European, 125, 221
evacuation, viii, 9, 17, 18, 39, 40, 42, 43, 45, 46, 47, 51, 52, 54, 55, 56, 60, 61, 64, 65, 66, 67, 74, 76, 77, 78
evening, 179, 184
event-related potential, 119
evidence, ix, 83, 85, 86, 108, 111, 113, 114, 115, 116, 140, 146, 149, 156, 160, 161, 165, 166, 167, 168, 169, 170, 171, 174, 178, 179, 190, 207, 212, 219, 221
evil, 222
evolution, 137, 140, 159
exchange rate, 70
excitotoxic, 117
exclusion, 97
execution, 92, 93, 95, 98, 100, 103, 110, 133, 149, 150
executive function, 108, 109, 159, 162, 163, 178
executive functioning, 108, 178
executive functions, 109, 159, 163
exercise, 169
experiment, 150
experimental condition, 218
experimental design, 151, 212
expert, ix, 123, 124, 131, 132, 133, 134, 135, 136, 137, 138, 139, 140, 141, 142, 143, 144
Expert System, v, ix, 123, 124, 131, 133, 134, 135, 136, 140, 141, 142, 143, 144
expertise, 131, 202
experts, 131
exposure, viii, 9, 10, 11, 12, 14, 17, 18, 39, 46, 47, 48, 49, 50, 51, 54, 55, 58, 61, 63, 64, 68, 69, 70, 72, 74, 75, 76, 108, 182, 216
external environment, 93
external validity, 183
extinction, 116
eye, 28

F

facilitators, 187
factors, 157
factual knowledge, 140
failure, viii, 107, 111, 121
false, 52, 90, 93, 95
family, 166, 167, 168, 181, 182, 186, 199, 200, 202, 204, 210

family history, 181, 182
family members, 199, 200, 204
family therapy, 186
fear, 161, 165, 168, 213, 215, 216, 219
fears, 212
Federal Emergency Management Agency (FEMA), 14, 51, 52, 76
Federal Register, 76
fee, 198
feedback, 109, 158, 184, 189
feeding, 119, 140
feelings, 178, 183, 205, 212, 213, 215, 217, 219
feet, 82
females, 114, 119, 184
fever, 170, 217
fillers, 85, 86, 88, 93
film, 183, 184, 186, 188, 189, 190
filters, 101
filtration, 52
financial support, 199, 200
finite volume, 21
finite volume method, 21
Finland, 197, 199, 208, 210
fire, 15, 49, 58, 77, 78, 84, 85, 98
fires, 39, 76, 78
fixation, 153
flexibility, ix, 21, 97, 145, 172, 190
flow, vii, 1, 2, 7, 16, 17, 18, 19, 20, 21, 22, 23, 24, 31, 42, 49, 52, 61, 68, 74, 76, 77, 91, 101, 108, 114, 115, 199
flow field, 17, 18, 21, 22, 23, 24, 31, 68, 74
FLUENT, 21
fluid, vii, 9, 16, 19, 21, 77
fluoroscopy, 6
fMRI, 111, 116, 121, 152, 154, 156, 159, 160, 162
focus groups, 186, 187, 188, 189, 190
focusing, 97, 99, 103, 158, 171, 207
food, 184, 185, 187, 188, 189
fractionation, 147
framing, 218, 223
France, 145
frequency, 157
friction, 11, 13, 45, 46, 65, 78
friends, 179, 201, 202
frontal, 146, 147, 152, 154, 155, 160, 161, 163
frontal cortex, 109, 116, 155
frontal lobe, 146, 147, 160, 161
frontal lobes, 146, 147, 161
frontal-subcortical circuits, 109
functional, 148, 154, 156, 158, 159, 160, 161, 162
functional magnetic resonance imaging, 118, 162
functional MRI, 158, 160
functioning, 159, 164
funding, 15, 190
funds, 199

G

gambling, 112, 113, 114, 115, 118, 119, 160, 162
games, 190
gas, vii, 9, 10, 12, 15, 18, 21, 22, 23, 50, 68, 70, 72, 74
gender, 113, 178, 183, 189, 215, 216, 220
generalizability, 183
generalization, 89
generation, 109, 125, 130, 133
genetic, 24, 159
Geographic Information System (GIS), ix, 123, 124, 125, 126, 127, 128, 129, 130, 131, 132, 133, 134, 135, 136, 137, 138, 139, 140, 141, 142, 143, 144
geography, 127, 140
Georgia, 173
geriatric, 209
Germany, 105
girls, 183, 186, 187, 188
glass, 187
goals, viii, 81, 89, 90, 94, 95, 98, 103, 180, 181, 185, 190
gold, 125, 170
government, iv, 15, 125
GPS, 127, 140
grades, 43
grading, 27
graph, 129
gravity, 11, 19
gray matter, 117
Greeks, 125
grids, 20, 21, 40, 41, 42, 128
groundwater, 24
grouping, 83, 86
groups, vii, x, 1, 3, 5, 52, 111, 149, 154, 155, 156, 160, 167, 179, 183, 186, 187, 188, 189, 197, 198, 211, 213, 215, 216, 217, 222, 223
growth, 158
guessing, 146, 158, 161
guidance, 169
guidelines, 15, 166, 167, 168, 189
gyri, 152
gyrus, 111, 117, 152

H

handedness, 161
handling, ix, 109, 123, 124, 131, 132, 135
hands, 201, 202

hanging, 188
hardness, 13, 45
harmful, 93
Harvard, 191
hazards, 76
head, 199, 200, 201, 205, 206
headache, 170
header files, 138
health, x, 51, 121, 124, 166, 167, 168, 169, 170, 172, 173, 174, 175, 179, 193, 197, 198, 199, 200, 206, 211, 217, 219
Health and Human Services (HHS), 107, 117
health care, 167, 173, 174, 198
health education, 169
health problems, 121
health services, 166, 198
health status, 166, 169
healthcare, 168
heart, 4, 6, 7, 117, 158, 160, 161, 204, 205
heart failure, 4
heart rate, 158, 161
heat, 12, 19, 21, 24, 70, 77, 171
heat transfer, 21, 24, 77
height, 48, 64, 92
hematoma, 118
hemisphere, 154
hemodynamic, 2, 6
hemorrhage, 119
heroin, 113, 117, 118
heterogeneous, 131, 133
heuristic, ix, 123, 124, 132, 216, 218, 219
high school, 179
high-level, 82, 97, 104
high-risk, 115, 158, 180, 182
hippocampal, 116
Hispanic, 183, 186, 188
history, 163
holism, 140
holistic, 140
Holland, 163
home care services, 208
homes, 199
homologous, 154
honesty, 205
hospital, 202, 204, 207
hospitalized, vii, 1, 4
hospitals, 16, 167
host, 115
household, 117
housing, 200, 205
human, 7, 39, 48, 49, 83, 96, 110, 112, 116, 124, 125, 131, 132, 146, 159, 160, 163, 209, 212
human brain, 146, 160

human cognition, 83, 96, 159
human information processing, 163
human reactions, 39
humans, 96, 110, 112, 114, 117, 121, 146, 147, 217
humidity, 19
hunting, 90, 94
Huntington's disease, 116, 118
hybrid, 105, 137
hydrologic, 142
hyperactivity, 118, 120, 155, 161, 162, 163
hyperbolic, 118
hyperemia, vii, 1, 2
hyperlipidemia, 3
hypertension, 3, 192
hypertensive, 108
hypnosis, 171
hypotension, 170
hypothesis, 98, 99, 100, 103, 104, 120, 156, 158, 216, 217
hypoxia, 116

I

IAC, 137
identification, vii, ix, 9, 10, 11, 12, 13, 17, 19, 24, 25, 27, 28, 31, 32, 33, 38, 56, 63, 74, 75, 145, 161, 221
identity, 178, 209, 210, 215
illicit substances, 180, 183
imagery, 204, 207
images, 128, 187, 188, 215
imaging, 5, 7, 111, 115, 118, 119, 121, 126, 155, 160, 161, 162
immediate gratification, 112
immersion, 171
impairments, 110, 158
implementation, 16, 95, 100, 101, 102, 103, 104, 109, 130, 138, 191
impulsive, 157, 178
impulsiveness, 119
impulsivity, viii, 107, 108, 110, 111, 114, 115, 119, 155, 162, 163, 178, 180
in situ, 156, 157, 183, 184
in vivo, 5, 182
inactive, 102, 103
incentive, 114, 120, 162
incidence, 170
inclusion, 95, 128, 150, 183
income, 199
incompressible, 19
increased access, 167
independence, 148, 178, 214
independent variable, 218

indication, 93
indices, 15, 16, 17, 27, 28, 48, 49, 54, 65, 67, 75, 219
individual differences, 160, 163
Indonesia, 143
induction, 216
industrial, 16, 78, 135, 139, 143
industry, 125, 133
infancy, 156, 158
infarction, 119
inference, 154
inferences, 82, 131
influence, 115
information processing, x, 163, 177, 178, 180, 182, 183, 185, 190, 191, 192
information system, 123, 140, 142, 143, 144
information systems, ix, 123, 124, 125, 126, 127, 131, 133, 134, 143, 144
informed consent, 166, 168
inhibition, ix, 110, 116, 117, 118, 119, 120, 145, 146, 147, 148, 150, 151, 152, 155, 159, 160, 161, 162, 163, 164
inhibitor, 3
inhibitory, viii, 91, 101, 103, 107, 108, 109, 110, 111, 115, 117, 120, 146, 147, 148, 149, 150, 152, 155, 156, 157, 158, 159, 161, 162, 163, 164
initiation, 93, 178, 179, 180
injection, 18
injuries, 212
injury, 11, 12, 18, 50, 51, 58, 68, 69, 70, 72, 110, 119, 121, 147
input, 129, 136
insight, 119, 146
inspection, 113
instinct, 212
institutions, 200
instruction, 214
instruments, 127
integration, ix, 49, 109, 123, 125, 129, 132, 134, 135, 136, 139, 141, 142
integrity, 119
intelligence, 43, 131, 133
intensity, viii, 9, 10, 12, 17, 19, 23, 24, 25, 27, 28, 31, 32, 33, 50, 52, 54, 55, 58, 65, 74, 166
interaction, x, 44, 45, 93, 102, 103, 113, 133, 148, 184, 185, 197, 198, 199, 200, 204, 208, 209, 218
interaction effect, 218
interactions, 146, 184, 185
interdisciplinary, 197
interest, 114, 115, 156, 197, 199
interface, 133, 135, 137, 138, 139, 140
interference, 97, 147, 152, 154, 155, 161, 163
intergenerational, 197
international, 77, 143

internet, 127, 137, 172
Internet Protocol, 137
interoperability, ix, 123, 125, 133, 134, 137, 138, 139, 141, 142, 144
interpretation, 85, 115, 130, 158, 181, 185, 190
interval, 110, 149
intervention, ix, x, 5, 165, 167, 177, 183, 190, 194
interview, 183, 185
intravascular, 5, 6, 7
intravenous (IV), 2, 162
intravenously, 2
intuition, 57, 216
investment, 211
Iowa Gambling Task, 157, 161
Iraq, 212
ischemia, viii, 2, 5, 107
ischemic, 108
ischemic stroke, 108
Islamic, 212
ISO, 134
isolation, 147
Italy, 105
iteration, 21

J

Japan, 1, 2, 76
Java, 130, 140
Jews, x, 211, 212, 215
judgment, 52, 76, 114, 124, 132
justice, 207

K

killing, 90
kinetic energy, 11, 19
knowledge, 199, 202

L

L2, 11, 50, 51, 69, 70, 72
labor, 129, 168, 172, 173, 174
laboratory studies, 213
labour, ix, 165, 166, 167, 168, 170, 171, 172, 173, 174, 175
Lagrangian approach, 40
lamina, 13, 19
laminar, 13, 19
land, 124, 125, 129, 135
language, 83, 133, 136, 137, 139, 140, 162, 186
large-scale, 132
latency, 110, 149

laterality, 161
laughter, 206
law, 16, 21
law enforcement, 16
lead, 94, 99, 132, 134, 146
learning, 105, 180, 181, 191
left hemisphere, 154
left ventricle, 2
left ventricular, 4
lesions, 112, 117, 121
liberalism, 212
life course, x, 198, 204, 205, 207
life cycle, 173
life span, 150, 159, 160
life style, 3
lifestyle, 193
life-threatening, 50
lifetime, 179, 186
light, 148
likelihood, 56, 93, 112, 115, 119, 178, 187, 188
limitation, 6, 70, 96
limitations, ix, 5, 6, 95, 96, 97, 104, 123, 124, 132, 141
linear, 23, 110
linkage, 134, 156, 180
links, 86, 89, 95, 135
liquor, 184, 187
literature, viii, x, 107, 108, 109, 112, 113, 114, 134, 147, 159, 166, 168, 173, 177, 179, 180, 182, 190, 197, 213
living arrangements, 202
localised, 170
location, 4, 11, 13, 16, 22, 24, 25, 27, 28, 32, 33, 37, 40, 41, 42, 49, 52, 54, 55, 56, 57, 60, 61, 63, 65, 76, 86, 124, 126, 127, 129, 186, 189
location information, 55
logic, 157
London, 14, 76, 77, 78, 108, 113, 116, 117, 118, 120, 143, 144, 163, 208, 209, 210, 222, 223
long-term, viii, 81, 84, 86, 110, 112, 119, 199, 204, 206
losses, x, 52, 147, 160, 211, 216, 217, 220
love, 206, 207
lumen, vii, 1, 2, 3, 4, 5

M

machinery, 93
machines, 138
magnetic, 111, 118, 160
magnetic resonance imaging (MRI), 118, 154, 158, 160, 162
mainstream, 130, 155

maintenance, viii, 81, 102, 103, 104, 181, 193, 201, 202
males, 113, 119, 184
management, 76, 130, 131, 140, 142, 168, 169, 171, 173, 174, 221, 222
manipulation, viii, ix, x, 81, 83, 103, 104, 126, 140, 145, 211, 213, 214, 215, 217, 218, 219, 220
mapping, viii, 81, 105, 130, 133, 152
marijuana, 113, 179, 184, 185, 186, 187, 188, 189, 190, 194
market, 125, 198
Maryland, 191, 208, 209
mass media, 215
Massachusetts, 105, 143, 144
mat, 155
maternal, 167, 171, 172
mathematical, 70, 163, 213
mathematical thinking, 213
matrix, 53
maturation, 146, 154, 158
meals, 201, 205
mean, 148, 154
meanings, 134, 199
measurement, vii, 1, 2, 3, 4, 5, 6, 7, 128, 149
measures, 108, 155, 159, 164, 170, 183, 188, 190, 214, 223
meat, 95
mechanical, 75
media, 166, 168, 189
medial prefrontal cortex, 110, 158
median, 148
Medicaid, 173
medication, 2, 5
medications, 166, 168, 170
medicine, 78, 193
membership, 128
memory, 84, 108, 109, 117, 136, 146, 148, 156, 157, 161, 162, 180, 181, 193
men, 2, 85, 215
mental model, 161
mental models, 161
mental representation, 180
mentorship, 191
messages, 136, 137
meta-analysis, 162
metabolic, 121
metabolism, 117
metaphor, 207
methodology, 113
methylphenidate, 155, 163, 164
Microsoft, 130, 134, 139, 142
midbrain, 158
Middle Ages, 125

midwives, 170
military, 15, 16, 125, 222
mines, 125
Minnesota, 142
misleading, vii
Missouri, 14
MIT, 163
mixed economy, 210
mixing, 30
MLD, 3, 4
mobility, 170
modalities, 190
modeling, viii, 9, 16, 21, 32, 39, 52, 65, 74, 79, 83, 126, 127, 128, 131, 134, 136, 140, 142, 144, 187
models, 16, 18, 20, 39, 40, 43, 52, 63, 83, 109, 114, 128, 129, 131, 137, 140, 142, 144, 161, 179, 180, 182, 184, 192
modulation, 90, 109, 110, 152
modules, 88, 135
momentum, 19, 21
money, 89, 190, 202, 205, 206
monitoring, 109, 114, 116, 146, 160
Monte Carlo, 150
morality, x, 197, 198, 207, 208, 209
mortality, x, 211, 212, 213, 214, 215, 216, 217, 218, 219, 220, 222, 223
Moscow, 15, 78
mothers, 173
motion, 42, 97
motivation, 114, 117, 181, 190
motives, 181, 192
motor control, 148, 155
movement, 19, 39, 40, 41, 42, 43, 44, 171, 213
MRI, 158, 160, 193
multiple factors, 112
muscle, 120
muscle cells, 120
mushrooms, 136, 144
music, 171, 187, 190
myocardial infarction, 4, 6, 119
myocardium, 2
myopia, 112
myopic, 113

N

naming, 154
narratives, 198, 200
Nash, 70, 77
national, 174, 193
National Academy of Sciences, 104, 117
National Institute for Occupational Safety and Health, 14, 15

natural, 139, 167
nausea, 170
Navier-Stokes, 14, 21
near-infrared spectroscopy, 154
needs, 201, 202, 203, 205
negative consequences, viii, 94, 107, 108, 112
negative outcomes, 178
nerve, 171
Netherlands, 78, 145
network, viii, 39, 81, 83, 87, 89, 90, 93, 94, 95, 96, 97, 98, 99, 101, 104, 105, 111, 114, 130, 131, 181, 201, 202
neural function, viii, 107, 115
neural network, 114, 115
neural networks, 114, 115
neural systems, 146, 147
neuroanatomy, 161
neurobiology, 120
neuroimaging, ix, 111, 114, 120, 145, 146, 152
neurons, viii, 81, 83, 84, 85
neuropsychiatry, 116
neuropsychology, 116
neuroscience, ix, 96, 145, 146, 159
neutral, 154
New Jersey, 142
New South Wales, 167
New York, 14, 76, 121, 142, 143, 144, 160, 161, 162, 163, 164, 191, 192, 193, 194, 209, 221
New Zealand, 143, 144, 168, 173
next generation, 133
nicotine, 113
NIH, 193
NIST, 76
nitrous oxide, 167, 171
nodes, 39, 42, 83, 84, 85, 86, 87, 88, 89, 90, 93, 94, 95, 96, 97, 98, 100, 101, 102, 103, 105
noise, 96, 161
non-invasive, 5
nonlinear, 70
non-linear, 19
non-pharmacological, 167
non-smokers, 119
non-uniform, 21
normal, 5, 50, 58, 59, 60, 63, 64, 102, 110, 146, 155, 162, 163, 167
normal children, 162
normal development, 163
nucleus, 110, 117, 120
nucleus accumbens, 110, 117, 120
nurses, 198, 199, 200
nursing, 199
nursing home, 199

O

obesity, 3
obligations, 200
observations, 27, 87, 93, 94, 126, 155
obsessive-compulsive disorder, 111, 121
obstruction, 2, 6, 12, 41
occipital, 154
occlusion, 6, 121
occupational, 179
oculomotor, 152
older people, 209, 210, 212
online, 17, 19, 24, 33, 56, 72, 74, 183
on-line, ix, 145, 146, 160, 169
open space, 43
openness, 133
operating system, 130
operations research, 52
operator, 103
opioid, 118, 171
opioids, 167
optimism, 13, 57, 58, 63
optimization, 70
oral, 110, 117
orbitofrontal cortex, 111, 114, 116, 120
Oregon, 177
organ, 127
organic, 120
organization, viii, 81, 83, 84, 103, 104, 109, 124
organizations, viii, 52, 123, 124, 134
orientation, 212, 221, 222
oscillations, 105
ostium, 6
Ottawa, 77, 78, 169
outliers, 27
outpatient, 186
outpatients, 118
output, 32, 126, 129, 133
OWL, 140
ownership, 129
oxygen, 171
oxytocin, 170

P

P300, 119
pain, ix, 165, 166, 167, 168, 170, 171, 172, 173, 174, 175
pain management, 172, 175
paper, 2, 76, 78, 168, 188, 199, 214, 216
parallelism, 158
parameter, 93
parents, 178
partial differential equations, 19
particles, 68
passive, 21, 23, 24, 68
pathological gambling, 119
pathophysiological, 119
pathophysiological mechanisms, 119
pathophysiology, 159
pathways, 89, 97, 103
patients, vii, 1, 2, 3, 4, 5, 6, 7, 112, 113, 116, 117, 119, 157, 158, 166, 168, 169, 171, 172, 174, 194, 197, 209, 217
pedestrian, 11, 12, 13, 44, 45, 46
pedestrians, 11, 12, 43, 44, 45, 46
peer, 178, 182, 183
peer group, 183
peer influence, 178
peers, x, 177, 178, 179, 181, 184, 190
penalty, 113
PER, 173
perception, 113, 215
perceptions, 187
perceptual, 150, 151
perceptual component, 150
performance, ix, 15, 39, 77, 78, 93, 96, 108, 110, 111, 112, 113, 114, 115, 116, 117, 120, 123, 136, 137, 146, 152, 154, 155, 157, 158, 160, 184, 215
performers, 154
perfusion, 5
perinatal, ix, 165, 167, 172
peripheral arterial disease, 7
permeability, 221
personal, x, 33, 39, 52, 61, 130, 166, 168, 169, 170, 178, 191, 211, 215, 216, 219, 220
personal communication, 178
personal computers, 169
personal control, 166, 168, 170
personal identity, 215, 219
personal values, 166, 169
personality, 114, 119, 178, 180, 181, 217
personality traits, 178, 180
perspective, ix, 113, 146, 163, 200
pharmacological, ix, 165, 167, 171, 173
Philadelphia, 175
philosophy, 96
phone, 203
photographs, 187
photon, 114
phylogenetic, 212
physicians, 175, 216
physiological, 2, 3, 112, 166
pilot study, 78
placebo, 111, 155

planar, 40
planning, viii, 81, 109, 125, 127, 146
plaque, 6
plaques, 5
play, ix, 99, 145, 147, 152, 185
plug-in, 140
policy makers, 167
policy making, 208
political, ix, x, 123, 124, 211, 212, 219, 220, 222
politics, 216
pollutant, 78
pollution, 65, 144
polygons, 128
poor, 33, 108, 179, 190
population, 11, 12, 39, 49, 50, 51, 54, 55, 58, 68, 114, 212, 220
Positive and Negative Affect Schedule, 217
positive attitudes, 212
positive correlation, 154
positive reinforcement, 114
positron, 114
positron emission tomography (PET), 114, 121
power, 21, 83, 125, 150, 199
predicate, 85, 86, 90, 91, 93, 94, 95, 97, 98, 101, 103
prediction, 16, 193
predictors, 179, 191, 194
pre-existing, 134
preference, 87, 113, 212, 217, 222
prefrontal cortex, ix, 103, 110, 112, 114, 116, 117, 120, 145, 146, 147, 152, 154, 155, 156, 158, 159, 160, 161, 162, 163, 178
pregnancy, 167, 170, 172, 173
pregnant, ix, 165, 167, 172
pregnant women, ix, 165, 167, 172
prejudice, x, 211, 212, 213, 214, 215, 216, 220, 221, 222
preparation, 158, 160, 166
preparedness, 15, 78
president, 222
pressure, vii, 1, 2, 3, 4, 5, 6, 12, 19, 189
prevention, 115, 190, 194
preventive, 216
prices, 130
primary, 149
primary care, 15
primates, 109, 114
primitives, viii, 81, 100, 101, 102, 103, 104, 133
printing, 130
private, 202, 203, 221
probability, 3, 11, 12, 13, 24, 26, 32, 43, 44, 45, 46, 50, 52, 56, 61, 90, 93, 95, 110, 169
probability distribution, 46, 52, 61
problem behaviors, 194

problem drinkers, 121
problem solving, 132, 134
problem-solving, ix, 109, 123, 124
procedures, 39, 97, 100, 103, 114, 124, 126, 170, 182, 183, 186, 190, 193
processing variables, 20
production, 125, 136, 187, 189
productivity, 130, 137
program, 21, 65, 77, 113, 131, 217
programming, 70, 137
programs, 159
promote, 138, 174, 223
propagation, 83, 86, 87, 88, 90, 91, 93, 94, 95, 96, 98, 99, 101
property, 101
protection, 49, 57
protocol, 136, 137, 140, 183, 187
prototype, 139
proximal, 2, 4, 6, 179
psychiatric disorders, 192
psychiatric patients, 194
psychoactive, viii, 107
psychological, vii, x, 39, 112, 163, 192, 193, 211, 216, 219, 222
psychological development, 163
psychological processes, x, 211, 216, 219
psychological review, 162
psychologists, 149
psychology, vii, 96, 120, 147, 161, 164, 213, 216, 221, 223
psychopathology, 119, 147, 155, 163, 178, 190, 191, 193, 194
psychophysiological, ix, 145, 159, 163, 164
psychosocial, 115, 178, 191, 212
psychosocial functioning, 115, 191
PUB, 77
puberty, 177, 178, 194
public, vii, 9, 10, 16, 17, 18, 51, 72, 74, 124, 170, 186, 189, 194, 198, 203, 216, 217
public funds, 198
public health, 124, 216, 217
public policy, 194
public schools, 186
public television, 189
publishers, 143, 144
Puerto Rico, 194
punishment, 82, 88, 90, 94, 112, 147, 157, 158
Pyszczynski, 211, 212, 219

Q

quadratic programming, 70
qualitative research, 43, 193

quality research, 169
quantitative research, 166, 169
query, 84, 85, 86, 87, 91, 98, 103, 129, 130

R

race, 148, 159, 183
racial groups, 183
racism, 214, 222
radical, 201, 203
radiological, 15
rain, 154
random, 61, 89, 101, 157, 162
range, ix, 15, 48, 61, 72, 97, 104, 113, 123, 125, 126, 130, 135, 141, 146, 150, 171, 180, 183, 188, 189
ratings, 187, 188, 189
rationality, 194
rats, 116, 117, 121
reaction time, 42, 43, 110, 148, 149, 160
reactivity, 180, 182, 184, 185, 188, 190, 193
real time, 56, 183
realism, 186, 187, 188, 189
reality, 112, 139, 209
real-time, 24
reasoning, ix, 82, 83, 85, 87, 91, 94, 96, 104, 105, 132, 133, 136, 139, 143, 145, 146, 157
recall, 121, 172
reception, 84
recognition, 90, 105, 199
recovery, 193
recreational, 179
reduction, 155, 192, 193
reflection, 208
regional, 15, 115
regression, 144
regular, viii, 107, 128, 186
regulation, ix, 146, 162, 178
rehabilitation, 119, 121
reinforcement, 88, 114, 120, 121
reinforcement learning, 88, 105
reinforcers, 110, 117
rejection, 220
relapse, viii, 107, 108, 113, 115, 179, 180, 182, 183, 191, 192, 193
relational database, 131
relationship, x, 84, 108, 112, 129, 134, 198, 200, 202, 204, 205, 207
relationships, 125, 129, 131, 139, 178, 180
relatives, 199, 200, 208
reliability, 5, 21, 183, 190, 214, 221
remodeling, 5, 7
reperfusion, 6
report, 154

research, vii, viii, x, 43, 47, 52, 75, 107, 108, 110, 111, 115, 134, 137, 142, 143, 147, 156, 158, 159, 161, 166, 167, 168, 170, 177, 182, 184, 186, 187, 188, 189, 191, 193, 197, 198, 216
researchers, 43, 83, 109, 125, 134, 158
residential, 113
resistance, 147
resolution, 39, 128
resonance, 154
resources, 99, 124, 129, 137, 212, 222
respiration, 48, 61, 64
respiratory, viii, 16, 107, 121, 171
respiratory failure, viii, 107, 121
response, ix, 145, 146, 148, 149, 150, 151, 152, 153, 154, 155, 156, 157, 159, 160, 161, 162, 163
response time, 161
responsibilities, x, 198, 200, 203, 208
responsibility, 207
retail, 16
returns, 57, 102
revascularization, 2, 7
reward, 146, 157, 158, 160, 162, 163
rewards, 54, 55, 93, 94, 112, 118, 163, 178
rhetoric, 209
right hemisphere, 154
rights, x, 198, 200
risk, viii, x, 3, 9, 10, 11, 16, 49, 50, 51, 54, 55, 56, 58, 61, 74, 76, 107, 108, 112, 113, 115, 137, 158, 169, 170, 172, 174, 177, 178, 180, 181, 182, 183, 185, 187, 188, 190, 194, 216, 217, 222
risk assessment, 76, 137
risk factors, 3, 181, 194
risks, 52, 170, 171, 179, 190
risk-taking, 112, 113, 178
rodents, 109
rolling, 184, 187
Roman Empire, 125
roughness, 13, 45, 46
routines, 136, 137
routing, 130
Royal Society, 120
Russian, 15
Ryan, Jack, 162

S

sacrifice, 98, 203
safety, 15, 43, 58, 78
salinization, 135, 143
sample, 27, 33, 108, 111, 113, 114, 115, 128, 150, 186, 188, 213
sampling, 32, 33, 38
SAS, 109

satellite, 128
satisfaction, ix, 90, 165, 166, 167, 170, 172, 174
scalable, 83
scarcity, 203
scheduling, 109
schema, 93
schemas, 109
schizophrenia, 111, 116, 120
school, 16, 179, 182, 186, 187, 188, 191, 192, 208, 213
schooling, 208
science, 125, 134, 139, 140, 146, 160
scientific, 111, 112, 113, 125, 131, 169, 183, 189
scientific community, 111
scientists, 109
scores, 113, 215
scripts, 187, 188, 189
search, 84, 85
searches, 69
secondary sexual characteristics, 178
security, 130, 217, 221
segmentation, 96
segregation, 161
seizures, 108
selecting, 98, 100, 103, 124, 139, 142
selection, 151, 160
self, ix, 114, 116, 193, 121, 146, 162, 222
self-consciousness, 212
self-destructive behavior, 114
self-efficacy, 182, 185, 190
self-esteem, 212, 221
self-monitoring, 116, 146
self-regard, 219
self-regulation, ix, 146, 162
self-report, 183
semantic, 134, 139, 142
semantic information, 142
semantic web, 140
semantics, 144
sensation, 112, 113, 178
sensation seeking, 178
sensitivity, 110, 160
sensitization, 120
sensors, viii, 9, 11, 16, 17, 19, 24, 25, 26, 28, 30, 31, 32, 33, 34, 35, 36, 37, 74, 75
separation, 215
September 11, 14, 72
sequelae, 108
series, 41, 86, 110, 125, 128, 129, 157, 173, 183
service provider, 202
services, 133, 136, 138, 166, 170, 198, 200, 202, 208, 209
SES, 137, 189

severity, 2, 5, 7
sex, 4, 160, 161, 189, 194
sex differences, 160
sex role, 194
sexual activity, 178
sexual development, 193
Shanghai, 75
shape, 105, 201, 202, 203
sharing, 88, 126, 127, 134, 135
shelter, 17
short period, 15, 68
short term memory, 105
short-term, 109, 171, 202
short-term memory, 109
sibling, 93
siblings, 161
side effects, 171
sign, 83, 103
signaling, 101
signals, 88, 110, 149, 150, 151, 158
silver, 170
similarity, 188, 222
simulation, 16, 17, 18, 20, 25, 31, 39, 40, 42, 61, 65, 76, 77, 79, 91, 93, 94, 98, 99, 100, 103, 104, 137
simulations, 24, 31, 33, 150, 159
sites, 132
situation, 156
skills, 125, 182
skin, 158, 160
skin conductance, 158, 160
smoke, 60, 77
smokers, 116, 118, 119, 120
smoking, 3, 116, 183, 188, 193
smoking cessation, 183, 193
sobriety, 186
soccer, 82
social, ix, x, 39, 40, 43, 114, 121, 123, 124, 146, 166, 167, 177, 178, 179, 180, 181, 182, 183, 184, 185, 186, 189, 190, 192, 194, 197, 198, 199, 200, 201, 209, 211, 212, 213, 215, 216, 217, 219, 220, 222, 223
social adjustment, 181, 192
social anxiety, 190
social behavior, 114, 146
social behaviour, 212
social care, 197, 200
social change, x, 177
social conformity, 181, 190
social construct, 211
social context, 180
social dilemma, x, 211, 213, 216, 217, 219, 220
social environment, 180
social factors, 215

social group, 184, 223
social identity, 216
social influences, 178
social information processing, 180, 182, 183, 185, 189, 190, 192
social network, 179, 201
social problems, 219
social psychology, 213
social situations, 179, 180, 181, 182, 183, 184
social work, 209
socially, 181, 192
society, 124, 125, 205, 206
software, 31, 61, 125, 126, 130, 133, 134, 135, 136, 137, 138, 139, 141, 144
soil, 135, 144
soils, 129
solutions, ix, 19, 123, 125, 129, 132, 135, 141, 188
somatic, ix, 145, 156, 157, 158
somatic marker, 156, 157, 158
South Carolina, 142
Spain, 211
spatial, viii, ix, 9, 40, 47, 52, 61, 75, 77, 108, 123, 124, 125, 126, 127, 129, 131, 132, 133, 135, 136, 137, 139, 141, 142, 143, 161
spatial analysis, ix, 123, 124, 132, 139, 142
spatial information, 143
specialists, 131, 217
species, 19, 23
specific knowledge, ix, 123, 124
specificity, 183
SPECT, 114
speed, 2, 12, 13, 40, 41, 44, 45, 46, 70, 82, 83, 108, 126, 148, 149, 150, 151, 153, 155, 156, 161, 162
sports, 16, 187
SPSS, 188
stabilize, 94
stages, 17, 18, 43, 54, 65, 163
standard deviation, 218, 219
standardization, 134
standards, 130, 134
statin, 3, 6
statistics, 52, 82
statutory, 197
steady state, 31
stenosis, vii, 1, 2, 3, 4, 5, 6, 7
stimulant, 116, 120, 155
stimuli, 149
stimulus, 110, 149, 153, 154, 186, 187, 188, 189, 190
stochastic, 43
stomach, 171
storage, 126, 129
strategies, 6, 52, 56, 63, 73, 109, 117, 126, 134, 141, 142, 146, 186, 194, 216, 217, 219, 221

strength, 84, 92, 93, 108, 132
stress, 161, 178
striatum, 158
stroke, 108, 110, 116, 118, 119, 121
strokes, 120
structural equation model, 190, 194
structural equation modeling, 190
structuring, 131, 140, 222
students, 179, 186, 191, 212, 213, 217
study, 146, 151, 152, 154, 155, 157, 158, 159, 160, 163
subdural hematoma, 118
subjective, 57, 58, 63, 114, 189
substance abuse, 110, 112, 113, 117, 186, 191, 192, 194
substance use, x, 177, 178, 179, 180, 181, 182, 183, 186, 187, 190, 192, 194
substances, viii, 107, 112, 121, 179, 180, 181, 183, 184
substrates, 159
suffering, 11, 50, 72, 88
supernatural, 212, 222
supervisor, 82
supply, vii, 9, 10, 16, 17, 18, 21, 22, 23, 29, 30, 59, 60, 68, 72, 197
suppression, ix, 145, 148, 152, 154, 155, 156
surgery, vii, 1, 5, 7
surgical, vii, 1, 3, 4, 6
survivability, 78
survival, 5, 212
susceptibility, 115, 147
symbolic, 83, 105, 132, 199, 212
symbolic meanings, 199
symbols, 133, 201
symmetry, 70
sympathetic, 207
symptoms, 5
synchronization, 83, 105
synchronous, 43, 83, 88, 96
syndrome, 194
syntax, 140, 144
synthesis, 147
systematic, 105, 113, 149, 159, 169, 172, 173, 174
systematic review, 169, 172, 173, 174
systems, vii, ix, 9, 15, 16, 17, 21, 58, 74, 105, 109, 116, 123, 124, 125, 126, 127, 130, 131, 132, 133, 134, 135, 136, 137, 138, 139, 140, 142, 143, 144, 146, 147, 159, 198

T

targets, 101, 103
task performance, 115, 154

tax collection, 125
taxation, 206
TBI, 118
TCP, 137
TCP/IP, 137
technological, 137, 140
technology, ix, 15, 123, 125, 126, 129, 130, 131, 132, 135, 136, 137, 138, 139, 141
technology assessment, 174
teens, x, 177, 178, 179, 184, 186, 190, 194
telephone, 130
television, 189
temperature, 12, 19
temporal, viii, 40, 52, 61, 75, 81, 83, 84, 86, 88, 93, 95, 105, 112, 117, 121, 206
temporal distribution, 40, 52, 61, 75
tensor products, 83
terminals, 16
terror management theory, x, 211, 219, 221
terrorism, x, 72, 211, 212, 219, 220, 221
terrorist, x, 14, 15, 72, 211, 212, 215, 219
terrorist attack, x, 14, 72, 211, 212, 215, 219
terrorists, vii, 9, 10, 11, 12, 15, 16, 17, 18, 68, 69, 70, 72, 74, 77
Texas, 107, 143
textbooks, 70
thalamus, 158
theoretical, 40, 109, 110, 180, 182, 190, 192, 212, 220
theories, 147, 161
theory, vii, ix, 9, 53, 96, 105, 118, 136, 140, 145, 148, 159, 162, 190, 194, 216, 221, 222
therapeutic, 183
therapy, vii, 1, 3, 6, 186
thermal, 19, 21, 29
thermal energy, 19
thinking, 39, 178, 215, 219
third party, 138
threat, x, 14, 72, 211, 213, 215, 219, 220
threats, 213, 215, 216, 219
three-dimensional (3D), 19, 29, 130, 192
threshold, 44, 50, 72, 94, 101
threshold level, 94
thresholds, 50
thrombus, 6, 118
time consuming, 190
timing, 149, 163, 207
tissue, 118
tobacco, 120
tobacco smoke, 120
Tokyo, 2, 77
tonic, 184
top-down, viii, 81, 109, 110, 147

topological, 132
Toshiba, 2
toxic, 11, 49, 51, 69
toxicity, 115
tracking, 99, 127, 149
trade, 125
tradition, 199
traditional, 147
traffic, 144, 148
training, 15, 184, 189, 208, 214, 215
traits, 178, 180
trajectory, 40, 42, 192, 203
transcendence, 221
transcription, 201
transcripts, 187
transfer, 21, 24, 77, 127, 135
transformation, viii, 81, 95, 104
transistors, 125
transition, 112, 163, 177, 178
translation, 97, 167
transmission control protocol, 137
transparent, 208
transport, 21, 24
transportation, 16, 124, 139
traumatic brain injury, 110, 119, 121
treatment, 163
trend, 150, 152
trial, 68, 99, 151, 169, 172, 174, 214
trial and error, 68
tribes, 199
triggers, 98, 111
trusts, 15
turbulence, 13, 19, 20, 21, 76
turbulent, 11, 13, 19, 21, 31
Turkey, 172
two-dimensional, 43, 65

U

UK, 15, 76, 78, 79, 143, 170, 172
ultrasound, 5, 6, 7
uncertainty, 52, 57, 63, 83, 90, 124, 140, 157, 158, 160, 169, 223
undergraduate, 213, 217
unification, 146
uniform, 21, 41, 47, 48
United States, viii, 14, 15, 75, 76, 107, 117, 194
United States Postal Service (USPS), 14, 15, 75
University of Sydney, 165
unpredictability, 172
updating, 43, 146
urinary, 170
urinary retention, 170

users, viii, 21, 107, 108, 110, 111, 114, 115, 130, 133, 140

V

Valencia, vi, 211
validation, 192, 193, 223
validity, 57, 183, 190, 221
values, x, 3, 12, 27, 28, 35, 37, 50, 55, 72, 88, 89, 90, 91, 93, 96, 168, 169, 171, 188, 189, 211, 212, 216, 221, 222, 223
variability, 114, 188
variable, viii, 13, 19, 50, 81, 83, 84, 95, 96, 105, 124, 171, 213, 218
variables, 20, 83, 104, 112, 114, 220
variance, 152
variation, 33
vascular, viii, 107, 120
vasculitis, 108
vector, 12, 19, 26, 40, 42, 128, 129
vegetation, 129
vehicles, 127
velocity, 12, 13, 19, 23, 30, 40, 42, 43, 46, 65
ventilation, vii, viii, 9, 10, 15, 16, 17, 18, 21, 30, 52, 53, 54, 55, 56, 58, 59, 60, 61, 62, 63, 64, 65, 68, 69, 70, 72, 74, 75, 76, 77, 78, 79
verbal fluency, 108
vessels, 5
victims, 16, 222
video, x, 169, 177, 182, 183, 184, 185, 186, 187, 188, 189, 190, 198, 199
Vietnam, 172
vignette, 184
violence, 117
viscosity, 13, 19, 21
visual, 2, 105, 121, 129, 139, 149, 162, 183, 186, 190, 213
visual stimuli, 149, 183
visual stimulus, 186, 190
visualization, 132, 140, 144, 162
vocabulary, 139
voice, 206
voicing, 202
volumetric changes, 156
vomiting, 170
vouchers, 200, 201, 202
vulnerability, 12, 50
vulnerable people, 11, 50

W

W3C, 140

Wales, 167
walking, 184
warfare, 16, 76
warrants, 113
watches, 103
water, 129, 171, 184
Watson, 191, 217, 223
WCST, 113
weakness, 132
wealth, 85
web, 140
Web Ontology Language, 140
weight gain, 88
well-being, 200
wells, 128
western countries, 167
wet, 82
white matter, 119
wilderness, 212, 222
wildlife, 142
wind, 216
windows, 138, 139, 160
wine, 187
winning, 103
wireless, 130
Wisconsin, 113, 117, 159
women, 2, 86, 165, 166, 167, 168, 170, 171, 172, 173, 174, 175, 213, 215
wood, 144
words, 112, 115, 154, 202, 205, 206
work, x, 147, 197, 198, 199, 200, 202, 203, 206, 207, 208, 209
workers, 200
working memory, 96, 103, 105, 109, 148, 156, 157
World Health Organization (WHO), 112, 121
World Trade Center, 76
World Wide Web, 140
worldview, 211, 222
world-view, 212
writing, 137, 182, 189

X

XML, 140

Y

young adults, 149, 150, 151, 154, 158, 159
youth transition, 178

Z

Zen, 194
zippers, 201
zoning, 131

BF
448
.P96
2008